The Transatlantic Zombie

The Transatlantic Zombie

Slavery, Rebellion, and Living Death

SARAH JULIET LAURO

Rutgers University Press
NEW BRUNSWICK, NEW JERSEY, AND LONDON

LIBRARY OF CONGRESS CATALOGING-IN-PUBLICATION DATA

Lauro, Sarah Juliet.
  The transatlantic zombie : slavery, rebellion, and living death / Sarah J. Lauro.
    pages cm. — (American literatures initiative)
  Includes bibliographical references and index.
  ISBN 978-0-8135-6884-3 (hardback)
  ISBN 978-0-8135-6883-6 (pbk.)
  ISBN 978-0-8135-6885-0 (e-book (web pdf))
  1. Zombies—History. 2. Zombies—United States—History. I. Title.
GR581.L38 2015
398.21—dc23

2014040924

A British Cataloging-in-Publication record for this book is available
from the British Library.

Copyright © 2015 by Sarah Juliet Lauro

All rights reserved

No part of this book may be reproduced or utilized in any form or by any means, electronic or mechanical, or by any information storage and retrieval system, without written permission from the publisher. Please contact Rutgers University Press, 106 Somerset Street, New Brunswick, NJ 08901. The only exception to this prohibition is "fair use" as defined by U.S. copyright law.

Visit our website: http://rutgerspress.rutgers.edu

Manufactured in the United States of America

A book in the American Literatures Initiative (ALI), a collaborative publishing project of NYU Press, Fordham University Press, Rutgers University Press, Temple University Press, and the University of Virginia Press. The Initiative is supported by The Andrew W. Mellon Foundation. For more information, please visit www.americanliteratures.org.

Turn and turn about; in these shadows from whence a new dawn will break, it is you who are the zombies.
—JEAN-PAUL SARTRE, PREFACE TO FRANTZ FANON'S
WRETCHED OF THE EARTH

For Joshua, Noah, and Sloane

Contents

	Acknowledgments	xi
	A Note on Orthography	xv
	Introduction: Zombie Dialectics—"Ki sa sa ye?"(What is that?)	1
1	Slavery and Slave Rebellion: The (Pre)History of the Zombi/e	27
2	"American" Zombies: Love and Theft on the Silver Screen	64
3	Haitian Zombis: Symbolic Revolutions, Metaphoric Conquests, and the Mythic Occupation of History	108
4	Textual Zombies in the Visual Arts	146
	Epilogue: The Occupation of Metaphor	187
	Notes	203
	Filmography	225
	Works Cited	229
	Index	257

Acknowledgments

I am grateful to many people from whom I have had the privilege of learning over the decade that this study was in development. Chief among them are my excellent advisers at UC Davis, Scott Simmon and Timothy Morton, and all the professors who helped to shape the project in those first years of nascent development, including Neil Larsen, Claire Waters, Joshua Clover, and Mike Ziser; supportive colleagues like Tiffany Gilmore who encouraged me to travel to Haiti and Karen Embry, an early and generous collaborator; and friends like Jesse Burchfield and Nick Sanchez, Natalie Strobach, and Mike Graziano, all of whom helped me to find out what I wanted to say by asking hard questions. A fellowship from the UC Humanities Center and a year as a postdoctoral lecturer in the English department of UC Davis were enormously helpful in this project's development and its beginning stages of revision.

But there are a few people from my days at Davis who were most responsible for this book: Colin Milburn, who was a kind and thorough mentor; Eric Smoodin, who has remained a steadfast supporter, reading chapters for me and advising me on the book's publication; and Marc Blanchard, who challenged me to keep Haiti the focus of this book. Marc's influence stayed with me well after he passed away. It is my great hope that he would approve of the direction this project took.

Two groups that deserve special mention are my fellow classmates under the graceful tutelage of Leela Gandhi during her seminar on anticolonial metaphysics at the 2009 Cornell School of Critical Theory and those who participated in the NEH summer program, "Slaves, Soldiers, and Rebels: Black Resistance in the Tropical Atlantic," at Johns Hopkins University in 2011. Both seminars radically reshaped my project.

This book has godparents, and they are Sean Goudie and Priscilla Wald, organizers of the First Book Institute (FBI) at Penn State. Without the sage advice, patience, and generosity of spirit of Sean, Priscilla, and the inaugural FBI cohort, Adrienne Brown, Todd Carmody, Danielle Heard, Samaine Lockwood, Theodore Martin, Christen Mucher, and Sonya Posmentier, this book would look very different, and it would be vastly inferior. Thank you also to Jonathan Eburne, for his participation in that event and attention to chapter drafts workshopped at the Institute. I owe this book to the FBI.

I am enormously grateful to the fine staff at Rutgers University Press, in particular, Lisa Boyajian, Carrie Hudak, and Leslie Mitchner; and to Tim Roberts of the American Literatures Initiative. Sheila Berg, copy editor of the manuscript, has also taught me much. I would be remiss if I didn't acknowledge Thomas Lay and the late Helen Tartar of Fordham University Press, who took a chance on the odd topic of the zombie to publish the collection that I coedited with Deborah Christie, *Better Off Dead: The Evolution of the Zombie as Posthuman*, in which I first worked out some of the ideas that appear here; and the University of Minnesota Press's Doug Armato, who has given me much guidance and counsel over the years as I began to figure out how to shape this book and others in the works.

My visiting assistant professorship at Clemson University allowed me to benefit from the wisdom of many individuals. As I grappled with the difficulties of teaching on "The Plantation," as some call the campus, I had a daily reminder not to lose sight of the slave in the contemporary zombie narrative. In particular, I want to thank Angela Naimou, who generously read materials for me, and Kimberly Manganelli, who taught me so much through our collaborations. The faculty writing group organized by Linda Nilson was enormously helpful in keeping me on task and self-motivated. There is hardly a member of that English department who wasn't a friend (Meredith McCarroll for instance), a mentor (Jonathan Beecher Field, Michael LaMahieu), a collaborator (Catherine Paul), or an inspiration (Susanna Ashton, Rhondda Thomas).

An old friend, Caleb Smith at Yale University, has played all those roles at various points, and I am grateful for both his precise input and his steadfast example.

The wonderful thing about a topic like zombies is that everyone has an opinion to share, and this project has been greatly enhanced by conversations with Ivy League professors at a cocktail party, as it has by chatting with my hairdresser, Kyle Vorst, a true horror aficionado, and talking to journalists like David Ovalle of the Miami Herald, or my terrific students. Some of the most important discoveries in the book came out of such disparate places as phone conversations with my best friend, Lise Aftergut, and a dinner in Port-au-Prince with Mario Delatour and new acquaintances. I am grateful to Max Beauvoir for meeting with me and to Carroll F. Coates, Patrick Bellegarde-Smith, Frantz-Antoine Leconte, Leslie Desmangles, and Colin Dayan for helping me to make connections and friends in Haiti. I am indebted to both Jaime Russell and Peter Dendle for their books on zombie cinema that were helpful guides and for their feedback on chapter drafts and to Jerry Gandolfo, Thea Munster, and the artists Debra Drexler, George Pfau, Jillian Mcdonald, and Ganzeer for fruitful conversations and permission to reprint their work here. Many librarians, particularly at the Williams Historic Center in New Orleans and at the Université Michel de Montaigne, Bordeaux III, were tremendously helpful.

There is scarcely a member of my large extended family (from Ban-Weisses, Delfosses, and Logefeils to Riordans, Waggoners, and Zertuches) who has not contributed in some way to this book. My father-in-law, Ron Waggoner, steered me to some of the best B-movies of the 1950s; two grandmothers, Agnes Hughett and Edna Lauro, regularly saved newspaper clippings about zombies to send to me; my dad read passages from a book about the Belgian Congo to me, aloud, over the phone.

My darling husband and my children, Noah and Sloane, have sacrificed much as I was writing this book. Josh, you have been a constant source of support, a springboard as well as an editor. I could not have done this without you. You hold every word in place.

Above all else, I am thankful to my parents, Don and Diane Lauro, for their enormous support—as grandparents, parents, and friends. My mother first imbued in me a love of the written word. My father's dedication to his field, public health, was my foundational model for how to be a scholar and a citizen of the world. I am grateful every day for the adventurous companionship of my siblings, Mujy and Jesse Lauro, and for the action our parents took that moved our family to West Africa in the 1980s. Those childhood experiences greatly informed my interest in this mythology, which, for me, is one of the many invisible ways that Africa pulses and thrives, undetected, in American culture.

A Note on Orthography

I use the spelling *zombie*, as it is written in popular American orthography, rather than *zombi* or *zonbi*, as one finds in Caribbean writing. I preserve the way that each author prefers to spell the word when using quotations, but there are certain occasions when I use the spelling *zombie* to designate the Americanized version of the figure, as contrasted with *zombi* in the Haitian idiom. Similarly, I use *Vodun* and *Vaudou* to refer to the Haitian religion, unless I want to explicitly draw upon the American conception of Voodoo. I use the lowercase to designate the voodoo that is a commodity of popular culture but uppercase when referring to US religious practices. Many Haitian words have alternate spellings, for example, *lwa* or *loa* (deities) and *bokor*, *bocor*, or *boko* (practitioner of Vaudou). In such cases, I have tried to keep one spelling as the standard throughout, except when quoting from a source. I also sometimes borrow the Haitian word *Blancs*, used to refer to non-Haitians; I find it a useful substitute for the problematic term *Westerners*. Unless I cite a book in translation or unless noted otherwise, passages quoted from French are rendered here in my own translation into English.

The Transatlantic Zombie

Introduction: Zombie Dialectics—
"Ki sa sa ye?" (What is that?)

Something strange was afoot in the first decade of the twenty-first century: the dead. Thousands of people made up to look like ambulant corpses took to the streets en masse in major cities across North America and around the globe. The world record for the number of zombies gathered in one place was first set in Monroeville, outside Pittsburgh, Pennsylvania, in 2006 and was verified again in 2007. Nottingham, England, took the title in 2008 for its gathering of 1,227 zombies at an event at GameCity, an annual video game festival. Pittsburgh reclaimed the title in 2009, but the record was overturned twice more that year, in Seattle, Washington, and then Ledbury, England. Many other cities worldwide claimed staggering records of zombie attendance—Dublin, Mexico City, Brisbane, Santiago, and Buenos Aires—but the figures were not confirmed by Guinness. As of this writing, the official record stands at 9,592 zombies, gathered in Asbury Park, New Jersey, on October 5, 2013 (www.guinnessworldrecords.com/).

It was this phenomenon, the zombie walk, inaugurated in 2003 in Toronto, Canada, that really solidified for me that I wasn't imagining it—the way you learn the etymology of the word *brazier* and then see them on every corner—something bizarre was happening; zombies *were* everywhere. Though participants may have claimed that the zombie walk wasn't a form of protest but was just for fun—they weren't gathering in public dressed as killer clowns or Guy Fawkes, that would come later—it is difficult not to see the act of playing dead as having significance.[1] Whether the impulse to dress as the living dead had to do with the turnover of the calendar to the new millennium or other events of social significance—political, economic, and environmental—I think we can now say that the era of the millennial zombie is over. Today one increasingly finds zombie walks replaced by zombie runs, geared to the participant who identifies not with the living dead but with the human who must outrun the zombie horde. This phenomenon, which transforms the zombie's purpose from an expression of dark fatalism to a narrative of survival, is also spreading worldwide. The first German zombie run was held in May 2014. The popularity of the television show *The Walking Dead* on AMC is another barometer of this sea change. It holds no interest for me precisely for this reason: it isn't about zombies but humans.

In an interview about his essay "The Funeral Is for the Wrong Corpse," Hal Foster warns of claims surrounding the "death of art": "It is easy to make claims about the end of this, that, and the other thing" (Schneider and Hussain). In that essay, Foster describes "our condition [as] largely one of aftermath" and proposes some new categories for thinking about art in the age of "aftermath," including the "spectral" (Foster 125).[2] Foster's argument is in line with Derrida's description of hauntology as "the dominant influence on discourse today" and as "the logic of haunting [that] would harbor within itself... eschatology and teleology themselves. It would *comprehend* them but incomprehensibly" and raises the question, "How to *comprehend* in fact the discourse of the end or the discourse about the end?" (Derrida 10; original emphasis). I'm not claiming that the zombie is dead. It never can be, and the zombie will almost certainly remain a convenient bogeyman. Indeed, its spectrality is similar to the model suggested by Derrida: "After the end of history, the spirit comes by *coming back* [revenant], it figures *both* a dead man who comes back and a ghost whose unexpected return repeats itself, again and again" (Derrida 37; original emphasis and brackets). For the zombie signifies both of these things at once, inseparably: the positive, resistive return of the revenant and the specter enslaved, doomed to repeat. Therefore, the zombie may be the most apt hauntological figure, representing both our adaptation to existence in a "condition of aftermath" and the futility of attempting it. Nonetheless, the era that for me was typified by millennial identification with the zombie has come to a close.

Perhaps it ended in October 2011, when a contingent of protesters who had been active in the Occupy Wall Street (OWS) demonstrations in New York City, many of whom had already been sleeping in tents in Zuccotti Park for weeks, dressed as zombies to express dissatisfaction with corporate influence over politics and the grotesque wealth inequality in the United States. In a missive from OWS headquarters, participants were encouraged to come to the financial district on October 3 "dressed as a corporate zombie!" Organizers wrote, "This means jacket and tie if possible, white face, fake blood, eating monopoly money, and doing a slow march, so when people come to work on Monday in this neighborhood they see us reflecting *the metaphor of their actions*" (Apple; emphasis mine). One zombie's makeshift sign better explains the "metaphor" protesters meant to make visible: "Money hungry fascists are dead inside" (*Daily Mail*). These zombies were not using the image of the living dead to represent themselves but creating a reflection of the Wall Street bankers whose policies they found abhorrent. This signals to me a change in how zombic imagery has been appropriated.

In addition to zombie walks, the living dead have been found at a number of public events over the previous few years: at performances and protests, at student rallies against fee increases, and at the royal wedding of Will and Kate, but the Occupy Zombie obviously draws upon the figure's ability to signify dissatisfaction with a capitalist paradigm that diminishes the rights of workers for the benefit of a master class. The articles in the mainstream media that were produced as a result of the OWS display drew largely, if not solely, upon the films of George Romero for reference.[3]

To many in the United States, the zombie belongs to cinema, and the word conjures images of figures lumbering stiffly across the cinematic landscape; a mob of moaning, half-rotten people greedily devouring the entrails of their friends; a snarling, blankly vicious look in the eyes of a child. But, as most zombie film fans already know, the legend of the walking dead that merged with Romero's cannibalistic "ghoul" is a folktale from Haiti, one that is deeply associated with the nation's history as a colony and the people's past as plantation slaves.[4] This book traces the history of the zombie myth, whereby a metaphor about slavery became transposed in cinema, pulp fiction, and US popular culture, and it teases out the various complications inherent in the myth's transformation. I may be wrong to think that we've laid to rest even the millennial zombie; as long as it serves a purpose, the figure may continue to darken our doors, but I can't help thinking that knowing the history of the zombie myth changes our relationship to it. The zombie, as we will see, is a creolized and creolizing figure.

The catalog of the zombie's appearances in transatlantic culture has become expansive. Indeed, after hundreds of years of transmission, transformation, and translation, the zombie cannot be called anything other than a "myth." I use the term myth to describe the development of the zombie narrative across the centuries and "mythos" when designating the diverse strands that today are yoked together to signify the recurrence of the theme in diverse media. I also refer to the "metaphor" at the heart of the myth, when the figure of living death is made into a symbol or allegory or is used in analogy to draw comparison between the animated corpse and something else. At various points, the zombie is all these things: a metaphor, a symbol, an allegory, a figure, and an icon, not to mention, as Ulrich Beck claims, a category.[5] Overall, its diverse usages as a figure are aggregated into an accumulated historical meaning that I call the zombie myth. The term zombie dialectics alludes to a kind of Hegelian Spirit of History that animates the zombie. Operating in one register of the zombie's dialectic (individual/collective), this accrued historical content signifies over and above solitary uses of the zombie metaphor. The zombie doesn't just mean whatever one wants it to mean; almost as if it had its own agency, it speaks over those who would wield the zombie metaphor. It is not my claim that this animation of the zombie metaphor is unique to the undead (as Heidegger said, "Die Sprache spricht," "Language speaks") but only that its historical content (as an appropriated imagery that resists its own appropriation) is uniquely in synch with its form, which originally represented a slave raised from the dead to labor, who revolts against his masters.

In order to start our exploration of the long and complex history of the rich myth of the zombie, we can take hold of that object, the Wall Street zombie, as a knot by which we can begin to grasp the zombie in its contemporary form. If we pull on the threads, certain things become visible that reveal the central core of this mythology: for example, the zombie is deeply connected to a colonial and postcolonial history of oppression; this is crystallized in that fraught term Occupy, which here is doubly laden, tacitly bearing the acknowledgment that the zombie only comes into US cinema because of the American occupation of the sovereign republic of Haiti (1915–34). Yet this zombie is neither, like its Haitian forebear, a critique of commodity production under a slave economy nor, like its cinematic parent, an allegory of the blind ingestion of the consumer capitalist. Rather, in this setting the spectacle of the zombie was invoked to protest corporate greed, Wall Street's special brand of conjuring: nothing is made but profits; nothing consumed but dollars. Nevertheless, the Occupy zombie is not so far afield from where the myth began, and even as it would overwrite the image of the living corpse with a new program (a trick that has been performed time and time again upon the zombie's body), the sight of the dead lumbering down a city block in New York preserves two aspects of the zombie mythology—those inseparably woven together as strands in our knot, forming the center of the zombie myth: the specter of the colonial slave and that slave's potential for rebellion. These two lines provide the tension of what I am calling the zombie's dialectic; and when it is a mode for thinking, zombie dialectics.

Zombie dialectics is not, like Theodor Adorno's *Negative Dialectics*, a means of understanding the production of knowledge; it is just a mode for understanding the zombie myth. In the zombie there is a tensile fluctuation between the disempowered, vacant zombie and the terrible, powerful zombie. The specter of potential violence is visible even in the most benign slave zombie; and even the most horrific, bloodthirsty zombies are, in some sense, pitiable. As with that other living dead, Frankenstein's monster, one sees concretized in the form of the zombie myth something like Hegel's Master and Bondsman dialectic: the fluidity of power, violence, and monstrosity.[6] It is rather more hopeful than Lars Bang Larsen's description of the zombie as a "collapsed dialectic" (2) and more in line with David McNally's single use of the phrase "zombie-dialectic" to draw out the relevance of Frantz Fanon to Hegel and Marx (265). In part, I embrace the theory of the transmissibility of colonial power structures—the zombie is never merely a cultural appropriation, but it also infects its occupying host—but I prefer the term dialectic here because I am eager that we should listen to the way that this myth speaks to us, over and above the fan, the film director, the *houngan* (Vaudou practitioner), or the individual author. The phrase "zombie dialectics" also conveys the back-and-forth motion that this cultural history of the myth traces, as a figure of Caribbean folklore (described in chapter 1) is taken up in Hollywood cinema (chapter 2), reclaimed in Haitian literature (chapter 3), and responded to in the contemporary visual arts of North America (chapter 4). Yet it is true that "zombie dialectics," by which I mean its inherent unity of opposites—of living death, of singularity/plurality, of enslavement/rebellion—only ever leads to stasis, not resolution or even progress. Above all else, zombie dialectics is something like Walter Benjamin's concept of the dialectical image: frozen, a snapshot of irresolvable oppositions.

One sees the zombie's dialectic between slavery and resistance at work in this example of the OWS protest: the danger of making use of the zombie as a signifier is in not keeping the terms in balance. Because the zombie is typically a futile, disempowered figure, the image of a walking corpse hardly seems effective as a figuration of rebellion: the zombie's use in social protest risks transforming a battle cry into a dirge. Thus, it seems, the zombie speaks over those protesters who would use its image, unwittingly invoking its complicated lineage. This is the more complex, lesser-known history of the zombie that is detailed in this book. If the zombie of twentieth- and twenty-first-century cinema can be said to be "about" capitalism, this is only because the much longer lived zombie myth that the film industry attempts to absorb is "about" colonialism. And the zombie myth is not just concerned with the disempowerment of the colonial subject but equally the dialectical exchanges between masters and slaves, between the colonized and the colonizer; and as such it is also about the cultural powers of the entirely real domain of the imaginary, as retained even by those who are described as socially dead. But before I go into more detail about how zombie dialectics works, let's take a step back.

The trope of men returning from the world of the dead is as old as narrative itself. The hero's voyage to the underworld is a general characteristic of the epic genre as evidenced by *The Odyssey*, *The Aeneid*, *The Epic of Gilgamesh*, and, of course, *Dante's Inferno*. The idea that the dead might be reanimated exists in religions and cultures throughout the world. Aside from the well-known resurrections of deities in Greek mythology, ancient Egypt, and Christianity (Dionysus, Osiris, Christ), which are bodies that defy death completely, examples of corporeal living dead that, like the zombie, straddle this hinterland between being and not-being include shape-shifting ghouls who haunt graveyards and assume the identity of those they devour; moldy grims that may turn out to be sacrificial victims buried alive to protect a church; fleshly revenants who return largely to complete unfinished earthly business such as exacting revenge; animate corpses deprived of rest due to sins they committed in life, a violent death, or an improper burial; and some kinds of vampires. There are also more joyful living dead, like the dancing skeletons of some Native American cultures or those seen in medieval *danse macabre* frescoes, but regardless, the fantasy that death, the ultimate inevitability, can be defied is a longstanding and ubiquitous trope in folklore and mythologies from around the globe. So why is it specifically the zombie, a figure with a lineage that can be traced to the African slave trade and which has deep associations with enslavement and rebellion, that is so prevalent in American culture today? And what is it about the zombie that made it seem (erroneously, in the case of OWS) like an apt icon for social protest?

There is a long-standing rhetorical connection between revolution and reawakening from death. Elias Canetti associates "reversals" (as of status, slave rebellions, peasant uprisings) with the idea of resurrection; he discusses them both as "reversal crowds": "At the center of this kind of promise [of spiritual reversal] stands the idea of revival. Cases of people brought back to life by Christ are reported in the Gospels. The preachers of the famous 'revivals' in Anglo-Saxon countries made every possible use of death and resurrection" (Canetti 60).[7] The discourse of "the last shall be first" or "the meek shall inherit the earth" is well known; as Canetti claims, this is interpolated, and the oppressed understand that "between the present state and that other stands death" (60). Frantz Fanon, too, refers to this biblical allusion directly in his discussion of the Haitian Revolution: "For if the last shall be first, this will only come to pass after a murderous and decisive struggle between the two protagonists" (Fanon, *The Wretched of the Earth* 37). This allows us to understand one reason why imagery of revival, rebirth, and resurrection is prevalent in discussion of social revolutions: the poor who were made to believe that they would have their reward in heaven perform their deaths and resurrection symbolically. They will not wait for death; they will claim their due on earth.

All living dead might be said to be figures of rebellion, for they are, at the very least, rebelling against the natural order and the laws of human mortality. Yet the zombie is not a resurrected body, like Lazarus, or restored to wholeness, like Dionysus, but an animated corpse: a body reduced to an object, stripped of its subject status, but which nonetheless maintains a type of agency. Most likely due to its association with Haiti, the site of what is problematically termed the world's only successful slave rebellion, the zombie, more than other undead figures, has become a trope associated with revolution. In the zombie horde of twentieth-century cinema, we see the specter of the angry mob; in the Haitian zombie, we see an allegory of slavery that is at the same time historically connected to the revolution. Reading the zombie pessimistically, one might say that rather than resurrection, which is equated with complete liberation, the incarnation of living death in the zombie represents revolutions that have not completely succeeded—an accusation that many have leveled at the Black Republic. The zombie thereby incorporates a people's history of both enslavement and political resistance. This becomes a paradox as striking as its living-deadness, the central antinomies of the zombie dialectic I describe here: slavery, rebellion, and living death.

The figure of the zombie as we conceptualize it today—as the walking dead; a vacant-eyed drone; a vicious, animated corpse; a rabid, dehumanized carrier of virus; or a toxic body that passes on its psychopathic behavior with a bite—began as a figure allegorizing the plight of the colonial slave. The contemporary zombie is the descendant of an immigrant mythology heralding from the French colony of Saint Domingue, which would become the nation of Haiti after a thirteen-year battle between rebel slaves and free blacks and several European armies. The zombie myth itself first took shape out of the raw material of many different kinds of African folklore and the new mythologies of the enslaved population of Saint Domingue; perhaps it was even inflected by European revenant legends and religious lore passed on by the French colonists. But hailing as it does from a predominantly oral mythology, the precise details of how the myth formed were lost along the passage of the ides.

The zombie's history is one that can be reconstituted only by sifting through the literary fragments of empire, histories written almost entirely by the colonial oppressors, slaveholders, and French and Spanish monks and chronicled in the exaggerated travelogues of curious travelers. A history of the zombie myth would chart its journey across the globe, as it was borne on slave ships across the Atlantic and sprouted among the sugarcane plantations of the Caribbean, as it was carried to Europe in the incendiary reports of missionaries, settlers, journalists, and anthropologists. In places one must read the interstices in the written records. Staring into aporias, we can only wonder whether the creature may have migrated to the American South during the Haitian Revolution, tied up in the kerchiefs of those unfortunates who were swept by their masters to climes kinder to the slaveholder. In places the zombie's history is irrecoverable, and we must admit our own limitations, confined as we are to one side of the story, that which was written down by Europeans, who usually were not objective ethnographers but had vested interests in representing the slave population as superstitious and savage. As with many figures of folklore, the zombie provides us with a case study that challenges definitions of history. Is the contemporary oral history of the zombie that survives in Haiti as valid as the written record dating to the colonial period? Is it valid as history, or as folklore? Because the Haitian zombie is in itself a representation of the people's history—as slaves and as slaves in revolt—this mythology is in a unique position to represent the people's deft navigation of history and myth and the complicated relationship between them.

The zombie's global migration and its evolution furnish a commentary on empire. On the macrolevel, the specter of the slave persists even within the much-changed zombie mythos, and this probably accounts for the enduring fascination with the figure: whether as a means of atoning for a deeply embedded cultural regret regarding the triangle trade or an unfortunate impulse to repeat the past sins of empires in the form of cultural conquest. For example, under the microscope the cinematic viral zombies of the present day remind us of the way we are slaves to our physical bodies, at the mercy of our instincts and drives, hosts to the parasites and bacteria that *colonize* us. Peering through the telescope of a distant vantage point, we must recognize that the zombie is a myth that was taken (up) from Haiti, where it represented a people's history of enslavement and oppression and was made to do the psychological labor for another group of people. The living dead zombie is essentially a metaphor that was commandeered by Europeans and Americans and put to service to represent their own concerns, as in George Romero's notable critique of consumer capitalism in *Dawn of the Dead* (1978). In tracing a cultural history of the zombie, we find that the zombie was not only a metaphor for slavery, but became a *slave metaphor* itself when it was forced to labor in cinema, carrying the psychic load of a formerly imperialist culture, made into a lamentation of capitalist greed rather than colonial servitude or postcolonial oppression. And yet this is only one of the forces in play in the zombie dialectic; the other parallels the figure's indivisible association with slave rebellion and reveals the way the metaphor rebels even against those who would make use of it for their own devices.

Along the way to providing the most fleshed out cultural history of the zombie myth to date, this volume questions the ethics and the efficacy of making use of the zombie's dialectical metaphor. Increasingly polyvalent in popular culture, the zombie (at various points and places a tenet of spiritual belief, a folkloric bogeyman, a cinematic cash cow) has come to be legible as a global mythology and interpolated in society nearly as a symbol, a kind of icon of disempowerment that can be made to signify everything from distrust of the government to fears of terrorist attack or viral pandemic to suspicion of science or a critique of consumerism. This multiplication of potential meanings, this semiotic fecundity of the zombie mythos, resembles many contemporary zombies: they keep coming. But though symbols are always more than what they seem, this cipher is an especially rare case. One can see this just at the level of its form. Both living and dead, the zombie is, like many monsters, always a border dweller, a hybrid character, in defiance of ontology, or as Jeffrey Jerome Cohen states in his seven theses on "monster culture," "the harbinger of category crisis" (6). The myth's history reveals that the zombie's ambivalence as living and dead is paralleled in its simultaneity as a figuration of both slavery and rebellion. The seventeenth-century African soul-capture myths out of which the zombie developed clearly respond to the people's experience of slavery, but the myth's historical connection to the Haitian Revolution has ensured that it is also always tinged by political resistance. Inherently and inseparably dual, the zombie symbolizes both the disempowered slave-in-chains and the powerful slave-in-revolt.

Cohen notes the way that, more broadly, the monster frustrates the typical dialectical model: "This simultaneous repulsion and attraction at the core of the monster's composition accounts greatly for its continued cultural popularity, for the fact that the monster seldom can be contained in a simple, binary dialectic (thesis, antithesis ... no synthesis). We distrust and loathe the monster at the same time we envy its freedom, and perhaps, its sublime despair" (17). Because of the zombie's suspension in contradiction and also because of the dialogic, communicable (in both senses of the word) mode of the zombie's transference, I refer to its conundrum as zombie dialectics.

What I am calling zombie dialectics is, in part, a mode of investigating the zombie, for its transmissions across space and time and the conversations that occur about power and possession in and through its movements and transformations. It is also shorthand for signifying the tension one finds in zombie narratives between representations of slavery and of resistance, of the difference between creolization, cultural merging, and appropriation, cultural theft. This book takes cues from Paul Gilroy's discussion of the "complex interpenetration" of cultures in *The Black Atlantic* (48), as it does from Homi Bhabha's discussion of the "ambivalence of colonial discourse" (122) in *The Location of Culture*. It takes as a perhaps unlikely model Eric Lott's *Love and Theft*, with its discussion of the "dialectical flickering" between envy and insult evidenced in the practice of nineteenth-century blackface minstrelsy (18). For cultural cross-pollination and ambivalences are inherently visible in the *content* of the figure in the zombie's transatlantic transmissions, when it signifies both resistance and oppression, or revolution and enslavement, as well as in its *form*, when the zombie-as-text oscillates between cultural appropriation and syncretism, or something in between.

Studying one of the most popular figures of pulp fiction and twentieth-century cinema that became increasingly visible in a variety of other media in the first years of the twenty-first century, together with its complex political history, is perhaps the best way to understand the persistence of colonialism in cultural form. The zombie has been ubiquitous, "cultural common coin" (as Lott said of blackfaced minstrelsy, 4), in the past decade; it has been so prevalent in the entertainment of North Americans that the fact that the majority remain unaware of its extraordinary postcolonial significance indicates a surprising (if not malicious) cultural blind spot. If minstrelsy was a "further commodification of an already enslaved, noncitizen people" in the nineteenth century (15), the zombie is a twentieth-century commodification of a people's narrative about their ancestors' commodification under transatlantic slavery and its persistence in the postcolony. In a way, then, the appropriation of the zombie myth in a display like Occupy Wall Street risks seeming like a kind of second-degree blackface, an appropriation of a people's cultural narrative of struggle and empowerment for entertainment purposes.

Differently from Bhabha and Gilroy, this study of one transatlantic myth highlights an explicitly national (in addition to racial and cultural) politics in its description of (to borrow yet another phrase from Lott) the "social unconscious" of zombies. For the zombie's transmission is deeply tied to the history of Haiti and its relationship with the world beyond, including its prehistory as a slave colony and its establishment as a free republic via the revolution, its military occupation (1915–32), and its (lasting) economic dependence on foreign powers and international corporations. Whereas Bhabha and Gilroy emphasize the transnational over the national in a spirit of looking at the creolization of cultures, in the case of the zombie we find a myth that is centrally important to the national identity of Haiti being appropriated by its former colonizers and occupiers. Differently from Lott, for whom blackface is "less a repetition of power relations than a signifier for them—a distorted mirror, reflecting displacements and condensations and discontinuites between which and the social field there exist lags, unevennesses, multiple determinations" (8), I read the zombie as both a reflection of existent power relations and a repetition of past ones: a cultural rehearsal enacted on the body of the metaphor that dramatizes the enslavement, colonization, appropriation, and occupation exercised over literal bodies. Akin to Lott's discussion of the "love and theft" evidenced in blackface, the zombie's transnational, transcultural, and transmedial travels reveal a "flickering dialectic" of repression and resistance not only in specific zombie narratives but also in the myth's transmission. Even as I claim that the figure was appropriated in an act of cultural piracy, I acknowledge that its journey simultaneously demonstrates the Afro-Caribbean culture's power, revealed in its infection and inflection of American cinema and popular culture.

Those participating as OWS zombies may have been, like most of the general public, un- or misinformed about the long history of this myth—that its ancestral roots can be found in African soul-capture mythologies, that it germinates among the slave populations of the Caribbean and is fed by the syncretistic religions of the region, that it is transplanted first in the United States as a direct result of the US occupation of Haiti. They may have been ignorant, in short, of the ways that the zombie's invocation draws upon a much larger, varied, and rich critique both of empire and of colonialism. Nonetheless, contemporary iterations of the zombie like the OWS protest often unknowingly parallel the colonial imperialism under which the zombie myth was born(e) even as they propose to critique the global economic system that is its heir.

The OWS zombie demonstration prompted a biting critique from the political blog gawker.com in a piece titled simply, "Hey Occupy Wall Street, Dressing Like Zombies Is Dumb!" (Apple). It argued merely that zombies are "played out," but I take the author's point to be a good one, namely, that zombies have been so co-opted by the mainstream as to be an ineffectual symbol of rebellion against commercial capitalism. But in another way, too, the zombie metaphor worked against those who donned zombie drag. An article in the *New York Observer*, a paper that caters to the most affluent denizens of Gotham, began with the rhetorical question, "What better way to engage the pros and cons of the Occupy Wall Street movement than to see it in terms of a zombie invasion?" (Grant). Effectively turning the metaphor against them, the author claimed that the protesters were the ones who were conformist zombies taking over public space. Obviously, the paper's conservative readership makes clear a motive for this deflection, but what both of these examples illustrate—in the *detournement* of the subversive potential of the imagery against those who would brandish it and in the accusation that the zombie's revolutionary valence had already been neutralized by the co-optation of the imagery by capitalist enterprise—is the much larger issue of how the metaphor has been and can be used: its capacity for signification and the history of its circulation, which is the subject of this book.

"Ki Zombi? Pou ki moun Zombi sa ye?" (Which zombie? Whose zombie?)

Cultures all over the world and across time have similar figurations of living death, like the Chinese hopping ghost, for instance. How and why do we isolate the zombie among so many others? What makes it worthy of study, and why study it in American literature or American studies (a category that for me denotes the various nations in the Americas, not the US exclusively)? One reason is that the zombie is perhaps the most "American" monster: it comes from elsewhere, and it is distinctly informed by slavery, colonialism, and occupation, and yet somehow this always gets relegated to the backstory rather than treated as *the* story.

In "The Monstrous Caribbean," Persephone Braham writes that the modern zombie symbolizes "the collective erasure that occurs in the Caribbean at the nexus of colonialism, patriarchy, and capitalism" (39). The zombie's blank stare conveys the evacuation of the subject under imperialism, but the zombie myth's history, its migration, and translation reveals (once more) that the occupier himself is colonized by the experience of colonialism.[8]

In her useful lecture on the zombie, published in *Fantastic Metamorphoses, Other Worlds*, Marina Warner writes, "The zombie's increasing salience since the nineteenth century results from the collision of forces in mercantile imperialism still clashing so turbulently in the present day" (120). Writing of the zombie metaphor's "currency" in 2001, she could not have known how much the figure's cultural capital would inflate in the first decade of the twenty-first century. And though Warner's study of the zombie stops short of an adumbration of the figure's dialectical valences, what she writes in the introduction to the published collection of her four Clarendon lectures is decidedly true of the zombie's most recent incarnations as well: "The argument that the contemptuous depiction of savage rites and superstitions gave the oppressor permission to oppress the subaltern as an inferior, a child, a barbarian does not take into account sufficiently the continuing and ever-increasing fascination above all with stories of metamorphosis and magic in evidence in ethnographic and literary texts. The emphasis on repression does not suffice either, it seems to me: the confluence of ideas and the resulting current offers more direct intellectual and cultural exchanges" (21).[9] Imperialist chronicles did not report instances of magic merely as a way of denigrating the colonized cultures as backward; rather, like the ambivalence of the love and theft exhibited in blackface minstrelsy, they were captivated by it as well, as the literature and poetry coming out of Europe at the time attests.

The zombie's dyad of slavery and resistance might be taken as just a further iteration of the master/slave dialectic, but the myth is equally about the bleed between occupier/occupied roles in colonialism, subject/object roles in biopolitics, and author/text roles in the creation of myth. Taking cues from Chris Baldick's treatment of Frankenstein, which he titles "The Monster Speaks," and his discussion of the way in which, through the other texts and interpretations it has inspired, Shelley's novel and all works of art "behave monstrously towards their creators, running loose from authorial intention and turning to mock their begetters by displaying a vitality of their own" (30), I investigate the way that the zombie's critique of power dynamics extends even to the dividing lines between author and text and between the imaginary and the real.

The zombie tells a story about how myths work and how, like Baldick said, narratives come to have a life of their own. The zombie also calls into question the category of historical truth. It is as much about the way histories are encoded in our stories as it is about the way our fictions have shaped history. For metaphors have weight and myths have real-world power: Have not accusations of cannibalism, the practice of dark magic, and even rumors of the raising of the dead justified various interventions and occupations of foreign lands, including the "birthplace" of the zombie, the island colony of Saint Domingue that became Haiti? In the figure of the living dead, as with most of its boundaries, the lines between history and myth, fiction and nonfiction, reality and the imaginary, blur.

Here at the outset I merely want to present the various considerations at issue in this study with a series of questions. If I am asking, "Which zombie? Whose zombie?," it is because the zombie's history stretches back in time to Guinea and extends farther in space than Haiti to a place incautiously called "the West." Does the zombie belong properly to one place, or time, or people? The zombie defies categorization as either singular or plural: evocative always of the crowd, is it a misnomer to ever refer to "the zombie" in the singular? Are we talking here merely of one zombie? Of the zombie (in the US spelling) or the zombi or zonbi as seen in Haitian texts? Or of all the living dead's incorporations? Am I seeking to trace this figure as a historical or cultural artifact? To study it as a myth or as a feature of a particular cosmology? And what method can we use to investigate the zombie's origins to respect its own voice?

WHICH ZOMBIE?

One sees the same struggle between themes of enslavement and of rebellion that is the main source of the zombie's dialectical flickering in other living dead, most notably, the Jewish Golem—which might not properly be considered living dead by some because it is not *reanimated* but merely animated from clay—and in Mary Shelley's *Frankenstein*. But, for the most part, there is no cultural push-me–pull-you over these other metaphorizations of living dead rebel slaves. Though Frankenstein's creature and the Golem share the zombie's ambivalences of content, particularly as regards themes of slavery and rebellion, there is not the cross-cultural drama of cultural absorption, the creolization, or the appropriation seen in the zombie's cultural theft.[10]

Of course, it is beyond the purview of this study to trace out exactly to what degree the one may have influenced the other, but many scholars have theorized that the "German ghost stories" that inspired Shelley's novel may have included references to the medieval Jewish folk legend of the Golem.[11] Shelley may also have been aware of the Haitian zombie's closest relative, in descriptions of Jamaican Obeah practitioners who claimed to be capable of raising the dead, when she wrote *Frankenstein*. Elizabeth Young's *Black Frankenstein* goes into some detail regarding the attention the author was paying to colonial empire (26–27), and Alan Lloyd-Smith directly addresses the Haitian Revolution and its probable influence on Shelley (219). But the monster's ambivalence as a creature that is both pitiable and terrible, as well as the inherent duality of his living dead being, a (n)ontology, troubles attempts to read the novel as purely abolitionist.[12] If the Golem influenced Mary Shelley's writing of *Frankenstein*, if tales of Caribbean sorcery did, too, these are instances of mythic transmission worthy of consideration, but I am interested in those moments in which a living dead figure made to stand for one political ideology is purposefully redirected and made to stand for its inverse: more than translations, this amounts to a willful redefinition of the sign. Yet the figure of the zombie is not so easily redacted.

The zombie's genealogy has its roots in seventeenth-century African folk beliefs, and it becomes associated with Vaudoun spiritual practices in the nineteenth century; nonetheless, over four hundred years the zombie narrative has transformed so much that it does not properly belong to any one cosmological or cultural framework anymore. Over time, the beings that have been labeled "zombies" have changed drastically in both form and function, most notably, in the fairly recent pivot of the "zombie" from an innocuous, pitiable walking corpse to a terrifying contagious cannibal. The basic structure of the narrative remains the same. A person dies or appears to die, or is infected/affected by curse, chemical, or contagion. He subsequently reanimates or transforms. Though it retains the same basic physical shape, the zombie is essentially emptied of its former self, leaving only a body on autopilot with the capacity to follow orders, thus making it an ideal slave, or with the most primal instincts, such as to feed or to transmit infection.

The idea that the zombie is secularized by American cinema is partly misleading. Although the zombie is deeply associated with the spiritual architecture of Haitian Vaudou, we might say that it is not a load-bearing pillar of that syncretist religion: while the zombie reveals the proximity of life and death within the cosmology or provides a useful illustration of the division in Vaudou between the *gros bon ange* and the *ti bon ange*, two types of souls possessed by all, the zombie's manufacture is always ascribed to the workings of the witch doctors rather than the gods. The Haitian saying, "Wanga, moun qui fait ca" (Herskovitz, Life 220), applies here: it is men (not gods) who make charms and spells. The zombie, to some degree, has long been the doing of man, often just a ruse perpetrated by the uses of poisons, not one enacted by the deities or evencreated by invoking them. Moreover, in Haiti the legend has been deeply divisive, concretizing, for some, the kinds of superstitions that have led many to discredit Vaudou as a spurious religion or associated, for others, irrevocably with the horrific regime of François Duvalier and the rumor that his Tonton Macoutes themselves were zombies. Although the zombie's association with Haiti is for me of the utmost importance politically, I am reading this figure not theologically but mythologically.

The zombie doesn't even really belong to Vaudou.[13] If we look further back in time than Haiti, or even Saint Domingue, we find this narrative's ancestry in colonial documents recording the people's fears of soul capture practiced by neighboring tribes in Angola. This was seventeenth-century West Central Africa, prime hunting grounds for Dutch and Portuguese slave traders. The myth serves as an attempt to explain life's cruel mysteries: Why were people disappearing? Where were they going? They were bewitched by sorcerers, their souls forced to labor in a desert land far away. Zombies at first explained slavery as an act of sorcery that steals the person's soul. Just as myths reconcile an unexplained natural occurrence (such as a solar eclipse) as having a supernatural cause, the application of this type of mythologization to a human phenomenon like slavery only further underlines the peculiarity of the "peculiar institution" as distinctly non-natural.

The Haitian zombie that is the zygote of all the forms that bear the name today was, like its progeny and predecessors, a myth about the political climate and social conditions of the people that shaped it. On the one hand, the Haitian zombie seeks to make sense of an incomprehensible reality: how could one people have had complete ownership and dominance over another group if not by means of sorcery? And yet, as we will see, the undercurrent of rebellion is inherently a feature of the myth from the very beginning, so that enslavement and resistance are locked in the same form in the body of the zombie. This is revelatory of the nature of power dynamics in general and the potential for political empowerment of the disenfranchised. On the other hand, the narrative provided a way of retaliating discursively, of creating an arsenal to combat that reality. This is not to say that zombies aren't "real"; they are, as are words, symbols, and rhetorical devices.

As a cultural history of the zombie this book traces the development of one figuration of living death, connecting diverse images that share common ancestors, spying those moments of influence, transmission, and translation—terms that I use here not interchangeably but to highlight subtle differences in the agency involved in the myth's adaptation—wherein the figure is hewn by emerging cultural forces or when one mythology grinds against another and is reshaped. But even as I call this a "cultural history" of the zombie myth, I use the term with some reservations. This is a history of a myth—a myth that is itself an index of a particular history of the transatlantic slave trade. The importance of the zombie myth is the way its migrations and transformations (from Haitian folklore to US cinema, for example) parallel its symbolic content: the figure first allegorized the displacement of the African to the cane plantations of the Caribbean and, under the glare of colonial imperialism, the transformation of the human into an instrument. Eerily, the zombie has a history—as a myth—that uncannily parallels its own substance, and it has a structure that appositely reflects the matter of the metaphor. The zombie most clearly translates the experience of the African slave into a folkloric figure—biologically alive but "socially dead," as the subjectless agent of another's bidding. This metaphor comes to be taken up in the twentieth century by the heirs of the oppressors to exorcize the demons of the descendants of empire. It is therefore not just a myth about slavery, but a "slave metaphor": usurped, colonized, and altered to represent the struggles of a distinctly different culture.

Questions about the zombie's history, about the conquest of this mythology and its subsequent countermanding, form a constellation, which, when traced out, reveals the way that myths, too, are battlegrounds of imperial and postcolonial struggle. If we were merely interested in the ways in which myths reveal the "contact zones" of colonialism and the cross-pollination of cultures that interacted under the auspices of empire, we might look at a figure like the African goddess Mami Wata for the way that ancient figurations of water spirits collided with European images of mermaids.[14] In the case of Mami Wata, and in many histories of a myth's transmissions, we can see the indices of various contact points of cultures drawn together by colonization. But as a mythic figure that was itself transported across the Atlantic and made to do (psychic) labor for another culture, the zombie presents us with a unique case because its content (the animated corpse as allegory of the slave's disempowerment) is mirrored by its history.

My interest is in looking at how this myth has transformed and yet persevered over time and in questioning if slavery is over why the myth is still with us (and today more ubiquitous than ever). Looking to this myth as an index of cross-cultural transmission under colonialism is revealing of the ways in which the history of the transatlantic slave trade is still very much a part of everyday life in the United States, the way we might say slavery "haunts" our cultural consciousness. But looking at the myth's endurance alongside its translations causes us to reflect on the material ways that slavery, imperialism, and occupation have not ended, either politically or economically, but have merely transformed under late late capitalism. This cultural history also charts other back-and-forths that occur over and within the body of the zombie, not only between cultures, but also within the larger mythos and its emergent trends, revealing tensions between definitions of historical "fact," for example, and the mythic reimagination of "history."

Above all, this is a myth about the power of myths. The zombie is exemplary of the way that myths are imported across national and cultural boundaries; that contagion and contamination became significant aspects of the mythos on its earliest transmission across media (into film) and across borders (into the United States) is telling. We see in the zombie's example the way narratives are leveraged and used in the field of conquest as if they, too, were natural resources that could be claimed, mined, hauled away, and refined into capital. But resisting forced labor, the zombie myth has a life of its own and contradicts those who would invoke it.

WHOSE ZOMBIE?

This book draws on the work of scholars who address monstrosity specifically, like Jeffrey Jerome Cohen, but also those who investigate the limits of humanism more generally in a variety of ways, such as the posthumanist treatment of cyborgs, animals, and objects. It is in dialogue with scholars who look for the wider political importance of horror film, like Steven Shaviro, Carol Clover, and Judith Halberstam. To a lesser degree, it is in communication with the many scholars who have looked specifically at zombie films, like Robin Wood, Gregory Waller, Peter

Dendle, Annalee Newitz, Kyle Bishop, and many others, but this book's contribution to the field is its step back from the zombie film to look at the history and the mechanics of the larger zombie mythos for what it reveals about the way that postcolonial myths work to preserve and to challenge imaginaries of subjugation and resistance. Indeed, like studies of the ghost that are informed by Freudian psychoanalysis or even Derrida's concept of hauntology, my interest is in emphasizing the materiality and real-world ramifications of the zombie, in a manner similar to Avery Gordon's spectral study, *Ghostly Matters*. Gordon writes, "The ghost is not simply a dead or missing person, but a social figure, and investigating it can lead to that dense site, where history and subjectivity make social life" (8).

Drawing directly from scholars of Haitian history, literature, and culture, this study of the zombie myth reveals the way that the transatlantic slave trade is preserved in our cultural imagination. Many works that address the subversive nature of Vaudou have been a great influence: Maya Deren's *Divine Horsemen: The Living God of Haiti*; Joan Dayan's seminal work, *Haiti, History, and the Gods*; Leslie Desmangles's *The Faces of the Gods*; edited collections by Frantz-Antoine Leconte, *Haïti: Le Vodou au troisième millénaire*, and Claudine Michel and Patrick Bellegarde-Smith, *Invisible Powers: Vodou in Haitian Life and Culture*. Many others, like Michel-Rolph Trouillot's study of Haitian history, *Silencing the Past*, have also shaped my thinking. This book is equally informed by postcolonial scholars who look at other places in the world where the history of colonialism and imperialism is written into (or out of) cultural artifacts and their interpretation, as it is by Foucault's theories of power dynamics and the Marxists of the Frankfurt school.

Any of the traits that emerge in the zombie's mythos, like contagion, or are effaced, like the connection to black magic, are worthy of study in and of themselves, and I know of other scholars working on different aspects of the mythology. My own interest, however, is in illustrating the substance and the history of the myth, which sets up a dyad between slavery and rebellion, the warring antinomies of the zombie's dialectic.

"Ki kote nou prale?" (Where are we going?)

The figure of the zombie embalms a particular narrative of slavery and rebellion. In four chapters, this book offers a "cultural history" of this aspect of the mythology, but it follows geographic and cross-disciplinary trajectories as well as chronological ones as I look at the zombie myth's transmissions across time, space, and media. One can plot key moments of the zombie's transformation on a timeline: when a spiritual enchantment becomes an explicitly botanical brand of sorcery; when it ceases to signify only the feeble slave and becomes capable of overturning the existing order; when, having made the trip to the United States, disseminated in published memoirs of US Marines stationed in Haiti during the long occupation, it becomes a binocular vision of the American factory worker as much as the African slave; when, hardly recognizable from its original form, it more clearly mirrors advanced capitalism rather than mercantile empire, looming on the incandescent screens of cinema houses, a monstrous by-product of corporate or government malfeasance, a slave only to its empty desire to consume; when in the twentieth century it is reconstituted and reclaimed in Haitian folklore and literature as a symbol of a distinctive history of resistance to political oppression; when it makes its appearance in contemporary political protests, and the symbolic register of the zombie inveighs against those who would wield its image for their cause.

To begin with, in chapter 1 I trace the historical moments that are preserved in the zombie's dyad of slavery and rebellion: in particular, the triangle trade and the Haitian Revolution. Looking primarily at historical and anthropological documents, this chapter examines nonfictional zombies belonging to spiritual cosmology and folklore to illustrate the way the political history of Haiti merges with ancestral mythologies hailing from Africa in the zombie narrative. In this chapter I begin to consider where the boundary between history and myth, political reality and social imagination, lies.

To imagine oneself as dead may not always be the kind of disempowering imagery that critics of Orlando Patterson's *Slavery and Social Death* have claimed it is. Vincent Brown's important book *The Reaper's Garden*—with its presentation of the role death played both in solidifying and challenging the established social order of the colonial sugar plantocracy in British Jamaica—can influence our reading of the zombie's history and its roots in the Haitian Revolution, during which death was embraced as a rallying cry in the rhetoric of rebellion. Acknowledgment of their own "social death" shored up the slaves' resistance, as in the rebel chant, "We have no mother, no child; What is death?" (Ott 39, 47). In chapter 1's discussion of the Haitian Revolution, during which death was equated with liberty and life with living death, enslavement is depicted as a kind of sorcery, a dream-in-death from which rebel slaves might awaken.

The Haitian scholar Laënnec Hurbon wrote in *Les mystères du vaudou* that there is a deep-seated connection between the Haitian Revolution and the people's practice of Vaudou: "Concerning Haiti, the news disseminated about the insurrection of 1791 and of the war for independence made evident an association between voodoo and savagery. The same theme, taken up again in the 20th century, would justify the American occupation and make of Haiti the funereal fatherland of the living dead" (51). This quotation brings to light two predominant areas of confusion concerning the zombie's history. First, there is much misinformation concerning when and how the myth of the walking dead came to be. The zombie does not first appear in those early twentieth-century texts that exoticized the island nation, which Hurbon suggests drummed up the myth of Haiti's walking dead to the degree that it served as justification for military intervention in a sovereign country. In actuality, as I also discuss in chapter 1, the word zombie and its orthographic variations have a history that reaches much further back in time than the American occupation of Haiti, though a paucity of reliable anthropological texts makes it difficult to tell precisely when the "zombie" took on the characteristics of the living dead.

Second, Hurbon's emphasis that it was the foreign writers of the 1920s and 1930s "[qui] fera d'Haïti la funestre patrie des morts vivants" ([who] make of Haiti the funereal fatherland of the living dead) raises the question of authorship (and thereby ownership) in an interesting but not decisive manner. Soon after its transmission to the United States, the subject of the second chapter here, the zombie became a cash crop for Hollywood, mostly because it provided a convenient topic that, due to its instantiation in nonfiction rather than fictional literature, would not require the studios to pay any royalties (Jaime Russell 19). The zombie was put in the cinematic spotlight precisely because it had no one author. In chapter 2, I examine the moment when the zombie narrative is translated in the United States.

Early zombie fiction developed within the horror genre with stories like G. W. Hutter's "Salt Is Not for Slaves" (published in *Ghost Stories* magazine in August 1931), August Derleth's "The House in the Magnolias" (in *Strange Tales*, July 1932), Vivien Meik's "White Zombie" (1933), and Thorp McClusky's 1939 story "While Zombies Walked" (in *Weird Tales* magazine). Many of these offerings tend to strike a nonfictional pose, often relaying the story within a frame narrative in which an experienced traveler or connoisseur of the exotic tells the narrator—or sometimes, it is assumed, author—of his experience with zombies. The nonfictional zombie's popularity—coupled with the fact that it required no copyright payments—would eventually lead to a uniquely "born in the USA" zombie, one that has continued to thrill moviegoers for nearly a century. This period of translation and the development of a cinematic zombie that still pays homage to its roots are addressed in detail in chapter 2. But although on film the zombie now bears only a distant resemblance to the originary mythology, the flesh-eating, contagious zombie of horror film nonetheless remains shaded by its direct lineage to its Haitian ancestor. Connecting the rare examples of films in which the Vaudou zombie narrative is preserved (or resuscitated) even after the mythology was co-opted and transformed in cinema, this chapter's study of zombies on film reveals much about racial prejudice, resistance, and attitudes to social justice as they evolved in the twentieth century.

Drawing attention to the conquest of the metaphor that was effected in its translation from Haitian folklore to American and European cinema, this book points out that this has not merely been a one-sided cultural conquest. Though, as Hurbon states above, "voodoo" and in particular images of "les morts-vivants" were used to denigrate Haiti as an exotic, savage, and superstitious country, in part to justify American involvement in the nation's politics, Vaudou and zombification have both at various points in Haiti's history crossed the threshold of the imaginary to have real-world political impact. Think, for instance, of Papa Doc's use of the iconography of Vaudou, coupled with the brute force of the Tonton Macoutes, to cement his people's fear of him. The zombie myth is reconstituted (or better, reincarnated) in contemporary Haiti in literature and folklore by means of what I call the meta-myth, the mythologization of the zombie myth's transformations, in a manner that empowers the Haitian people and depicts US culture *as having been colonized by* the zombie narrative. In chapter 3 I examine the era of Duvalier and his legacy for the recuperation of the zombie that occurs in Haitian literature after the reigns of Papa and Baby Doc. One has to look to the way the zombie is depicted in twentieth-century Haitian literature, and the manner in which twenty-first-century witch doctors characterize the mythology, employing it post hoc against the US occupation to fully understand the weight of the zombie metaphor as a tool of empowerment. This is the project taken up in chapter 3.

In chapter 4 I look to a recent trend wherein the zombie has ceased to be associated merely with film, folklore, and literature and has instead infiltrated a variety of media, including even the visual arts. Often, the return of the dead, as with ghosts, is equated with the enduring trace of the past. In some zombie narratives, the return of the dead becomes translated into an insistence on (or a tropological use of) repetition and revision to create a sense of narrative or even structural déjà vu, underlining the way that the past, in effect, is not only psychologically but also, on some level, *materially*, present or at least effective and affective—capable of producing both real-world effects and feelings in the here and now. The exact connection between themes of colonization and revolution and the use of repetition to represent these states is excavated most completely in chapter 4, where I articulate a category of "textual zombies" that seemingly critiques the metaphoric conquest and redirection of this myth. Suggesting the open wound of the post/neo/colonial condition, textual zombies employ narrative repetition or structural parallelism to intervene in as well as illustrate the ever-presentness of the past.

In the epilogue I briefly address the uses of zombies in live events like zombie walks, where an element of social protest is clearly visible, or the uses of the imagery of zombies in overt political demonstrations, like Occupy Wall Street, taking into consideration what is at stake in this use of the metaphor. Does it in some way pay homage to the zombie's heritage, or is it merely a culturally insensitive "occupation" of a people's symbol of resistance to colonial oppression and enslavement? In most films, zombies are deprived of speech, but, indeed, the zombie myth itself often seems to speak against those who invoke the metaphor of living death, even at times, as with the OWS protesters, perhaps directly contradicting them. At other times, the zombie refuses to talk.

The back-and-forth structure of the chapters also informs my use of the term zombie dialectics, as I transcribe the global conversation that has occurred over the ages in the form of this one particular myth. Along the way, I extrapolate grander questions from the myth and its place in popular culture: What is at stake in the zombie's suspension of the opposite concepts of slavery and resistance in dialogue in one form? What does this myth reveal about power through this maintained tension? And what can we learn from the zombie about the way that especially transnational myths negotiate political power more broadly?

I said earlier that the zombie embalms a particular narrative of slavery and resistance. An embalming isolates and makes visible a particular historical moment, but it also ensures that this moment continues to have relevance, continues, in a sense, to have life. An embalmed object of medical study, for example, continues to *work*, as it is used to teach successive generations of doctors. Likewise, the zombie crystallizes a narrative about a particular historical moment but is held up in different time periods to suit new purposes of comparison. This book looks at the enduring importance of this one cultural artifact for what it tells us about our relationship to the history of slavery and the practice of resistance, including even the practices of resistance that are made possible by myths and mythmaking.

So prevalent in popular culture today, the zombie makes but a few, murky appearances in the annals of previous centuries, existing only in written records preserved by the colonizers, the oral texts being lost to time. This book is not a recovery project that seeks to uncover the "authentic" zombie; indeed, coming as the earliest iteration of the mythology does out of an oral tradition would make this type of project impossible, unless we were to privilege certain types of information above others.

We cannot wrest all the answers about how the zombie myth solidified in the Caribbean colony of Saint Domingue, amid the influence of various African peoples as well as European modes of thought, by looking to the extant documents. I resist what I see as an imperialist epistemological impulse by beginning with the acknowledgment that the archive will not yield all the answers; there is, perforce, much about the zombie's history that is unknowable. That it refuses to be found in the written record should not be a source of frustration to us but should be celebrated as an indication of a people's own resistance to the colonial apparatuses that were recording (intentionally and incidentally)—in the journals of slaveholders, in the published accounts of missionaries, and in travelogues—the queer beliefs of the slaves.

Admitting, in essence, that there is a history of the zombie that is lost to us (or better, that refuses to be found), I am attentive to the way the zombie myth itself intervenes in, messes up, and resists "history." In a manner similar to the way all monsters trouble taxonomy, the zombie myth flouts the empirical impulses that seek, in labeling, categorizing, and defining, to conquer intellectual territories. One way this book resists the theoretical implications of a definitive "history" is in its structure. Although the arrangement of the chapters moves forward in time, each chapter centers on a different medium, so that we can defy the impulse to read a narrative of progress and instead think of this study as moving laterally across genres and modes rather than linearly through time. Therefore, chapter 1 focuses on the folkloric zombie; chapter 2, on the zombie in film; chapter 3, on the zombie in literature; chapter 4, on the zombie in the visual arts; and, to further resist a linear structure, the epilogue comes full circle, suggesting a return to the folkloric zombie in its examination of the zombie's use in contemporary social protest and communal performances.

Observing rather than overriding those moments when the zombie refuses to be found in the historical record, I concentrate instead on the instances of transmission, when the zombie narrative passes between cultures, for what is revealed about the ways each is changed by transaction. In doing so, I ask a series of questions: What is the payoff for those effectively borrowing, absconding with, or making use of a mythology that seemingly doesn't belong to them, as in the United States remaking the zombie in its own image in cinema? What is at stake in movements that appear to "reclaim" that mythology? Above all, I want to know what motivates assertions of authenticity or ownership of the myth, especially those that seek to erase the known past of the zombie's migration and overwrite it with a new semiotics.

The zombie myth bears witness to mythic and cultural transmissions, endemically furnishing a commentary on colonization, but it also comments on its own transmissions as a myth. The zombie is not just a myth about a particular history of enslavement and imperialism, but, more grandly, it is a myth about the way myths work in the (post)colonial era: as sites of cultural conquest and resistance. Specifically, the zombie illustrates the way myths allow us to intervene in history (itself always a myth), resist it, or question it, atone for or master it, holding open (in apology or defiance) an aperture through which to reflect on a society's past.

Reading the zombie in the light of its full historical, anthropological, and mythological context suggests how we might rethink other myths and symbols and their sources in order to look at a wider range of unintended significations. The zombie's resistive strategy is visible in those instances when the zombie "talks back." At least, this is how the US appropriation of the figure has been interpreted by some: not as colonization of their Haitian resources but, like something out of a horror movie, a curse that follows the oppressor home. The zombie's dialectic suggests a shift in thinking that might apply to elements of US American culture as diverse as the commercialization of Cinco de Mayo, with its oversized sombreros and tequila shots, or the way the Hindu bindi or Native American headdress has been made into a fashion accessory sported by pop stars. To merely call these out as appropriations is to ignore their influence. They are compelling narratives and captivating objects, and it is for this reason that capitalism seeks to commodify them, to dispel their power. This book emphasizes the way fictions and myths like the zombie have contributed in a very real manner to an alternative strategy of colonial and postcolonial resistance: the counteroccupation of mythical space.

1 / Slavery and Slave Rebellion: The (Pre)History of the Zombi/e

No slavery! Long live Death.
—BATTLE CRY OF HAITIAN REVOLUTIONARIES, IN LAURENT DUBOIS AND
JOHN D. GARRIGUS, *SLAVE REBELLION IN THE CARIBBEAN*

On July 30, 1789, a wealthy colonist from the French-controlled side of an island that had previously been known as Hispaniola and that was currently divided between France and Spain, spoke before the one-month-old National Assembly. He said, "The glorious epoch is now arrived when France quits her chains, emerges from her darkness, and is warmed to animation, by the bright beams of the Sun of Liberty" (*European Magazine* 208). Some might say that it was callous of the Martinique-born white Creole, Messr Médéric-Louis-Elie Moreau de St. Méry, to draw a comparison between France's monarchical system and the chains of enslavement, between a nascent republic and a freed slave, when wealthy French colonists like himself had no intention of lessening the plight of the Africans who worked, and would continue to work, the cane-rich colonies of Saint Domingue for their exclusive profit. To Moreau de St. Méry, as in much of the discourse surrounding the American Revolution, the slave's irons seemed a good metaphor to inhabit, but he wouldn't want to literally live there.[1]

Moreau de St. Méry's statement is an image of resurrection as much as liberation: France is "warmed to animation by the bright beams of the Sun of Liberty." If we make nothing else of this, we can note that his words intimate that those who are not free are not quite living. And yet it was just a few years later that he would flee to Philadelphia, where in 1797 he would publish his *Description topographique, physique, civile, politique et historique de la partie française de l'Isle de Saint Domingue*, the text in which, according to most dictionaries of French etymology, the word zombi appears in print for the first time. There would have been an interested market for such a volume at the time. In Saint Domingue, the cane fields were burning. The slaves, unwilling to wait for the "Sun of Liberty" to shine on them, were warming themselves to animation by the light of their own fires, a blaze that would become the Haitian Revolution.

Most historians typically begin to tell the story of Haitian independence with the description of the Bois Caïman Vaudou ceremony, a gathering of slaves that involved the sacrifice of a black pig and a blood oath swearing them to carry out rebellion on their own plantations. Antoine Dalmas, who purportedly wrote the first account of the Bois Caïman ceremony in his 1814 *Histoire de la Révolution de Saint-Domingue*, describes "a black pig, surrounded by objects [the slaves] believe have magical power, each carrying the most bizarre offering, [that] was offered as a sacrifice to the all-powerful spirit of the black race. The religious ceremony in which the nègres slit its throat, the greed with which they drank its blood, the importance they attached to owning some of its bristles which they believed would make them invincible reveal the characteristics of the African" (qtd. in Dubois and Garrigus 90).

Leaving aside the overt bias of its author, this characterization of the Bois Caïman ceremony as uniting the slaves' religious practice with the spirit of rebellion is not isolated. The witness accounts of the rebel slaves and the early histories of the revolution emphasize that Vaudou played a part in instilling in the insurgents an indefatigable spirit. Jacques Nicolas Léger writes that the Vaudouists, "in order to inspire the slave with confidence in them[,] . . . pretended to possess supernatural powers, such as being able to insure happiness, to make their enemies impotent, and defy death itself by becoming invulnerable" (356). Many ascribed to Vaudou the manufacture of charms—alluded to by Dalmas himself in his reference to hog bristles taken as souvenirs—which slave-soldiers during the rebellion and revolution believed made them invulnerable to bullets. As I discuss, there is a direct line that connects the metaphysical tactics of the Haitian revolutionary and the Vaudou zombie.

In contemporary accounts of the Haitian Revolution, the ferocity of the rebels was denigrated: they were less than men; they were animals or machines run amok. This is the transformation by which the dehumanized slave becomes the inhuman rebel. In contemporary accounts penned by Europeans and former colonists, the rebel slaves were not bestowed with a comparison to the Resurrection, though this vocabulary, as we see in the impassioned speech of Moreau de St. Méry, was the natural conclusion of the narrative when it was a metaphoric slave shaking himself free of his shackles. Similarly, the zombie is not a figure of resurrection but only of living death, and insofar as the zombie metaphorizes both slavery and slave rebellion (an argument I've been making since the publication of my coauthored piece "A Zombie Manifesto" in 2008), its ability to represent not merely enslavement, but liberation from that state, is tempered by its irresolvable dialecticality.

The larger project of this book is to illustrate the way that, at various points in its mythology, the figure of the zombie clearly represents one or the other: the history of a people's enslavement or that of their fierce resistance to oppression. More than a decade after a black pig was slaughtered in the Bois Caïman ceremony and the cane fields were burned, the first black republic declared its independence on the first day of the year 1804, proclaiming that all its citizens would remain forever free of the bondage of slavery. Out of the ashes of a war that had raged for thirteen years and in full view of an empire that had been brought to its knees by the conflict, a new subject did indeed, as Moreau de St. Méry suggested in his address before the National Assembly, come forth out of the darkness, freed of his chains, to take his place among the citizens of the free world, but as a member of the republic of Haiti. This, a nation's inauguration out of what was once a colony of displaced slaves—a moment redolent of images of birth and rebirth, animation, and resurrection—is also a flash point in the history of the mythology of the soulless, living dead that today we call the zombie. Significantly, the Haitian Revolution is the big bang that gives rise to two dialectical theories of power relations: one we associate with Caribbean folklore, the other with Continental philosophy. Neither pair of oppositions is as simple as it would seem.

Hegel's theory of the master and the bondsman—which we know from Susan Buck-Morss's landmark piece, "Hegel and Haiti," was written as Hegel read, in Jena from 1803 to 1805, accounts of the Saint Domingue slave rebellion that had bloomed into a war for independence (844)—clarifies, first, that the identity of the master is dependent upon the slave for definition and, second, that the consciousness of the slave comes to being through a process of realizing its negative constitution of the master's existence.[2] In the abstract sense in which self-consciousness is concerned, Hegel's master becomes the slave and the slave, the master.

Furthermore, this turnabout is achieved through a "trial by death," important, Buck-Morss emphasizes, for its direct implication of slave revolt (849). It is in the process of seeking the death of the other and being willing to risk one's own life that they each "raise the certainty of being for themselves to truth" (Hegel 114). Hegel writes, "And it is only through staking one's life that freedom is won.... The individual who has not risked his life may well be recognized as a person, but he has not attained to the truth of this recognition as an independent self-consciousness" (114). But the gain of this life-and-death struggle, in Hegel's description, comes to seem like a vanishing point: "This trial by death, however, does away with the truth which was supposed to issue from it, and so, too, with the certainty of self generally. For just as life is the natural setting of consciousness, independence without absolute negativity, so death is the natural negation of consciousness, negation without independence, which thus remains without the required signification of recognition" (114). The self, therefore, may have established itself in its willingness to die, but it will not be around to enjoy the victory.

In the inseparability of the identities "master" and "bondsman," and in this description of the "trial by death," for what comes to seem like an infinite deferral of resolution, the master/slave dialectic finds a murky reflection in the figure of the zombie and the zombie's dialectic. The zombie, as much as it represents life and death in one form—a two-headed monster, a terrible miracle—is also an incarnation of the slave and the slave-in-revolt. At all moments, the zombie's paradoxical nature—as living dead, neither fully conscious nor completely inert—suggests the inseparability of these figures. In the most negative reading, the zombie's pathos, its irresolvable dialecticality, seems an apt reflection of a people denied a right to life by their oppressors, many of whom would have to fight to the death for their freedom, leaving the survivors to face a host of challenges in a postcolonial state. Typically, the zombie is not liberated but merely deanimated, though myths can be rewritten.

In a more positive interpretation, the duality of the zombie also makes visible what Michel Foucault would later articulate about the dynamics of power relations. Although Foucault writes, in "The Subject and Power," "Power is exercised only over free subjects, and only insofar as they are free ... [for] slavery is not a power relation when man is in chains, he adds, "There is no face-to-face confrontation of power and freedom which is mutually exclusive (freedom disappears everywhere power is exercised), but a much more complex interplay" (221). He continues: "The relationship between power and freedom's refusal to submit cannot therefore be separated.... Rather than speaking of an essential freedom, it would be better to speak of an 'agonism'—of a relationship which is at the same time reciprocal incitation and struggle" (221–22). And later: "Every power relation implies, at least in potentia, a strategy of struggle, in which the two forces are not superimposed, do not lose their specific nature, or do not finally become confused. Each constitutes for the other a kind of permanent limit, a point of possible reversal" (225). One might contend that the wall separating and yet joining the slave and the rebel, as well as the master and the slave, is not a wall at all: it is fleshly, seeping, and porous. It is this movable boundary that we should look to for delimitation of the power relations involved in the institution of slavery, and in its resistance.

One of the central claims of this chapter—and of this book—is that the zombie is not merely an allegory for slavery, but is also representative of resistance; indeed, the zombie itself is an embodiment of one mode of resistance, mythmaking. When we think more broadly about what constitutes slavery and what constitutes resistance, the zombie's living dead state suggests the difficulty of separating the slave from the slave-in-revolt, an idea that has had traction in the field of slavery studies for some time, with the suggestion that demonstrations of agency aside from overt rebellion are worthy of consideration as acts of resistance, no matter the political or social impact. The zombie's dual metaphorization of slavery and rebellion continually conveys that the roles are not crystallized, forgive the expression, in black and white: even the docile slave is sometime a rebel and the free man, sometimes still a slave. The same duality is visible in postcolonial Haiti: sometimes, as we will find in studying the zombie myth's machinations, resistance masquerades as subjugation, the better to fight undetected. Yet similar to Hegel's "trial by death," which immediately negates that which it established (being-for-itself), the zombie's dialectic (always already undead) ultimately refuses any kind of definitive synthesis. The zombie is, after all, not a concrete weapon but a myth, and thus remains mired, like an example of dialectics-at-a-standstill (to borrow a description of Walter Benjamin's concept of the dialectical image), in a balancing act on, as Max Pensky puts it, "the unresolvable cusp of oppositions" (193).[3]

How the zombie functions in US cinema and popular culture today is a complicated issue, for it acts simultaneously as a dramatization of disempowerment (often in the form of a frustrated critique of capitalism) in line with its previous incarnation of slavery and as a fantasy of rebellion against the hegemonic order. The zombie of American cinema is epitomized in George Romero's oeuvre—from the mall-haunting ghouls of *Dawn of the Dead* (1978) to the undead legions that follow their leader, a zombie in a workman's uniform, in *Land of the Dead* (2005). As in these two examples, the cinematic zombie is a slave to its drives, but it is also redolent of the rebelling mob. It has but one function—to blindly consume—and yet it is relentless in this pursuit. It is a blank, subhuman, negative image of man, and yet, as depicted in World War Z (2013), in a swarm it is powerful, even posthuman. It may stand for the faceless crowd at a distance, but up close the zombie typically bears identifying marks, the traces of its former self—like Johnny with his driving gloves in Night of the Living Dead (1968). In representing simultaneously the individual and the horde, it also tacitly suggests the duality of the state's mechanism of control as Foucault described it: "both an individualizing and a totalizing form of power" (213). But because life persists where it should not, the zombie is inherently resistant, if only to the forces of nature. This is the most elemental way that the zombie recalls, at one and the same time, enslavement and rebellion. Just as it exists in a state of living death, it dramatizes (non)existence; it belongs completely to neither category; it is ontologically defiant at the same time that it is a nonentity.

Books describing how the zombie morphs from the folkloric somnambulistic slave to the cinematic contagious cannibal have been written for a popular audience, and most well-read zombiephiles now know that the zombie migrated to the United States in narratives written by journalists like William Seabrook (1884–1945) and in the memoirs of Marines stationed in Haiti during the American occupation (1915–34). But the connection between the Haitian zombie and the political history of the country that spawned both it *and* Hegel's master/slave dialectic is not merely incidental to its narrative structure; rather, the zombie's history, its connection to Saint Domingue, the most profitable slave colony in the New World, and to Haiti, site of the slave rebellion that became a national revolution, *informs* its symbolic mechanism, its dramatization of the dialectic between disempowerment and resistance. This first chapter of the book concerns the history and, what has previously been untold, the prehistory of this figure, looking specifically to the zombie's ancestors in Africa and its parallels in the Haitian Revolution in order to explain the larger significance of a being that is perplexingly, paradoxically, simultaneously an archetypal figure of subjugation and of active resistance, like the revolutionary's creed, "Long Live Death!"

This chapter provides an archaeology of the zombie, excavating its African ancestors and in doing so examining the origins of the slave/slave rebellion dichotomy that is so central to the zombie's history and to its currency today as a cultural metaphor. Tracing the zombie's earliest migration (not to "America" but to the Americas) and the initial transformation that accompanied this move at last clarifies many inchoate questions concerning the zombie's association with Haiti and the zombie's resonance with themes of resistance. As I trace this path, we will see that the zombie's association with rebellion is actually endemic to the figure and its forebears.

Resistance was always, in some sense, a feature of the zombie's makeup. The history presented here is critical to an understanding of the ramifications of the zombie's (mis)translation for Euro-Americans in the early twentieth-century remaking of the myth in cinema, presented in the next chapter, so that we can fully account for the zombie's transformations, the redactions of certain aspects of the myth and the ramifications of its redirection to suit the aims of a new audience. The zombie's capacity to symbolize resistance will seem all the more trenchant when those moments are revealed in which the myth itself resists appropriation, refusing to have its historical associations with colonial resistance leached out of it, and instead retains its dual significations.

Yet—with the zombie there is always a "yet" or a "but," or a "however" and a "nonetheless"—the irresolution of the zombie's dialectic (not master/slave but slave/rebel-slave) continues to thwart attempts to read the figure as wholly resistive. Mapping the zombie onto the motif of living death in the Haitian Revolution, as I do in the second part of the chapter, reveals that on either side of the binary—for both the historical slave of Saint Domingue in the characterizations of the colonizers and the cinematic zombie—one is confronted not with depictions of men but with nonhuman objects. But if synthesis is impossible in the living dead zombie, catharsis may still be offered, for the myth may have real-world power. This is the field of inquiry that surrounds the zombie's dialectic, and it will take the full span of several centuries (and the length of this book) to illustrate precisely how it works.

The Zombie Slave

The true history of the technique of zombification, as it was described in Wade Davis's work in the 1980s, including *The Serpent and the Rainbow* (1985) and *Passage of Darkness: The Ethnobiology of the Haitian Zombie* (1988), which made legible the zombie as the victim of a pharmacological arsenal employed by a witch doctor, necessarily invokes the herbal expertise that was a weapon of the rebel slave.[4] One might suppose that it was only once the raw material of the zombie myth—fragments from multiple points of origin (European legends, African religion, indigenous knowledge)—came together in the Caribbean by means of the slave trade and colonial rule and had been melded in the conflagration of the Haitian Revolution that the zombie solidified as an anticolonial mythology as well as the product of empire. In the longer passage from which comes the Haitian author René Depestre's now well-worn aphorism, "The history of colonization is the process of man's general zombification," he explains that the zombie myth is deeply rooted in Haiti's history as a colony (qtd. in McAlister, *Rara!* 108). But the inverse may also be true: the zombie takes on a special significance in Haiti because of its defining history of slave insurrection.[5]

It seems that if we can approximate any sort of birthdate for the zombie, a figure that combines the oppression of the slave with the image of slave revolt, it would surely be the moment when the Haitian republic declared its sovereignty. The paltry archive of early written fragments recording this originally oral mythology bears witness to the fact that it was only after the Haitian had obtained the potion that liberated him from slavery that the mythic zombie could take up this valence and represent the people's dual struggle: oppressed slaves who had transformed themselves into slaves-in-revolt. And yet to understand the full import of the zombie's dialectic, and what, for me, is its ultimate irresolution, one must retrace the zombie's path back in time and space, from the Caribbean colonies to Africa.

THE HISTORY OF THE "ZOMBI"

The history of the zombie is one that has to be written not just by connecting dots on a line, but by pointing to the effacements, the blank spaces and the omissions in our knowledge, as if—appropriately for a hybrid creature such as the living dead—we have to trace its history as much through its absences as its presences. The earliest iteration of the word *zombie* (in any language) appears in the title of a book published in France in 1697 but possibly published earlier in the Antilles. *Le Zombi du Grand Perou* was later attributed to the French writer, serial criminal, and gigolo who was called the "Casanova of the seventeenth century," Pierre-Corneille de Blessebois (1646–1700). This novel, composed in both prose and verse, was largely considered obscene, but it has garnered some interest because it is thought to be a roman à clef lampooning historical figures such as Dupont, one of the wealthiest planters in the French Caribbean colonies (Garraway 175–76). The principal plot concerns a jilted Creole countess who has been wronged by her lover, the marquis of Grand Perou (a locality in Guadeloupe, a French colony that neighbored Saint Domingue), who broke up the countess's marriage, used her for carnal pleasure, and began dragging his feet on promises to marry her. She seeks help from the narrator, a supposed sorcerer, to make her invisible so that she can exact her revenge, and she exchanges sexual favors for these charms.

The sorcerer only pretends to make her invisible, which leads to great comedy as the household servants have to pretend that they cannot see the creeping woman overturning chairs. In the end the countess learns her lesson about fooling with black magic when naughty "zombis" keep her up all night. These are actually only accomplices of the sorcerer tormenting the woman, but here zombi denotes biting, pinching, hair-plucking spirits that try to get the victim to open his or her eyes or make a noise. If they succeed, they will have the power to do worse (Blessebois 45–46).

There are no soulless embodied zombies in this text, though the word zombi is used at various points to mean "un fantôme, un esprit, un sorcier," as the author of the introduction writes (xxxviii). The word is also attached to spirits that walk around having left their bodies resting elsewhere (41), charms that render the person's body invisible, and maleficent entities ("Zombis de ronde") that pester and can lead one to do evil (41). There are also flying zombies that always carry torches (47) and even mentions of wax figures that were used to torture people by European witches (27)—an early reference to voodoo dolls, perhaps, which illustrates an instance of syncretism between European and Caribbean witchcraft.

In the end, the sorcerer does not fare well. He is picked up by the marquis's henchmen and thrown into a dungeon for his crimes, at which point he mounts the following defense: "But there is nothing supernatural in my productions; there is only imprudence and indiscretion, and I have no fear of my false witnesses" (57–58). The text seems to serve as an indictment of the local superstitions, which is a common theme in the writings of colonists and missionaries of the period. But as Doris Garraway writes in *The Libertine Colony*, "Blessebois's text corroborates the close association between indentured servitude and witchcraft[,] . . . selling one's body to the master and selling one's soul to the spirit of evil" (Garraway 182). Whether or not the sorcery described in the text is meant to be understood as real or illusory, and despite the lack of zombies as we think of them today, there is still a similar commentary on servitude, power, and magic.

In the scenes in which various characters recount their experiences with the supernatural forces of the island, Garraway writes, "the zombi accrues meaning as a frightful entity in the colonial imagination, one that is believed to shape shift, or metamorphose, in myriad ways" (180). Although folklorists emphasize that the word came to have a double meaning in Haiti—signifying a body without a soul as well as a soul without a body—there is no timeline available that can pinpoint precisely the evolution of the concept.[6] And though there is a central divide between embodied and disembodied zombies, both might be said to represent the slave in certain instances and the rebel in others. For example, the zombie's soul, called elsewhere the "zombi astral," can be captured and imprisoned in a bottle to do work for its master as a "Zombi bouteille."[7] It seems logical that the French colonists may have had more to fear from invisible, powerful zombi spirits like those described in Blessebois's narrative, which were similar to the ghosts, specters, and spirits of their own superstitions, than the counterpart slow-witted soulless zombie laborer one encounters in later fiction. Perhaps this explains the embodied zombie's absence in texts written by libertines like Blessebois. Regardless, the word zombi very seldom appears in conjunction with either type of being until much later in the written record.

The next earliest published reference that one finds to the "zombi" is Moreau de St. Méry's aforementioned *Description . . . de la partie française de l'Isle de Saint Domingue*. In fact, this is the typical reference that we find cited for the period, "un comte de *Zombi*, mot créole qui signifie esprit, revenant" (*Trésor de la langue française* 1:52). Moreau's use of the word does little to clarify whether the "Zombi" was at this time only considered a spirit or whether it also signified a body emptied of its soul.[8] That Moreau de St. Méry compares the zombi to the medieval revenant seems to signify that it could be fleshly. The second edition of the *Dictionnaire infernal*, published first in 1818, claims that "un revenant se trouve toujours froid quand on le touche," a revenant is always cold to the touch (de Plancy 577).[9] Nonetheless, it is impossible to know when these Europeans' definitions are accurate and when they reflect the inability of the chroniclers to translate a belief system that was so foreign and much more fluid in terms of the categories of the spiritual and material into their own Judeo-Christian vocabulary, wherein spirit and body were diametrically opposed.

One can trace a variant spelling of the word zombi to the 1765 French *Encyclopèdie*, where it is mentioned only in passing, under the entry titled "nègre." The article specifically investigates the behavior of the *nègre* as it pertained to managing slaves in the colonies. Under the subheading "Caractère des nègres en général" is written, "If by chance one encounters honest men among the *nègres* of Guinea, (the majority are nonetheless vicious.) [sic] they are for the most part inclined toward debauchery, vengeance, theft, and lies. Their stubbornness is such that they will never admit their faults, no matter what punishment one makes them submit to; the fear of death moves them not at all. Despite this kind of immovability, their natural bravery doesn't guard them against fear of sorcerers and spirits, which they call *zambys*" (11:82).[10]

The subject of "sorcerers and spirits" here comprises a large category tented under the broad signifier "zambys." In the same entry of the *Encyclopèdie*, the author writes of the "Arada," an African population living in Saint Domingue, "many of [whom] know perfectly the good or ill properties of various plants unknown in Europe. The Arada principally use the venom of certain insects to compose a poison for which there is no known cure.[11] The effects of which are so singular, that those who use it pass continually for sorcerers among the inhabitants of the land" (11:81). Here we see an oblique reference to what will come to be the accepted, secularized definition of the Haitian zombie put forth first by colonists and missionaries and later by foreign journalists, anthropologists, and scientists who ventured to study the phenomenon: it is not a body literally raised from the dead but merely the victim of poisoning in the guise of sorcery. This will doubtless seem like a leap, unless we take the time to connect the dots and bridge the gaps between these earliest references to the zambys/zombi and the travelers' tales that would interpret and interpolate the zombie for the "Western" imagination.

Some trace the origins of the word zombi back to the Congolese deity Nzambi, "an invisible being with origins in the Bantu and Bankongo tribes in the Nzambi Mpungu region of the lower Congo River area, who reportedly oversaw the people of the region," which could be related to the variant spelling zambys (Boon 50–51). In Congo bad spirits are still known as "mpeve zambi" (Bockie 64), though an evil dead somewhat closer to the horror film's zombie (in that they torment their living ancestors) are Nkuyu (Bockie 131–32). In contrast to the French etymology, the word Zombi first appears in print in English in Robert Southey's *History of Brazil (1810–1819)*, though there it is used to refer to the Angolan deity. Samuel Taylor Coleridge, the author's brother-in-law, converses with Southey in the margins of his copy, now preserved in the British Library, on the subject of this deity. There is, therefore, likely an earlier reference to which they were both referring, possibly Sebastião de Rocha Pita's 1730 *History of Portuguese America*, which is mentioned in Coleridge's margin note.[12]

Zombie has a complicated etymological history. The word is sometimes, incorrectly, I think, associated with the Spanish sombra (shadow),

Indian words like zemi, or the West African duppy, a shape-shifting ghost derived from the spirits of the dead.[13] Though the zombie may have evolved from aspects of African religions, be they guardians of the people like the Angolan Zombi, Congo's Nzambi or zambi, or the Vaudou lwa Damballah, called Li Gran Zombi in New Orleans, or even malicious ghosts like the duppy, this etymological research does not clarify the origins of the zombie as a spiritless body, though it situates the word as African in origin.

My own hypothesis is that the unnamed ancestral myth closest to what we today consider a "zombie" hailed from West Central Africa, where, in close proximity, there is a region called Zombo, a deity called Nzambi, and a Congo practice of creating bottle fetishes called Zumbi. Betraying the syncretism that happened perforce due to the transatlantic slave trade, it may be that a Loangoan belief in soul capture by sorcerers became conflated with other concepts, like the talismanic objects of its African neighbors, or the Congo bottle fetish Zumbi (called "nkisi" in nearby Loango) may have merged at some point with the concept of soul enslavement, for we certainly see its relative in the Zombi bouteille, previously mentioned. This is supported by Vincent Brown's description of the Loangan nkisi, spelled here minkisi, "spiritual charms [that] could be used to effect one's will in the world" (Reaper's Garden 144). Here Brown quotes from Robert Farris Thompson's *The Four Moments of the Sun: Kongo Art in Two Worlds*: "The nkisi [was] believed to live with an inner life of its own. The basis of that life was a captured soul.... The owner of the charm could direct the spirit in the object to accomplish mystically certain things for him" (37).[14]

The best comprehensive resource on the etymology of zombie is Hans-W. Ackermann and Jeanine Gauthier's article "The Ways and Nature of the Zombi," which includes fumbi, the Yoruba word for spirit; mvumbi, a Congolese word for a cataleptic person; and nvumbi, the Angolan term for "a body without a soul," as probable relatives of the zombi. Another possibility might be that the word arose from a common ancestor of one of these, like vumbi, translated in Adam Hochschild's book on the Belgian Congo, *King Leopold's Ghost*, as pale "ancestral ghosts" (15). Hochschild records that Africans of the region mistook the first white slavers that they saw for *vumbi* "since the Kongo people believed that a person's skin changed to the color of chalk when he passed into the land of the dead" (15). That this belief, in some capacity, was transmitted to Haiti is evidenced in Dany Laferrière's novel *Pays sans chapeau*. The narrator says at one point that the ever present dust in Port-au-Prince is one of the things that makes the population seem like the living dead, for his grandmother had explained to him that the dead are always covered with a fine white powder: "It's because the road that goes there"—a path that the narrator himself will later travel on his journey to the land of the dead, *pays sans chapeau* (lit., "land without hats"), so called because no one is buried in his hat—is "long and dusty. That oppressive white dust" (69). That zombification is often effected by aspiration of a powder—as depicted in the 1988 film based on Davis's nonfictional account, *The Serpent and the Rainbow*, in which the zombie powder is blown in the victim's face—may suggest a possible link between the powdery white vumbi and our zombie.

But of the exact route the word zombie took to the Americas, and what it signified along the way, we have no precise record. Because the *Oxford English Dictionary* lists it as one of the first appearances of the word zombi in English, many scholars of zombie film trace the word only as far back as Lafcadio Hearn's perhaps misleadingly titled essay, "The Country of the Comers-Back," published in *Harper's Magazine* in 1889. Hearn's essay is on Martinique, not Haiti (which is traditionally considered the birthplace of the zombie), but more important, by Hearn's definition, a zombi does *not* resemble "one who comes back." In answer to his question about the zombie, he receives the following reply:

'Zombi? Mais ça fai désòde lanuitt, zombi!'
'Ah! it is Something which "makes disorder at night."'
Still that is not a satisfactory explanation. 'Is it the spectre of a dead person, Adou? Is it one who comes back?'
'Non, Missié,—non, çé pas ça.' (57)

Indeed, in Hearn's account, the "zombi" is nothing like a "revenant," still less like a walking corpse. Among the list of things he cites that might be a zombi in disguise are a woman fourteen feet tall (57), a very large dog (57), a horse with three legs (58), and a child growing taller by the minute (59). There is also a tale told of fires that seem to recede ever farther into the distance as you approach them. These are called "Evil Fires,—*mauvai difé*"; they are purportedly set by zombis, and if you follow them they will lure you off the edge of a cliff or into a cavern (58).[15]

Therefore, at the point at which Hearn is chronicling, and in neighboring Martinique rather than Haiti, the word zombi is associated with a shape-shifting spirit rather than the zombie as we know it today.[16] Later in the text, the zombi is distinguished outright from the returned dead: "zombis go everywhere: the dead folk remain in the graveyard. . . . Except on the Night of All Souls: then they go to the houses of their people everywhere" (57). Therefore, these Martiniquan zombis are quite clearly mischievous beings, but they are not the spirits of men, certainly not the reanimated bodies of the dead.

Hearn himself makes evident the duplicitous nature of the island's moniker by beginning his 1890 volume, *Two Years in the French West Indies*, with an epigraph from le Père Dutertre (1610–87), a French missionary who published "Histoire générale des Antilles habitées par les Français" in 1667: "The manner of being in the country is so agreeable, the temperature so good, and one lives there with a liberty that is so honest, that I have not seen a single man, nor a single woman, in whom, upon returning, I did not remark a great enthusiasm for having returned" (frontispiece).

Hearn includes an explanation: "He who first gave to Martinique its poetical name, Le Pays des Revenants, thought of his wonderful island only as 'The Country of Comers-Back' where Nature's unspeakable spell bewitches wandering souls like the caress of a Circe,—never as the Land of Ghosts" (148). We see in this quotation the admission that the lure of the island was its natural charm, not anything having to do with the supernatural.[17] In fact, this malapropism ironically mirrors the evolution of the zombie concept, wherein something first associated with occult powers changed to one anchored in natural phenomena in the zombie myth's association with poisons endemic to the region; in the misinterpretation of the epithet, the Caribbean island's reputation for natural beauty is eclipsed by its reputation for harboring strange, spectral goings-on.

The name "Le Pays des Revenants" has also been attributed to Père Labat (1663–1738), another French missionary posted in the Caribbean who in 1722 published a book on his voyages titled *Nouveau voyage aux isles de l'Amérique*.[18] Both Dutertre and Labat wrote extensively on the habits and superstitions of the slave and native populations of the Caribbean islands. Yet among the nearly thousand pages that Labat left on the French islands of America," which describe, often in excruciating detail, the dress of natives, the dances of which the slaves were most fond, and the flora and fauna, there is no reference to the word zombi or the concept of the *corps cadavre*, "ko kadav" (walking dead). This seems especially strange given that there are extensive sections devoted to "Les Vaudoux" (vol. 2, pt. 5, chap. 7) and the religion of the slaves (vol. 2, pt. 4, chap. 5), as well as the history of "quelques nègres sorciers" (vol. 1, pt. 2, chap. 3). Nonetheless, there are many references to diverse superstitions and beliefs: people who can make it rain (1:153–54); people who can make objects talk (1:156); people demonstrating supernatural insensibility to pain (2:45); and even some vampirelike Negresses who cause the death of people by eating their hearts without laying a hand on them (2:45–47).[19] The author claims that "almost all the Negroes who leave their country having reached manhood are sorcerers, or at least have some taint of magic, sorcery and poison" (2:44). Like the description of the Arada from the French encyclopedia, this is in line with a long tradition that equated poison with magic in descriptions of the slaves' occult powers, yet there is nothing among Labat's tomes that resembles the walking dead. One way to account for this striking absence in such an exhaustive catalog of the slaves' practices, and particularly of their strange beliefs, is that the myth of the enslaved soulless corpse had not yet attained the kind of currency it would hold, after the revolution, among the population of newly manumitted slaves in the Caribbean.

Though it is asserted by many that the myth of a body separated from its soul likely migrated from Africa with the slaves, the word zombi is not commonly attached to this concept until later. A time line of references to the "zombi" in the French texts coming out of the colony of Saint Domingue and other Caribbean isles has to take into consideration these events: (1) Blessebois described various kinds of bodiless spirits as "zombis" in 1697; (2) Labat published his book in 1722 without giving this name to any of the various spirits, forces, and charms that he describes, and neither is there an assertion that sorcerers are raising the dead. Here the absence of the zombi may be counted as a negative presence, signifying that the concept may not have had the circulation it would later attain (3). By 1797 Moreau de St. Méry had described the zombi as "a spirit, a revenant," obscuring whether it was then understood as material rather than disembodied. There was yet no revelation in the writings of colonists and missionaries that the zombie was a corpse raised and put to work by a sorcerer. By 1809, however, the word zombie had become allied with an entity that could explicitly take on human form.

In his 1809 *Voyage d'un naturaliste . . . (1799–1803),* M. E. Descourtilz devotes a section to familial relationships. He is recounting the story of a young man who returned home from a period spent serving as a soldier to find his mother living in abject poverty. Repulsed by her situation, he denounces her: "il la repousse en disant que cette vielle zombie n'avait jamais été sa mère" (140). He pushed her away, saying that this old zombie had never been his mother. This passage, dating from 1809 but recording anthropological research from a decade earlier, represents the earliest text that explicitly references a "zombie" in the sense that we now think of one—as *embodied* rather than intangible and taking human form rather than that of a god or some other spirit. One might even stretch the words on the page to suggest that the zombie, by this time, could resemble or replace someone once familiar, a trope that is now commonplace in the zombie's idiom. If we follow the line of thought that suggests that the zombified were people who had been found guilty of crimes or immoral behavior and were a source of shame to their families, the young man may be using the term as a means of disowning his mother.[20] His invocation of the term zombie probably serves as a figurative denouncement rather than a literal accusation that she is the walking dead. But whether the son is claiming hyperbolically that this woman is zombielike because she brings him social embarrassment or that the accused was missing her soul or whether Descourtilz's zombie is more akin to the West African shape-shifting duppy and is merely a being impersonating his mother, this example illustrates that the European's understanding of the word was expanding.[21] In any case, it seems that by this time the "zombi" was comprehended as a spirit that could take on flesh or a specter that yet looked identical to the person it once was.[22]

If it is difficult to pinpoint exactly when the word zombi became allied with the walking corpse, it is more difficult to trace how the concept solidifies into a myth of a body unburied—with the insinuation of the involvement of various paralyzing poisons—and forced to labor interminably. As with the etymological history, the earliest narratives describing elements that become key ingredients of the zombie's makeup are preserved only in a few scant texts written by colonizers. Until the Haitian Revolution, that is. As a sovereign nation, Haitians would define (and then redefine) the zombie and its role in society; its emphasis would oscillate from the enslavement of the living corpse to the technology of zombie-making and its potential as a weapon, depending on the most pressing political, social, and cultural concerns of the Haitian people.

THE ZOMBIE'S JOURNEY

That the nation of Haiti was home to sorcerers who attempted or pretended to raise the dead was documented definitively in 1835 when the Penal Code appeared on record as part of Haitian law (Hurbon 56). In it was the strange and now-infamous Article 249: "Also shall be qualified as attempted murder the employment which may be made against any person of substances which, without causing actual death, produce a lethargic coma more or less prolonged. If, after the administering of such substances, the person has been buried, the act shall be considered murder *no matter what result follows*" (103; qtd. in Seabrook, translation his). Though the word *zombie* is absent from Article 249, this description forecasts the zombie as William Seabrook's *The Magic Island* would present it, a century later, to the Blancs.

This passage, oft-quoted on zombie film fan sites, confirms, if not the widespread acceptance of the zombie legend by the first third of the nineteenth century, then at least the fact that people in Haiti were being administered substances that gave the illusion of death and that the problem had become so prevalent that it required legislation. Article 249 makes clear that a person found dispensing such drugs would be charged with murder if the person were buried, "no matter what result follows." Seabrook's 1929 account, "Dead Men Working in the Cane Fields," marked the decisive union of the word zombie with the walking corpse—a coupling that would captivate American audiences from the first films in the 1930s to the present day. But before the ultimately inaccessible, obscure point and time of its collision with the word zombie, the concept of the walking dead, or *corps cadavre*, was on its own journey.

Though we can trace the roots of the word zombi to Africa, it is harder to establish a definitive connection between the Haitian zombie and the apparitions described in African folklore that may in fact be directly related but whose histories evade anthropological and ethnographic records. Yet there are other genes legible in the zombie's ancestry that can be more easily mapped. For example, many African religions have beliefs that involve the stealing of souls, both of corpses and of live persons. Wyatt MacGaffrey writes in *Religion and Society in Central Africa*:

> Witches may suck out or draw off (vola, hola) all or part of the soul, depriving all or part of the body of its inner essence, so that in a short time it will be seen to sicken or die.... [T]he soul is removed from its ordinary container and enclosed in another in such a way that its energy is at the witch's disposal.... A person in this kind of captivity is called the 'soldier' (soldat) of his witch master. His soul may be enclosed in a charm so that his anger at the way he has been treated may be turned against his master's victims. Or he may be sold to another master or even shipped to America to be put to work in factories making textiles and automobiles. (161–62)

Despite the fact that the source material here is younger—the author draws on his own fieldwork from the years 1964–70, as well as an archive of ethnographic research compiled by Swedish missionaries from 1912 to 1919—the figure described above seems like distant kin of the Haitian walking corpse, more closely related to the Zombi Bouteille. The text even depicts suspicion of American industry in its assertion that a soulless body might be shipped to America to work in a factory, uncannily similar to Seabrook's description of Haitian zombies working in the American-controlled sugar industry, furnishing a commentary on modern capitalism rather than colonialism (see chapter 2).

Indeed, in Africa there remain traces of a narrative similar to the zombie that perhaps developed out of a common predecessor mythology. The difference between these cousins seems to be that while the African myths only obliquely describe the sorcery that put the worker into such a state, the zombie that developed on the island of Saint Domingue is linked to the natural herbs and poisons endemic to the isle. Melville J. Herskovitz, for example, notes the similarity to the Haitian zombie of a phenomenon he chronicles in *Dahomey, an Ancient West African Kingdom*: "the essence of sorcery lies in obtaining control over a human spirit to do the bidding of the worker of evil magic" (243–44). The being described sounds very similar to the zombie, though there is no explanation given for how he came to be that way: "It was recounted several times how one individual or another, who was thought to be dead, had been encountered in Togoland or on the Gold Coast or in Nigeria. Such individuals, however, did not recognize their old friends, even though addressed by name. They were soulless beings, whose death was not real but resulted from the machinations of sorcerers who made them appear as dead, and then, when buried removed them from their graves and sold them into servitude in some far-away land" (243). Though the African sorcerer creates a false demise, this is linked, in Herskovitz's description, to spiritual techniques of soul capture rather than poisons giving the appearance of death.

In their important article "Alien Nation: Zombies, Immigrants, and Millenial Capitalism," Jean Comaroff and John Comaroff trace several mythologies of African "zombies" for their critique of the treatment of the worker. There is the *dlukula*, mud-eating beings bewitched and set to work in mines in nineteenth-century Mozambique. The South African *shipoko*, described in 1927, were shape-shifting nocturnal workers also in the control of witches who take the form of children during the day. And among the Bakweri of West Cameroon, the *vekongi*, displaced living dead workers who sheltered in tin houses and labored for the profit of greedy relatives, began to appear around World War I. The Comaroffs trace the way these mythologies, and especially the resurgence of a zombielike figure in contemporary South Africa, metaphorize class struggle, capitalist exploitation, and labor migration. Though these are not "zombies" as the Haitian describes them, they share with the zombie an embedded critique of social conditions whereby one set of people profits from the labor of another. The zombielike figures that the Comaroffs describe and the nameless "soulless beings" that Herskovitz classifies as a kind of ghost may even share a common ancestor with the zombie, in an early African soul-capture myth.

This description of the natives' beliefs is from Olfert Dapper's 1686 *Description de l'Afrique*:

> But nothing is more ridiculous than the opinion they hold that there is no natural death, and that no one dies except by the malice and enchantments of his enemy, who by means of the same spell, resuscitate him, transport him to a desert place and make him work there for the enemy's own profit. That the murderer there feeds him meats without salt, because if the resuscitated were to taste salt, he would pursue his killer relentlessly. The imagination of some others is no less absurd, they think that by these spells one can transport souls from one country to another, and one principally accuses the inhabitants of Gobbi of this crime. (334; Dapper, translated from the French)

One can see in this quotation, which describes the fear that souls were kidnapped and forced to labor across the sea, the ancestor of our modern zombie, giving credence perhaps to the Haitian assertion that the knowledge of zombification was passed down as a part of African heritage (see chapter 3). The obvious allusion to slavery is contemporaneous with and reflective of the African population's experience.[23] In an entry titled "Camma" the *Encyclopaedia* describes Camma and Gobbi as "two provinces of the kingdom of Loanga in Africa. The inhabitants are continually at war with each other. . . . The chief town of Gobbi lies about a day's journey from the sea. The principal commerce with the natives is in logwood, elephants teeth and tails, the hair of which is highly valued, and used for several curious purposes" (62).[24] Living only a day's journey from the sea, these warring peoples were an ideal trading partner for the Europeans. And though the main commodities exchanged for the gunpowder and other weapons of war furnished by the Dutch to the Gobbi are listed in Dapper as elephant teeth and tails and logwood, the fear of being sold into slavery by one's enemies is nonetheless evidenced here, a common practice all along the slave trading coasts.[25] The entry titled "Kingdom of Loango" in volume 16 of the 1760 *An Universal History* expands on the Dutch slavers' trading practices with the natives of this region and their neighbors, who share the same superstitions (Sale 281–82).

This myth, which I believe is the earliest ancestor of the zombie we have yet found, responds directly to colonialism and empire. It even contains a detail shared by the Haitian zombie about the liberatory properties of salt. Here salt will turn an imprisoned soul against its master in overt rebellion. Therefore, built into this myth was the potential for upheaval, resistance, rebellion, if only the slave came into contact with the right material. The sometimes oblique reference to the properties of salt is but one of the ways that the zombie mythology makes overt the threat of slave rebellion.[26] Another is the direct implication of the zombie as a product of poison, for there was a long-standing record in the Caribbean of slaves poisoning their masters.

The houngan's powers were more often viewed and depicted by outsiders as medicinal, pharmacologic, and, thus, secular technologies.[27] This emphasis on the natural rather than supernatural character of Vaudou is seen plainly in the eighteenth century's widely read anthropological texts coming out of the Caribbean colonies, for example, those by Bryan Edwards and Edward Long, wherein practitioners of the occult arts—namely, Myal men, Obeah workers, and Vaudouists—were depicted as charlatans, not truly capable of raising the dead, but only of pretending to do so.

Both Bryan Edwards's 1793 *History of the British Colonies* and Edward Long's 1774 *History of Jamaica* describe the key ingredients of the Caribbean zombie myth: the induction of a deathlike state that is later removed, effectively giving the appearance that the witch doctors (or houngan or Obeah men, or here "Myal men") were capable of bringing the dead back to life—even though neither of these works describes a figure that resembles the soulless walking dead. Instead, the emphasis is placed on the undeserved worship garnered by the sorcerer. Long writes of the Jamaican slaves, "The most sensible among them fear the supernatural powers of the African obeah-men, or pretended conjurors; often ascribing those mortal effects to magic, which are only the natural operation of some poisonous juice, or preparation, dexterously administered by these villains" (416).

Edwards chronicles the technique that we now associate with the zombie in his *History of the British West Indies*. Writing of Jamaica, he describes the Myal men of the Caribbean who "by means of a narcotic potion, made with the juice of an herb (said to be the branched Calalue or Solanum) which occasions a trance or profound sleep of some duration, endeavor to convince the spectators of their power to reanimate dead bodies" (21). This is the text that Mary Shelley read in 1814 and again in 1815, shortly before she would write her novel about a scientist capable of raising the dead.[28]

As Marina Warner notes regarding Samuel Taylor Coleridge's "The Three Graves," he too had read Edwards's *History of Jamaica* (121).[29] Though I do not claim that Coleridge's animated dead of "Rime of the Ancient Mariner" are zombies, the similarity to later instantiations of the zombie myth comes to seem eerie, given the work's combination of themes of colonialism, nature, and plague. Coleridge's interest in the West Indies is well known and illustrated in his public lecture on slavery.[30] In Alan Bewell's interpretation of the text, the dead rise because they have been "redeemed" by the Mariner's realization that colonialism is fundamentally wrong (106). Bewell asserts that the lesson the Mariner learns is that if God loves all creatures "great and small" (such as the sea snakes), then surely he would not sanction colonialism, which subordinates some men's rights to those of others. Thus we might claim that this African-born mythology had influenced European culture far earlier than the zombie's introduction via cinema in the twentieth century, indeed shaping some of the most canonical Gothic texts via colonial accounts of the slaves' beliefs—even before the Haitian Revolution solidified certain aspects of the zombie narrative.

Lacking the crucial element of the resurrected's enslavement to a master, these protozombie myths stress the capacity of magic and medicinal herbs to aid the resistance effort. If in the reports coming out of the colonies before the Haitian Revolution occult knowledge and its alleged command over the body is emphasized as charlatanism, subterfuge, and deception, the Vaudouist's impressive knowledge of the botanical life of the island is underlined as a potentially dangerous weapon, with which the slaves were armed. Long, too, illustrates that Myal men effect their deception by the same means described by Edwards, "a cold infusion of the herb branched colalue" (Long 416), and asserts that their demonstration subjects are not really dead but only paralyzed by the agent. But the mixture was also thought to have other properties, "particularly that it rendered the body impenetrable to bullets; so that the Whites would be perfectly unable to make the least impression upon them, although they were to shoot at them a thousand times" (417).[31]

Despite the fact that both Long's and Edwards's histories concern the British colony of Jamaica rather than the French colony of Saint

Domingue, the accounts are concerned with similar social conditions, and both anticipate what would become a central element of the Haitian Revolution: the repository of resistance that was to be found within the spiritual practices of the slaves and the dangers posed by their herbal acumen. Though in these prerevolutionary texts the emphasis is placed on the sleight of hand perpetrated by the Obeah men—who on Saint Domingue would be called Vaudoux—one sees the potential for use in overt rebellion in the claim that the Myal society possessed a command over death, that they could create charms that would make the slaves "invulnerable" to the white man, "and, although they might in appearance be slain, the obeah-man could, at his pleasure, restore the body to life" (Long 416).

Edwards writes directly of the propensity of these Obeah practitioners to use their powers to incite rebellion, recalling a case "in the year 1760, when a very formidable insurrection of the Koromantyn or Gold-Coast negroes broke out in the parish of St. Mary, and spread throughout almost every other district of [Jamaica], an old Kormantyn negro, the chief instigator and oracle of the insurgents in that parish, who had administered the Fetish, or solemn oath to the conspirators, and furnished them with a magical preparation which was to render them invulnerable" (Edwards, "Civil and Commercial History" 23). Although these accounts of Obeah do not mention any kind of soulless body, walking corpse, or enslaved laborer, they show that the posture of sorcery and the reality of herbal potions such as we find in the zombie myth were deeply linked to political resistance. Sensationalized accounts of Vaudou and Obeah men (like that of Three-Fingered Jack) were motivated by different agendas: the demonstration of the inhumanity of the slave or, like Coleridge's "Rime of the Ancient Mariner," an indictment of the institution of slavery itself.[32]

After the revolution was won and Haiti had declared its independence, Europeans were understandably curious about the phenomenon of the Black Republic, and inflammatory writings drew a large readership. Works intended for European and American readers promoted rumors of occult practices like grave-robbing and Vaudou potions that could make people appear dead temporarily; such texts sought to denigrate the Haitian as backward and (in an obvious lament of the loss of colonial domination over the region) incapable of self-rule. From the mid-nineteenth century, coinciding with the beginning of the decade-long dictatorial rule of Faustin Soulouque, a fervent adherent of Vaudou and self-proclaimed emperor of Haiti, European journalists became invested in painting the Haitian people as cruel, cannibalistic, savage, and even "satanic" (Hurbon 52). Though we do not yet find zombies overtly described in these pieces, a technique of poisoning similar to that later directly connected to zombie making is visible in their descriptions of the Caribbean cannibal.

Spenser St. John's *Hayti, or the Black Republic* (1884), the biggest offender propagating the stereotype of the bloodthirsty Haitian cannibal, describes the pharmacological technology that would later be attributed to the zombie's creation, the "great knowledge shown by Vaudoux priests of herbs as poisons and antidotes" (232). Mostly, in St. John's estimation, poisons giving the appearance of death are used so that the body could later be exhumed without cause for suspicion; the person could then be carried away to act as a sacrifice in a Vaudou rite, or be carved up at mealtimes.[33] St. John's libelous characterizations were echoed by James Anthony Froude in *The English in the West Indies* (1888: 162, 303), in Hesketh Pritchard's *Where Black Rules White: A Journey Across and About Hayti* (1900: xvi), and, one presumes, elsewhere. By all accounts, these sensational accounts of Vaudou rituals involving cannibalism are fabrications calculated to stoke the fires of empire's grand regret.

Though the religion is denigrated as savage and the people as animalistic, St. John does not appear to accuse the Vaudoux of charlatanism, as both Long and Edwards had done, but neither is he claiming that there is anything supernatural about their powers. Rather, in his 1884 account the knowledge of herbal properties is presented as scientific knowledge put to nefarious and beneficent purposes alike. Among the writings of this former British minister, there even seems to be the implication that the Vaudoux can sometimes raise from the dead even those who have met a natural end: "To show how the knowledge of herbs is extended throughout the population, I will insert here an account of an incident brought in evidence at a trial which took place in Hayti on the 3rd June 1887:—'The dead child was carried to the house of this officer, who had it placed in the presence of Pierrine, and who pressed her to restore it to life. Pierrine gathered some herbs in the neighborhood, and made with them a curious beverage, which she administered to the child, who immediately recovered consciousness'" (235).[34] No further explanation is given as to how this woman revivified the small child; but, on the whole, the text emphasizes the people's knowledge of a wide range of cures and poisons, which allow them also to bestow a variety of ailments (including impotence, paralysis, madness) on an adversary at any time (233–34). That its practitioners should have at their fingertips such potent herbal knowledge is obviously part of the lure that makes the Haitian Vaudouist a bogeyman.

These narratives about pharmacological trances that can be imposed and banished at will are part of the zombie's heritage. They describe the very same technology that twentieth-century studies of the science of zombification articulate as employed by the Haitian bokor to zombify his victims: the introduction of a potion that induces a deathlike trance to provide cover for kidnapping and toxicological enslavement in which the victim is reduced to a state capable only of performing the most menial tasks. During the period that we might call the second major wave of zombie dissemination during and just after the US occupation, discussed further in the next chapter, the Haitian zombie was consistently described as a being that awakened from death (or, rather, a drug-induced appearance of it) to a state of constant servitude and thus was clearly analogous to the African slave.[35] But in the documents of the colonial era, what I think of as the first wave of descriptions of the (proto)zombie, command of herbal and spiritual knowledge was used by Myal men and Vaudoux to demonstrate their power over the white man's aggression, and the practice was invoked by those who had a deep-seated mistrust of the slaves' religion and then of the Black Republic. In both contexts, descriptions highlight the occult arsenals of the African: one represents the power to enslave his enemies; the other, the sorcerer's ability to cast off this curse, for a paralyzed body waking from the dead neatly suggests the slave's rebellion. In the hands of black bokors, it may have seemed that retribution for crimes past was within their grasp.

I have already established that the zombie not only symbolically emblematizes the slave but also is historically connected to the transatlantic slave trade in its transmission to the Caribbean and its development out of ancestral African mythologies. I have shown here that the zombie is symbolically legible, too, as a symbol of slave rebellion. What remains to be drawn out a bit further is the degree to which we can think of the zombie as also historically related to strategies of resistance. The zombie deserves to be read in light of Vaudou's association with political struggle and the actual legacy of the herbal knowledge that was employed in slave rebellions.

Moreau de St. Méry warned Europeans with a stake in the stability of the Caribbean in his *Description . . . de la partie française de l'Isle de Saint-Domingue*, "Nothing is more dangerous than this cult of Vaudoux. The ridiculous idea that the ministers of this being know and can do everything could be transformed into a terrible weapon" (Dubois and

Garrigus 62). His words would have proved prescient were it not for the fact that they came too late.

Living Death and the Haitian Revolution

On January 1, 1804, Louis Boisrond-Tonnerre, secretary to Jean-Jacques Dessalines, read the Haitian Declaration of Independence, which he had penned the night before, to a crowd gathered at Gonaïves. It began:

> Citizens:
>
> It is not enough to have expelled the barbarians who have bloodied our land for two centuries; it is not enough to have restrained those ever-evolving factions that one after another mocked the specter of liberty that France dangled before you. We must, with one last act of national authority, forever ensure liberty's reign in the country of our birth; we must take any hope of re-enslaving us away from the inhumane government that for so long kept us in the most humiliating stagnation. In the end we must live independent or die.
>
> Independence or death . . . let these sacred words unite us and be the signal of battle and of our reunion. (Qtd. in Dubois and Garrigus 188)

The crux of the argument is simple: live free or die. But this is not merely a directive to die rather than serve—as it was in Patrick Henry's "Give me liberty or give me death" or in the slogans of the French Revolution, "Live Freely or Die" and "Rather Death than Slavery."[36] In the context of the Haitian Revolution, such slogans also draw an equation between slavery and death. The idea that slavery was death and that therefore slaves had nothing to fear from a literal death was a major rhetorical, political, and even spiritual tenet undergirding the revolution.

Writing about the slave rebellion that became the revolution of Saint Domingue, Gustave d'Alaux wrote in *L'Empereur Soulouque et son empire* (1834):

> Was it the magic word of liberty that pushed these unarmed and half-clad Congoes beneath the feet of the horses to which they clung, into the points of the bayonets that bit into them, down the mouths of the loaded cannons where they plunged their arms until they could touch the ball, crying the while with mad hilarity, soon interrupted by the explosion that would dismiss them in tatters:

Moé trapé li, (I have got it, I hold it)? No, it was a bull's tail, an enchanted tail, it is true, and that their leader, who knew his people, brandished among the ranks to turn back bullets and change cannon balls to dust.... [T]he sorcerers who formed the major component of Hyacinthe's group soon after announced in loud cries that *the dead resuscitate in Africa,* and a new human spray would joyously add himself to the pile of corpses. (13–14; emphasis added)

Because an African belief system holds that the dead join their ancestors, many supposed that death would involve a return to Africa; to "return to Guinee" meant simply to pass on. It is probable that Hyacinthe's call to arms, "the dead resuscitate in Africa," was intended to shore up the troops' courage by reminding them that in death they would return to their ancestral homeland. However, we must also recall the myth related by Olfert Dapper and wonder how many on the battlefield shared the sentiment of the Loangans, that slavery was an unnatural death, the effect of witchcraft suffered by those who found themselves enslaved in a foreign land; that they were in some sense dead already. Remembering, too, that "by sorcery one can transport souls from one country to another" (Dapper 334), it seems that in this exclamation overheard amid the cannon fire, what one finds is an inversion of a mythology that clearly once symbolized a people's fear of being kidnapped, sold into bondage, and transported far from their homes. Standing this myth about the capture and transportation of souls on its head, the slaves now proclaimed that there was no risk of "death" in rebellion but that they would awaken in Africa, finally free from the curse of a living death.

D'Alaux's acerbic intimation that the slaves are not fighting for the Enlightenment ideal "liberty" but out of the misguided belief that their magic would protect them fails to grasp the slave's nuanced understanding of the dialectical opposition between liberty and death; what for a Blanc like Patrick Henry may only have been a metaphor might have been literal to the slaves: if slavery is death and it is only once a slave is dead that he is literally free of his enslavement, then, in fact, to die is to become liberated. It should not shock that the unarmed slave managed to defeat three of Europe's strongest armies (France, Spain, and Britain): "Liberty/death" is replaced by liberty-in-life/liberty-in-death. With such options, how could he lose?

Going further than Orlando Patterson's equation of slavery and social death, an argument that has been criticized for depriving the slave of agency,[37] we can read this particular slave—he who perceived himself as dead, as having been transported to this foreign land and made to work for the bounty of others in an act of sorcery[38]—as resistive. For him, the way to "reanimate" and to return to Africa was to expire in battle for his freedom, another form of Hegel's "trial by death" but one that restores the subject to "life," or at least, in his death, ownership of himself. Regardless of the outcome, this discursive operation—by which a myth (here not explicitly the zombie but related soul-capture figurations), which once stood for the reality of one's oppression, comes to be reshaped as a device of empowerment—is the same movement we detect in the reclamation of the zombie as a figure of resistance more broadly. In the example above, one finds that those who are literally dying become empowered through an appeal to myth: "We are not dying," they say—or perhaps, "We are already dead"—we will reawaken in Africa. This posture of identifying oneself in bondage as nonliving can therefore be thought of not, as many have said of Patterson's theories, as profoundly disempowering but instead, along the lines described in Vincent Brown's study of Jamaica, *The Reaper's Garden*, as embracing death in an act of rebellion, whether that means being literally willing to die or just claiming, as in the rebel chant below, that one's existence in the state of servitude is as unnatural as living death.[39]

> Grenadiers to the assault
> What is death?
> We have no mother
> No child
> What is death? (Laroche, "The Myth of the Zombi" 55)

The rebel's call to return to Guinée in death is in line with Patterson's arguments about kinship under the institution of slavery, but it simultaneously turns this most horrific aspect of enslavement into a narrative strategy spurring on defiance. The slave's embrace of the posture of living death is a tactic that enables his literal resistance.

The charismatic/talismanic figure described above in d'Alaux's text is Hyacinthe, an houngan active in the slave rebellion, who is not to be confused with General Hyacinthe Moise (1769–1801), Toussaint L'Ouverture's cousin. Here is how Carolyn Fick describes the young leader: "Although he was only twenty-two years old, he was already a revered voodoo leader who had gained the confidence and respect of the slaves throughout the region. Armed with only pointed sticks, knives, machetes, and various farm implements as weapons, the blacks marched on Croix-des-Bouquets in the thousands, defying the onslaughts of cannon and artillery fire. Hyacinthe carried with him a talisman made of horsehair, which he waved before his troops to protect them and to reinforce their defiance and determination, crying, 'Forward! Don't be afraid; it's only water coming out of the cannon'" (139).

Some version of this account of the rebel slaves' use of Vaudou is repeated in nearly every history of the revolution, and many elaborate, noting, for example, that the Vaudou priest "profits by his oftentimes great knowledge of the medicinal herbs and tropical plants to gain the confidence of his clients" (Léger 36). Elsewhere it is written that talismans of the kind used by Hyacinthe contained animal hair, herbs, and bits of bone (Fick 111). Such statements question the exact content of the charms and the physiological effects of their medicinal properties, but that they had a psychological impact on the insurgents is well documented.

One of the most important early twentieth-century sources on Haitian Vaudou, the anthropologist Melville Jean Herskovitz's 1937 *Life in a Haitian Valley*, briefly mentions the use of Hyacinthe's oxtail in the 1792 uprising, providing some insight into the modern Haitian understanding of such charms, which they refer to as a *drogue*, and the role they played in solidifying the young nation. That the name for such charms means "drug" would seem to suggest that they had an explicit pharmacological property. Herskovitz writes:

> The most powerful type of protective magic is known as a *drogue*. One of the most potent of these—of the type referred to by Léger in commenting on the ox-tail carried by Hyacinthe, or such a one as tradition holds Christophe possessed, which gave him immunity from all but silver bullets—makes it possible for the owner to go to war without being harmed.[40] Even were the possessor of such a drogue to be struck by a bullet, the wound would be a minor one; while the thrust of a machete or saber would leave him unscathed, poison placed in drink or food would be impotent, and a trap set against the warrior would be ineffective. (226–27)

This description adds little to what I have already said of Hyacinthe, but Herskovitz's research makes a direct correlation between "drogues" and raising the dead. He describes a man who had used a drogue in fighting against the Marine occupation in the early twentieth century: "The grandfather of this man was said by him to have owned a drogue which came from Guinée. He knew how to resuscitate those who had met their death from unnatural—magical—causes" (227).[41] As I discuss later, this narrative of Vaudou empowerment, specifically, the technique of zombification, extends to allow the Haitian to fend off postcolonial aggression even today. Herskovitz's description of the drogue from Guinée also resembles the antidote that Wade Davis describes as the counterpoison that is administered by the bokor in order to bring his zombie out of the preliminary false death. Therefore, a definite lineage can be traced from the apparatuses employed by soldiers in the Haitian Revolution to the *technē* of the zombie's production—whether or not they, or the myth itself, work by virtue of the production of a spiritual result, a physiological response, or a psychological one.

But if the line that connects the Haitian revolutionary to the zombie yet seems faint, what cannot be doubted is the role that Vaudou played in the slave rebellion. Any history of the revolution will make clear that "voodoo constituted . . . an important organizational tool for resistance. It facilitated secret meetings, as well as the initiation and the adherence of slaves of diverse origins, provided a network of communication between the slaves of different plantations who gathered clandestinely to participate in the ceremonies, and secured the pledge of solidarity and secrecy of those involved in plots against the masters" (Fick 59).

David Geggus writes that "voodoo in Saint Domingue . . . has always been presented as a vehicle for revolution" (17); indeed, the practice of Haitian Vaudou ought itself to be considered a form of slave resistance, for it had been strictly prohibited since the Code Noir of 1685 was instituted by Louis XVI.[42] Still other scholars illustrate the way that after the revolution Vaudou integrated the history of the people's resistance into the fabric of the religion: "Songs sung to the lwa carry histories of slavery and revolution, sometimes evoking the names of Boukman, who led the first revolts in 1791, or of L'Ouverture and Jean-Jacques Dessalines. The internal conflicts of the revolutionary period are remembered, for instance, in a song that describes how 'Dessalines left the north, carrying an ouanga nibo (a kind of charm)' in order to kill an enemy" (Dubois, *Colony* 434).[43]

It was said that the slaves' courage in battle, a source of amazement to the European soldiers, was often attributed to the occult mechanism of Vaudou. The sadistic French general Rochambeau, whose cruel tactics included the feeding of captured slaves to man-eating dogs, purportedly stopped a battle to commend the black general François Capois for his resolute bravery. The courage of the rebel slaves was described by witness accounts as *unnatural*, as is evidenced in this case of the "fearless black general," called "Capois-la-Mort by reason of his indomitable courage"

(Léger 140). Some accounts of the famous battle at Vertières, in which Capois-la-Mort (Capois the Dead) charged the French, say that when his horse was killed beneath him, he continued the charge on foot; he was shot twice through the hat, giving the appearance that he was taking bullets to the head and still continuing forward, perhaps earning him his nickname.[44] There are many such stories of invulnerable Vaudou soldiers, and in its reconstitution after the revolution the zombie myth absorbs a new element: the living dead becomes legible both as subhuman beast of burden, a reminder of the nation's past and of literal threats of reenslavement to new tyrants, and as a threat to others, an unstoppable force reminiscent of Capois-la-Mort's relentless drive and a reminder of the nation's bloody birth. But the association between the zombie and revolt can be traced back much further in time, to earlier modes of resistance, by invoking the history of poison and rebellion.

As stated at the outset of this chapter, most accounts of the Haitian Revolution set the dates from the initial widespread slave rebellion—the coordinated attack that began after the Bois Caïman Vaudou ceremony led by Boukman, in which slaves on neighboring plantations killed overseers and owners and burned the properties to the ground—to the declaration of Haitian independence (August 21, 1791–January 1, 1804), a period of some thirteen years that involved three European armies. But for centuries slave resistance had taken many forms other than overt rebellion. Geggus writes that "resistance to slavery covered a broad spectrum. Armed revolt was only one extreme of a continuum which stretched from satire, lying, feigning illness and working slow, through tool-breaking, theft, flight and strikes, to self-mutilation, suicide and infanticide, arson, poisoning and physical assault" (1). Escaping or committing temporary desertion was called *marronage*. Among legends of rebellious slaves, few stand as tall as the marron leader Makandal.

François Makandal (d. 1758) was a one-armed escaped slave with considerable knowledge of herbs and tropical medicine who began manufacturing and distributing poison through elaborate channels.[45] Historians' accounts differ as to whether he was missing only a hand or a whole arm, though most report that the injury was the result of an accident working at a sugarcane refinery. Sources also differ on whether a "makandal," which came to mean poison or talisman, was named for the man or whether he took this as his name because of what it signified.[46] Nonetheless, the man known as Makandal (or Macandal) organized and facilitated a mass poisoning of the white colonists of Saint Domingue. He was worshipped by the slaves as a prophet, and his followers, many of whom he instructed in the ways of making poison, believed that he had the ability to change his physical form into that of an animal. Despite his promises to transform into a mosquito if he was ever captured by whites, Makandal was heard of no more after he was captured and burned at the stake in a public square in 1758.

In his historical fiction about the turmoil surrounding the formation of Haiti and its early governors, the Cuban novelist Alejo Carpentier begins his novel *The Kingdom of This World* with the story of Makandal, "Lord of Poison" (30): "One evening, after his afternoon repast, the master of Coq-Chante plantation had suddenly dropped dead without any previous complaint, dragging down in his fall the clock he was winding. Before the news could reach the neighboring plantations, other owners had been struck down by the poison, which lurked, as though waiting to spring, in glasses on night tables, soup tureens, medicine bottles, in bread, wine, fruit, and salt" (28).

Like a commonplace of the contemporary zombie film, in which the city square, the shopping mall, or the suburbs become the backdrop of a horror show, what this passage emphasizes is that the banal objects of everyday life—soup tureens, saltcellars—have been made terrifying. We might say that in this passage objects—a carafe of water on a nightstand, a medicine bottle—are themselves like zombies waking from the dead, or like slaves, human objects turning against their masters, animated by the menace they inwardly conceal. This emphasis on objects is underscored in Carpentier's poetic license, as the victim "drags down in his fall the clock he was winding." In fact, it is his clock that has run out.

If many historians of the Haitian Revolution provide little more than a footnote on the mysterious figure named Makandal, Carolyn Fick believes that the series of poisonings he orchestrated set a precedent for the revolution, a first attempt at a wide-scale rebellion. This was a coordinated effort that was to be followed by an all-out attack: "the day and the hour were set when the water of all the houses in le Cap was to be poisoned" (Fick 62). Fick describes at length the panic, paranoia, and terror that Makandal and his followers inspired in the whites. Most effectively, perhaps, the poisonings continued unchecked after Makandal's death, thereby giving his legend credence, or at least making his work seem larger than life. In Carpentier's magical realist retelling of his execution, Macandal (as it is spelled in Carpentier's novel) is capable of taking various forms: "His powers were boundless. He could as easily cover a mare as rest in the cool of a cistern, swing on the swaying branches of a *huisache*, or slip through a keyhole" (36). Because his physical shape is malleable, the slaves who attend his execution reject the idea that he has, in fact, been burned at the stake; they "returned to their plantations laughing all the way. Macandal had kept his word, remaining in the Kingdom of This World. Once more the whites had been outwitted by the Mighty Powers of the Other Shore" (46). Macandal's resistance extends even to his corporeal substance; he purportedly could not be physically destroyed because he was so spiritually powerful.

In reality, slaves and livestock were destroyed along with slaveholders in Makandal's attempt to bring down the entire plantation system. Fick quotes Gabriel Debien, who suggests that the terror aroused by the rash of poisonings granted the slave power over the slaveholder; he recounts how small doses of toxins were sometimes administered to a master as a warning if he was mistreating slaves (Fick 71). Thereby, the threat of poisoning, after Makandal, allowed the slave a kind of psychic dominion over the whites who oppressed him daily.

Fick laments the lack of documents that would provide us with an exact history of Makandal and other slave-orchestrated poisonings and questions the veracity of the records that do survive, many of which are slave testimonies procured under torture. Still, she concludes that "however loose or rudimentary the Makandal affair may have been, it was neither a spontaneous eruption, nor was it only blind terrorism, but rather a deliberately organized plan of revolt that appears to have taken concrete form within a concurrent context of widespread, often unexplained, poisonings that he and his followers had done much to create" (70).

In the contemporary record, the writings of the colonists associated the poisonings with highly guarded African herbal knowledge and with the practice of sorcery (Fick 66, 69). The Makandal affair deserves to be read in conjunction with the Haitian Revolution for its overt and violent rebellion but also for its portrayal of magic and herbal medicine as the *technē* of both the rebel slave and the houngan who claimed command over life and death. Whereas prerevolutionary accounts emphasized the bogus nature of the Vaudou man's herbal arsenal, Makandal's toxic tools could not be doubted. During and after the revolution, accounts of Vaudou remain tainted by the tone of the Blanc's salacious interest in denigrating Haiti's citizens (as in St. John and d'Alaux), but soon after they begin to reflect genuine curiosity, and something more. The accounts of Vaudou practices, in particular, those later implicated in the creation of zombies—death-defying demonstrations, suspicious body snatchings, the inducement of paralytic trances—were henceforth interpreted as a weapon decidedly not supernatural but terrifying nonetheless, signifying the leaders' possession of a complete command of the natural poisons and antidotes endemic to the island. Fick writes, "Whether the poisons that slaves obtained and used with such alarming proficiency were actually toxic herbal potions derived from certain plants and prepared by African blacks who held the knowledge and highly guarded secrets of herb medicine; or whether they were simply compositions of an arsenic base, disguised by the presence of various colonial herbal substances, remained for the colonists a matter of dispute" (66). Nonetheless, an added element of the psychic damage wrought by the poisonings may have been the colonists' subconscious sense that their own actions had been turned against them. African slaves had been forcibly imported to the Caribbean to work the land, to coax from it sugar and indigo and cultivate its riches for the benefit of others. Now they were harvesting a crop invisible to their white masters but far more potent.

Fick's description of Makandal's reign of terror, which was characterized by contemporary observers and early chroniclers as both physical and psychological, resembles the myth of the zombie, which we might think of as a discursive weapon that employs the technology of the *contrapassum*, retribution, counterthreat. There is a need for a term other than psychic "terrorism" when we are discussing rhetorical devices invoked in the name of subverting the dominant paradigm and flipping the (post)colonial hierarchy. A neologism like *phobia-technē* could work here (not to be confused with "technophobia"). This is the way the zombie works in Haiti today: by inspiring fear in the nation's enemies, cultural sovereignty is ensured even when its political power is undermined.

The link between the mythic zombie and the historical reality of the Haitian Revolution is made by Colin Joan Dayan in her seminal work, *Haiti, History, and the Gods*, in the figure of Jean Zombi, a mulatto warrior famous for his brutality against whites. Jean Zombi incarnates the nonhuman rebel slave, with his "'vile face,' 'red hair,' and 'wild eyes'" (36). Dayan cites Zombi's fearsome appearance in the early witness accounts of the revolution, such as that by Thomas Madiou (quoted above), and in later histories, such as that by Hénock Trouillot, to illustrate how Zombi's exploits became the stuff of myth and his figure an amalgam of various hybridities at play in the revolution: "Variously reconstituted and adaptable to varying events, Zombi crystallizes the crossing not only of spirit and man in vodou practices but the intertwining of black and yellow, African and Creole in the struggle for independence" (36).[47]

Despite her recognition that the zombie myth may have preexisted this warrior, coming to the island from slaves of Dahomean legend,

Dayan implicates Jean Zombi in the development of the Haitian zombie, which she states is an "incarnation of negation or vacancy" (37). Here is how she draws out this association: "The name zombi, once attached to the body of Jean, who killed off whites and avenged those formerly enslaved, revealed the effects of the new dispensation. Names, gods, and heroes from an oppressive colonial past remained in order to infuse ordinary citizens and devotees with a stubborn sense of independence and survival. The undead zombi, recalled in the name of Jean Zombi, thus became a terrible composite power: slave turned rebel ancestor turned lwa, an incongruous, demonic spirit recognized through dreams, divination, or possession" (37).[48]

Dayan suggests that Jean Zombi, in sharing the name of the figure that is "the ultimate sign of loss and dispossession" (37), in some capacity involves a recuperation of the zombie, enacting upon the signifier a movement similar to that seen in the revolution whereby the mortal slave became a hero and then an immortal legend. Here, the zombie, the "most powerful emblem of apathy, anonymity, and loss" (37), becomes associated with action, enduring glory, and victory over the oppressors. But, as we have seen, the zombie's capacity for rebellion is perhaps endemic to the African origin tale from which it likely sprouted. Dayan, therefore, rightly calls the zombie both "a terrible composite power" (37) and "a marvel of ambivalence" (38), but here I wish to clarify that this duality is as inherent to the figure as its living deadness.

Dayan is right, nonetheless, in noting that the "composite power" of the zombie that is always latent in the figure becomes more visible after the Haitian Revolution. In the zombie's association with Jean Zombi, the word takes on a powerful valence, emphasizing its rebellious potential. This is a significatory attachment, but there may have been a historical link between the zombie and the fearless warriors of the revolution, if only in the attribution of herbal properties to their success and the zombie's later emphasis as a production of similar herbal knowledge.

In contemporary accounts of the Haitian Revolution, the ferocity of the rebels was denigrated: they were less than men, bloodthirsty "cannibales" (Dalmas 2:142) and "tigres humains" (Descourtilz 126).[49] Figures like Hyacinthe, Capois-la-Mort, and Jean Zombi, along with accounts of the rebels' impressive resistance of torture, raise the question of the source of this mental and physical endurance.[50] In the contemporary documents, the slaves' comportment is often presented as otherworldly.[51]

There seems to be the intimation in the writings of some European witnesses that there have must been an anesthetizing agent that was used to spur soldiers on to do battle and to calm the nerves of those about to be executed, to ease fear, or at least physical pain, for the rebel slaves are characterized as either superhuman and uncannily courageous or subhuman, blindly following orders. In a letter in the Archives nationales from Pierre Mossut to the Marquis de Gallifet dated September 19, 1791, a slaveholder describes the rebellion on his and his neighbor's plantation. He says of the rebelling slaves, "There is a motor that powers them and that keeps powering them and that we cannot come to know. All experienced planters know that this class of men have neither the energy nor the combination of ideas necessary for the execution of this project, whose realization they nevertheless are marching toward with perseverance. . . . [W]e have executed many slaves, among them ten from your plantation; all have observed their obstinate silence when questioned about who armed them and incited this odious plot, though they admit to being guilty and having participated in it" (qtd. in Dubois and Garrigus 94).[52] Here the choice of a mechanistic metaphor contributes to the idea that the slaves are machines run amok, inhuman, incapable of agency, the intimation being that they are under the control of an unseen force. When the blame for France's loss wasn't being laid on yellow fever, to which a majority of the European soldiers succumbed, references to Vaudou were invoked to explain the slaves' impressive defeat of the foremost militaries in the world in a discursive move that would at once denigrate the slaves' barbarous religion as backward and suggest that their powers were the province of prerational, base animality, or even, as with Jean Zombi, demonic forces. Yet if they were successful in shoring up the rebels' resolve, the Vaudou rituals had real-life, physiological outcomes as well as symbolic, metaphoric, and psychological ones.

I have often wondered whether a study might produce a detailed pharmacology of Caribbean resistance, including a description of the role that herbs, intoxicants, and poisons played in the slave resistance and its combat—from the imbibing of taffia mixed with gunpowder in the aggressive "Don Petro" Vaudou dance, to the doling out of rum by slave holders when they wanted to induce lethargy in their slaves, for example, immediately before the arrest of Makandal.[53] One might also investigate the use of abortive herbs to deprive the slaveholders of more human capital, as well as the mysterious talismans carried by the rebel soldiers. In such a study, the herbal science made use of by the "Black Jacobins" would fall on the same line as the zombie's "black magic."[54] The epidemics of poisoning strategically coordinated and carried out by Makandal and others could be compared to postcolonial legends of zombified white generals, exterminated as retaliation for their intervention in Haiti. For, as we will see in chapter 3's address of Haitian literature, the zombie is repossessed as a discursive weapon in Haiti after the US conquest of the myth and its abuses by the dictator François Duvalier. I imagine these diverse points—the threat of a dose of deadly nightshade, a story about a white zombie—as nodes in the same network of resistance, much like the mesh of lines that constitutes a *veve* drawing, a Vaudou symbol drawn in cornmeal or another kind of powdery substance. It matters little if one type of rebellion is documented, a verifiable historical event, and the other unwritten, the stuff of oral history or even legend, for to my mind they both achieve real-world results.

Let's return, once more, to this chapter's epigraph. The motto "Long Live Death" is a paradox that simultaneously illuminates the slave's sense of his own unnatural existence and the type of metaphysical resistance afforded by his spiritual belief system.

The rhetorical device of the battle cry, "Long Live Death," at once recalls the slave's existence in a kind of living dead human-object state and suggests the embrace of the alternative, literal death, over the symbolic death of slavery. At one and the same time, death is the problem (in metaphor) and the solution (in practice), whether turned on one's enemies or oneself.[55] This reads as both an empowering rallying cry—promising to become the agent of destruction of the oppressors or conveying that the rebels will have no king but Death—and a disempowering acknowledgment that for the warrior slave himself there may have been no alternative, as the only available path to liberation was through the death of the body, his own consignment to the past in order to ensure a future for others.

In a literalization of the equation of slavery with death and liberty with self-sacrifice, the invocation of images of living death in the Haitian Revolution bifurcates in such a way that it can metaphorize both enslavement and rebellion, strength and subjection, triumph and loss, the individual and the collective, often simultaneously. In the end we know who won the war. But for the zombie such resolutions are refused: there is rarely the promise of the resurrection in liberty but more often only the soul's release from bondage to eternal rest. In its relationship to the history of slavery and slave rebellion, the zombie metaphor represents the human subject treated as object: either a walking corpse that is a stand-in for the slave—and thus a tool laboring for the benefit of another—or a crazed cannibal, the most denigrating image of the rebel-slave: not the agentic leader, but the foot soldier, the machine run amok, whirling in pure fury. The pathos of the zombie is like the rebel's cry, "Long Live Death," a paradox from which there is no escape. It is in making use of the zombie—either in claiming to possess the art of zombification or in ownership of the myth and its capacity to terrify one's enemies—that resistance is possible.

Dayan writes of the "phantasm of the zombi—a soulless husk deprived of freedom" (37):

> In Haiti, memories of servitude are transposed into a new idiom that *both reproduces and dismantles* a twentieth-century history of forced labor and denigration that became particularly acute during the American occupation of Haiti. As Haitians were forced to build roads, and thousands of peasants were brutalized and massacred, tales of zombies proliferated in the United States . . . to justify the "civilizing" presence of the marines in "barbaric" Haiti. The reimagined zombi has now been absorbed into the texture of previous oral traditions, structurally reproducing the idea of slavery in a new context. (37–38; emphasis added)

Dayan's substantive discussion of the zombie ends here, justly suggesting that its uptake in pseudoanthropological texts leads to its reconstitution in film and fiction outside of Haiti as a figure capable of inspiring fear, as well a symbol of the country's backward superstitions.

Dayan has unearthed the skeleton; it now remains for it to grow flesh. The mythic figure of the zombie very definitely "both reproduces and dismantles" slavery itself. Unfortunately, it also "dismantles and yet reproduces" slavery. As the next chapter illustrates in detail, the zombie myth operates on more than just a symbolic register in its uptake by the Blancs; its ability to signify enslavement is literalized as the zombie becomes *a slave metaphor* in the service of American interests, as well as a metaphor about slavery. Just as Moreau de St. Méry had borrowed the slave's chains for his characterization of the French Republic's liberation, filmmakers would appropriate the figure of the zombie for their own narrative purposes. As with the Creole slaveholder, however, the metaphor could turn against them.

2 / "American" Zombies: Love and Theft on the Silver Screen

Down among the dead men, Down among the dead men, Down, down, down, down, Down among the dead men let him lie.
—TRADITIONAL SONG, WORDS BY JOHN DYER (1700–1758)

"Jazz great Jelly Roll Morton was a zombie," the curator and owner of the New Orleans Voodoo Museum, Jerry Gandolfo, said to me when I spoke with him in spring 2008.

"Pardon?" I begged.

This required explanation. No, he wasn't a zombie in the sense I was hoping to find, a walking corpse reanimated from the dead to labor for others, in an obvious allegory for slavery dreamed up by a people enslaved, colonized, and, later, oppressed by tyrants both foreign and domestic. "He was a *give-man* zombie," Gandolfo clarified.

The give-man zombie, as it is described by Zora Neale Hurston in her ethnographic portrait of the Caribbean, *Tell My Horse: Voodoo and Life in Haiti and Jamaica*, is more like the Faust myth: a soul is given to a powerful sorcerer in exchange for good fortune in life.

> Now this "Ba Moun" (give man) ceremony is a thing much talked about in Haiti: It is the old European belief in selling one's soul to the devil but with Haitian variations. In Europe the man gives himself at the end of a certain period. Over in Haiti he gives others and only gives himself when no more acceptable victims can be found. But he cannot give strangers. It must be a real sacrifice. . . . There are lurid tales of the last days of men who have gained wealth and power thru "give man." (184)

The give man is made in the same way as the other type of zombie, when "a plantation owner has come to the Bocor to 'buy' some laborers" or "an enemy wants the utmost in revenge" (182): "Alone [the Bocor] makes the ceremony to call the soul of the person who is to be sacrificed.... [He] will soon place his lips to the crack of the victim's door and draw his soul away. Then will follow the funeral and after that the midnight awakening. And the march to the hounfort for the drop of liquid that will make him a zombie, one of the living dead" (189).[1] In Hurston's account of the creation of the Ba Moun it seems that the give-man entails the literal zombification of the sacrifice. However, in the related Hoodoo belief system of the American South, the give-man zombie may look different from the walking dead, even if the principle of soul capture is the same.

Jelly Roll Morton may be the best example we have of an original American zombie—free, that is, of the influence of the Haitian mythology—and even his story falls short of clarifying the particulars of the cultural transmission. The laboring living dead zombie is exceedingly rare in the South prior to the Haitian zombie's introduction in the 1930s. For example, although Hurston chronicles the phenomenon of zombification in detail in her study of Haitian Vaudou, *Tell My Horse*, there are no zombies described in the one-hundred-plus pages devoted to Hoodoo in her *Mules and Men*, a study of the folk tales and beliefs of southern African American cultures. Conducting much of her study in New Orleans—"the hoodoo capital of America," where "great names in rites that vie with those of Hayti... keep alive the powers of Africa" (*Tell My Horse* 229)—Hurston became the assistant of several different practitioners. She underwent months of apprenticeship and performed laborious initiations, many of which involved fasting for days. Her tutelage under Kitty Brown corroborates what Jelly Roll says about the "give man" aspect of Hoodoo initiation, as Kitty tells Zora, "In order for you to reach the spirit somebody has got to suffer. I'll suffer for you because I'm strong" (297). The majority of the cases that Hurston recounts concern people seeking recompense for wrongs done them when the law would be ineffectual or uninterested in their plight, such as a woman whose husband had taken all her earnings and left her for another (280). Of the many instances she relates, either from personal handling of the procedure or from interviews with those practicing in the field, there are only a few that recall Haitian zombification, and many differences between Vaudou and Voodoo or Hoodoo are underlined. For example, in the United States the use of salt is key in ceremonies, so much so that the noun becomes a verb—"to salt" someone is to lay a curse. But whereas the Haitian zombie is either liberated when it tastes salt or, as Hurston herself states in *Tell My Horse*, made to speak (183), in Hoodoo salt inhibits a person's freedom: throwing salt in someone's direction, for example, can encourage him to leave town (*Mules and Men* 233).

Hurston also addresses the use of poisons, which we consider the primary technique of zombification in Haitian Vaudou, but she says that in Hoodoo to be "poisoned" usually just means to be "cursed" or that someone is working magic against you. Hurston notes that Haitian zombification is likely the "semblance of death induced by some drug known to a few. Some secret probably brought from Africa and handed down from generation to generation" (*Tell My Horse* 196). But although she provides an appendix of herbal remedies and their uses at the end of *Mules and Men*, titled "Prescriptions of Root Doctors," the entry under "Poisons" states of US practice, "There are few instances of actual poisoning. . . . Juice of the nightshade, extract of polk root, and juice of the milkweed have been used as vegetable poisons, and poisonous spiders and powdered worms and insects are used as animal poisons. I have heard of one case of the poison sac of the rattlesnake being placed in the water pail of an enemy. But this sort of poisoning is rare" (343). The various compounds implicated in Haitian zombification—puffer fish venom, the Datura plant (a nightshade), and poisonous toads—seem not to be directly implicated in the US South for the same purposes they are in Haiti.[2]

Hurston's study of Hoodoo nonetheless catalogs powers that resemble zombification, such as one detailed account related to the author by a "two-headed doctor" (i.e., a practitioner) about a wealthy white plantation owner who was habitually nasty to his servants. When he rashly strikes and kills the daughter of a servant named Old Dave, "known to dabble in hoodoo," Dave gets his revenge by turning the family members of the plantation owner insane: They become homicidal and violent toward their husband and father—but not anyone else—routinely trying to kill him, until he is forced to live apart from his loved ones.

Hurston also chronicles the abilities of Marie Laveau, the "voodoo queen" of New Orleans, to control people and even the police who come to arrest her: "First one come, she stretch out her left hand and he turn round and round and never stop until some one come lead him away. Then two come together—she put them to running and barking like dogs. Four come and she put them to beating each other with night sticks. The whole station force come. . . . She did work at her altar and they all went to sleep on her steps" (241). But though we might find the odd resemblance to Haitian zombification in the image of the New Orleans police force put into a state of suspended animation, or a white family turned into agents of revenge for a wronged servant, there is little evidence to suggest that the practice of zombification existed outright in American Hoodoo at the time of Huston's study, that is, before the zombie entered popular consciousness via literature and cinema.

One of the difficulties of tracing the cultural transmission's development is that such histories tend to be rewritten. Elsewhere, Marie Laveau is said to have had knowledge, if not of zombie-making, then of tetrododoxin, the zombie poison.[3] Ina Johanna Fandrich reports a tale told her by a community historian that Laveau would feed inmates a special gumbo prepared with the zombie poison and then, after they had been presumed dead and buried, dig them up and help them escape to freedom (Fandrich 166–67). Whether or not the detail about tetrododoxin is a "recent addition to the Laveau legend" as other historians assert (Long 159), it is nice to think of Laveau using the zombie-making poison not to enslave but to liberate. Even in relating this tale, however, Fandrich assumes that Laveau would have obtained the powder from Haiti, noting that "there was a close connection between the French Afro-Creoles in New Orleans and the people of Haiti . . . until Reconstruction" (167).[4] Zombie-making is thus emphasized as belonging primarily to Haiti.

Nonetheless, the tale of Jelly Roll Morton, inventor of jazz and giveman zombie, provides an unexpected link between southern Hoodoo and Haitian Vaudou and sets the scene for the complex drama of the myth's appropriation. Jelly Roll Morton's "Dead Man's Blues" echoes the traditional folk song quoted in the epigraph to this chapter in both content and form: it calls attention to the same space, "Down among the dead men," and like its predecessor has insistent repetition, repeating a single word for the whole of a musical line. I'm not asserting here that Morton, or his companion Anita Gonzalez, who it is said penned the words (Pastras 20), was intentionally alluding to the traditional ballad; Dyer's lyric emphasizes the importance of enjoying life, claiming that the man abstaining from the joys of women and whiskey is as good as dead—"Down, down, down, down,/ Down among the dead men let him lie"—while Morton's song more plaintively reminds the listener "that the world was built on bones." Nonetheless, the similarity reminds me of the significance of jazz as a kind of cultural métissage.[5] Both songs are calls to action, but Morton's may refer to Voodoo, its spiritual and physical appeal to the ancestors, in the lines, "Bones! Bones! Bones, bones, bones, bones!/ Dig 'em up, (Dig 'em up) . . . / Take 'em home (Take 'em home)."

Gandolfo told me that Jelly Roll's godmother, Laura Hunter, a.k.a. Eulalie Echo, was a reputed witch doctor. Like the living dead zombie described in chapter 1, the give-man zombie allows someone to profit from the reclamation of another's soul, and it is said that "Lalie" kept his soul, the source of her power, in a jar underneath her bed. In *Mister Jelly Roll*, the folklorist Alan Lomax writes of Echo's encouragement and love and the extent to which the famed musician believed, at a certain point in his life, that he had been damned by his godmother's Voodoo doings.

> The woman, Laura Hunter, who raised Jelly Roll, was a voodoo witch. . . . She made a lot of money at voodoo. People were always coming to her for some help and she was giving them beads and pieces of leather and all that. Well, everybody knows that before you can become a witch you have to sell the person you love best to Satan as a sacrifice. Laura loved Jelly best. . . . Jelly always knew she'd sold him to Satan and that, when she died, he'd die, too—she would take him down with her. (260–61)

According to Anita Gonzalez, Lomax's source for this point in his biography, that is exactly what happened. Morton would tell Lomax, "Here, late years, I have often thought many of my troubles came from my being around during those séances when my godmother fooled with that underground stuff" (10). Lomax later concludes that "Morton never felt certain whether voodoo or big business had ruined him; both were mysterious forces which finally overpowered his tiger" (222). The conflation is telling; after all, both involve, in Marx's terms, fetishes, reification, and the alienated laborer who is concretely personified in the form of the zombie. Lomax continues, "Usually he delivered his economic tirade, but once, in a confiding moment of weariness, he told the following fantasy—a poignant story of his final attempt to be a New York big shot, a story of a voodoo curse that shadowed Mister Jelly Roll along the Great White Way" (222).

The narrative Lomax recounts in the chapter titled "It Like to Broke My Heart" concerns a former business partner Morton refers to only as "the West Indian," who betrayed him, stealing and selling his music to "a big, high-powered firm" behind his back to profit exclusively from the sales. When Morton confronted the scoundrel and fired him, he had a conjure man put a curse on his former boss, the evidence of which was discovered in the form of noxious powders placed all around the office. Hoping to counter the curse, which Morton believed was causing him to feel "blurry" and bringing with it a string of bad luck—like leaving trunks full of valuables at hotels while touring—Morton gave hundreds of dollars to a practitioner named Madame Elise, whom he would eventually believe was in league with his enemies. Of this Voodoo woman, Morton said, "I seen her put her hand on a woman's head and this woman went out like a light and stayed out for thirty minutes. That put a fear into my heart" (226). It seems, in fact, that Morton was more than just the type of sacrificial zombie that Hurston describes. Under the control of the West Indian, and perhaps even of Madame Elise, he had lost his will.

> I just wasn't myself anymore. I walked around in a stupor. I went back to see Madame Elise. Pretty soon I was bringing big bags of food to her. . . . I told her about the condition in my office—how people couldn't walk in the door. She took some turpentine and scrubbed the walls, but this only made things worse. Then I resolved to take action and to beat the West Indian to death, because Madame Elise told me it would help if I caught him and drew blood.[6] But every time I got to the guy I couldn't raise my hands. (227)

The kind of disempowerment Morton felt at his partner's betrayal—songs were sold out from under him, his creations put to labor for the financial betterment of another—is neatly woven in this yarn as a kind of zombification, be it psychosomatic or the workings of sorcerers. The details of this case, the use of powders, for example, do recall Haitian zombie lore in part.[7] Is this story a shibboleth that allows us to access an authentic Voodoo or Hoodoo zombie belonging properly to the American South, or was the influence of the cinematic zombie already at work when in 1938 Morton told this tale to Lomax? It may be impossible to say.

Is there such a thing as an "American" zombie endemic to the African-derived spirituality found in the United States, or does the zombie merely come to us through the channel opened during the US occupation of Haiti? And if it's the latter, what are we to make of the neoimperialist way the figure enters US culture, especially in light of the fact that the zombie is immediately and then repeatedly refashioned? To reprise the line of inquiry introduced earlier, is this appropriation, as Eric Lott wrote of blackface minstrelsy, cultural theft? Or is it love, betraying, perhaps, a profound respect for Haitian Vaudou or at least a fear of black wisdom and power? Is it a productive syncretism that melds mythologies? The zombie complicates our understanding of appropriation, not just its underlying motives, but also where the agency lies in the transference.

My purpose here is to record the transmissions of the zombie from Haiti to the United States and to catalog its translations within folklore and popular literature, especially in film. The zombie of cinema has rapidly evolved over its nearly century-long tenure as one of our most prominent movie monsters, taking on various significations to represent different cultural anxieties but also, as many have noted of late, gaining speed—literally, as the shuffling, shambling zombie of yesteryear is replaced by a fleet-footed, frenzied goblin. This chapter emulates the frenetic pace of the contemporary zombie, covering much cinematic ground in little space, chasing after the flickering specters that have been projected onto film screens, seeking not to outrun them, but only to make sense of their appearances, their absences, and their adaptations.

In order to understand the zombie's capture on the silver screen and to define the "American zombie," if there is such a thing, we first have to listen to tales like that of Jelly Roll Morton and others to isolate the zombie's transmissions from the chatter. And as we'll see, it's not a one-sided conversation.

Zombies in the American South

If there is there evidence of a properly American zombie—that is, one that grew out of the ancestral African mythologies the way the Haitian zombie had done but germinated instead in the bayous of Louisiana and the swamps of Florida or under the Spanish moss of the Carolinas, not a transplant landing on our shores after the American occupation of Haiti forced its migration as a cultural curiosity but a myth of the living dead endemic to our own slave cultures—I haven't found it. Of course, this is not to say that it doesn't exist. All the difficulties of tracing the history of a predominantly oral culture, discussed in the previous chapter, weigh equally as heavily here. But the lack of zombies in the US South may also confirm what we know about the demographic diversity of slaves, the confluence of African American cultures, and concern about the influence of the Caribbean on the American plantation.

The rhetoric that revolution is contagious is well known. Many colonists surmised that the French Revolution had ignited a rebellious spirit in their slaves. In fact, rumors about the political strife in France led to whisperings that the government had given slaves more rights or even abolished slavery but that colonial governments were refusing to implement these new rules; such misinformation was directly responsible for some slave rebellions, including one in Martinique in 1789, just a month after the storming of the Bastille. Laurent Dubois recounts a story about the capture of an insurgent a mere week after the rebellion of 1791 began in Saint Domingue. On his person were "pamphlets printed in France, filled with commonplaces about the Rights of Man and the Sacred Revolution" (Dubois, *Avengers* 102).[8] Many claimed that the slaves had caught revolution fever from their owners, who wanted to see a French Republic instantiated that would give the colonies a more substantial role in governance.

People feared, too, that the slave rebellion would spread beyond the islands. Though the second president of the United States, John Adams, had recognized the sovereignty of Saint Domingue even before the revolutionaries declared their independence, Thomas Jefferson withdrew it, fearing that Haiti's model would encourage slave rebellion at home (Dubois and Garrigus 159–62). In *Avengers of the New World*, Dubois describes how masters in Jamaica were made nervous by the fact that their slaves began singing songs about the Bois Caïman rebellion only a month after it happened; within a few years, slaveholders as far away as Virginia blamed Saint Domingue for what they said was growing insubordination (304).

Some southern states instituted an embargo on slaves imported from Saint Domingue after the rebellions, fearing that the spirit of revolution would be transmitted to their own shores. Louisiana remained a Spanish colony in the 1790s, and "Spanish officials feared the introduction of slaves from St. Domingue would increase the possibility of slave insurrections" (*Common Routes* 87–88). In fact, it was not until June 1809 that "territorial governor William C. C. Claiborne personally approved the entry of slaves (accompanied by their owners), into Louisiana, as well as the entry of free blacks. . . . Claiborne's decree transformed New Orleans from a secondary destination to a primary port of call" (88–89). This reversal came just as those Haitian planters who had been refugees in Cuba since the revolution began were being expelled, and they now traveled en masse to the Crescent City. They brought with them their unfortunate slaves, whose emancipation had been forfeited when they were forced to accompany their fleeing masters to Cuba. After a twenty-year embargo and five years after the first Black Republic was established, these slaves, who had missed the storm of the revolution and had been put out of the path of history's sweeping change, began pouring into New Orleans. Yet the living dead zombie seems not to have been among them.

As Ron Bodin writes in *Voodoo: Past and Present*, published by the Center for Louisiana Studies, "Many of the slaves accompanying these planters were snake worshippers and devotees of 'Vodu'" (11). In fact, it was not only the rebellions that had frightened American administrators concerning immigration of slaves from the Caribbean. Robert Tallant notes, "As early as 1782 Governor Gálvez of Louisiana prohibited the importation of Negroes from Martinique because he believed them to be steeped in Voodooism and that they 'would make the lives of the citizens unsafe'" (9). By 1809, Louisiana relaxed its immigration policy, and Voudou came to the American South via the unmanumitted slaves who had been previously routed to Cuba. This demography will be important to bear in mind as we consider which aspects of Vaudou took root in the South and which did not, as these individuals bore a much different relationship to resistance and revolution than those who had remained in liberated Haiti.

"Louisiana possessed a unique culture, a unique environment," Bodin writes. "In this very different world emerged a unique brand of Voodoo—less organized than the Haitian model, influenced by the mysteries of Catholicism and the basic beliefs of European superstition, and business-oriented" (12–13). Bodin claims that slaves were mostly well cared for in American-controlled Louisiana because of the planters' view that they were an investment to be protected; there was less need for the knowledge of the "root doctors" because traditional medicine was at hand. Robert Tallant notes, too, "De Bienville's Black Code had previously provided that the Negroes should be branded with the fleur-de-lis, whipped, or put to death if they were caught meeting together. So gathering for Voodoo or any other rites was impossible in those days" (10). As we saw in the previous chapter, the association between Vaudou and revolution was deep-seated. Prohibitions against assembly were often couched in terms of the danger of the practice of dark magic, though political and economic motivations clearly undergirded such bans.

It was therefore mainly after slavery was abolished that Vaudou, or, as it is more often transliterated in the US context, Voodoo, began a resurgence in New Orleans in a "less Africanized" and more economic form: "Voodoo represented one of the few ways for blacks to gain economic and personal power in a racist and chauvinistic world. A number of blacks discovered this reality and thus started the business of Voodoo in Louisiana" (Bodin 18). Bodin notes that though the fascination with Voodoo remains, the practice of it as a structured religion in Louisiana died out by the 1920s (27). Though Vaudou may have made the journey from Haiti to New Orleans, thereby becoming Voodoo, the zombie seems not to have made the trip, which perhaps lends credence to the idea that the slavelike zombie only became an integral part of the fabric of the Haitian cosmology sometime during or immediately after the revolution, when the population of slaves who would carry the belief system to the United States were already exiled.

The zombie is not a significant aspect of Louisiana's brand of Voodoo. Where it exists today in commercialized voodoo tourism, it has clearly come into the mythology backward, through the popularity of the zombie in horror film and its associations with Haitian Vaudou. In authentic descriptions of Louisiana Voodoo, the appearance of the word Zombi is typically connected to "Le Grand-Zombi," which bears no resemblance to the walking dead but is, rather, another name for the lwa Damballah Ouedou, who is associated with the icon of the snake.

A Voodoo priestess cares for a snake, which is worshipped as a symbol of the serpent god and is involved in the ritual practice, being brought out to lick the queen's face and induce visions (Tallant 12–13). Tallant writes that this comes into Voodoo directly from Dahomey legend that the human race was born blind and that the serpent bestowed sight on man (13). He describes the rituals that called forth the presence of the Grand-Zombi: "On other occasions the king lifted the box [containing the snake] and shook it, and from the numerous bells which always adorned it came a magic tinkling that induced the hypnotic state desired by the devotees" (13). The shared name might suggest a connection between the state of the walking dead, under the blind control of a bokor, and the trancelike state induced in the viewer of these rituals, but this seems unlikely given the predominantly negative connotations of the zombie and the overwhelmingly positive associations of the Grand-Zombi snake deity. (The words probably share a common ancestor in Nzambi/Zombi, Congo and Angolan names for deities; see chapter 1.)

The only zombie reference in Newbell Niles Puckett's comprehensive *Folk Beliefs of the Southern Negro* is to "Le Grand Zombi," the spirit god, and there is no mention of the corps cadavre or any other walking dead.[9] Tellingly, in Rod Davis's *American Voudou*, there is but one reference to "zombis"; Davis states explicitly that this comes from Haiti and implies that it is not found in US Voodoo (125). Still, in folklore of the South one can find zombielike figures, though affixing the term zombie to them occurs only after the cinematic monster solidifies its popularity. Ackermann and Gautier cite the example of a headless "zombie" said to walk in New Orleans that is believed to be the spirit of a British soldier; but this seems a mashup of several mythologies, including the American legend of the Headless Horseman. Their source is B. A. Boktin, *The Treasury of Mississippi River Folklore*, published in 1955, after the zombie is well established in American cinema, and the same narrative, called "Zombi of Batture du Diable," is recounted in Hewitt L. Ballowe's 1948 *Creole Folk Tales*, in which the author makes direct comparison to the Haitian zombie. Ballowe also includes two tales of "Duppies" in his 1947 book, *The Lawd Sayin' the Same*, but these bear no resemblance to the zombie; rather, in these Creole tales the duppy (see chapter 1) is a protective or destructive spirit that can take the form of an animal.

In the folklore section of Hurston's *Mules and Men*, she briefly discusses a zombielike tale called "Raw-Head-and-Bloody-Bones and High Walker," but of these living dead figures she says, "nobody knew them but the old folks" (231). Though some say that Rawhead is a bogeyman of Celtic origins, in the version related here a character named High Walker who is capable of causing the bones of the dead to stir is taught a lesson by the corpse of a black man who had sold his soul to the devil. The moral of the story seems to be about showing solidarity against the white man, suggesting that the difference between black and white is greater than the difference between the living and the dead. At the end of the tale, High Walker is killed by his master, joining Rawhead in living death, the white man is scared off, and the last line is, "De Bloody Bones say, 'We got High Walker and we all bloody bones in de drift together'" (219–20).

References to anything resembling the walking dead in accounts of Louisiana Voodoo prior to the Haitian zombie's twentieth-century introduction are scarce. A reference to an old Voodoo priest who was caught digging up a corpse (*Daily Picayune*, March 17, 1914) is otherwise explained: François Pierre "has the reputation of being a voodoo doctor, and it was declared by his neighbors he wanted to use the head of the body to concoct his potions." The body had been dead eighteen months, so it is unlikely that the seventy-nine-year-old Voodoo priest was attempting a resurrection; further, grave dust is a common ingredient in conjury, a tradition reaching back to African tradition (J. R. Young 163). Another case, reported in the New Orleans Bulletin on May 29, 1875, and included in Lyle Saxon's nearly six-hundred-page volume, *Gumbo Ya-Ya: A Collection of Louisiana Folk Tales*, smacks of the zombie, though it is not depicted as such: "Buried Alive. Sickening Tale of Our Hospital Dead. A Man in the Charity Wagon Revives. He Attempts to Get out of his coffin. The Driver smothers him." Was this the victim of a zombie poisoning who suddenly revived? No, just a case of mistaken death during a smallpox epidemic and an overzealous hearse driver, who hit the man with a brick, claiming, "I have a doctor's certificate that you are dead, and I'm going to bury you" (Saxon 342).

And yet the concept must have existed in some form in the southern states, for the word Zombi is cataloged, after *mosey* and *cavort*, in

Maximilian Schele de Vere's 1872 book, *Americanisms: The English of the New World*: "Spanish terms may appropriately come to an end with the word *Zombi*, a phantom or a ghost, not unfrequently [sic] heard in the Southern states in nurseries and among the servants. The word is a Creole corruption of the Spanish *sombra*, which at times has the same meaning" (138). Though the etymology here is false (see chapter 1), this entry stands as proof that the word Zombi was used in the South in some form other than to refer to the snake deity prior to the introduction of the Haitian zombie into popular culture in the twentieth century. Its incorrect association with Creolized Spanish probably signifies that the word was found in slave populations that had come via the Caribbean. But here the word seems more in line with earlier uses of the term zombi to signify a kind of ghost rather than specifically the reanimated dead.

A thin book titled *Louisiana Voodoo* by Andre Cajun nonetheless establishes a real connection between the Vaudou zombie's creation and the use of an herbal, pain-killing remedy. A rural Louisiana ritual is described in the entry "The Zombi."

> An ordinary Negro [is] made to play the part of a Zombi at a cult's spiritual service. Weather permitting it takes five days to complete this make-up. The face is blocked, and the ears pinned back with a prepared mud. The lower teeth are covered with a paste of powdered charcoal; the upper teeth and gums are edged with the same paste. The lower lip is coated with mud whereby it may be given the corrugated effect. The upper lip is raised and held in place by a roll of cotton steeped in honey. The eyes are of shell and held in place by mud....
>
> The body of the man who plays the part of a Zombi is rubbed seven hours daily for five days with a "Zombi Salve," a concoction brewed by Voodoo doctors. The salve makes the man immune to minor pain caused by pin pricks, burning matches, etc. The long hours of rubbing with this "salve" makes the body feel ice-cold to the touch. Whenever possible the Zombi is made up to represent some one who has recently died.
>
> Shortly before the collection plate is passed the Zombi walks among the Negroes like a mechanical man; thus, he fills them with mortal fear, and they dig deep for that last dime. (Cajun 32)

This "Zombi" of rural Louisiana resembles the Haitian zombie in this demonstration of the powers of the Vaudou cults, but the difference here is that this zombie is a man chosen to play the part of the resuscitated dead. He is made up to look like a walking corpse, with recessed and cracked lips, mud caked on his skin to resemble decay. White shells in place of his eyes, a convention that is seen in some of the early zombie films, give the appearance of an always vacant stare. Regardless, this, too, is a late example, dating to 1946, and therefore may have been influenced by the cinematic zombie rather than the other way round.

Yet this pretend zombie is not unlike like the real thing, treated with an herbal concoction. It is not clear from this description whether "Zombi Salve" is derived from the same elements used in the production of real zombies or whether it only works to make one resemble the walking dead; nor is it obvious whether the faithful indulge the fantasy, viewing it as merely symbolic of Voodoo's powers, or believe that the man is truly a zombie. The mysterious salve that Cajun describes is capable of dulling the senses, so that, it must be presumed from his oblique description, if a member of the congregation were to challenge the authenticity of the Zombi's performance by pricking him with a pin or burning him with a match, the actor would feel no pain and could remain in character. If this salve indeed contains the same mixture as that which, in a more potent concoction, can produce a state that appears like death, then this is the first description connected to the fabrication of (real or ersatz) zombies I have found that overtly suggests the affected also becomes insensible to pain. It is tempting to associate this poultice with the various herbal armors used by rebel slaves in the Haitian Revolution.[10]

That the living dead zombie is not found in the Voodoo belief system of New Orleans might lead us to conclude that the zombie myth solidified in Haiti during or after the Revolution. According to Jerry Gandolfo, owner and historian of the New Orleans Voodoo Museum, the zombie's scarcity in the annals of Crescent City suggests that prior to Haiti's declaration of independence the slave culture had little narrative need for the folkloric zombie and that the central purpose of the Haitian zombie is related to its use as a punishment for social infractions. It was only when the people began to govern themselves as a sovereign nation, he claims, that they had need of the zombie myth as an imagining of the worst kind of punishment that could be dreamed of by a culture consisting of former slaves. As I discuss in the next chapter, although the zombie's use as social punishment is evidenced by later anthropological research—Max Beauvoir described it to me as a convenient alternative to imprisonment (Beauvoir pers. comm.)—I have not found that the earliest accounts of the zombie bear this description.

Therefore, it seems unlikely that the living dead zombie as we know it only arises, as Gandolfo suggests, out of a need for a punitive system in postrevolutionary Haiti. Instead, I think that the myth preexists the revolution and that evidence like de Vere's 1872 definition indicates that a few seeds were carried on the wind before the twentieth-century popular interest in the zombie myth flowered. That the myth really takes root and begins to disseminate after the revolution is proof that living death is an expression of the perceived continuity between colonial slavery and the capitalist system that succeeded it. Maximilien Laroche writes, "A man becomes a zombi when, as a result of certain ritualistic practices, a spell is cast over him by an individual possessing supernatural powers. But the reasons for transforming a man into a zombi appear natural indeed to the individual who casts the spell: he wants to possess a being who will serve him, work his fields and constitute a truly low-cost work force. To put it bluntly, he wants cheap labour" ("Myth" 55). To put it more bluntly, what he would prefer to cheap labor is a slave. What the Haitian zombie makes evident is that the brand of international capitalism that replaced France's dominion over Saint Domingue was just colonialism in sheep's clothing.

Though the zombie may not have been a substantial part of American Voodoo prior to the cinematic introduction of the Haitian Vaudou zombie, it certainly made a significant impact on the cultural imagination, as a fictional if not folkloric figure. In the earliest wave of zombie fiction to hit American shores, slave rebellion was an especially pertinent element. This association between the zombie and revolution continues. Aren't we when confronted today by the cinematic zombie mob and the zombie's contagion reminded, if only on a subconscious level, of the infectious specter of rebellion? In the next section of this chapter, I present the way in which revolution was preserved as the primary economy of the zombie myth in its earliest exchanges outside of Haiti and explore the catharsis provided to white film audiences anxious about narratives of black empowerment.

Over the past decade, especially, many critics have considered the zombie's current incarnation of present-day horrors. In a 2008 article, "A Zombie Manifesto: The Nonhuman Condition in the Age of Advanced Capitalism," Karen Embry and I sought to illustrate that at its most basic level the living dead zombie represents a defiance of the binary categories imposed by Enlightenment reason, many of which, like the self/other distinction, undergird capitalism. Because of its historical associations, the zombie always carries with it the wraith of rebellion and of Age of Revolutions; in its basic irresolvability the zombie bears the marks of the dawn of modernity as it resists classification as either living or dead, inanimate or animate, subject or object, human or animal. But here I am more interested in exploring what it means to say *what* the zombie signifies. The zombie myth itself became a kind of slave when it was abducted by American and European filmmakers, voided of its previous associations, branded as a new signifier, and made to bear a very different psychic load. The important thing for me to draw out here is the way the zombie admits and resists its own appropriation.

Zombies in Early Fiction and Film

Though zombies may have existed in Saint Domingue long before the outside world knew of them (except for a few oblique references in the writings of former colonists), the Haitian zombie was formally introduced to the American imagination in 1929 with the publication of William Seabrook's travel narrative, *The Magic Island*. Although entities called "zombies" had previously been discussed in print, Seabrook's text is the entry point through which the walking dead zombie passes into American cinema. The promise that Seabrook's Haitian guide delivers to his readership is the revelation of "dead men working in the canefields" (23), and this phrase is sometimes used as shorthand for the early wave of zombie lore in which the zombie is primarily a somnambulistic laborer. Despite the passage's enduring popularity among zombie-film fans, there are several aspects of Seabrook's description that are usually overlooked.

Though the image of dead men working in the cane fields doubtlessly calls to mind the plantation system imposed in agrarian Haiti, and the fact that it was once a colony ruled by the French and populated by slaves, Seabrook's description of the zombie is closely tied to modern capitalism, global commercial exchange, and industrial technology.

> "If you will ride with me tomorrow night, yes, I will show you dead men working in the canefields. Close even to the cities there are sometimes zombies. Perhaps you have already heard of those that were at Hasco..."
>
> "What about Hasco?" I interrupted him, for in the whole of Haiti, Hasco is perhaps the last name anybody would think of connecting with either sorcery or superstition. The word is American-commercial-synthetic, like Nabisco, Delco, Socony. It stands for the Haitian-American Sugar Company—an immense factory plant, dominated by a huge chimney, with a clanging machinery, steam whistles, freight cars. It is like a chunk of Hoboken. It lies in the

eastern suburbs of Port-au-Prince, and beyond it stretch the canefields of the Cul-de-Sac. Hasco makes rum when the sugar market is off, pays low wages, a shilling or so a day and gives steady work. It is modern big business, and it sounds it, looks it, smells it.

Such then, was the incongruous background for the weird tale Constant Polynice now told me. (23–24)

I leave it up to the reader to decide whether such a link in fact proves to be "incongruous." The story that Seabook relates directly implicates Hasco, established in 1912, in the hiring of zombies; it even suggests that the company may have been indirectly responsible for the creation of these undead unfortunates. In 1918, an overabundant cane season led Hasco to begin issuing bonuses to workers who brought in new laborers. To take advantage of the bonus, a man named Ti Joseph came to work with a gaggle of ragged, vacant-eyed laborers, who had to be cared for and prodded continually by his wife.

That this narrative of the Hasco zombies becomes the prime example of the zombie myth's transportation to the United States is extremely important, as it implicates global capitalism from the very beginning of American interest in the zombie. Many assume that it is only in the later films of George Romero that the zombie metaphor is transformed from being about the African slave subsumed under colonial empire to being about the alienated worker oppressed by industrial capitalism. However, both are explicitly visible in Seabrook's account, and the twin vision of the colonial slave and the corporate employee is held in parallax perspective in Seabrook's description of the zombie. Later in the chapter, he describes seeing zombies with his own eyes: "They were plodding, like brutes, like automatons" (29). This description makes explicit the zombie's dual capacity to represent both the dehumanized slave and the factory worker reduced to the repetition of a mechanized gesture; it refers at the same time to Haiti's predominantly agrarian economy and its past as France's cash crop colony, as well as to the formidable sugar factory Seabrook has just described and the militarily sustained commercial alliance between Haiti and the United States that Hasco represents. It should not be forgotten, moreover, that the factory was a permanent fixture on the sugarcane plantations of Haiti, dating to before the revolution, because of the need to refine the cane shortly after harvesting it.

That the first major wave of zombie fiction to hit US shores coincided with the country's worst economic disaster is telling. Seabrook's story was published in 1929, the same year as the major market crash that economic historians identify as the beginning of the Great Depression, and interest in this strange mythic figure soon manifested in both fiction and film. American intervention in Haiti, primarily in the form of military occupation, had also sparked a rash of autobiographical and pseudo-anthropological travel accounts published throughout the 1930s, many of which mention the folkloric zombie.[11] In the first few years of the 1930s the zombie outgrew its containment within journalistic accounts of exotic climes and foreign superstitions and took up residence onscreen, on air, and in the pages of horror magazines.

In the initial rewriting of the zombie that occurred as it was adapted to the medium of horror and fantasy and rebranded for an American audience, the theme of slave rebellion was foregrounded. The accepted Haitian folklore typically mentions that a zombie is forbidden from tasting salt as this will break the zombie's trance: the corpse will realize that it is dead and seek its grave. Seabrook's book recounted the now-famous story of Ti Joseph's wife, Croyance, who, in her husband's absence, took pity on the zombies they controlled and gave them a candy that unbeknownst to her contained salt.

> But the baker of the *tablettes* had salted the *pistache* nuts before stirring them into the *rapadou*, and as the zombies tasted the salt, they knew they were dead and made a dreadful outcry and rose and turned their faces toward the mountain.
>
> No one dared stop them, for they were corpses walking in the sunlight, and they themselves and everyone else knew they were corpses. And they disappeared toward the mountain.
>
> When later they drew near their own village on the slopes of Morne-au-Diable, these men and women walking single file in the twilight, with no soul leading them or daring to follow, the people of their village, who were also holding *bamboche* in the marketplace, saw them drawing closer, recognizing among them fathers, brothers, wives, and daughters whom they had buried months before. . . .
>
> But the zombies shuffled through the market-place recognizing neither father nor wife nor mother, and as they turned leftward up the path leading to the graveyard, a woman whose daughter was in the procession of the dead threw herself screaming before the girl's shuffling feet and begged her to stay; but the grave-cold feet of the daughter and the feet of the other dead shuffled over her and onward and as they approached the graveyard, they began to shuffle

faster and rushed among the graves, and each before his own empty grave began clawing at the stones and earth to enter it again; and as their cold hands touched the earth of their own graves, they fell and lay there, rotting carrion. (27–28)

Seabrook's prose seems to emulate the oral storyteller's cadence, with a heavy reliance on coordinating conjunctions and a long final sentence that parallels the winding path of the zombies trudging up the mountain, undeterred by the attempted interventions of family members in their quest to find their final resting places. In a sense, this determined march of the zombies, single file, to freedom, might be read for its insinuation of slave rebellion or marronage, but it is the end of the fable that most closely echoes both the Haitian Revolution and more recent political coups.

The mourning family members, newly alerted by the zombies' appearance in their home village to the reality of the false deaths suffered by their loved ones, band together and raise money to pay a bokor to curse Ti Joseph the zombie maker with a death-bringing *ouanga*: "And in case the needle *ouanga* be slow in working or be rendered weak by Joseph's counter magic, they sent men down to the plain, who lay in wait patiently for Joseph, and one night hacked off his head with a machete" (28). This end of the zombie master directly parallels the first night of the slave rebellion, when the instruments used for cutting cane were turned on the slaveholder and the plantation overseer. The combination of Vaudou and physical force that the offended parties draw on also recalls the Haitian Revolution, but this scene would perhaps have recalled for contemporary readers the prevalence of mob violence and political assassinations that had become commonplace in Haiti at the time of the US occupation.[12]

In Seabrook's work this narrative is presented as a story believed to be true by the people of Haiti and recounted to the author by the "peasant" Polynice. But shortly after Seabrook's work drew the attention of a wider audience to this mythological figure, it began to take on a life of its own, in fiction produced and even set outside of Haiti. In August 1931, *Ghost Stories Magazine* published G. W. Hutter's short story "Salt Is Not for Slaves."[13] Borrowing from Seabrook's tale, which the author had elsewhere critiqued, this work of fiction uses a frame narration in which a zombie named Marie recounts—a rare example of a talking zombie—the story of a zombie rebellion to an unnamed narrator, presumably a foreigner.[14]

The story that Marie relates conflates the Haitian Revolution with a narrative of zombie rebellion, so that, troublingly, they are rendered equivalent. Marie was one of six zombies among a plantation of slaves controlled by a bad master. They had been warned never to taste salt, but when the fire of rebellion began to take hold, incited by the words of "Christophe" and other leaders encouraging the slaves to claim their freedom, her fellow zombie and lover, Tressaint—an obvious allusion to Toussaint L'Ouverture, as Christophe is to Henri Christophe—opens the master's stores up to the slaves and zombies. Unaware of exactly what result it will yield, he encourages his fellows to partake: "Here, my friends, in one hand you have the salt, in the other the wine to wash the curse away" (47).[15] Rather than free them from living death, however, a similar result, if more gruesome, is produced; as in Seabrook's text, the flesh falls off their bodies, and the pitiful zombies, now little more than walking skeletons, begin to howl and fly toward their graves. The rebellion of zombies, thus, leads inevitably to their destruction.

In Seabrook's account and other versions of Haitian folklore, such as that in Inez Wallace's series of journal articles, "I Walked with a Zombie," on which the 1943 Val Lewton film of the same name was partly based, the zombie's state is emphasized as one that is worse than death—so that when the zombie tastes salt, its release from this state is accepted as liberation, a release from enslavement. In Hutter's story, by contrast, the zombies are lucid, they are stronger than slaves, and they do not get sick. They even take lovers and feel emotion, so the fact that the rebellion leads to their destruction connotes its failure. Indeed, it was not the outcome that Tressaint was expecting, just as, it may be Hutter's intimation, the contemporary state of Haiti was not what Toussaint L'Ouverture had wanted for the nascent republic. This is a complex and highly problematic position to take, but the story was produced during the American occupation of Haiti, which had justified itself by creating a discourse about the state of near-constant political turmoil that had been suffered by the Haitians since declaring their independence in 1804. The political commentary couched in such narratives is obvious, produced at a time when the dominant political rhetoric was that Haitians could not be trusted to run their own country: the slaves' revolution was depicted as a Pyrrhic victory, just as the rebel zombie earned only his place in the cemetery.[16] Nevertheless, Hutter's zombie strengthens the link between slave rebellion and the zombie myth. As the zombie continued to infiltrate American fiction, this element of the mythology would evolve.

In July 1932 *Strange Tales* magazine published a story by August Derleth titled "The House in the Magnolias" that relocated the zombie from the Caribbean to the southern United States, setting the tale on a plantation about four miles outside of New Orleans. Derleth's tale drops the anthropological posture adopted by earlier zombie fiction. A young painter comes upon a house that he wants to make the subject of a landscape; when he knocks on the door to ask permission of the owners, he finds there is something strange about the unspeaking servant who first opens the door. The young Creole mistress of the house, named Rosamunda, intrigues him, and he is pleased to gain permission to undertake the painting, but odd occurrences lead him to discover that all is not right with the inhabitants and their servants. He learns that the plantation is owned by Rosamunda's Haitian aunt, who moved her to the United States when she was just a child, and that Aunt Abby keeps zombies who work the fields at night when no one will see them.

Yet there is one zombie who stands out; this is explained only by Rosamunda's cryptic comment, "Over Matilda Abby had no power—it often happens that way" (157). The young couple hatch a plan to return the dead to their graves. Rosamunda instructs the painter to give the zombies candies with salt in them, but they have more sinister plans in store for the zombie master: "Rosamunda's eyes suddenly went cold. She said: 'Matilda can be directed to Abby. Only I can direct her. Matilda hates Abby as I do. Abby is a fiend—she has robbed these dead of their peace'" (158).

Most of the zombies are given the salted candy and released from their state to seek their graves, but before Matilda can have hers she is given one final instruction: "Above there is Abby, Matilda. Long ago she took you away from where you were—took you to be her slave. You have hated her. Go up to her now. She is yours. When you come down, there will be a candy on the table for you" (159). The pair escape the house in the magnolias with the sounds of the "shrill screaming of a woman in deadly terror" filling the night behind them (160). The plantation is found burned to the ground the next morning, echoing the slave rebellion.

This tale of zombie revolution is, like Hutter's, perturbing. First, though the niece is Creole, the author makes a point of having her say of her aunt, "She brought me from Haiti when I was just a little girl. I cannot remember anything. She is much darker than I am; she is not a Creole" (148). The intimation may be that she is not actually the niece of this woman but was kidnapped by her as a young child. Regardless, that the zombies and their master are both identified as black and the niece as mixed race, while the protagonist is presumably white (though this is never explicitly stated), lends the troubling insinuation that the zombies, to continue reading this fiction in light of contemporary US policy on

Haiti, represent disempowered Haitians who need the help of whites to attain their freedom from local tyrants. For Matilda commits the act of revenge while still a zombie, not after she has eaten the candy, which suggests that the violent act of resistance is possible only as the following of a directive; in this tale, too, the liberated zombie has the ability only to seek its grave.

Current assessments of the American occupation hold that it effectively stabilized an ineffective and unpopular government because US interests feared that a change of power would put at risk American investments in the country, particularly Hasco, the profitable sugar company to which Seabrook alluded. However, the popular line of the day portrayed the Americans as saviors rescuing the peasant class from another brutal dictatorship.[17] And Derleth's tale only perpetuates this narrative.

One can find other stories among the pages of horror magazines during the 1930s that wrestle with the political implications of the Haitian occupation and the complex legacy of slavery and colonialism and its extension into postcolonial economic imperialism. For example, interest in slave rebellion in horror fiction of the period extends beyond the zombie.[18] A tale by the pulp legend Manly Wade Wellman, "Song of the Slaves," was first published in *Weird Tales* in 1940. Set in the 1850s, it features the walking corpses of drowned slaves who have come back from the dead to exact revenge on a cruel slave trader, who, to escape discovery by a British patrol fleet, chained his forty-nine slaves to an anchor and threw them overboard to drown—a detail that is obviously meant to recall the horrors of the Zong massacre of 1781. Despite the theme of slavery and several allusions to rebellion, these living dead are not quite zombies—for they were never the enslaved dead—but are more like revenants, seeking revenge for wrongful death. Nonetheless, the story combines many of the themes prevalent in zombie fiction. In particular, there is a recurring motif of the power of the mob.

The American slave trader, Gender, being of a uniquely capitalist mind-set, has come to Africa to kidnap his own slaves in order to cut the middlemen out of the slave-running profit. But from the moment of their capture until their execution he is perturbed by his captives' constant singing. He is told by a deckhand that the African natives believe that they are capable of singing someone to death.

> "I've heard it said," Gender replied, "that they sing together because they think that many voices and hearts give power to hate, or to

other feelings." . . . "[H]eathen foolishness," snapped Gender, and his lips drew tight.

"Well, in Christian lands we have examples, sir," Dunlapp pursued. "For instance, a mob will grow angry and burn or hang someone. Would a single man do that? Would any single man of the mob do it? No, but together their hate and resolution becomes—" (48–49)

The speaker is interrupted by Gender and advised to change the subject, but the reader gets the point. What is more difficult to ascertain from the vantage point of our contemporary perspective is what such a reference to the crowd would have signified to the pulp fiction readership at the end of the difficult decade of the 1930s. Despite the association made between slavery and rebellion, there is no direct reference to Haiti in this story; it seems more likely that this would have been interpreted as an oblique reference to the power of the proverbial people. Given Gender's greed and the pervasiveness of critiques of capitalism in the era, I wonder if this wouldn't read to some at the top of the economic hierarchy as an oblique threat.

Gender does indeed get his comeuppance. At the story's end, he is pursued to Charleston, South Carolina, by the rumor of his actions and is ostracized by the community, but this is not punishment enough. One night, sitting alone in his empty house, he begins to hear the song of the slaves. Their water-logged corpses march up to his house and drag him outside to drown him in the ocean, as he had done to them. This is their rebellion, carried out postmortem. In a struggling US economy, the living dead slave—and the zombie in other stories—was a convenient symbol both for individual servitude in an unjust system and the futility of rebellion against it.

Perhaps early zombie narratives afforded a space in which American readers could exorcise their demons regarding the nation's past reliance on the transatlantic slave trade or the military's contemporary involvement in Haiti, but more likely, I think, the audience was invited to compare the figure of the zombie-slave to the American worker's abuse under the capitalist system and the government's abandonment of the poor during the early years of the Depression. This is the primary pivot on which the Haitian zombie is turned to represent the concerns of US audiences. With this came the first of several adjustments to the mythology that pulled the focus of the zombie narrative from the institution of slavery and its long-suffering descendants still oppressed under postcolonialism and policies maintaining racial inequality to the concerns of a different, and mostly white, population.

The earliest zombie films, *White Zombie* (1932), *Ouanga* (1935), *Revolt of the Zombies* (1936), *King of the Zombies* (1941), and *I Walked with a Zombie* (1943) put white characters into foreign settings where they must oppose the creation of zombies or their own zombification. Liberties are taken with setting: zombies are not only associated specifically with Haiti or a vaguely defined Caribbean isle but also begin to crop up in places like Cambodia (*Revolt of the Zombies*). One strange trend discovered among the cache of early zombie narratives, folkloric, literary, and cinematic, is the explicit concern with both white zombies and white zombie makers.[19]

Dr. Gordon Bromley's magazine article for *American Weekly* provides a transparent account retold to him in 1936 by a Frenchman, Henri Champley, who is writing a book on interracial relationships: "He was frankly alarmed at the intercourse of white men with coloured women, and—what seemed more serious to him—that of white women and the coloured men. He could understand, he said, the German revulsion against this biological revolution" (104). Unsurprisingly, this racist informant then recounts a story of a white woman kept as a naked zombie in a Harlem apartment by "an old Negro" performing a "Congo exhortation." The white zombie is shown to an African American acquaintance of Champley's in New York "as an example, for him not to fear the power of the whites" (107). Yet the descriptions of the zombie's nipples, white as "the roots of some plant," and her hairless nude body are clearly meant to suggest the "Negro's" sexual threat as well as a supernatural one.

As in Bromley's piece, Inez Wallace's nonfiction article series, "I Walked with a Zombie," includes a white female zombie and an implicit warning about interracial relations. In one of the many brief anecdotes related by Wallace, a jilted *amante* thrown over for a white woman zombifies her replacement and sets her to work in the cane fields. Both of these purportedly nonfictional accounts depict white people zombified by black magic workers, inhabiting the zombie's position as victim and thereby offering it as a space to be occupied by the white reader fearful of an always sexualized black power. However, in the extrapolation of the myth in fictional stories published in horror magazines, the tables are turned further.

The British author Vivien Meik's 1933 story, "White Zombie," set in colonial Africa (first published in his short story collection *Devil's Drums* in the Creeps series and named *after* the Halperin film), describes a white woman who has zombified (with the help of an African witchdoctor) her plantation's workforce and her husband for the purpose, it is implied, of sating a "perverted lust" (93). In Meik's sensational fiction, then, the Afro-Caribbean command of the dark arts is commandeered by a white woman. And in Thorp McClusky's 1939 offering from *Weird Tales* magazine, that power is further displaced to the hands of a white man, a former minister, who zombifies blacks and whites alike for the purpose of gaining both sex (from Eileen, a young white girl affianced to the protagonist) and wealth, as he tries to take over a cotton farm from an ailing man.

In these cases, the power of zombification is redistributed to the arsenal of the white antagonist. Yet, as in many of the early tales of Haitian bokors, the zombies are freed in the end. McClusky's reverend is ultimately unsuccessful; as in Derleth's story, the zombies are freed by white protagonists and return to their final resting place when the zombie master is killed. The black arts presented as an anthropological mystery and demonstrated by the Harlem resident in Bromley's account as a source of alternative power are thereby not only appropriated by white villains in zombie fiction but also defused by white heroes.

This trend of rewriting both the zombie's creation and its rebellion as powers belonging to white characters is seen throughout both pulp fiction and film. See, for example, Stan Lee's "Zombie!" in the July 1953 issue of *Menace*, in which a white zombie rebels against his white master, proclaiming, "For the first time in history a zombie has slain his master!" (111). The same dynamic sketched here in terms of early zombies in literature is true of zombies in film: the first zombie films listed previously all feature white people or Creoles in control of the forces that raise the dead. If black characters are present, they look on, reduced to disempowered victims or humorous sidekicks. Creole characters may have been intended to be perceived as of mixed race but were played by white actors, like Bela Lugosi in *White Zombie*, or very fair ones, like Fredi Washington in *Ouanga*, a light-skinned African American actress playing a character of mixed descent in a film that repeatedly emphasizes the lightness of her skin. Scholars have examined many of these early films for their deeply troublesome representations of race and especially for their depiction of the sexual threat to white women of black men.[20] But I am troubled by the fact that although one finds disempowered black zombies from the very beginning, Hollywood would not conjure a powerful black houngan as zombie master for four decades: The cinematic manipulation of the zombie myth reveals much about contemporary racism, even after the zombie film seems to cease being about race.

In her essay "New South, New Immigrants, New Women, New Zombies," Ann Kordas theorizes, "The depiction of blacks as helpless creatures was undoubtedly appealing to many white Americans.... Fear of physical harm at the hands of African Americans and fear of economic hardship as the result of the inability to command African American laborers led many white southerners in the late nineteenth and early twentieth centuries to yearn for a black labor force of contented, willing, docile workers" (19). This doubtlessly accounts for one reason that the early fictional zombie narratives were popular among a certain demographic. But we also typically find that in these films the white protagonists save themselves, free the zombies, and help other impotent African American characters (many of whom are there for comic relief, as in *The Ghost Breakers* [1940], *King of the Zombies* [1941], and *Revenge of the Zombies* [1943]) from a powerful white or mixed-race character depicted as neither properly black nor white.

To my mind, this maneuver, in which the white character becomes the savior and liberator of blacks and/or zombies, risks seeming like a rehearsal of the freeing of the slaves and is part of a larger, insidious cultural exercise that allows the white filmgoer to perform a kind of vicarious redemption for the evils of slavery and its lingering effects—whether this comes in the form of self-flagellation, provided by a film like *12 Years a Slave* (2013); the atrocious celebration of white characters helping black ones, as seen in *The Help* (2011) or *The Blind Side* (2009); or, even, what I like to call "the *Django* effect" (after Quentin Tarantino's 2012 *Django Unchained*), when white audiences are invited to pat themselves on the back for rooting for violence perpetrated by a black character against white ones.[21]

Early zombie films place black characters in a position of disempowerment and dependence, and at the same time they reallocate to whites a power associated specifically with black knowledge. But as early as the 1940s filmmakers discovered they could make a zombie movie that included neither Vaudou nor black bodies. I think here of the 1942 film *The Living Ghost*, with its one mention of the word zombie and a tale of brain damage inflicted to secure a wealthy man's fortune while keeping him in a subdued state. This signals the next move in the cultural chess match for possession of the zombie: the erasure of its blackness and its origins altogether. Indeed, it is not long after the initial films are set abroad that one finds the zombie transplanted to the United States in films like *Voodoo Man* (1944) and *Revenge of the Zombies* (1946). Swiftly thereafter the figure begins to take on resonances beyond the occult zombie, with its themes of "going native," of the cultural and racial "contamination" that was a much-feared result of inhabiting the contact zones of colonial empire.

As we will see below, as the economic woes of the 1930s gave way to a second global war and then the Red Scare, horror fans found other bogeymen more terrifying. The zombie remained, but it came to represent other evils: infiltration of the nation by outsiders, manipulation of the multitudes by a lone dictator, communist brainwashing, concerns about technology and science in the service of evil. The titles of zombie films took on the vernacular of the space and arms races: *Zombies of the Stratosphere* (1952), *The Creature with the Atom Brain* (1955), *Astro-Zombies* (1968).

The narrative of the Vaudou zombie waxes and wanes throughout the decades and makes scant appearances in cinema, even today. Yet as the zombie receded from Vaudou within Hollywood's idiom, it gained more and more power. The early cinematic zombie only rarely (and then, feebly) attacked onscreen in films like *King of the Zombies* (1931) or *The Zombies of Mora Tau* (1957); otherwise, they did no violence to humans. Overt revolt of zombies against their masters is still more rare in this early period. One reason for this might be the taboo against the depiction of any kind of violence visited by a black body on a white one. Yet that the US appropriation of a Haitian myth was originally intended to give the white majority a sense of command and control over black culture (within and outside the nation's borders) is incontrovertible when one considers the paucity of black witch doctors in American zombie cinema.

The 1935 film *Ouanga*, elsewhere called both *Love Wanga* and *Crimes of Voodoo*, which was actually shot in the West Indies, presents an exception to many of the conventions of early zombie cinema. Doubtless, if this film were easier to find, it might be written on more often. The plot, highly reminiscent of Wallace's "I Walked with a Zombie," concerns Clelie (Fredi Washington), a mixed-race plantation owner who is in love with Adam, a white man, and tries to prevent his marriage to the white Miss Langley. Clelie is repeatedly told by LeStrange, Adam's mixed-race overseer (played by Sheldon Leonard, a Jewish actor) who is in love with Clelie himself, that like should marry like. The film has some great lines about the complicated politics of interracial relationships coming out of the institution of slavery and is a useful time capsule for examining the racial stereotypes of the period. Clelie tells Adam, "Don't draw away from me as if I were a black wench in your fields!" And, comparing her own fair skin to the zombified Miss Langley, Clelie asks her mockingly, "Can a placid, white-blooded thing like you make Adam happy?" In the end, naturally, the Vaudou priestess is out-voodooed and the mixed-race characters, Clelie and LeStrange, kill each other, leaving the white couple to marry, happily after all. But before this happens, in a rare display of black (or at least mixed-race) power, Clelie raises zombies from the dead, puts Miss Langley into a trance, and nearly sacrifices her to get her out of the way.

The film is only the second offering in cinema to portray zombies, and it does so with great artistry. Especially notable for its formal elements is the scene when Clelie raises the dead to do her bidding: a V-shaped wipe transitions the viewer to a low-angle shot of Clelie standing over the graves, with only tree branches and sky behind her, waving her hands as she subtly and suggestively wriggles her body and performs a silent incantation. The next shot shows two zombies sitting up in their coffins; they are framed opposite each other so that as they rise their bodies create the shape of a V, a parallel to the wipe effect that revealed Clelie standing above the grave site. The film also makes wonderful use of black and white and dark and light: there is a repeated and hauntingly effective shot of a drummer whose black body is hidden in shadow until he bends forward to beat the drum and is bathed in the key light coming from below. Most significantly, the film doesn't shy away from showing contact between black and white bodies, as in the juxtaposition of the white face of Miss Langley covered by the black hand of a zombie as he abducts her. When Adam bursts in on the Vaudou sacrifice just in time to save his fiancée, too, the crowd at the ceremony rushes him—showing blacks and whites struggling—before the police force breaks it up and order is restored. Though the zombie is associated with resistance in this picture—namely, Clelie's resistance to the expected social convention that the mulatta lover will gracefully recede from view when the white mistress comes on the scene—the black zombies themselves are docile, completely in the control of their mixed-race mistress. Despite the film's ending, that Clelie is a powerful, nonwhite character in control of zombies makes this film notable.

Even as late as 1964, in a film like *I Eat Your Skin*, which remains faithful to the Vaudou zombie narrative in its Caribbean setting, the true villain overseeing all the zombification and virgin sacrifice turns out to be a white man.[22] The closest one comes to depicting a man of color with the power to zombify prior to 1970 might be an episode of the television show *The Man from U.N.C.L.E.*, "The Very Important Zombie Affair"

(1964), in which a brutal dictator named El Supremo (obviously meant as a stand-in for Fidel Castro), who has the power to zombify his enemies, tells the protagonists not to be fooled by his blue eyes, for "the jungle drums are in my veins!"[23]

Finally, the 1974 film *House on Skull Mountain* returns a genre that had since moved on to its Vaudou roots with a story line about a black bokor, a descendant of the Haitian president Alexandre Pétion (1770–1810), who is killing off the American ancestors of Roi Henri Christophe (1767–1820). Yet even here, in this seemingly brave depiction of a powerful black man, all the violence is perpetrated against other black bodies, and it is the "honky" anthropology professor among the group who ultimately saves the day, using his knowledge of Haitian Vaudou to convince the zombie Tomas Pétion has raised to terminate him instead of the surviving Christophe ancestors.[24]

Wade Davis's *Serpent and the Rainbow* was made into a film in the 1980s, at last illustrating a break from the taboo and returning the zombie to its original context in the control of Haitian bokors; before the film, the television series *Miami Vice* would produce an episode about the zombie poison in season 2, 1985. "Tale of the Goat" features a powerful Haitian crime lord, called Legba, who takes a dose of tetrododoxin so that he can enter the United States in the guise of a corpse for burial, perhaps pointing to cultural insecurities about Haitian immigrants. Naturally, Crockett and Tubbs are victorious in the end.

Even more problematic than Hollywood's long-standing squeamishness about powerful black men is the narrative that George Romero's decision to cast a black actor, Duane Jones, in the lead role in his 1968 film, *Night of the Living Dead*, and the film's subsequent subtext of civil rights issues "rebooted" the genre, as the film historian Mark Harris claims in the unfortunately titled documentary *Birth of the Living Dead* (2012). That the film showed a black man saving white people indicated, this line goes, that the zombie wasn't racist anymore, that it was antiracist, or better, says Barbara Bruce, represented race "ambivalently": "the binary conceptions of race at play in the film demonstrate the problems associated with depicting 'blackness' in American mainstream cinema" (60).[25] Leaving aside the particulars of this now-classic movie—it is the hagiography that has developed around Romero that is troubling to me, not the film itself—I present in the next section the consequences of claiming that Romero's film constitutes the "birth" or even rebirth of the living dead.

Before and after Romero

Almost universally, today's zombie is the inadvertent consequence of scientific malfeasance or technological innovation, or the result of a virus, often engineered by humans. This trend is said to have begun with George Romero's *Night of the Living Dead* (1968), in which the cause of the zombie outbreak is suggested as radiation from a human-made space probe orbiting around Venus.[26] But, in fact, Del Tenney's earlier film, *The Horror of Party Beach* (1964), contains many of the elements that people commonly associate with Romero's reinvented zombie: the creatures, which are explicitly called "zombies," though they have giant fish heads, are identified as both living and dead, and they are the result of badly disposed of toxic waste that reanimates human corpses underwater. They attack humans and drink their blood, which turns the victim himself into a zombie. This is somewhat difficult to ascertain at first—probably due to budget restrictions and the difficulty of producing several of the fish-headed zombie costumes—because more than two zombies are rarely shown in the same frame until the film's end, when the protagonists find the hive of the sea-zombies and destroy them with the only effective weapon: sodium, a possible nod to the Haitian zombie's deanimation with salt. There are more explicit references to Haiti in the film: the protagonist's African American maid, Eula Belle, tells the doctor who is trying to solve the mystery of these creatures, "The Voodoo, that's what it is"; and the film ends with a shot of a voodoo doll on the heroine's nightstand. This campy flick admits not only its own indebtedness to the folkloric zombie but also its relationship to zombies in cinema.

The film is, as the title suggests, part horror picture and part beach movie: several musical numbers interrupt the action, including a song called "Zombie Stomp" performed by a musical group on the beach where the first zombie is seen. Frolicking teens begin a choreographed dance performed with outstretched arms, in imitation of the predecessor cinematic zombie, as the film intercuts shots of the reanimate fishman drawing closer to his first victim, sunbathing on a rock. The band sings, "Oh, everybody do the zombie stomp: just let your foot down with an awful thump. You reach out further, further, stepping closer, closer. . . . It's the living end!" Tenney's film thus recognizes its intervention in a preexisting genre. That it depicts a community overrun by contagious, flesh-eating zombies certainly diminishes the novelty of Romero's *Night of the Living Dead*, which was made several years later and yet has been lauded as the origin of the apocalyptic zombie narrative, what has since become the most prevalent form of the genre describing an outbreak of contagious, cannibalistic living dead. Most of the contemporary elements— the implication of the role of human science in the zombie's creation, the communicability of the zombie's state, and its appetite—are already visible in Tenney's film and others, so why the canonization of Romero as the zombie's new houngan?

Let us begin to answer the question by putting Romero's picture in context. Like the films of the 1930s and 1940s, some of those produced in the 1950s and 1960s still portrayed Vaudou as the primary cause of reanimation: this trope lingered even in films such as *Plague of the Zombies* (1966), set in an English tin mine, drawing an obvious parallel between the Haitian slave and the British laborer. At the same time, films also continued to imagine scientific resurrection enacted by a lone man, à la *Frankenstein*, and the movies increasingly fantasized, especially as the space race began, that alien technology might be capable of raising the dead for their own nefarious purposes. Many of the living dead resurrected during the aftermath of World War II and the onset of the Cold War began to weave distrust of military technology into the material of the mythology. In the 1950s, for example, one sees films that link the creation of living dead to atomic power, as in *Creature with the Atom Brain* (1953), in which a scientist uses atomic energy to raise the dead to do his bidding, or *Plan Nine from Outer Space* (1958), in which aliens reanimate corpses to mount an attack on humanity.

Though the latter Ed Wood B-movie is much maligned, it makes explicit what most of the zombie films of this period covertly represent: fears that human technology has exceeded its natural domain. As the alien leader, Eros, explains, humanity is developing weaponry at a rate that exceeds its maturity. Fearing that humans are on the verge of developing a weapon that could wipe out not only their own planet but also those of other intergalactic species, the alien explains to the humans that they are too "stupid" to be in possession of such technology.

The real breakthrough in films like Tenney's and Romero's is the association of the zombie with what was already a long-standing trope in science fiction: the harrowing notion that our own scientific achievements and technological advances could have unpredictable, and sometimes horrible, ramifications. In this iteration of the zombie, American audiences confronted a living dead that was not, like Frankenstein's monster, a mad scientist's "abortion" but that took on the traits of the trope "nature run amok," already a staple of science fiction (Shelley, *Frankenstein* 276).

After Romero, the zombie was definitively rebranded as the result of a horrifying accident caused by man's interference in the natural world.[27]

Elsewhere I have traced the way the zombie dovetailed with the trope of the mad scientist in cinema and popular fiction, in a lineage begotten by Mary Shelley's *Frankenstein*, which was itself perhaps informed by imperialist tales of Vaudouist reanimation.[28] It was the year after the release of James Whale's *Frankenstein* (1931), which translated Shelley's iconic and archetypal man-made monster for the filmgoer, that the Haitian zombie—heretofore the exclusive province of anthropological studies of the Caribbean—was imported to Hollywood. Victor Halperin's *White Zombie* (1932) introduced audiences to a kind of strange living dead somewhat vaguely defined as being made by a witch doctor's potion but seemingly also controlled by the use of hypnosis. One can trace the way in which these different mythologies—the mad scientist's living corpse and the Haitian zombie—became tangled, merged, and exchanged traits to produce a "new," "Western" zombie. Still, the trend of the lone scientist attempting to raise the dead, though no longer the predominant method of zombie creation as it was in the 1930s and 1940s, does not entirely dissipate but remains a mainstay of horror. Then, films often combined a doctor's passion for science and a Vaudou theme, as in *King of the Zombies* (1941), *Voodoo Man* (1944), *Zombies on Broadway* (1945), and *The Face of Marble* (1946).

What lies behind nods to dark magic, "savage" superstitions, and folk knowledge from the supposed "uncivilized" parts of the world in stories of mad scientists may be the admission that science and technology had trespassed into the province traditionally deemed the domain of divinities. We see in science fiction and horror of the midcentury and beyond the modern era's grappling with its own advances: at worst, the development, since the beginning of the twentieth century, of weapons of massive devastation and mass destruction, but even advances in surgery such as organ transplants may have caused existential anxiety for their ability to extend life past its natural threshold.

As it developed in the second half of the twentieth century, indebted to both its mad scientist father and its black magic mother, the nouveau zombie became an expression of angst concerning the powers that scientific knowledge bestowed on humanity: to destroy his fellows and to profit from their abuse. Misuses of science and technology became the most common engine associated with the reanimation of consciousness-lacking corpses, and zombies morphed into beings enslaved only by their desire to consume human flesh. Cannibalism is the ultimate symbol of the human preying on his fellows—an image long tied to slavery and colonialism—but it may also, as Chera Kee has argued, signal the originary mythology with references to Caribbean anthropophagi.[29] The new man-eating zombie is likewise employed in plots concerned with science's use for military or political gain and absorbed into narratives critiquing technological misuse for profit. For example, a subgenre I have called the Eco-Zombie may include films as diverse as Jean Rollin's *Les raisins de la mort* (1978), in which zombies are created by pesticides used in agriculture; or 2005's *Severed*, in which the logging industry's use of a genetically engineered growth hormone on trees causes the outbreak, or even (another of my personal favorites) *Dead Meat* (2004), an Irish film about the food industry and mad cow disease. As the zombie becomes allied with tales about naturally occurring viruses, this critique may seem to recede, but mistrust of for-profit science remains a constant thread in the zombie films of the twentieth and twenty-first centuries.

The viral zombie exists in many permutations: Lucio Fulci's biochemical virus unleashed in *Zombi 3* (1988); the *Resident Evil* video game and film series that first became popular in the 1990s, with its Tyrant virus (and various others) developed by the Umbrella Corporation; Danny Boyle's *28 Days Later* (2002), which introduced audiences to the zombie-making "Rage virus"; the Thai production *SARSWars: Bangkok Zombie Crisis* (2004), which fantasizes the zombie's evolution from the real-life SARS epidemic; Bruce LaBruce's *Otto: or Up with Dead People* (2008), with its subtext of AIDS.[30] The viral zombie extrapolates the contagion narrative associated with Romero's biting living dead, making the zombie definitively the victim of a wide-scale epidemic but often in a way that still questions science in the hands of the military, the motives of capitalist industry, and political infrastructures' abilities to cope with a global crisis, a precedent that Romero indeed set in his films.

Consider the monologue delivered by the helicopter pilot, John, in Romero's third installment in his zombie franchise, 1985's *Day of the Dead*, in which the character presents his theory of why the dead have begun to walk: "We're being punished by the Creator. He visited a curse on us, so we might or could have looked at what Hell was like. Maybe he didn't want to see us blow ourselves up and put a big hole in his sky. Maybe he just wanted to show us he was still the bossman. Maybe he figured we was getting too big for our britches, trying to figure his shit out."

John's theory that God is demonstrating his power as punishment for man's misdeeds (against once another, the earth, and the divine himself) represents a popular strand in contemporary zombie films, even if the rhetoric is most often secularized and references to God are watered down or fully replaced by a narrative of crimes against Nature. This is seen in tales of mad scientists, like *Dr. Blood's Coffin* (1961) and the cinematic version of Lovecraft's tale, *Re-Animator* (1985), as it is in the viral zombie nightmares, which draw particularly on a historical connection between plague narratives and divine retribution. It is not incidental that the monologue quoted above from *Day of the Dead* is spoken by a black man from the Caribbean who wears a machete at his hip: this is a wink to the zombie's longer lineage, its relevance to themes of enslavement and rebellion, and, I think, Romero's acknowledgment of his own complicated intervention in such a mythos.

The term zombie had been legible in American cinema for decades when Romero's *Night of the Living Dead* was released in 1968, and the word had already begun to take on broader significations than association with Vaudou or Haiti. Take, for example, a film like *Teenage Zombies* (1959) in which a nerve gas is used by a scientist to make students into slaves; or *Astro-Zombies* (1968), in which an international cabal attempts to steal an experimental device that can turn any person into a mind-controlled minion. For a long time, I have been suspicious of those who call Romero the "father" of the modern zombie genre.[31] Peter Dendle's word choice here is telling and problematic: "Romero *liberated* the zombie from the shackles of a master" (6; emphasis added).

On the one hand, as in the example of Tenney's film, we can see the development of most of the elements that we associate with Romero's contagious cannibal zombie developing over a period of decades. I think of *The Zombies of Mora Tau* (1957), one of the films about white zombies—there isn't a black person in the movie, despite its setting in Africa—who are the result of a curse laid on them for trying to steal native treasure. The film thus maintains ties to the anticolonial theme of the early zombie narratives but changes the myth significantly. Like Romero's relentless zombie droves, these indefatigable walking dead can be kept back with torches. They surround the protagonists as they are holed up in the captain's quarters onboard a ship, banging on the walls and breaking through a window in a scene that is reminiscent of the squatters in Romero's farmhouse in *Night of the Living Dead*. Even the innovation of making zombies indestructible unless the brain is destroyed, with which Romero is often credited, is suggested (in dialogue only, though not shown onscreen) in the 1943 film *Revenge of the Zombies*, in which a Nazi doctor is trying to raise an army of the dead as super-soldiers for his country.[32] Therefore, I wonder at the impulse to dub Romero, a small-time filmmaker in Pittsburgh, the zombie's author, as the *New York Times* film critic Jason Zinoman does explicitly in *Birth of the Living Dead*, claiming, "All zombies come from Romero." To me, this impulse to rewrite the zombie, to stick a flag in this cinematic monster and reclaim it as "ours," seems directly contrary to the lessons that the zombie myth imparts. Romero is to the zombie what Columbus is to America.

On the other hand, maybe there is room in our consideration of Romero's living dead to look at the way the zombie's previous associations with the rebel-slave is given new life in its American reincarnation. Romero himself has been candid about his influences and the collaborative process of filmmaking. In particular, he cites Richard Matheson's novel about a plague of vampirism, *I Am Legend*, as one of his major influences: "It seemed to me that it was about revolution, underneath."[33] Romero says of his own film, "The dead are coming back to life, *that's* the revolution" (*Birth of the Living Dead*; original emphasis).

Romero had not intended the creatures to be considered zombies but called them "ghouls" in the first film; nonetheless, his living dead were swiftly identified as "zombies" by audiences and critics—not unlike what happened with Danny Boyle's 2002 film, *28 Days Later*, and its preference for the term infected. This communal recognition that Romero's ghouls were in fact zombies interests me most: for contrary to those who claim that Romero reinvented the zombie, fantasizing that one auteur set a genre on its feet, it was the moviegoer who saw that Romero's monster was not something new but merely walking the same path of an established narrative, one using living death to represent both disempowerment and rebellion.

What made Romero's monsters "zombies," despite the lack of Vaudou and exotic colonialism, were the film's palpable subtexts of both slavery and revolution. This duality remains consistent throughout the zombie's transformation before, in, and after Romero. The zombie's enslavement would be transformed in Romero's oeuvre and in the trend of the contagious cannibal that followed, as the zombie became the mindless slave of its own innate drive to consume, the high point of which remains Romero's *Dawn of the Dead* (1978), set in a shopping mall. It was not so much a transformation of the mythology as a translation to express a different kind of servitude, under advanced capitalism and its culture of consumerism, though to be sure, this is just an extension of the rapacious appetite of colonialism.[34] Rebellion, too, is legible to various degrees in Romero's films, most notably in *Land of the Dead* (2005), in which an African American zombie named Big Daddy leads a band of evolving zombies in an attack on the ruthless humans.

We might say that in American cinema the figure of the Haitian zombie was slowly bled of its previous associations and embalmed with new ones. Cross-cultural transmission need not always be suspect, but whenever one finds "exchange" coming from a culture of former slaves into an imperialist culture by means of a military occupation, then one must tread lightly. The zombie is a myth about the capture of souls and the reduction of the body to a machine. Therefore, its redirection in American cinema was, it could be said, an appropriation of a *critique* of human appropriation—bitterly ironic—a cultural theft of an artifact that was itself about cultural theft. In fact, it seems that there are three phases to this process of the zombie's appropriation: (1) *cultural aggression*, when in the first films the Caribbean is demonized as a backward and superstitious culture (this, in line with a much longer history of denigrating Vaudou); (2) *erasure*, midcentury, when the Caribbean and its complex history drops out of the new cinematic zombie narrative; and (3) *reinscription*, wherein film critics and audiences claim that the zombie is their own invention or so wholly different from the original zombie as to be considered an entirely different animal.

How the cinematic zombie (at some point) comes to shoulder diverse significatory burdens has been only roughly sketched here—whether it be a critique of American consumer culture, fears of a global pandemic, or concern for various capitalist industries' interventions in nature. The real zombification occurred when the myth was taken up by Hollywood, beginning in the 1930s, to be reprogrammed as a mouthpiece declaring the concerns of US culture.

And yet there is something important about Romero. For me, Romero marks the starting point of an important tropological return. The cannibal zombie reprises the revenant's long-standing associations with divine retribution, creating an undead that is the accidental result of human innovation and that delivers to humanity its comeuppance for tampering with nature— thereby, Romero's living dead may help us to better understand, looking backward, the Haitian zombie as an articulation of the transatlantic slave trade's secular sorcery, its crimes against Nature, God, Humanity, during a time when men were made into objects. Romero's films trace a line from the past to the present, if we follow their gaze, and implicitly identify capitalism as the legacy of colonial slavery and imperialism. Nonetheless, in the form of the zombie, the metaphor of a slave culture was repossessed and pressed into service for the psychic benefit of an entirely different population. Therefore, we might choose to read Romero's addendum as a kind of tacit admission of what had happened to the zombie metaphor in American cinema: a myth about precapitalist and postcolonial empire was cannibalized by US culture. Doesn't the Romero zombie at least admit to cinema's own swallowing of the Haitian slave?

Or maybe this gives Romero too much credit. The man himself was puzzled that his film *Night of the Living Dead* should be shown, in 1969, in a double bill with Herbert J. Biberman's *Slaves*, a film about a rebellion and escape carried out on a plantation. This pairing is what first drew critical attention to the film as worthy of more than just the grindhouse circuit.[35] Although Romero has consistently stated that the casting of a black man in the lead role was incidental—that the part wasn't specifically written as an African American character—this happy accident is precisely what makes the film socially conscious. In large part because of the casting of Duane Jones in *Night of the Living Dead*, the key elements of the traditional zombie narrative, slavery and rebellion, were legible to film audiences from the beginning, whether or not Romero intended his ghouls to be "zombies." It also reveals the way notions of authorship have changed in the modern era. I like to go one step further than the Death of the Author and see this as proof of the "un-life" of the zombie myth. Suffice it to say that the zombie narrative has a kind of vitality working beyond individual intent at the level of collective forces, on the horizon of the social unconscious.

It is true that the contemporary cinematic zombie bears such little resemblance to the original folkloric figure that we might say it is a "zombie" in name only, but the name was important territory to conquer and hold. Imagine the hue and cry that would be raised if I were to claim here that, in deference to the colonial and postcolonial history of aggression toward Haiti, the word zombie should no longer be used to refer to cannibalistic walking dead. Since I've received hate mail from zombie-film fans just for daring to interpret the larger significance of the zombie, something I discuss more in the book's epilogue, I'm guessing it would be a bad move to anger the type of people who get emotionally invested in narratives about individual survival in the face of total governmental collapse, where you're only as safe as your ammo stockpile is plentiful.[36] But I'm not stopping short of calling for the abandonment of the term zombie out of concern for my personal safety; rather, I think it is more productive to consider the ways that the zombie's origins speak despite the myth's reconditioning and the manner in which the Haitian element survives and even resists the myth's abduction and acculturation. Romero didn't reinvent the zombie; the zombie reinvented Romero.

Resistance in Zombie Cinema

At this point in the chapter, the reader may be inundated, her mind crowded by the various individuals who people this discussion—from Jelly Roll Morton to the Hasco cane laborers to mad scientists and Ed Wood's aliens to Romero's ghouls—but when dealing with zombies, to feel mobbed is an appropriate response. The important thing is to stay ahead of the unruly throng, and so we push forward. The revolutionary element of the zombie myth has been there from the beginning; it has only to be activated by a transformation in the way we view the zombie. We must read it as a symbol of resistance rather than for its threat of enslavement. To that end, this final section of the chapter calls forth yet more figures into the horde: those that acknowledge the zombie's origins, or resist the typical frame-up of the zombie in American cinema and instead emphasize the zombie's capacity for resistance, or even, in returning the zombie to its previous associations, effect what we might think of as counter-appropriations of the zombie narrative.

The potential for resistance in the zombie narrative is made clear in a bit of dialogue in the first zombie film, *White Zombie* (1932).

> "But what if they regain their souls?"
> "They would tear me to pieces. And that, my friend, shall never be."

Disappointingly, Murder Legendre (Bela Lugosi) turns out to be right: they merely walk off the side of the cliff when he is unconscious, and the world would have to wait to see zombies, in what would surely have been clear to contemporary audiences as an allusion to slave rebellion, turn against their master.

Even films with titles promising the "revolt" or "revenge" of zombies rarely depict violence by black bodies on white masters. In *Revolt of the Zombies* (1936) the victims are Cambodian, and they only revolt after the spell is broken, when they have, in this adaptation of the myth, ceased to be zombies. In *Revenge of the Zombies* (1943), which is set outside of New Orleans, the zombified white American wife of a German Nazi retains the ability to talk back and refuse orders. She ultimately leads a revolt against the master, but although there are both black and white zombies that join her, it is she who drags her husband into the swamp to kill him. In *The Incredibly Strange Creatures Who Stopped Living and Became Mixed-Up Zombies* (1964), white "zombies" disfigured by acid and kept under the hypnotic spell of a gypsy woman, Madame Estrella, rise up against their keepers—including Ortega, a grizzled man with a fake hook nose and a bicorn hat, in an obvious nod to the colonial era—and begin attacking them in a scene of rebellion. But the zombies here are white and the masters of some vague Hispanic origin, perhaps Caribbean. Yet that the very next scene is a shot of a girly revue in which the dancers are doing a number dressed as Africans (complete with feathered skirts and spears) seems to bespeak an acknowledgment of the appropriation of the myth.

In places we find a zombie that remains faithful to the Haitian living dead slave, if only through the preservation of the theme of slavery or political revolution. There are some cinematic zombies that were raised to be put to use by others; some reverberate with the language of conquest or call to mind, explicitly or implicitly, the political situation that was produced out of colonial empire. Yet only a handful of films overtly recall slave rebellion with their depiction of zombies in revolt. Even fewer contribute to a different kind of zombie resistance and emphasize themes of social justice that resonate with the original folkloric zombie. A few films might even be said to depict resistance not merely within but beyond the frame of the screen, by means of a narrative apology, or lament, for the zombie's appropriation that returns the myth to its original context.

In *Fido* (2006), a Canadian film that I would be remiss to elide completely, even though it contains not a single character of African descent, zombies unintentionally created by space radiation are put to use as household slaves, a callback to the Haitian mythology. Their hunger for human flesh is controlled by means of collars they are made to wear, and docility is imposed.[37] But these devices fail on occasion, and the humans themselves are under so many restraints by ZomCom, the company that maintains order, that they resemble prisoners in an idyllic township. The onscreen violence of the film's zombie uprising does not properly qualify as a zombie revolt, however, as the living dead are really used as weapons by the nonzombies to gain more freedom for themselves, which properly amounts to further exploitation. At the film's end, the slave zombies are not freed from their condition per se, though they are treated more like family members or, as the titular character's name suggests, pets.

Another North American offering, the Cuban film *Juan de los Muertos* (2011), or *Juan of the Dead*, deserves much more critical attention than I can give it here for its complex political critique. Juan is a Cuban ne'er-do-well who has his own criticisms of the country, but unlike his friends, he has no desire to leave his home for Miami. When zombies attack—they are regularly called "dissidents" in the film, as this is the way that the media spins the sudden appearance of the cannibal dead, as US-backed political or anarchic insurgents—Juan and his team of outcasts capitalize on the events by running a business that dispatches the zombies caught in people's houses. Juan repeatedly shows himself to be a wily capitalist: he profits from the disaster and charges certain people, like those who have relatives overseas, double the normal fee. As the situation deteriorates, there are wry, lingering shots of propagandist billboards, like "Cuba Libre" and "Revolution or Death." The human civilization around them is crumbling, and Juan and his comrades eventually have to face the fact that they must, like so many disaffected before them, set sail for the United States. Nonetheless, at the end of the film Juan refuses to abandon Cuba and chooses instead to die there. Though *Juan*'s zombie is obviously the American-made, contagious cannibal variety spawned in US cinema, that this film returns the zombie to the Caribbean, in what is tempting to read as a political allegory, is resistive in itself. That Juan ultimately prefers to join the zombie horde (or die in battle) rather than go to the United States is the ultimate act of defiance, even if his politics and economic philosophy seem to run counter to this grand gesture.

The zombie's origins are alluded to, but barely, in the highly popular television series on AMC, *The Walking Dead*. I will not discuss it at length here, as it has already drawn much critical attention, with volumes of collected essays devoted just to this narrative and the subsequent video game based on the ongoing graphic novel series.[38] The only character from the series that interests me is Michonne, an African American woman who keeps two armless, jawless zombies shackled as "escorts" while she travels in search of food and supplies to detract from the attention she would otherwise draw from the "walkers." Beyond the "colonial gaze" that Gerry Canavan says is inherent to all zombies, these chained walking dead, under the control of a black woman, create a visual reminder of the zombie's origins, calling to mind images of the bokor leading his undead charges (437).

There are other films that make specific reference to the zombie's Haitian origins and its potential for political commentary, like the previously discussed *House on Skull Mountain*, which pits the ancestors of the Pétions and Christophes against each other. An inferior example, and one of the worst movies I've ever seen (and that's saying something!), is *Shrunken Heads* (1994). It depicts zombified, decapitated heads of adolescents that take revenge on their murderers and other "malefactors" in the community, turning them into zombies that clean up trash and paint over graffiti. The witch doctor here is at least a Haitian, but, problematically, Mr. Summatra is a former member of the Tonton Macoutes who keeps a signed picture of François "Papa Doc" Duvalier at his newsstand. He enters the lair of a crime kingpin to save the day with his army of zombies at the film's end, saying, "There's an old Haitian proverb... when the Tonton Macoutes come knocking, don't answer the door." Yet such callous glorification of the Duvaliers' gestapo hardly amounts to the kind of counter-appropriation of the zombie that I am interested in investigating.

Some zombie films are resistive in other capacities, like recognizing their own role in the zombie's cultural appropriation. As mentioned above, in *Ouanga* the mixed-race character called LeStrange is played by the white, Jewish actor Sheldon Leonard. That Leonard was cast in another zombie movie, *Zombies on Broadway* (1945), alongside Darby Jones of *I Walked with a Zombie* and Bela Lugosi of *White Zombie*, is key to understanding this film, which for me is implicitly about the commodification of the Caribbean folkloric zombie in cinema and its broader commercialization in American culture.[39]

The basic premise of the comedic zombie film *Zombies on Broadway* is that Ace Miller (Sheldon Leonard), a gangster turned entrepreneur, is opening a nightclub called the Zombie Hut. Mike and Jerry, the PR men whom he has hired to hype the opening, have promised that a live zombie will be present on opening night despite the fact that, as it becomes evident, neither of them know exactly what a zombie is. Not wanting to be made a laughingstock, Miller and the muscle behind him force the agents to go to San Sebastian, where they have heard that a Dr. Renault is doing experiments that involve zombies, in the hope of obtaining one for the club's opener.

Though this movie was made little more than a decade after the zombie made its cinematic debut, it is rife with references to other zombie movies. Even the name of the fictitious island they travel to is borrowed from Lewton's film *I Walked with a Zombie*, released just two years earlier. The fact that the film is about people who want to make use of the zombie's popularity, casts further light on its well-worn trope of the scientist attempting to discover the secret of zombification for his own purposes, a hybrid of the Frankensteinian and Vaudou zombie narratives. These metafictional elements emphasize US culture's adoption of the zombie as an appropriation akin to the scientist's confiscation of black magic secrets.

Here, Dr. Renault, played by Bela Lugosi, is trying to develop a zombie-making serum, but he has been unable to render the zombie's state permanent. He is attended by Kalaga (Darby Jones), a native-made zombie, who turns against his master in one of the first true onscreen zombie revolts. No explanation is given for why, when Renault orders Kalaga to kill his opponents, the zombie turns instead against the doctor, hitting him with a shovel and burying him in the grave intended for his own failed experiments. Nonetheless, the zombies in this film are resistive in a couple of different ways: just as Kalaga presents an early onscreen dramatization of slave rebellion, the film itself resists the larger narrative of the Vaudou zombie's appropriation—by acknowledging it and by lampooning it—as it critiques many of the elements the moviegoer had already come to expect of zombies in cinema. Yet I don't wish to belabor the point that this farce radicalizes the cinematic zombie—the film does, after all, contain an extremely offensive scene in which one of the press agents dons blackface to escape detection at a Vaudou ceremony—but nonetheless the characters' fascination with the zombie rings true of US culture's plunder of the Haitian myth. Their first appropriation is cultural—capitalizing on the popularity of the zombie in cinema—and the second is literal, when they go to San Sebastian to obtain a real zombie. In the end, in fair turnabout, it is Miller himself who ends up being the real zombie at his club's opening, when he is given a dose of Renault's only temporarily effective zombie serum. That the attempt at appropriation is turned back on themselves and that it is a black zombie, Kalaga, who saves the day—dispatching the white doctor who was trying to extract the secret of zombification from his country—makes this film novel for its time and its critique, still relevant today.

The blaxploitation film *Sugar Hill* (1974), called "*Foxy Brown* with zombies" by Mikel J. Koven, is perhaps the closest one comes to a reappropriation of the Vaudou zombie in American cinema, though, as Koven notes, the fact that a white anthropologist is consulted in the film preserves (like *House on Skull Mountain* in this regard) the trope of "white authority determining the understanding of black folk religion" (126). The plot concerns Diana "Sugar" Hill (Marki Bey), a beautiful African American woman and successful fashion photographer who takes revenge on Mr. Morgan, a white mogul who murders Diana's fiancé, Langston, at the beginning of the film when he refuses to sell their nightclub, aptly called Club Haiti. Diana seeks the help of Mama Maîtresse, an old mambo. In a graveyard, they summon the Vaudou lwa Baron Samedi, keeper of the cemeteries, to raise an army of zombies to assist them. Baron Samedi (Don Pedro Colley) announces himself as "Slave and Master, Master and Slave," a perfect illustration of the zombie's dialectical paradox. The dead he awakens are the corpses of African American slaves: they still have shackles on their wrists, hold machetes, wear simple cloth dress, and have strange, metallic eyeballs, harkening back to the earlier convention in zombie cinema of depicting the living dead with unblinking eyes made of wood or shell.[40] The film thus celebrates and preserves the zombie's lineage as a narrative strategy for processing Haiti's historical relationship to slavery and to rebellion.

But resistance is not merely narratological in the film: Sugar Hill and her undead accomplices stage various revenge plots against Morgan and his henchmen, and though her hair is normally worn straightened, when she battles an enemy she appears with a grand Afro hairdo. Morgan himself is drowned in the swamp, recalling *Revenge of the Zombies*, by a new crop of undead, his former henchmen, many of whom are white and are demeaned by Diana with terms like "whitey" as she exacts her revenge with her platoon of "zombie hit men," as the publicity poster touted the film.

The setting of the climax on the ancestral lands of Diana's people and the developed subplot wherein Morgan tries to get Diana to sell Club Haiti to him serve as the backdrop of a film that is about various appropriations. It refers simultaneously to the appropriation of labor that defined the peculiar institution in the image of the slave zombies, and of land under colonialism and imperialism, in light of the white man's efforts to control Club Haiti. It could even be said to include commentary on appropriations from black culture, for the film reclaims the zombie as a tool of black empowerment, as it was in the beginning: a slave culture's metaphorization of their social, political, and personal disenfranchisement under institutionalized slavery and colonialism, one that all the while preserves the capacity for resistance.

In the end, we come full circle, if not to Jelly Roll Morton, then at least to New Orleans. In the third season of the television series *American Horror Story: Coven* a collective of witches who are the descendants of Salem become embroiled in a battle with the local Voodoo Queen, Marie Laveau. The series is not set during Laveau's lifetime (1794–1881) but in the present day. In the show, Laveau (played by Angela Bassett) becomes an immortal whose past dealings with Madame Delphine Lalaurie (1775–1842) continue in the twenty-first century. Madame Lalaurie was a notoriously cruel slaveholder whose French Quarter mansion has become a locus for fans of dark tourism: in real life she grotesquely tortured her slaves and was driven from her home by a mob of enraged citizens. The series imagines that instead of fleeing to Paris, as the historical Lalaurie did, she was made immortal by Marie Laveau and imprisoned in a coffin underground, until the present day, when the Supreme of the coven, Fiona (Jessica Lange), unearths her and makes her a maid. The show's treatment of these historical figures is not without its problems. Kathy Bates's portrayal of Lalaurie is so entertaining that it risks giving the real-life woman a kind of absolution by proxy. In one delightful scene, the old racist cries pitifully when she discovers that Barack Obama is president of the United States—and, as much as the viewer is encouraged to enjoy her suffering, the character sometimes seems on the brink of real transformation as her friendship with the African American witch Queenie develops. Leaving aside the show's problematic portrayal of Lalaurie and the fact that it disappointingly consigns both Lalaurie and Laveau to Hell in the season's conclusion, here I am mainly concerned with the reclamation of the Vaudou zombie that is achieved in the series.

Whereas the real Marie Laveau probably had no connection to the Haitian zombie but only to the Grand-Zombi snake and its incarnation of the god Damballah Ouedou, in *American Horror Story: Coven* her incantations cause the dead to walk. In performing the zombie-raising ceremony, Marie Laveau, dressed in the traditional dress and headscarf of the Haitian *hounsie* and mambo, draws *veves*, quaffs a potion, and takes talismans out of her Voodoo cabinet. Staff writer John Gray explains the backstory in "American Horror Story: Inside the Coven," acknowledges the zombie's origins in Haiti, and states that the original Vaudou zombies were more like "puppets." Gray reveals that each talisman Laveau holds is meant to represent a former enemy of hers, over whom she retains control. This is not, therefore, a random selection of walking corpses but an army of her antagonists, including Lalaurie's daughters, raised from the dead to attack the coven where their immortal mother is doing penance for her past, under Fiona's orders, as Queenie's "slave." True to the Haitian zombie, these undead are at first innocuous marionettes, and episode 4, "Fearful Pranks Ensue," ends with a long shot of the witches' academy surrounded by these upright cadavers, standing outside as listless as plants swaying in a breeze. It isn't until episode 5, "Burn, Witch, Burn!," that, in a levitating trance, her irises as milky as moonstone, Laveau orders them to attack, and they begin to resemble the ferocious cinematic zombie. And although it is a white witch, Zoe, who beats back the dark army, first with a chainsaw in an obvious allusion to Sam Raimi's cult classic *Army of Darkness* (1992) and then with a spell that knocks Laveau out of her trance, I nonetheless interpret this entire sequence as a reappropriation of the zombie from Hollywood that returns it to its roots.

In all three of these examples of resistive zombie narratives—*Zombies on Broadway*, *Sugar Hill*, and *American Horror Story: Coven*—allusions to other zombie films draw our attention to the tenuous line between homage and appropriation. In *Coven*, images familiar from recent zombie cinema—a locked door shaking with the fury of a zombie on the other side, a blood-splattered hero(ine) battling the undead—are rehearsed, but in so doing, they return the zombie to its original context. Despite the witch's temporary victory over the Voodoo Queen, *Coven* attempts the kind of counter-conquest of the zombie that we see achieved most effectively (and described at length in the next chapter) in Haitian literature of the last half of the twentieth century.

In *Coven* the zombie is associated explicitly with slavery, particularly in the colonial and Confederate zombies amid the horde, and with the slave's various means of resistance, both metaphysical (in the practice of Voodoo) and corporeal (in rebellion). The sight of zombies surrounding the coven's New Orleans mansion purposefully summons the specter of slave rebellion; it also recalls the historical mob that ousted the evil slaveholder Lalaurie from her home, which was recast in the series explicitly as a slave revolt. The twinning of such images suggests both halves of the zombie mythos: as much as the zombie myth is forever darkened by its historical association with slavery, in its vision of vacant-eyed puppets under someone else's control, it also illuminates a heroic past of slave rebellion, when—as in *Coven*—undead beings stumble in from the fields to surround the big house.

Those who would claim that Romero is the founder of a new zombie mythos should bear in mind the distinct possibility that the zombie cannot be rid of the mark of its former history: the scars of colonialism, occupation, and enslavement remain. As I have shown, as the zombie morphed it remained redolent of the imagery of both slavery and rebellion. This is seen in the zombie that is relentlessly driven to fulfill its compulsion to consume human flesh and in the zombie droves that recall the angry mob. Even the zombie associated with contagion or virus can be said to exemplify tyranny, if only Nature's own, which shackles man to a vulnerable, mortal body, as to his base, animalistic drives. The elemental infrastructure of the zombie narrative came out of the transatlantic slave trade, furnishing commentary on the appropriation of human labor and charging us to resist it: that zombic mechanism refuses to be rewired.

3 / Haitian Zombis: Symbolic Revolutions, Metaphoric Conquests, and the Mythic Occupation of History

> *La memoire est un revenant dont on ne peut se debarraser.*
> *[Memory is a revenant of which we cannot be rid.]*
> —JACQUES STEPHEN ALEXIS, *ROMANCERO AUX ETOILES*

This is a story about ... baseball. Visiting Haiti in fall 2013, I asked about the lack of industry in contemporary Port-au-Prince and its environs when I noticed the dominance of the red and white logo of Digicel—a company that makes cheap, disposable cell phones—with their little kiosks on nearly every corner for the purposes of "telecharger," reupping one's minutes. My friend Mario said, in answer to my question, "No, there haven't been sugar factories for decades. Once, they made baseballs. Do you know Rawlings, the company that makes the official balls for the sport? All of their balls were made here in Haiti, and you could tour the factory, and it was like a ballet, all of the men, in rows..." He mimed a worker sewing the signature stitches by crossing his arms in the air in a kind of vertical breaststroke. I could almost see the red thread. "But they closed the factory, moved production to China or something, I don't know, said it was too unstable here, politically. But do you know what Haitians say? That year was the only time that there hasn't been a World Series. They had to cancel it. Haitians say it was their doing, for taking all of those jobs away!"

I love this tale, whether or not it *was* Vaudou that caused Major League Baseball to cancel the Fall Classic in 1994, for only the second time in a century. I leave this anecdote here without further analysis, for the elements that resound in this study of the zombie are hopefully clear: the colonial legacy and postcolonial dependence on foreign investment and the uses of Vaudou as a tool of imagined might. My point in beginning this chapter in this way is to emphasize that as much as this is a book about the zombie, it is not just a book about the zombie but equally about the sorcery of appropriation and the conjure work of counter-appropriation that exist not only in slavery and (post)colonial occupation but also in mythmaking, folklore, and culture, in the stories that we tell ourselves.

All the work done in chapter 1 to call forth the history of the zombie myth—from my investigation of the etymological roots of the word zombie to the tracing of the mythology's ancestors in soul capture narratives to speculation on the invocations of imagery of living death in slave rebellions and the Haitian Revolution—must now be forgotten, as far as this is possible. For one of the most poignant lessons that the study of the folkloric zombie teaches us is the difficulty of ever coming to know, with certainty, the "history" of a myth that is ever evolving and that comes out of a predominantly oral tradition. Further, the figure of the zombie itself, the reanimated dead, suggests the way that in Haiti history becomes incorporated into the culture's rich folklore as more material that can be reclaimed, reconstituted, and put to new use. Just as an emptied wine bottle, or water jug, may become transformed into an ornate zombie bottle, housing the captured spirit of an enemy or a victim, various zombie narratives, many of them manufactured in the West, are recycled in present-day Haiti.[1] There are therefore two issues at hand when we discuss the zombie's capacity for replay in Haitian literature and culture: its sense of the return of history to haunt the living and, quite contradictorily, the willful redirection of the past to new ends.

Like the ghost, the folkloric zombie is a specter that reverberates with disconcerting repetition: it is that which should be past, dead, gone, returning to the here and now. Building on the African origins of the myth, the materiality of the walking dead Haitian zombie is usually interpreted as an allegory for slavery, as the houngan or mambo retains power over the soulless, revivified corpse and forces it to labor for his or her profit.[2] To most, the zombie symbolizes either the threat of a return to slavery or a nightmare in which servitude extends into the afterlife, prohibiting the eternal rest that was to be the slave's final respite from forced labor. As such, the zombie's dizzying sense of repetition may suggest the foreclosure of progress that is a central concern of Haitian literature, as is foregrounded by the epigraph above from the author and political activist Jacques Stephen Alexis.

The myth of the zombie is laden with political connotations from various contexts of Haitian history, suggesting, in part, the frustration that the newly established citizens felt as they discovered that although they were made "free" by their rebellion and revolution, their enslavement did not end. The reality of Haitian history, in fact, preserved their servitude well into the nation's establishment.[3] Under Toussaint L'Ouverture and Roi Henri Christophe, Haitians remained, like the dead men working in the cane fields of William Seabrook's *The Magic Island*, driven beneath the yoke and whip of domestic tyrants and foreign powers.

But as folklore coming out of a predominantly oral tradition, the zombie also questions what "history" is and who gets to define it. The difficulty of tracing a myth with a scarce paper trail is that its history is constantly rewriting itself. For example, some claim that this myth was actually in the service of slaveholders prior to the revolution, acting as a cautionary tale that might prohibit slaves from committing suicide. In an op-ed in the *New York Times*, Amy Wilentz writes, "It is thought that slave drivers on the plantations, who were usually slaves themselves and sometimes Voodoo priests, used this fear of zombification to keep recalcitrant slaves in order and to warn those who were despondent not to go too far." But for others, like Jerry Gandolfo, the zombie is understood as a role in a punitive system that was only put in place in the nascent Black Republic and forced upon those who had violated the social contract, returning freed men to the subhuman status of the slave.

The zombie's use as social punishment for those who have crossed a moral boundary line, with the permission of the community from which the person is being ostracized and often even at the behest of the victim's own family members, is evidenced by later anthropological research such as that conducted by Wade Davis.[4] Laënnec Hurbon writes, "Zombification is held by the voudouist as the supreme punishment, because it returns the individual to the condition of the slave, against which, precisely, the voudou practitioner dedicated himself" (62). Yet this element of the mythology, that he who is zombified is guilty of some social infraction and that his removal from the community is a benefit to the whole, only seems to develop in the second half of the twentieth century.[5] Writing in the late 1950s, Maya Deren described the way that fears of zombification directly result in elaborate burial rituals, some of which ensure the body will be useless to any would-be zombie maker, which indicates that a central element of the zombie's horror was the theft of the bodies of innocents taken without the community's permission (42). In the more recent iteration articulated by Michel Laguerre and Wade Davis in the 1980s, whereby zombification becomes a means of punishing those who transgress social mores, the Vaudoun community draws a firm line delineating acceptable behavior.[6] What has transpired between these two very different accounts, wherein zombification is depicted as a threat that comes from outside the community or a device wielded by the community to punish the wicked, is the regime of Duvalier *père* and *fils*.[7] We might see, then, in this transformation of the uses of zombification, a deflection of the Duvalier regime's adoption of Vaudou as a symbol of its inestimable powers. At the end of the terrible reign of the Duvaliers, zombification is rhetorically repossessed as something belonging to the people; only those who have done wrong to their family or village need fear it. This is one stage in the zombie's late twentieth-century metamorphosis into a narrative technology by means of which Haitian identity could be solidified: the symbolic revolution that is the subject of this chapter.

We might first, on historical grounds, challenge the assertion that the zombie myth was used before the revolution as a scare tactic warning slaves not to seek freedom from slavery by means of their own literal deaths. Wilentz writes merely that "it is *thought* that slave drivers on the plantations" may have used the zombie as a threat. The difficulties of tracing the history of a predominantly oral myth has already been discussed, and one might wonder whether there wouldn't be some mention of the figure, a striking enslaved animate corpse, in the colonial record if this belief were widespread. On the other hand, focusing on the historicization of the zombie in present-day folklore yields more concrete discoveries about this oral mythology, or at least about what the contemporary culture achieves by it. If it is currently supposed that the zombie was once a tool in the possession of the slave drivers—which would be in line with the African ancestral beliefs discussed in chapter 1 as well as the initial analysis that the zombie-maker is analogous to the slave master—and has only more recently become a means of protecting the integrity of the wider community, this suggests that the technology of zombie making had at some point been wrested from the aggressors and reclaimed by the *peuple*, even if it is only secret societies that possess the sacred knowledge, as Davis and others claim. I use the term meta-myth in this chapter to designate these second-generation mythologies that describe how Haitians reclaimed zombification as a part of their cultural heritage, the way the myth has traveled, whom it affects, and the effects it has on its hearers. The meta-myth seen in Wilentz's account amounts to the capture and redirection of the slave master's tools, in the form of the process of zombification.

I cannot verify the claim made by Wilentz in the extant documents that the generation fighting their war for independence worried that they might be zombified by the slaveholders or the Vaudouists in their employ. In fact, I would say that the strong association between Vaudou and resistance to slavery in the eighteenth and nineteenth centuries makes this interpretation dubious.[8] But what this example reveals is a two-part lesson: first, we have to acknowledge that the zombie myth has had a long oral history and that it has likely undergone various transformations that cannot be definitively traced on paper; and second, that more important than the historical trajectory is the way history is absorbed into folklore to become a technique for processing (even if that means rewriting) the past.

The implications of the historicization of the folkloric zombie seem far more relevant than trying to determine the historical accuracy of the claims made, which bring to bear all the difficulties of establishing what sorts of knowledge may have been available to whom and deciding which kind of records count for historiography. Working in a similar manner in her study, *Ghosts of Slavery*, Jenny Sharpe reminds us that "as a living memory, oral histories do not exist in a fixed form but change across time, often bringing into their narratives new evidence, published sources, and more recent events" (14). And she cautions that attributing legitimacy to facts only on the grounds of the written documents of the oppressive, occupying culture is highly problematic. Sharpe writes, "As a scientific form of knowledge, historiography gains authority over the temporal unknown—a past that is irretrievably lost—by conquering the primitive space of folklore, magic, and superstition" (2). Ultimately, although I have tried to provide the most thorough sketch of the zombie myth to date, knowing its complete history is less vital than understanding its cultural history, which emphasizes the fascinating way that its history, zombielike in its own right, is continually reinhabited and repurposed. Therefore, here I examine the living history of the zombie myth as it exists today, looking to Haitian literature as an index of the way the myth has changed as it is told and retold, in order to illustrate that even its own history as a myth is revised in contemporary Haiti to reflect contemporary concerns.

We saw in the previous chapter that there is a wide chasm between the American zombie of present-day horror film and his early cinematic cousin. And there is every reason to believe that much like the modern monster of the silver screen, the Haitian zombie of folklore evolved rapidly to address the culture's concerns. We cannot talk in the same sentence about the zombie investigated by Hurston in the 1930s and that discussed by Davis in the 1980s without acknowledging both the frame of the foreign anthropologist's gaze and the fact that the zombie has morphed over time to suit the culture's psychological needs. All bogeymen are a way of exorcising our demons, and therefore the zombie of the Duvalier era (1957–86) is very different from the zombie under Jean-Bertrand Aristide (1991; 1994–96; 2001–4).

One of the central claims of this chapter is that the much bandied about claim that the zombie is always a mark of the Haitian people's disempowerment is woefully out of date, or at least it fails to take into account the rich evolution of the myth and its capacity for signifying the empowerment of the people. But that being said, the zombie's evolution is not always readily apparent, especially to those outside Haiti, and one must be mindful of the standard caveats that come with anthropological study of another culture's oral folklore. If we cannot always be certain of the zombie's historical evolution, we can look to the zombie's transformation in Haitian literature for its evolution as a symbol.

Like the anecdote about the Rawlings factory and the cancellation of the World Series, the zombie mobilizes a symbolic revolution where a literal one may be impossible. Here is an example of one such use of the figure. The French anthropologist Franck Degoul, who chronicled contemporary understandings of the zombie myth in Haiti during his fieldwork in 2001–3, cites an anecdote related to him by a source named Colbert: "At the time of the American occupation . . . well, there was an old saying, an old story saying that the first general or colonel—I don't know—who had walked on the soil still works at Léogâne, in the sugar fields. . . . That's why those whites there fear our country" (Degoul, "'We Are the Mirror of Your Fears'" 29). This narrative, whether or not it dates to the US occupation of Haiti, makes a direct association between the zombie myth and anticolonial resistance. Here the intimation is that the first American officer to walk on Haitian soil has been zombified and, in a neat reprisal, made into a slave on a sugar plantation.[9] The US occupation was enormously destructive to the Haitian people, but whether or not this tale of the white zombie general actually dates to the early decades of the twentieth century or is a more recent innovation, repeating the tale today both rewrites that past and reconfigures the contemporary US diplomatic or UN "peace-keeping" presence in Haiti in the mode of a rhetorical and retroactive insurgency, in the space of mythological resistance.

On the most elementary level, because the zombie dramatizes the way the dead still occupy the space of the living, it recalls the famous words of

William Faulkner from the play *Requiem for a Nun* (act 1, scene 3): "The past is never dead. It's not even past" (92). I agree fiercely that, as Wilentz notes, the zombie illustrates that Atlantic cultures are haunted by the specters of the slave trade that built our present and also represents the way that, in our contemporary moment of advanced capitalism (the age of outsourced employment, sweatshop labor, and strike-breaking), slavery seems a warm body that has not yet been lowered into the cold ground.[10] However, it should not be overlooked that the figure of the zombie is also reactivated as a rhetorical weapon that Haitians wield to solidify their sense of sovereignty, as in Degoul's anecdote. This aspect of the myth is seen most concretely in a Haitian president's threat that he would use zombies against President Bill Clinton's invading forces—a moment stranger than fiction to which I turn my attention later in the chapter.

Many of the texts that are taken up here were written after the zombie had become an international import, first used to symbolize the backwardness of the Caribbean and then recalibrated to serve US interests. Mindful of Sharpe's preference for the term tactic in her discussion of slave women's resistive practices, I refer to the practice I am describing as the zombie's discursive technē. Working almost like the contrapassum of Dante's *Inferno*, the zombie turns against its master and rewrites itself as a colonizing force. It was not, after all, kidnapped and made into a slave metaphor; rather, it was so powerful that it *infiltrated* the cultural imagination of its occupiers.[11] This is not just a tale of dead men walking, or a story about neocolonial servitude. It is equally about the power of stories, about mythmaking and the malleability of history; it is about the conquest and counterconquest of metaphors that occur not only in what Mary Louise Pratt calls "contact zones" but also, beyond the geographic, in the metaphysical space of the imaginary.

If this chapter is concerned with the way that myths about zombification themselves become activated as tools, discursive apparatuses that enable symbolic revolutions, we have to examine, first, the way that the living dead stands as an icon of history's return in Haiti—a broader literary and political concern, as seen in the example of Carpentier's *Kingdom of This World*; because we must, second, excavate the ramifications of such an association between the zombie and the recurrence of the past, typically figured as a negative commentary on Haiti's political history; in order to, third, marvel at the transformation of the zombie's significance in Haitian literature, as seen in the way that the zombie, ante- and post-Duvalier, is wrested from Papa Doc's legacy and turned against him.

The myth of the zombie is remade to respond to the country's present-day struggles. Contemporary narratives that explain the zombie's history and its significance may explain Haiti's politics or even, at times, rewrite, remix, and thereby re*master* that history. I equate this turn with the proverbial salt thought to "cure" zombies. To my mind, this salt is the (re)making of myth and the mythologization of history. It recasts the hollow-eyed zombie that is a dim reflection of the Haitian's past enslavements as a material monument to his heritage, one defined by active resistance. Indeed, this treatment of history might itself be deemed an act of rebellion, or of sorcery. Rather than accept that the past exists independently of myth, ritual, and folklore, one finds that the two often intertwine.

History's Houngans

From the work of Ignace Nau (1808–45) to the contemporary author Gary Victor (b. 1958), Haitian literature often bears the literary traits associated with magical realism. Jacques Stephen Alexis (1922–61) wrote of magical realism's importance to postcolonial environments. According to Alexis, magical realism has four central attributes: praise of the homeland and its natural formation, rejection of art without social content, use of the creative and expressive means of the people, and translation of their current struggles into symbolic terms that could be widely appreciated. Alexis sees this as crucial to the identity formation of the nation: "The treasury of tales and legends, all the musical, choreographic and plastic symbolism, all the forms of Haitian popular art are there to help the nation in solving its problems and in accomplishing the tasks which lie before it" ("Of the Marvellous Realism of the Haitians" 197). Such a style acted as a kind of unique literary voice that Nau and the first generation of Haitian writers were seeking. Later in this chapter, I examine works of this ilk by Nau, Depestre, Alexis, Dany Laferrière, and others for their use of Haitian folklore, and specifically zombification, to take account of both the past and the present. To understand how the zombie is reclaimed in later twentieth-century Haitian literature and folklore as a symbol of empowerment after a long-standing association with colonial oppression and slavery, one must appreciate the relationship that Haitians have to history and myth and the relationship between the two.[12]

We often speak of the ghosts of cultural trauma. In *Ghosts of Slavery*, Sharpe quotes the Jamaican American writer Michelle Cliff. "'The past coexists with the present,' declares Cliff about the memory of slavery in the United States, 'in this amnesiac country in this forgetful century'" (xii). In contrast, in his essay "What Happened in Haiti: Where the Past Is Present," Paul Farmer writes, "Haitians *remember*: they consider themselves living legacies of the slave trade and the bloody revolt, starting in 1791, that finally removed the French" (12; emphasis added). Farmer makes clear that the past is not just legible in the present; it is alive in Haiti's contemporary economic woes. Writing in 2004, Farmer described the indemnity that saddled Haiti with a massive debt: "In 1825, under the threat of another French invasion and the restoration of slavery, Haitian officials signed what was to prove the beginning of the end of any hope of autonomy: King Charles X agreed to recognize Haiti's independence only if the new republic paid an indemnity of 150 million francs and consented to the reduction of import and export taxes for French goods" (13), an unjust obligation that was still being paid off in 1947. Thus the history of this former slave colony drastically shaped its present.[13]

In the same essay, Farmer alludes to the way that Haitians turn this sense of living with the past into an asset. On his forced removal from power on February 28, 2004, Aristide said, "I declare in overthrowing me they have uprooted the trunk of a tree of peace, but it will grow back because the roots are Louverturian." In doing so, he was echoing Toussaint L'Ouverture: "In overthrowing me, you have cut down in San Domingo only the trunk of the tree of black liberty. It will spring up again by the roots for they are numerous and deep" (qtd. in Farmer 12). That Aristide was evoking the final words spoken by L'Ouverture on his kidnapping by the French, Farmer emphasizes, resounds with great import as Aristide's removal was likewise orchestrated by a foreign government (24).[14] This rhetorical maneuver acknowledges at one and the same time the inescapable influence of the past on the present, and yet it effects a strategy pertaining to the symbolic, recasting that pervasive past in a resistive register. Aristide's statement resembles the kind of narrative work that the zombie myth accomplishes in Haitian literature: by means of the figure's inherent duality—as both living and dead; as both an eternal slave and, if fed salt, a rebel—it symbolizes history as both oppressive and liberating, as when history can be preserved and yet altered through storytelling.

Zombies are only briefly mentioned (and obliquely at that) on one page of Carpentier's magical realist novel about the Haitian Revolution and its aftermath. In the section of the book about the disappearance of Makandal, the infamous poisoner of the slave owners, Carpentier writes,

"Others stated that the *houngan* had got away on a schooner, and was operating in the region of Jacmel, where many men who had died tilled the land as long as they were kept from tasting salt" (35). *The Kingdom of This World*'s treatment of the haunting return of the past is similar to those works that specifically use zombification to metaphorize the Haitian's relationship to history. That is, even though there is a paucity of literal zombies, the recurrence of the past—the selfsame force that animates many figurations of the zombie myth—structures the philosophy of history presented in the novel. Despite the lack of zombies in Carpentier's novel, the reimagination of the revolution and its afterlife reveals much about the way the figure of the zombie functions in modern Caribbean literature.

The Kingdom of This World describes a time line that should span at least seventy years, by my calculation, in four sections: (1) the one-armed slave Makandal whose knowledge of the herbs of the island allowed him to create poisons used to assassinate the slaveholders—what we might think of as the precursor to the revolution; (2) Boukman's Vaudou ceremonies, which inaugurated the wide-scale slave rebellion, and the subsequent travails of both colonists and would-be citizens during the yellow fever plagues; (3) the callous cruelty and ridiculous pomp of Henri Christophe, self-declared king of Haiti who ruled in the manner of the French despots whom the people had just overthrown, and his eventual ousting by the subjects he effectively reduced to a state of slavery; and (4) in a brief dénouement, the return of the central protagonist, Ti Noel—a former slave through whose eyes the reader has experienced most of the novel—now a very old man, to his plantation, where he imagines himself as ruler of the broken remains and incongruous vestiges of both colonial rule and Haitian monarchy.

From the very first image that Carpentier presents to the reader, we are given clues that this story, like Haitian history itself, is girded by disturbing parallels and haunting juxtapositions, by eerie patterns that give one a queasy sense of déjà vu. At the novel's opening, the young slave Ti Noel notices that three shop windows, all in a row, present a startling continuity: a barber's window contains faceless wax heads meant to hold wigs, the butcher's shop displays the severed heads of cows, and a bookstore presents the profiles of the ruling heads of state on the covers of magazines. This is not just foreshadowing the Haitian Revolution and Dessalines's command to "koupe tet" (cut off heads), but it also establishes the novel's use of repetitive motifs: things are given a sense of recurrence by means of doubling, pairing, narrative echoes, and literary rhyme. As the protagonist recognizes an emergent sequence from the wax models to the severed heads of cows to the profiles of the sovereigns, the reader is taught how this book is to be read, for patterns. The repetitive structure is symbolic of the way that in Haiti the living trace of the former event is written on top of the present. It is emblematic of the characters' (and the nation's) tendency to be haunted by its past, either in the sense that the country cannot seem to get shut of its origins as a slave colony or in the pervasive feeling that history is always repeating itself, lent in no small part by the fact that Haiti has suffered from thirty-two political coups in its two centuries.

The use Carpentier's novel makes of literary form—repetition to represent the living past of the Haitian Revolution—is deeply revelatory of what I perceive to be the main work of the zombie's insistence on repetition and return. Like the zombie myth, too, the repetition in *The Kingdom of This World* suggests both the people's empowerment and their disempowerment at various points in the text and sometimes simultaneously.

Primarily, the novel's arc builds toward its (by all accounts, highly accurate) representation of Henri Christophe. The theme of repetition reaches its apex in Roi Christophe's de facto reinstitution of slavery and his nearly farcical imitation of the French court. Ti Noel soon discovers that both his newly bought freedom and the young republic's assurance of the freedom of all—as it was established in the Haitian declaration of independence—now count for naught. The people have been reduced to slaves, forced to labor for no pay for the sake of the king's construction of his palace, Sans-Souci, and the prison Citadel La Ferrière. This extension of slavery beyond national liberation illustrates the sense of tragic repetition that the Haitian people must have suffered—elsewhere symbolized in the zombie's plight in that slavery extends past death—but there are other moments in the text where the echoes resound with triumphal rebellion.

The sacrifice of the black pig that was a central element of Boukman's ceremony at Bois Caïman, which began the slave rebellion in 1791, is unintentionally evoked in the sacrifice of the bulls demanded by the tyrannical Haitian king, so that their blood can be mixed with the mortar to make the Citadel La Ferrière impenetrable. In a sense, it is this symbolic boomerang that seems to make the overthrow of Henri Christophe possible: "Not for nothing had those towers arisen, on the mighty bellowing of bulls, bleeding, their testicles toward the sun, at the hands of builders well aware of the deep significance of the sacrifice even though they had told the ignorant that this represented an advance in the technique of military engineering" (119).

Like the sacrifice of the bulls, which suggests to the workers their nation's past and reminds them of the possibility of insurrection, the beating of the drums that announces the mutiny against Henri Christophe reverberates with the echoes of previous scenes of rebellion, recalling, too, the blaring of the conch shells that the slaves on Ti Noel's plantation had used to coordinate their attack on the master's house so many years before. If the text's use of literary parallels sometimes represents the people's seeming inability to escape oppression, it nonetheless at other points reminds us of their past glory.

Just as Christophe was unaware of the symbolism he was invoking in mixing the blood of bulls into the bricks to make his prison, he does not see that the fact that he has made a Versailles of Sans-Souci leaves him open to the potential of another revolution, another storming of the Royal Palace, which is precisely what happens.[15] This historical novel takes some poetic license in its emphasis on repetition, but many of its most incredible elements, including Christophe's suicide by silver bullet, believing himself invulnerable to anything else, are entirely true.[16]

After the death of Christophe, Ti Noel returns to the plantation and discovers that the "mulattoes" are forcing the blacks to work for free under the threat of bodily harm, in the same manner that the late king had ordered the construction of his palace and the Citadel that came to be his final resting place. Yet Ti Noel notes the difference in this new brand of race-motivated enslavement: "Not even Henri Christophe would have suspected that the land of Santo Domingo would bring forth this spurious aristocracy, this caste of quadroons, which was now taking over the old plantations, with their privileges and rank" (171). Thus Carpentier's novel would seem to support the more negative interpretation of the axiom "History repeats itself," as, like the Hydra of ancient Greece, one tyrant succeeds another. This weighs heavily on Ti Noel: "The old man began to lose heart at this endless return of chains, this rebirth of shackles, this proliferation of suffering, which the more resigned began to accept as proof of the uselessness of revolt" (171–72). As much as the repetition of events is cast as a disheartening revelation that power corrupts, there is a way we can read the repetition as an effort to master the situation, revising it via replay.[17]

Ti Noel carries back to the plantation many items that he and the mob looted from Sans-Souci, which he now uses to adorn the ruins of the plantation where he makes his solitary shelter: "The pride of the old man's heart was a dress coat that had belonged to Henri Christophe, of green silk, with cuffs of salmon-colored lace, which he wore all the time, his regal air heightened by a braided straw hat that he had folded and crushed into the shape of a bicorne, adding a red flower in lieu of a cockade" (164). Planted in the ruined mansion, among the strange collection of trifles he carried off from the Royal Palace, Ti Noel now poses himself as the king, "holding a guava twig in his hand as a scepter" (165).

In Ti Noel's make-believe kingdom, there is no strife; he is a kindhearted despot, generous with his people. When the light-skinned surveyors begin to cross through the countryside forcing the people into bondage, our protagonist is devastated: "Try as he would, Ti Noel could think of no way to help his subjects bowed once again beneath the whiplash" (171). His last act in the novel is to declare war and order his subjects to march against these new masters, and in the final paragraph the remnants of the plantation and the palace, now joined in Ti Noel's collection, tumble to the earth, as if to suggest that as long as history repeats itself in presenting the Haitian people with tyrants, they will follow suit and rebel against the oppression.

What we see in Ti Noel's final rebellion is the kind of symbolic conquest of the master's tools that is a cornerstone of Haitian literature and folklore. Here a former slave dons the lush frock coat of a fallen monarch and turns his own symbols (the bicorne hat, the cockade, the scepter, which were, in turn, merely imitations of the French rulers) into a counter-appropriation meant to signify opposition to tyranny. I read this as the project of the novel as a whole: Haitian history is itself appropriated in Carpentier's fiction as a substance that can be worked over in a creative effort.

It is not my intention to become embroiled in the larger debate about history, resistance, and authority in Haitian culture; this is a very broad issue that has already been taken up by the foremost postcolonial theorists in other contexts, Homi Bhabha and Edward Said, among others. Nevertheless, Michel-Rolph Trouillot's words on the subject seem important to bear in mind: that rules regarding what constitutes historical truth "are not the same in all times and all places has led many scholars to suggest that some societies (non-Western, of course) do not differentiate between fiction and history. That assertion reminds us of past debates among some Western observers about the languages of the peoples they colonized. Because these observers did not find grammar books or dictionaries among the so-called savages, because they could not understand or apply the grammatical rules that governed these languages, they promptly concluded that such rules did not exist" (6–7).

I do not mean to suggest that there is no difference for the Haitian people between myth and history; rather, I wish merely to convey all that is at stake in the remaking of the zombie myth as it contributes to a larger trend within Haitian literature and culture—that of the revisitation and revision of the past in the space of myth, as in the rituals described by Deren, Dayan, McAlister, and many others. If the ongoing war against empire, past and present, is fought not only in the street, the corporate boardroom, or the legislative hall but also in the territories of ceremony and symbol, within the walls of the Vaudouist's temple, or *houmfort*, and among the pages of the national literature, one of its battlegrounds is the zombie myth itself.

A discursive maneuver allows the metaphor of the zombie to be repossessed within Haitian literature and folklore, dramatizing a revision of Haitian history along the lines represented in the narrative recounted by Franck Degoul about the zombified American general. In his anthropological study, "Dos à la vie, dos à la mort" (2006), Degoul also presents different origin stories of the zombie as they are preserved in the contemporary Haitian imaginary. Reporting interviews conducted with journalists and some of the most prominent houngans, Degoul explores divergent views, giving a story and a voice to respective positions, and concludes that Haitians consider the zombie as existing in a direct lineage either with Christian resurrection myths or with the Egyptian myth of Osiris and Isis's postmortem reanimation. In combination with either of these origin points, most houngans believe and promote the idea that the zombie was bequeathed to the slave by his African ancestors to use as a weapon against the white slaveholders. Fene, a houngan of forty years who believes that "the process of zombification" begins with Christ's resurrection of Lazarus, claims, "We are the descendants of Africa, and this comes from God.... Jesus Christ was an *oungan*!" (Degoul, "Dos à la vie" 243). What is immediately visible on examining Degoul's ethnographic archive is a disparity between the assessment of the myth that depicts it as a people's response to their enslavement and subjugation under colonialism and capitalism, in which the zombie is primarily identified with as a symbol of disempowerment, and this narrative, which emphasizes the capability of zombie creation as divinely granted, a source of strength.[18]

In narratives concerning the zombie's transmission to Haiti, given voice in Degoul's ethnography by a source named Chantal, the Haitian zombie is born out of direct confrontation with the French slaveholders. This story claims that the first generations of African slaves—who may have been worked to death—were improperly buried; thus the French unwittingly released their wandering souls into the atmosphere, after which their heirs had at their disposal "all these souls to help us do whatever we want to do!" (248). The speaker says explicitly that at the time of the struggle for independence, the souls of the African ancestors were a major factor in the revolutionary strategy and were appealed to for information about how to defeat the French: "It was because these people of the old times who had been killed could transmit all the techniques that they could experiment: they knew how to take a zombi, how to take the body, because they had understood how to do this. After having understood, they killed the whites with this! Do you understand?" (248). This description of a dialogue with the spirit world bringing about the rebels' knowledge of the zombification technique correlates with the people's historical reliance on Vaudou and folk knowledge in various modes of resistance (see chapter 1). This meta-myth chronicled in Degoul's archive explicitly ties the zombie's creation to anticolonial strategy.

Chantal's story even insinuates that Makandal was a part of this receipt of knowledge from the ancestors. Therefore, the zombie is connected to the resistance of rebel slaves, and the technique of zombie making is associated with the poisoning of slave masters. This is a symbolic operation that works both on the present and on the past: it isn't just a reshaping of the contemporary mythologization of the zombie, but it also rewrites history and definitively inserts the zombie into the Haitian Revolution to establish zombification as a technique of resistance.[19]

Degoul describes at length the houngan's assessment of zombification, a narrative recuperation of slavery that puts the power into the hands of the oppressed, colonized, occupied people rather than the aggressor. Haitian zombification is both narratologically based on the slavery system—a body deprived of its soul and made to work for the profit of another, which is clearly analogous to the forced labor of Africans in European colonies—and, in this origin story, narratively indebted to slavery: the souls of dead slaves communicated to their living heirs the *recette* (recipe) for creating zombies, enabling them to employ zombification and other practices as strategies in their struggle for freedom, national independence, and local dominion or general security (250).

Degoul's research was conducted during the second presidency of Aristide, when Haitians were beginning to reclaim Vaudou as a part of their cultural heritage, wrenching it free from memories of its abuses under the Duvalier regimes.[20] Papa Doc's use of Vaudou to solidify his power involved making use of the symbols of Haitian Vaudou, intimating that he had the lwa (or loa, the Haitian dieties) in his control and using the regionalized structure of the houmforts of Vaudou as extensions of his power into rural areas. In the chapter "Voudou Is His Arm" in their book, *Papa Doc,* Bernard Diederich and Al Burt write, "He has mounted Haiti as the loa does his 'horse.' The ride has been disastrous, even for voudou" (357). At the time Degoul was gathering his data, Haiti had not had an army since Aristide disbanded it in 1995, and Vaudou may have offered an alternative source of state protection. In tracing the transformations of the zombie myth, one finds moments when the mythology morphs from having a historical to a contemporary value as a discursive weapon that solidifies national identity. According to Degoul's sources, zombification is also used to hold firm the frontier shared by the Dominican Republic.[21] In their understanding, zombification is a weapon, a technology, and a science that the Haitians wield, à la Makandal and his secret poisons.

In Degoul's essay "'We Are the Mirror of Your Fears,'" an informant asserts, "Dominicans are afraid of us: It is for this reason [zombification]" (31). Citing a recent music video by a group called Koudjay that depicts a zombification, Colbert quotes the song lyrics, "'We are waiting for you.' Yes. We are waiting for you! Keep your armored tanks and your weapons ... we are waiting for you"(31).[22] To the Haitians that Degoul has made the subject of his study, zombification and the legend of the zombie are a source of pride and strength, one that fortifies their borders and prevents unwanted intervention even in the absence of military force. And as the anthropologist notes, "Everything continues as if the fear of zombification displayed in North American literature and cinema had been confirmed in Haiti, legitimated by an affirmation of the reality of the object of terror. Americans fear zombification, express it in all sorts of mediums, and are right to perceive the object of their fear in this way: zombification is precisely that which escapes them, and which simultaneously constitutes Haiti's mysterious power amid the neocolonial effort by which the North American hegemony had attempted to establish itself" (Degoul, "'We Are the Mirrors of Your Fears'" 29–30). Therefore that which at first appears to be yet another example of American imperialist greed in Hollywood's annexation of the zombie (whereby the Haitian myth was mined from its source, extracted of its original meaning, transposed to a different idiom, and set to serve the cultural needs of an entirely different population) in this Haitian meta-myth becomes just the opposite: Americans did not *abduct* the Haitian zombie; they were *invaded* by it. The prevalence of the monster in film, in comic books, and in video games only proves how deeply it terrifies them. This cultural operation on the zombie myth represents for me the second phase in the zombie's technē. If the first is a reconciling and remastering of history, as concretized in the example of the white American general laboring as a zombie in the fields of Léogâne, the second—symbolized by the reach of Haitian power into the American imaginary—I think of as analogous to what Frantz Fanon refers to as a "literature of combat" insofar as it represents the use of narrative as a strategy of national protection, or even sovereignty: to effect expansion of the country's borders, if only in mythic space.

A Literature of Combat

In "In Search of the Lost Body," Michael Dash claims that at one point in *The Wretched of the Earth* "Fanon equates a reanimated body with the liberated voice of the revolutionary intellectual" (296). If Fanon's language recalls the reanimated corpse, this is apt for our discussion of the zombie myth, for here he is discussing the development of national literatures in postcolonial environments as awakenings that provide the people with a kind of discursive arsenal. This even resembles the contemporary zombie's duality in creation and in purpose: the literature of combat, in Fanon's description, is a display of life where there was none; it threatens its enemies, and yet it has the capacity to awaken others from inanimate states. Fanon describes the development of a national literature and its transformation of the mode of the storyteller in a manner that leads to direct critique of the regimes in power, which results in (aside from edicts to arrest griots in some cases) the revolutionary awakening of the people:[23] "This may be properly called a literature of combat, in the sense that it calls on the whole people to fight for their existence as a nation. It is a literature of combat, because it molds the national consciousness, giving it form and contours and flinging open before it new and boundless horizons; it is a literature of combat because it assumes responsibility, and because it is the will to liberty expressed in terms of time and space" (*The Wretched of the Earth* 240). In Fanon's own rhetorical maneuver, the awakened social consciousness that finds its outlet and its mode of transference in literature is equated to a return to life.[24]

The zombie myth provides an example and a further clarification of how a "literature of combat" might work. There are two different stages in the literature of combat that is engineered through the zombie myth, just as there are two phases in the zombie's liberation. First, a zombie must be fed salt, given *goute sel*, so that he may realize he is dead; only after can he turn away from his work and turn against his oppressor.[25] Likewise, the first phase in Haitian literature's use of the zombie metaphor *reveals* the people's sources of oppression. Only afterward can the myth itself be reconstituted and transformed into a rhetorical weapon to be used against one's enemies.

Hénock Trouillot provides a useful introduction to Ignace Nau's *Isalina*, first published in 1834, celebrating Nau's important contribution to early Haitian literature. Trouillot writes that "Ignace Nau inaugurated in Haiti the literary genre of historical fiction" (17). Combining the historical novel with the fantastical elements of local folklore, Nau was one of the first to implement what would become a central feature of "la literature antillaise." At the time there was conflict between the elites, who wanted to distance themselves from rural superstition, and those intellectuals who refused to copy the model of Europeans; Nau was one of the first to embrace what he called *le merveilleux creole*—that is, the indigenous sorcery of the island—as a means of representing the authentic Haitian experience.[26]

In his introduction, Trouillot quotes an anonymous author who writes of the pleasure of discovering a Creole expression on a page of literature. The author contrasts the Haitian's experience of reading the national literature to the experience of watching the traditional Carnival: "Because, in seeing the carnival marching through the streets, 'The costumes of all the centuries and of all the people,' he also begins to smile. But what he admits is that 'our ideas are produced within a form that is not our own; it's a foreign garb in which we dress ourselves!'" (Nau 14–15). Carnival, which itself mythologizes the nation's history by representing various moments in the culture's development, furnishes here a comparison of postcolonial oppression with being dressed in the clothes of another. Like the costumed participants in the parade, this author felt that to write not only in French but also perhaps in the custom of the European tradition was to don the vestments of the oppressor.[27] As Fanon would say, what was needed was a national literature that could serve as a literature of combat, holding firm the symbolic front between the Haitian's own cultural identity and those associated with imperialist interests and the colonial past. And yet, as we will see, the precise manner in which Carnival melds history and creativity in its active retelling of the past provides such means: it is not just a parade; it is a display of might. Like Ti Noel, the protagonist of Carpentier's novel, who in the end sports the bicorne hat of the fallen king, dressing in the clothes of the oppressor can also be a strategy of resistance—signifying the power of the act of imaginative (re)appropriation and even, in regard to the zombie, cultural infiltration.

In Edwige Danticat's *After the Dance*, a description of the traditional annual Carnival in Jacmel, Haiti, the reader is introduced to the various figures that one will encounter in the parade, from people dressed as colonists and slaves to a float representing the US Coast Guard turning away Haitian "boat people" to those wearing papier-mâché masks representing a variety of historical figures and animals to ghosts, zombies, and other mythological characters and even a personification of AIDS. But what she says of the zombie is revealing of one of its most striking associations in Haiti:

> Watching the carnival zombies on Sunday, I would also remember my uncle's wife, Tante Denise, waking me up one morning some twenty years ago to listen to the radio as an announcer reported that a few dozen zombies had been found wandering the northern hills of the country in a semicomatose state and that their loved ones should come claim them and take them home....
>
> Like many people Tante Denise had concluded that these found zombies were actually former political prisoners ... who were so mentally damaged by dictatorship-sponsored torture that they had become either crazy or slow. Tante Denise, like many others, had doubted that any relatives would go get them, for fear of being locked up themselves. (69–70)

The zombie's deep association with the Duvalier dictatorship is a part of its history. And if we were to imagine a carnival of the various zombies present in Haitian culture, we would have to include alongside the bokor with his rope-led zombies, like a painting by Hector Hyppolite, an image of the Tonton Macoute in his uniform—mirrored sunglasses, dark denim shirt—perhaps led by Papa Doc as Baron Samedi. What follows is like my own zombie carnival: an overview of the figure's appearances in and transformation throughout Haitian literature, one that pays special attention to the zombie's uses, abuses, and reboot after the Duvalier regime. Over the next several pages, I present a by no means exhaustive catalog but at least a macabre parade of some of the most recognizable Haitian zombies in order to illustrate the narrative function of the zombie in a literature of combat, its reshaping and repurposing in prose.[28]

Although Ignace Nau's "Isalina, ou une scène créole" (1836), seems to be more of a tale of entrancement than a true zombie story—the exact nature of the spell under which the titular character is placed is unclear—it is possible to interpret Isalina as a quasi- or even full zombie. This is a short story, roughly forty pages, about a young woman who is all but engaged to her love, Paul. His close friend and "frère de baptême," Jean Julien, becomes enamored of her and suffers from lovesickness and jealousy. He waits for her in a cemetery one night and attacks her, causing her to hit her head on a stone; afterward she is discovered bathed in her own blood and much changed. One character overhears the townspeople talking of her. They say, "Il y a des zombis dans ceci, qu'en pensez vous?" (There are zombies in this, don't you think?) (42). But it is not clear from this statement whether they mean merely evil spirits (as in the earlier meaning of the word discussed in chapter 1) or whether they suspect her of *being* a zombie. The attack that changes the protagonist occurs by a cemetery (33), and her injuries are such that some might think she died of her wounds and exists now in a living dead state. His comrade replies only, "Cela se peut bien" (It's quite possible).

The majority of the tale concerns a battle between sorcerers wherein the skills of one must surmount the other's "science," which consists of "their advice and their drugs" (49). Regardless of whether Isalina is a zombie proper or merely entranced, the cultural critique works to similar ends. The difference between the two seems to be negligible in this regard, as the text describes a soul controlled by another, a state that may apply alike to a living dead zombie and to the entranced: "the soul, obeying either its instinct or the magic of its master, as one wishes" (48). Isalina is noteworthy because she is perhaps the first of a pantheon of female zombies in Haitian literature that includes those of Alexis and Depestre, to which we turn in the final section of this chapter, but also because the cultural critique launched by Isalina's zombification/entrancement is located in the setting of this story. This particular *scène créole* takes place in the environs of a sugarcane factory.

Nau describes a town situated around a factory and details the way it structures the people's lives. Particularly telling is the description of "the young girls destined to constantly nourish the greed of the cylinders" (28). The pairing of the image of a young woman put into a trance by a romantic suitor and the young women of the village who spend their lives toiling in the factory draws on an obvious analogy, one that will become a staple of the zombie genre. In our parade, Isalina represents the way the zombie, an erstwhile image of colonial slavery, first began to be adapted as a reflection of postcolonial capitalism. As discussed in chapter 2, this sentiment is also the subtext of Seabrook's sketch of the cane field zombies in *The Magic Island*, and these Hasco sugar zombies also deserve representation in our carnival. The comparison made in "Isalina" personifies the claim that slavery yet existed, albeit in a different form, in the nineteenth century, materialized in the image of the Haitian factory worker toiling in the sugarcane industry.

In Graham Greene's famous 1966 novel, *The Comedians*, by contrast, zombies are explicitly connected to the Duvalier regime, as the threat of economic, imperialist power is replaced by fears of Papa Doc and his gestapo. The narrator, Brown, a European hotelier living in Port-au-Prince, describes a world in which "no one dared move on the roads at night; it was the hour when only zombies worked or else the Tontons Macoute" (93). Early on in the novel, Dr. Philipot, secretary of social welfare, who has fallen out of favor with Duvalier, kills himself in Brown's swimming pool rather than be caught (and presumably tortured to death) by the Macoutes. After his body is stolen by the secret police during his funeral, Mr. Brown has a conversation with one of his hotel employees.

> 'What good to them is a dead man in a coffin? Were they afraid that people might have laid flowers on his grave?' . . .
> 'The people they very frightened,' Joseph said, 'when they know. They frightened the President take their bodies too when they die.'
> 'Why care? There's nothing left as it is but skin and bone, and why should the President need dead bodies anyway?'
> 'The people very ignorant,' Joseph said. 'They think the President keep Philipot in the cellar in the palace and make him work all night. The President is big Voodoo man.'
> 'Baron Samedi?'
> 'Ignorant people say yes.'
> 'So nobody will attack him at night with all the zombies there to protect him? They are better than guards, better than the Tontons Macoute.'
> 'Tontons Macoute zombies too. So ignorant people say.'
> 'But what do you believe, Joseph?'
> 'I be ignorant man, sir,' Joseph said. (126–27)

As the character Joseph recounts, it is often said that the Tonton Macoutes were in fact zombies; their mirrored sunglasses, which hid their eyes, helped to complete this image.

The idea that Duvalier kept the bodies of his political enemies to make them into a zombie army for his protection (or, at least, that he purposefully perpetuated this rumor by visibly stealing their corpses) is also referenced in the 1974 novel *Le nègre crucifié* by Gérard Etienne, in which zombies are explicitly forced brought back from the dead by the president to protect him: "Twenty thousand zombies surrounded him. Even if a bullet were fired, it wouldn't reach him. The zombies are there to eat the bullet" (119). This novel is discussed for its treatment of themes of the individual and the collective in Lucy Swanson's "Zombie Nation?," so I won't go into great detail here, but the narrative makes evident this moment when both the zombie and Vaudou more broadly were denigrated as elements of the people's oppression rather than their salvation: "If God weren't absent, I am sure that he would give me the forces to massacre the President's zombis. He would give me the same power to kill all the *roinègres* ('negro-kings') who dance, calling upon the gods of the Vaudouists. It would be my gesture of protest against a world of torture, tears, crimes, injustices, against the desiccation of Haiti, despite this rain that ravages beasts for eating and houses for living in" (Etienne 105). In these examples, we have a further development of the zombie myth, from the pitiable slave zombie under the control of a sorcerer for the exploit of personal profit, often tied, allegorically if not directly, to corporate interests like foreign investment in the sugar industry to the zombie explicitly under the control of Duvalier, whether as an army of the dead kept out of sight in his palace to protect him if needed or as the blank-eyed, heartless, and seemingly omnipresent Macoutes.

But Duvalier's grasp on Vaudou was not constant throughout his reign, and this, too, is represented in Greene's novel. When Brown and Mr. Smith, a naive American bent on establishing a center for vegetarianism in Haiti, brings up the issue of Philipot's interrupted funeral to a government official, he is told that the funeral was a sham and the coffin full of stolen bricks that the police were merely repossessing.

> 'Then it's not true what the people think—that the body of Doctor Philipot is in the palace working as a zombie?'
> 'All that is Voodoo stuff, Mr. Brown. Luckily our President has rid the country of Voodoo.'
> 'Then he has done more than the Jesuits could do.' (154)

Duvalier had not, in fact, rid the country of Vaudou (as the reader sees later in Greene's novel), but his relationship to it, as the book suggests, was far more complex than many histories allow: Papa Doc used some elements of Vaudou to secure his power and the fear of his people but prohibited the practice when it might be a threat to his regime. Taxes dating from the anti-Vaudou campaign of the 1940s were enforced when it suited his interests, so that all but the wealthiest were prevented from hosting Vaudou ceremonies, which had served as convenient meeting places for insurrectionists since the days of slavery. And it is, indeed, at the lone Vaudou ceremony described in Greene's narrative that the rebels gather, including Philipot's nephew, saying, "The gods of Dahomey may be what we need" (179). The "conflicting feelings" about Vaudou at the time of Baby Doc's ouster can be seen in the *Los Angeles Times* article "After Duvalier: A Scary Time for Voodoo," by Dan Williams, published on March 7, 1986, which describes the sacking of temples and murder of houngans, with calls such as "Down with Voodoo. Free the Zombies!" graffitied on walls, at the same time that other Vaudouists were given credit for demonstrations against Duvalier and his removal. This confusion is visible in the treatment of literary zombies during the Duvalier regime.

In places, the zombie is depicted not as a threat issued from within the dictatorship but one associated with the general lawlessness from which the regime might be the people's only protection. In a novel titled *Les Zombis en furie*, by Romulus Pierre and published in May 1978 in Port-au-Prince during Baby Doc's control of the nation, a retired police captain is enlisted by a concerned citizen to stop the evil machinations of a local gang and their leader, Purificatè, who like all good villains is given to extemporize in long monologues (against, for interest, the importation of American and European goods) and who hopes, by means of his own zombie forces, to infiltrate the government and implement his vision for the nation. This thin volume seems to amount to anticommunist propaganda in the guise of a hard-boiled detective novel (complete with cheesy love subplot), but regardless, the zombies here are explicitly in the control of the government's enemies, and it is the long arm of the law, or its surrogate, in the form of Captain Alain Foucauld, that saves the day. The zombies under Purificatè's control (accomplished by the use of a plant serum injected intravenously and not, as traditionally depicted, introduced by means of powders) are not really as "furious" as the title suggests, or not in the way that I had hoped. Indeed, it is hard to think of it as anything other than a puff piece for the government, one in which the zombies are associated with mindless communists—unsurprisingly, for the Duvalier dictatorship was long at war with the Parti unifié des communistes haitiens (PUCH) and its supporters, though the elder often used his diplomatic ties with Castro as leverage when the United States threatened to cut off aid (Diederich and Burt 140).[29]

The definitive literary revision of the Haitian zombie occurs in Frankétienne's *Dézafi* (1975) and its subsequent French "rewriting" as *Les Affres d'un défi* (1979). Thematically, scholars agree that *Dézafi* is an allegory for the reign of Duvalier that uses zombification to metaphorize the effects of his tyranny. As Diederich and Burt write, "The most outstanding job of zombifying people, it has been pointed out repeatedly, is the job Duvalier has done on Haiti. His method of total domination of rural Haitians has been accomplished by superstition and fear" (357).[30] In his "Note on Frankétienne's *Les Affres d'un défi*," Carrol F. Coates cites Charles H. Rowell's interview with Frankétienne: "*Dézafi* has symbolically exploited the phenomenon of zombification in order to denounce the horrors and alienation bred by all forms of tyranny and totalitarianism. In this novel, the salt used by one of the protagonists to awaken the zombis from their lethargy plays the role of a powerful symbol: the symbol of full awareness and recaptured memory" (761). Formally, however, Frankétienne's work recalls the zombie's association with return in its heavy use of repetition and, in the author's own revisions and "transcreations" of the text, reminds us of the zombie's capacity for transformation into a symbol of resistance.

Rachel Douglas describes the importance of rewriting for Frankétienne's work. The very structure of Frankétienne's *spiralisme*, a movement he founded with René Philoctète and Jean-Claude Fignolé, emphasizes the repetition, reworking, and recycling that are major components of folkloric narratives and which have been made use of by various Caribbean authors. However, as Douglas emphasizes, whereas many rewrite the texts of others in a manner that suggests the openness and mobility of narrative in oral traditions, Frankétienne practices revision and reworking of his own texts. The treatment of zombification, Douglas claims, is broadened in the French version of the novel, drawing the parallel to slavery and imprisonment more generally (44).[31]

Frankétienne's novel is a work that has already been studied at length, and those interested in the formal aspects of the spiralist text and its revisions should see Douglas's important book. In terms of its zombies, Kaiama Glover's important address of the novel in *Haiti Unbound* is foundational. Because there is such a wealth of scholarship already devoted to this text, its complex form, and its publication history, especially its criticism of Duvalier, I'll keep my remarks here minimal.[32]

As Glover and others note, Frankétienne's is not only a book that has been reworked, but it also modifies the myth of the zombie as it had formerly appeared in Haitian literature and culture. Glover writes of the novel, "While the zombie's subjugation is profound, it is not necessarily definitive. Rather, the zombie is a creature within whom coexist an utter powerlessness and an enduring chance for rebirth" (*Haiti Unbound* 60). When the zombie's full history is taken into account, it becomes apparent that this statement is true of the myth broadly, at least in any iteration in which salt is presented as a cure. *Dézafi/Les Affres d'un défi* nonetheless transforms the literary zombie, for Frankétienne's "zombi" is an overt figure of revolution. The story concerns a cruel zombie master, Saintil, whom Glover writes "is both what he is—an exploitive houngan—and an allegorical stand-in for the dictator Duvalier" (65) and his daughter, Sultana, who becomes enamored of one of the zombies, Clodonis, and feeds him salt, after which he gives it to the others, bringing about a rebellion: "Revived by the salt, the former zombies, become *bois nouveau*, carried forward by a vengeful rage, shook, destroyed, ransacked, completely tore down to the ground the house of Saintil" (191).

After tasting salt, these zombies do not just stumble off the plantation and seek their graves, as in some versions; rather, they tear their former captors into pieces in bloody rebellion: "Bodies torn into innumerable scattered bits. Spectacle of jawless pieces, thrown here and there in the dust of the thoroughfare: the pan of a mandible, a few teeth, the ends of arms, fragments of thighs, a gaping skull, sections of... intestines, phalanges, cuts of ears and lips" (193). The scene is gruesome, and reminiscent of the kind of harrowing detail provided by early historiographers of the slave rebellion.[33] By making the former zombie an active agent of its master's destruction and in providing such a visceral description of the destruction of the slaveholder's body, Frankétienne reworks the zombie as a figure of explicit resistance, where before it most often represented merely the innocuous slave or was associated with Duvalier's sadistic henchmen.[34]

The zombies in Frankétienne's work undergo a complete metamorphosis from "zombis" to "bois nouveau"—literally, "new wood," but also probably having the connotation of something like "citizen," as their town is called Bois Neuf—which he defines in a glossary in the book: "all persons who have ceased to be a zombie, after having regained their lucidity thanks to the absorption of salt" (230). This represents a major intervention in the zombie myth and one that seems far more optimistic about the potential for successful resistance to oppressive power structures, because whereas the myth usually offers only two avenues to the zombie given salt—he seeks his grave, or he seeks revenge and then his grave, presumably—Frankétienne's narrative emphasizes in the designation of the category "bois nouveau" that there is a kind of existence possible on the other side of zombification, one in which even lucidity returns.

This is not to say that there isn't always power in the zombie and the zombie metaphor—at least for whomever brandishes it—there is. But Franketienne's intervention imagines a zombie's restoration to a position of power, which is a rarity indicative of the people's desire to be reborn after the long subjugation of the Duvalier era. Former zombie Clodonis will also address his fellow bois nouveau, convincing them to "avoid . . . gratuitous violence" (193) and to unite with the *paysans* to form one collective bent on liberty for all. Jérôme, a persecuted student, addresses the crowd of bois nouveau and paysans at the novel's end: "We must in all times and all places, learn to live to share the salt. Many other zombis are languishing in poverty, and unconsciousness at the base of mountains, the interior of plains and even in the cities. Let us go wake them with salt" (199). Clodonis and the bois nouveau that join together make perhaps the most revolutionary contribution to the carnival of zombies.

One finds neither a lucid nor a truly awakened post-zombie in the Cuban and Puerto Rican author Mayra Montero's 1995 novel, *In the Palm of Darkness*. The book concerns an American herpetologist, Victor S. Grigg, who travels to Haiti in 1992 to seek a species of frog, the *grenouille du sang*, before it becomes extinct. The plot of the novel describes this quest in a time of great political turmoil—after the 1991 coup d'état that overthrew the immensely popular democratically elected Aristide—wherein bodies are found daily in the streets, even just outside the Hotel Oloffson (58). The narrative is divided between the American scientist and his Haitian guide, Thierry, who relates many stories from a life lived under the Duvaliers' shadow. There are parallels drawn throughout the book between the various species of frogs that are disappearing and the tortured past of the Haitian people, and the book offers an important contribution as postcolonial eco-criticism, but most important for our purposes here, in the analepses related by Thierry the book describes the terror of the Tonton Macoutes and a range of the people's poisons and their powers, including zombification.

Though there is no explicit connection drawn between the capability to zombify and the reign of the Macoutes, the portrait of zombies drawn here nonetheless suggests an evolution from the wholly pitiable, impotent creatures of yesteryear. Thierry, who is an old man in 1992 and whose brother was a Macoute in what must have been the 1960s—the book rarely clarifies the time line—was just a boy when his father served as a *pwazon rat*, a zombie hunter sent to find wayward zombies to prevent their taking "vengeance" on their masters, called "cattle owners" (50). The pwazon rats, like Thierry's father,

> checked to see if perhaps there were any among them who could be returned to their packs, but they almost never could return any of them because by the time they got to Chilotte most had spent days and days wandering the coast, rolling around in the poisonous shade of the black mangroves, licking the salt that crusted the foliage. It was the salt that woke them, and when they woke they saw themselves as they really were, they remembered what they had been, they were desperate to be that again. They went into a rage: They started in kicking, they started in biting, they started in scratching, and since they couldn't even be dragged back to the village, the hunters just pulled off that little piece at the back of the neck where they had the mark of their pack. In exchange for that, the cattle owner would give them money. (50–51)

The zombies are captured, their brands are removed, and then they are herded into a cave and killed. This narrative includes many fascinating elements that suggest a merging of Haitian folklore and the Hollywood cinematic zombie: the hunters cannot go out on a hunt if they have an open wound—fearing contamination it seems (52); and the zombies are described as "hungry and bloodthirsty" (55), though there are no signs that they are actually cannibals. Thierry's father is killed by a pack of savannah zombies that leave him flayed of his skin, in a passage that recalls, if not Frankétienne's bois nouveau, then at least the B-movies that had been common fare for decades prior to the novel's publication (55). These salt-fed zombies are not those returned to enlightened revolutionary consciousness, turning only against their oppressive masters; rather, they have, more like the zombie of cinema, just gone off the rails. But this parity still contains political commentary. When a man described as having "the soul of a macoute" later skins a woman in Jérémie, Thierry asks, "Does that remind you of anything?" (138). The intimation seems to be that the gangs terrorizing the countryside in the early nineties, whose calling card is the body part they take as a trophy from their victims, are not unlike the zombies—mindlessly destructive. This book thus provides, similar to *Les Zombis en furie*, an equation drawn not between zombies and dictatorship or foreign control but between zombies and that which is exterior to the government, or general lawlessness.

And yet at the time in which Montero's novel was set there was also a power play by the acting Haitian government to harness the zombie for its own uses. Belonging not to the pages of novels written in and about Haiti but to newspaper headlines, Emil Jonassaint's zombie army deserves representation in our parade for its claim to the zombie's mythic and military might. Faced with the threat of US invasion after Aristide's removal from power and increasing unrest, Jonassaint, acting president from May until October 1994, made repeated declarations that American troops landing in Haiti would be forced to contend with the full Vaudou arsenal at the country's disposal, including "three battalions of zombies" invisible to the naked eye and "voodoo spells" that would protect the country from air strikes (Joseph; French). A short article in the *Miami Herald* summarized Jonassaint's many threats over the summer: "For months, he has warned that Haitians would meet the invading troops with a special powder that would turn them into zombies and that, with the gods on their side, they would be given special power to repel the invading armies of the international community" (Colon). The piece seems to give Jonassaint's threats some credit, mentioning the recent running aground of the *USS Monsoon*, two emergencies at the White House, and even Vice President Al Gore's torn Achilles' tendon as potential signs of Vaudou at work.

This is referred to directly in Dany Laferrière's novel *Pays sans chapeau*: "Ah! I remember this army of zombies that the old President had threatened to launch against the Americans if they dared to put a single foot on Haitian soil. The general of the dead army. I remember this episode very well. I was in Miami at the time, and the *Miami Herald* had reported the words of the old President" (64).

Pays sans chapeau is what Swanson calls one of Laferrière's "autofictional" (25) novels, about the return of an author, Laferrière himself, to Haiti after an absence of twenty years, having been, like his father before him, in political exile. The chapters are divided, oscillating between descriptions of the *Pays Réel*, as the narrator rediscovers the land of his childhood and old friends, and the *Pays Rêvé*, as he investigates the ghost world that is nearly superimposed on the city of Port-au-Prince and details the people's beliefs and superstitions. Acting as a kind of journalist chronicling his adventures in the Pays Rêvé, Laferrière eventually finds a way to enter the pays sans chapeau, the land of the dead. This is an intensely rich novel, full of valuable commentary not only on Haiti's politics but also on the importance of spirituality in the culture.

Early in the novel, the narrator begins interviewing professors about various mysteries of his *pays natale*. Stories abound, about an American soldier married to a Vaudou goddess (192); about a group of people in Bombardopolis who have no need for food (93), the intimation being, it is later made clear, that they are a kind of living dead (251–52); and about the American scientists who have come to discover the secret of their survival (193). But importantly for our purposes here is the duality of the uses of living death, as a means both of characterizing life under Duvalier and of solidifying national power beyond his reign of terror.

Reunited with his mother after more than two decades, the narrator is told, "You cannot know, you weren't here, but it's even more grave than you know, what happened here, in this country. We had the impression of being already dead, here. The killers are no more living than the killed. We are all already dead" (102). The same sentiment is echoed later, at a point at which the narrator recounts a meeting with his father in the United States, when he said to him, "Il n'y a que des morts en Haiti, des morts ou des zombis" (244). Having left Haiti under the control of Duvalier père, his father's impression is that "there are nothing but zombies in Haiti. As if the country were ... nothing more than an immense cemetery" (244).

At the same time, the book's repeated references to an "army of zombies" (93) act as what Swanson calls "an emblem of the persistence of intra-national and inter-national myths," and she rightly notes the way the zombie signifies national power: "the 'armee morte' is portrayed as an integral part of Haiti's extant power structures, commanded by the president and reinforcing his control, while the nation's borders, which can be inferred from the emphatic statement 's'ils osaient mettre un seul pied sur le sol d'Haiti' are ostensibly reinforced by the dead" (28). Yet Laferrière pushes the matter, for the US troops had in fact "dared to put a single foot on Haitian soil" (64).

> Where, then, was this army when the Americans disembarked?
> My mother's face became subtly grave.
> "It was there," she finally articulated. "It was awaiting orders. In the end, the old President made a pact with the young American president. The American army would occupy the country during the day. The army of zombies would have the night at their disposition." (64)

It would seem, then, that the government at last conceded the insufficiency of their spectral forces. Or do the Haitians have the last laugh? Consulting Professor J. B. Romain (a nod to the author of *Quelques moeurs et coutumes des paysans haitiens*, 1975) about the veracity of the story related to him by his mother, the narrator is told the tale of a recent peasant uprising against a wealthy landowner who is abusing his control of the region's water and who summons the police to his aid.

> They demanded the paysans to leave the place. They refused, drawing their machetes. So the soldiers fired, at the height of the men. Once, twice, three times. The paysans continued to march upon them. The soldiers shot again, before fleeing. . . .
> And how did they explain this phenomenon? . . .
> I can only reveal to you one single fact. . . . It seemed that one of the soldiers recognized a paysan.
> And?
> And, according to the soldier, this man had been dead for a long time.
> So, a zombi?
> That's it.
> But this is nothing new in Haiti, professor. And this is not the first time either that land owners have made zombies work in their fields.
> Yes, but it is the first time that we've seen a revolt of zombies. . . . Generally, the zombi has no will. He can't even hold his head up. He can't do anything but obey.
> And this, was what?
> That's a state secret. (73–75)

The power associated with the zombie is depicted as something that comes directly from the people; it is a power that the government would like to commandeer but has perhaps not entirely mastered, and one that the United States is equally eager to acquire. This novel is the first in which there is a *revolt* of zombies—not, as Swanson points out, salt-fed bois nouveau. These rebel zombies carry a previously unseen standard: for it is the zombie itself, not the post-zombie, that is associated with resistance.

Various Caribbean "zombies" not described here (from the pages of the Martinican writer Patrick Chamoiseau or the Guadeloupian Simone Schwartz-Bart or the Jamaican Canadian Nalo Hopkinson) are also worthy of critical attention, but for the present study I am attempting to call forth only the embodied dead of Haiti that serve as a people's expression of their disempowerment or a crowing boast of their capabilities for what they reveal about the "corrective power" of the imagination and especially about the capacity of a literature of combat to make and remake a mythic arsenal and to draw history, the spirit world, and the narratives of others together in its battery.

As a final example, I want to address one of the most famous zombies of Haitian literature, René Depestre's Hadriana. As Danticat notes in *After the Dance*, all carnivals have a queen or several, and ours is no exception, for Hadriana is not really singular but plural: she belongs to a narrative that is a retelling, and its multiple layers are in line with the zombie's duality.

In Depestre's novel *Hadriana dans tous mes rêves*, a character says in the primary narrator's hearing, "Dans notre pays, pour sûr, l'histoire se répète plus que partout ailleurs" (In our country, for certain, history repeats itself more often than it does elsewhere) (93). Depestre's careful framing of this claim recognizes that it is a loaded and a nuanced statement. One understands what it means to say this of a country with such a tumultuous political past. Though the student of Haitian history may find dizzying the successive coups, the various tyrants who have often seemed doomed to repeat the mistakes of previous regimes, and the occupations and interventions (political, social, and economic) that characterize the nation's two centuries, Haitian literature, like Haitian culture, has found a way to metaphorize this uncanny sense of history repeating. As I have already touched on in this chapter, many have noted the prevalence in Caribbean literature of an insistence on repetition, revision, and the restaging of history in literature; others have reflected that myth, narrative, ritual, and ceremony work to enact a cathartic labor. Depestre seems to acknowledge in this quotation the theory that, like the repetition compulsion—the psyche's attempt to master a traumatic event over which it had no control, *selon* Sigmund Freud—the Haitian people replay their travails and tragedies in myth and in literature even more often than most cultures.[35]

In Depestre's literary oeuvre one finds various metaphoric and literal zombies, as well as a category I elucidate further in the next chapter, textual zombies.[36] Playing on the troubling sense of cultural déjà vu that Depestre alludes to in the statement above, *Hadriana dans tous mes rêves* is in part a remake: it is highly reminiscent of a short narrative included in Alexis's *Romancero aux etoiles*, which may itself be based on a folk legend, recounted in Hurston's *Tell My Horse*, of "the most famous Zombie case of all Haiti," which concerns the zombification of the "beautiful daughter of a prominent family" (Hurston, *Tell My Horse* 194).

Appropriate to the theme of the return of history, and to the oral tradition of storytelling in which narratives evolve over time in their retellings, Depestre's *Hadriana* is a novel that reproduces a particular tale about a woman zombified on her wedding day. Its rehearsal operates in multiple ways: first, it repeats a familiar plot—the same subject as Alexis's piece, similar even to Nau's "Isalina," and based on a regional myth of Jacmel.[37] It is a theme that harkens back even to the medieval trope of Death and the Maiden, juxtaposing the eroticized young woman to the ghastly image of death. The structure of the novel itself also relies on repetition, retelling the central event multiple times, and the narrative also reverberates with echoes of Haitian history at various points.

The precedent story that influenced Depestre's formation of the plot of *Hadriana*, Alexis's "Chronique d'un faux amour," also describes a bride zombified on her wedding day, and both narratives relate the experience from the point of view of the would-be zombie. In Alexis's narrative, an upper-class Creole girl is poisoned on her wedding day by the dark-skinned uncle of her fiancé who objects to the match. The uncle is thought to be a kind of medicine man; earlier, his garden is described as containing many potent herbs, including "concombres-zombis," the poisonous jimson weed, and he prepares for her a toxic bouquet. Upon smelling the flowers, the bride collapses and is pronounced dead, but throughout the rest of the story she relates that she could hear and even feel everything that was going on around her. The narrative is related analeptically, from a point in the future, when the zombified bride has been institutionalized in a convent where she is cared for by nuns. She was presumably a zombie slave for a time, but she was found wandering when the zombie master died and was removed to the nunnery. The story oscillates between lucid flashbacks, which ostensibly occur when the girl is sleeping and which relate her zombification and the circumstances that led to it, and her present state at the convent, where she suffers in a semivegetative madness, fearful of the dreams that come when she falls asleep.[38]

As with *Hadriana*, Alexis's story relies on repetition. The narrative of her monochromatic life at the convent is interrupted by descriptions of her efforts to keep herself from falling asleep by tapping a silver spoon against her gold wedding ring. The pattern is repeated several times throughout the fifty-page story, and the continual tapping of the spoon against the ring, her ritual, becomes a refrain. As this chapter's epigraph explains, for the narrator, "memory is a revenant of which one cannot be rid," and in her sleep Hadriana is subjected to these memories and forced to relive her past. In this phrase, Alexis makes a direct comparison between history and the zombie revenant.

Both Alexis and Depestre were leaders of the *indigeniste* movement in Haiti and they collaborated on *La Ruche*, a dissident literary paper with Marxist and surrealist leanings (Williams 177). Alexis was assassinated by Duvalier's police in 1961, and Depestre lived in exile for much of his life.[39] One imagines that publishing *Hadriana* in 1988, after the end of the long Duvalier regimes, his retelling of Alexis's story, was also a tribute to his friend. It seems fitting that Depestre should choose such a tale to rewrite: in doing so he alters the significance of the narrative's structural repetition, from one symbolizing a people imprisoned by their past and doomed to repeat history to a triumphant story of the possibilities inherent in the production and reproductions of narratives. By working through the past, a people can free themselves of it, and make for themselves a new future. Here, the folkloric zombie, a figure of altered return, both contributes to and represents this mode of cultural resistance.

Depestre's novel is divided into two parts, the first of which is told from the perspective of a young Haitian boy named Patrick who has loved Hadriana since early childhood.[40] He describes the town and the residents' belief system, the celebratory preparations that are made in anticipation of Hadriana's wedding, the subsequent mourning of the townspeople when she appears to drop dead at the altar, and her funeral, which coincides with the traditional Jacmelian Carnival planned to occur with the wedding but which the town elects not to forgo when events take a disastrous turn. In the next section, he recounts the growing suspicion, born of the moment when her grave is discovered empty, that she has not died but has instead been zombified. Patrick documents his own research into zombification and his lifelong struggle to deal with her disappearance. At the end of his narrative, thirty years from the novel's opening, he is reunited with Hadriana, and the final section of the book relates her perspective, recounting the same course of events that the reader has already followed in the first section but from her point of view, when, paralyzed by the sorcerer's poison, she was laid in her coffin, presumed dead.

That the structure of the novel replays actions already described by Patrick in the first part undergirds the pivotal statement made about Haiti in the book: "In our country, for certain, history repeats itself more often than it does elsewhere" (93). But the lesson the novel ultimately teaches is that repetition need not carry the connotation of failure, as a statement such as this would certainly intimate, but can instead offer potential for revision, catharsis, mastery.

Most tellingly, and bringing this chapter full circle, the reader sees how history is replayed in Haiti in Depestre's long description of Carnival, in which people wear costumes and masks to represent the entire history of the island: from the native dress of the Arawak peoples who were the island's first inhabitants, forced to labor for the first waves of colonists and subsequently decimated by diseases, to the cowls of the French and Spanish monks who served as missionaries in the seventeenth and eighteenth centuries to caricatures of Napoleon Bonaparte and Toussaint L'Ouverture to imitations of the dress uniforms of the American GIs who occupied the country at the time the novel was set. The panoply represented by the costumed revelers is shown three times in the novel: first from Patrick's perspective, then from Hadriana's point of view, and later echoed again in symbolic form.

The novel creates a sense of narrative déjà vu when Hadriana describes an out-of-body experience she underwent while lying zombified in her casket. The sorcerer responsible for her state leads her to a cavern, explaining to her that her *petit bon ange*, soul, will be imprisoned here in a bottle, and her body will be made to labor for her zombie master. Showing her a collection of containers, her captor tells her:

> Here, I will enumerate for you at random some of your companions in imprisonment. In this old jar of Vicks Vaporub salve a petit bon ange captured from the cradle, the baby of a Levantine shopkeeper. In this pitcher a speculator of commodities meditates. The host of this carafe made of Bohemian crystal is a Marine Corps sergeant. This milk jug contains the good little angel of a little cobbler. The gentleman enclosed here is the soul of brother Jules, a schoolteacher from Brittany. His neighbor is the soul of an ex-president of the Republic. Further down, in the liquor bottle, a surrealist poet reflects; in this beaker officiates an Anglican bishop. In this seltzer bottle is detained a faggot painter, in the Chianti, a colonel of the Haitian Guard. (161–62)

Appropriately, the bottle chosen to house the petit bon ange of Hadriana is a magnum of French champagne, making reference to her heritage, the French colonial oppression that profited from the sweat of the African slave. The list of those zombified includes not only foreign aggressors, outsiders with commercial interests in Haiti, and foreigners who may have exercised undue influence over Haitian culture but also the elements—homosexuals, artists—that would be suppressed under some of the most repressive Haitian regimes and those who might be ousted, oppressed, or taken advantage of by would-be tyrants: a Haitian president, a member of the National Guard, a poor cobbler. This cabinet of zombies parallels the carnival, providing a menagerie of historical oppression.

In the hands of Depestre's houngans, zombification is the tool of the immoral, power-hungry element within the society of sorcerers. Though there is an obvious theme of retribution in the story, Depestre's zombie is not, as it is in Frankétienne's or Laferrière's novels, the symbol through which this revolutionary transformation is achieved: *Hadriana dans tous mes rêves* does not alter the zombie from an embodiment of slavery to slave rebellion; instead it is the novel's architecture that conveys revolutionary potential: foundationally, in the way the text appears to be constructed on top of Alexis's narrative and in the overlapping narratives of Patrick and Hadriana and the variegated patterns of narrative repetition. If there is no definitive redirection here of the zombie myth per se, then at least the novel makes use of the figure's association with return to house its commentary on the uses of literature, storytelling, and myth to revisit the past.

Alongside the visuals of the carnival—signifying the capacity to create and re-create at the community level—and its dark doubling in the individual zombie maker's catalog of victims, there are various ways that Depestre's *Hadriana* makes the point that it is not merely that history repeats itself in Haiti, but that it can be *replayed* that is significant, allowing the people a modicum of control over the past in their contribution to its retellings. In the middle section of the book, which depicts Patrick's quest for information on zombification, the story with which William Seabrook famously introduced the zombie to a European and US readership in *The Magic Island*, is related by Patrick's uncle Fefe. The very same narrative that touched off a flurry of pseudo-anthropological interest and cinematic exploitation of the Haitian myth, of Ti Joseph and his wife, Croyance, who accidentally feeds the zombies salt, is retold here, and if the zombies are not more powerful in this iteration, at least its inclusion here returns the story to the Haitian parole.

Back from the dead, the zombie may immediately suggest the ubiquity of Haiti's past. As an enslaved corps cadavre deprived of its death and forced to live in an unconscious present, it has long stood, to some, for Haiti's inability to be freed of the ghosts of colonial empire that spawned it. The scholar Rafaël Lucas has called the zombie "the archetypal figure of failure, the *creature* par excellence of the will to power," and he explains that some writers use the figure of the zombie to "question the meaning of the country's tragic historical path" (65; original emphasis). He quotes Louis-Philippe Dalembert's *Le songe d'une photo d'enfance*

(1993): "And what if the history of this Caribbean island were to continue to be a long tale of nightmares of bogeymen, flying ants, zombies, and the endless quest for the salt of true life?" (65; Lucas's translation). But this question is best answered by Depestre's already quoted line: "The history of colonization is the process of man's general zombification. It is also the quest for a revitalizing salt capable of restoring to man the use of his imagination and culture." The goute sel, first and foremost, restores to man his domain, mythic space. The narratives that abound about zombification offer a manner of wrestling with history, yet *Hadriana* is not merely about the Haitian's enduring past but also equally about the mythmaking and storytelling that we do (and I include in this category the trope of the zombie, and its *re*making). For this is the use of "imagination and culture" that is ultimately, for Depestre, the testimonial of a free people.[41]

As we have seen, the zombie, once a figure of disempowerment, both spiritual and political, and a symbol of the complete powerlessness of the people has become in recent years a demonstration of force. Within Carnival historical moments of national pain, like the US occupation, can be reclaimed. This is the type of symbolic revolution—a mythic conquest of historical events—that is seen in the transformation of the zombie myth as it reconstitutes postcolonial history and stakes a claim for the Haitian culture's sovereignty over its political oppressors, becoming less about a former slave state and more about its vibrant national imagination. To illustrate this point further, I bring together two long passages, one from Patrick Chamoiseau's introduction to *Creole Folktales* and the other from Dany Laferrière's *Pays sans chapeau*.

Chamoiseau introduces his collection of folktales thus: "Our stories and our Storytellers date from the period of slavery and colonialism. Their deepest meanings can be understood only in relation to this fundamental period in the history of the West Indies. Our Storyteller speaks for a people enchained: starving, terrorized, living in the cramped postures of survival" (*Creole Folktales* xii). Chamoiseau emphasizes the artistry of the griot, the storyteller, who had to craft stories that could be overheard by the master without causing alarm and yet still communicate his message to the slaves: "The Creole Storyteller is a fine example of this paradoxical situation: the master knows of his tales and allows him to tell them, and sometimes even listens to them himself, so the Storyteller must take care to use language that is so opaque, devious— its significance broken up into a thousand sibylline fragments ... to help camouflage any dangerously subversive content. And here again,

Edouard Glissant is right to emphasize that the Storyteller's object is almost *to obscure as he reveals*" (xiii; original emphasis).

In its early incarnation, the zombie had to speak of revolution without speaking of revolution; it had to suggest the slave's potential reservoir of power to be discovered even while it resembled an admission of complete subjugation, as in the narrative of the pathetic zombie and his grain of salt. This metaphoric fracture was retained in the zombie's commentary on dictatorship and postcolonial oppression. It is preserved in the zombie's dichotomy (slave/rebel) that is visible even in its uses in US cinema today, despite the fact that this is so often overlooked.

Consider now this passage from *Pays sans chapeau*, in which the narrator converses with one of the professors he has consulted.

> Have you forgotten the so-called anti-superstition campaign of 1944, in which the Church tried with all its force to destroy vaudou? They destroyed the temples, put in prison all the houngans, uprooted the mahogany, those great trees that house our memories....
>
> If they did all of that, how did you survive?
> By deception, my friend, we bypassed the enemy.
> How so?
> We made the Christian churches into vaudou temples.... Ha ha! hahahaha! ... we made the Christian saints into Vaudou gods. That's how Saint Jacques became Ogou Ferraille. The Catholic priests saw us in their churches thinking that we had abandoned our faith, when really we were actually in the process of worshipping, in our own way, Erzulie Dantor, Erzulie Fréda Dahomey, Papa Zaka, Papa Legba, Damballah Ouèdo.... All the gods had insidiously taken on the forms and the faces of the Catholic saints. We were "chez nous chez eux," at home at their place! (268–69)

As we saw in the previous chapter, Hollywood has been preoccupied by the zombie for nearly a century; and as we'll see in the next chapter, this fascination has only escalated in the new millennium. The Haitian zombie is definitely *chez eux chez nous*.

The figure of the zombie in part symbolizes history's enduring influence on the present and the persistence of (neo)colonial oppression despite the end of Empire, but it also allows for a mythic space in which change to the existent power structures can be conjured. In the mythologizations of the zombie narrative, symbolic revolutions transpire and conquests of metaphors are waged, with the end result that a nation's present condition can be reimagined and even the past can be retroactively reclaimed. I think of this as the technē of Carnival: the intentional donning of the vestments of the oppressor, the infusion of the Vaudou gods into the Catholic saints, the cultural colonization of spaces that have been historically oppressive and geographically off limits. I like to suppose that aside from the invisible army of zombies that waits to protect Haiti should any nation dare to threaten its borders, a very real, very visible zombie epidemic—the veritable obsession with zombies that we have seen take hold especially over the past decade not just in the United States, but internationally—is proof that we have all been occupied by the Haitian imaginary. And more than that, we didn't even notice, for we were enchanted by the griot, hearing only a lamentation of his subjugation when really he was celebrating his resistance.

4 / Textual Zombies in the Visual Arts

> *"Shadowing" by artistic precedents is primordial; it is the primary element that allows any art to be constituted as such, as a discipline that lives on at all. But often the shadowing in contemporary art is more literally spectral.*
> —HAL FOSTER, "THE FUNERAL IS FOR THE WRONG CORPSE"

I wanted to write this chapter (really, this book) without having to talk about Jean Rhys's *Wide Sargasso Sea*. In part, this was because I felt it was such an obvious choice, since it is one of the few Anglophone canonical literary works that includes a handful of references to zombies, including descriptions of people with "eyes like zombi[s]" (50) or looking like they had seen a "zombi" (100), imagery of live burial (after a character is poisoned, 137) and comparisons of the main character, Antoinette, to a blank-eyed doll or marionette under the control of other forces (149–50). But more than this, I could hardly add to the substantive discussion that has taken place in the past few decades regarding the zombie theme in this novel.[1] In a chapter titled "Obeah Nights" in her book *Jean Rhys at "World's End,"* Mary Lou Emery claims that "Antoinette has become a zombie, a dead person while living" (44), and many others have read the zombification in the text as literal, figurative, empowering or disempowering. In her important book *Fantastic Metamorphoses, Other Worlds*, Marina Warner writes, "Jean Rhys recuperates the phantoms that haunt the forest in *Wide Sargasso Sea*," rightly noting that "in a recursive move characteristic of postcolonial strategies, the zombie has been claimed as a figure not of servitude, but of occult and diffuse potency" (159). In the previous chapter, I illustrated this maneuver in Haitian literature, but I can offer little that hasn't already been said regarding this novel by the Dominican-born Anglo author.

More important than the zombies in the work, however, is the literary zombification the novel practices of Charlotte Brontë's *Jane Eyre*. Emery writes that its intertextuality "questions the moral values" of the classic novel (36). Sandra Drake calls the book "deliberatively derivative, an imitation, a copy. Its very existence derives from the English classical literary canon. It is a novelistic colony" (Drake 99). In the *Cambridge Introduction to Jean Rhys*, Elaine Savory describes *Wide Sargasso Sea* as "mostly a prequel" (79): "Rhys revisioned *Jane Eyre*'s lurid description of the Creole wife, which reflected nineteenth-century British stereotypes about white Creoles.... *Wide Sargasso Sea* is a writing back to *Jane Eyre* done before such intertextuality became identified as a widespread postcolonial response to colonial literary canons" (79–80).

Indeed, the practice of "revisioning" or "writing back to" precedent texts in a postcolonial maneuver is now well established. In "Postcolonial Literatures and Counter-Discourse," Helen Tiffin writes, "The rereading and rewriting of the European historical and fictional record are vital and inescapable tasks. These subversive maneuvers, rather than the construction or reconstruction of the essentially national or regional, are what is characteristic of post-colonial texts, as the subversive is characteristic of post-colonial discourse in general. Post-colonial literatures/cultures are thus constituted in counter-discursive rather than homologous practices" (99). Tiffin is describing here the postcolonial revision of canonical texts, what she calls "canonical counter-discourse" (100), in which category she specifically considers Jean Rhys's *Wide Sargasso Sea*, with its literary intervention in *Jane Eyre* that provides the backstory of Bertha Mason (née Antoinette Cosway) in the Caribbean, as the archetypal example. One might think of Rhys's unauthorized "prequel" alongside "allographic revisions" (11), as Rachel Douglas uses the term from Gerard Genette to describe works by Aimé Césaire, Edouard Glissant, and Derek Walcott, and this applies to others, like the South African author J. M. Coetzee's *Foe*, a revision of Daniel Defoe's *Robinson Crusoe*.

Rhys's *Wide Sargasso Sea* makes blatant the latent colonial context in Brontë's classic text, which—in the figure of Bertha, Rochester's Creole wife consigned to the attic—tied fears of racial miscegenation to Victorian concern with bloodline contamination, illness, and madness. Tiffin explains, "It has become the project of post-colonial literatures to investigate the European textual capture and continuing containment of colonial and post-colonial space and to intervene in that originary and continuing containment" (101). This phrase, "the textual capture and continuing containment of colonial and postcolonial space," is also an accurate description of what has happened to the zombie myth since the US occupation of Haiti. In thinking about cultural conquests in such terms, as seen in the case study of the zombie, one must work hard to clarify when something is intended as a subversive appropriation, or syncretic cultural creolization, and when is it merely cultural theft.

Rhys's work would be the most obvious choice to include in this study because of its direct references to the zombi and to Obeah more broadly, alongside its intervention in the lives of the characters created by Brontë. The novel recalls in its technique the zombie's return, or the redirection of a body now under new management.[2] As such, the novel *Wide Sargasso Sea* provides an example of a category I seek to label "textual zombies" when a revision or appropriation also makes use of the zombie or zombie imagery in a concrete way. In the best cases of textual zombies, the living dead act as a kind of calling card, illustrating the self-awareness of the maneuver and offering up a critique of acts of cultural conquest such as we saw enacted on the Haitian figure of the living corpse; but in many of these strange territories where dead narratives are reanimated in popular literature, there is no indication that such a rich vein runs beneath the surface.

The zombie, as a body that returns from the dead, neatly suggests figures of return and revision. This is why Meghan Sutherland's assertion of the cinematic zombie, "In some sense, every zombie film is a kind of remake" (64) rings especially true: *all zombies are inherently remakes.*[3] The zombie has been used as a means of literalizing a larger trend within literature, art, and popular culture: the propensity to revisit and rewrite canonical texts. I don't think this is merely because the zombie comes back from the dead, unlike, say, the vampire or the werewolf, but also because of the figure's long history as a narrative tool, one that, as we have seen, has been remade several times in the image of its user.

Like the Haitian zombie that was raised from the dead to serve as the witch doctor's slave, textual zombies are reanimated texts that are pressed into service by a different author to express the concerns of a new generation, or even another culture. A hallmark of postcolonial postmodernism, "restatements" or reanimations are widely found in literature and art—and although most make no reference to the living dead, in the case of what I call, using the terms textual zombie or textual zombification interchangeably, the content parallels the form: a reanimation of another's text directly references the zombie in order to reflect on its own process of appropriation. At best, such revisitations can be acts of resistance, providing insight into the problematic ways commodified culture depicts occupation or the conquest of both intellectual property and physical space.

To provide a complete taxonomy of textual reanimations here would amount to little more than an identification of a particular curiosity, and it is not my intention to fully sketch this rare phenotype. To do so, one would have to provide a complete species study of all zombified texts. On one side of the shelf, we would have to put those treasured revisions, like Césaire's *Une Tempête*, that do not contain any actual zombies but perform the gesture of zombifying a precedent text (in this case, Shakespeare's *The Tempest*) while putting special emphasis on themes of sorcery and conjure in what might be a similar gesture of recognition. On the other end of the shelf, one might find popular textual reanimates like "The Zombies of Lake Woebegotten" by Harrison Geillor (Night Shade Books, 2010), a takeoff on Garrison Keillor's *Lake Woebegon*; *Alice in Zombieland,* of which there are two versions, one by "Lewis Carroll and Nickolas Cook" (Sourcebooks, 2011), and one by Gena Showalter, a part of the White Rabbit Chronicles for Harlequin Teen (2013); *The Undead World of Oz* credited to "L. Frank Baum and Ryan C. Thomas" (Coscom Entertainment, 2009), and an entire series called Blood Enriched Classics many of which infuse zombies into classic works of literature, including, most horrifyingly, *The Adventures of Huckleberry Finn and Zombie Jim* by "Mark Twain and W. Bill Czolgosz" (Gallery Books, 2011).[4] My hesitation to write the chapter this way comes, in part, from a deep-seated nausea at the thought of putting Césaire on the same figurative shelf with a character named Zombie Jim, an obviously problematic reincarnation of the character often called "Nigger Jim" from Mark Twain's classic tale.[5]

While the trend has roots in fan fiction, the marketability of such revisions, or zombified texts, became clear with the 2009 best-selling publication of Quirk Books's *Pride and Prejudice and Zombies*. Eckart Voigts-Virchow describes the "recent afterlife of Austen" as but the latest instantiation of a much longer established trend, describing various Austenian appropriations, adaptations, mash-ups and fan-fic, of which *Pride and Prejudice and Zombies* is categorized under "Alternative Universe," "Pastiche" (for its imitation of Austen's style), and "generic crossover" (43). Although Voigts-Virchow notes, "It is probably not worthwhile to subject *Pride and Prejudice and Zombies* to a close reading New Criticism-style" (48)—a sentiment with which I reluctantly agree—we can note a few points of interest in the text's approach.[6]

Seth Grahame-Smith did not title his revision "Pride, Prejudice, and Zombies" but rather *Pride and Prejudice and Zombies*. Just as the word "Zombies" is tacked on here polysyndentonically, Grahame-Smith's contributions to the text come largely in the form of insertions of passages. Chapter 55, for instance, is very nearly Jane Austen's original text reprinted verbatim; chapter 56 begins following the original book word for word, but some pages in, one finds a slight alteration:

> "Miss Bennet," replied her ladyship, in an angry tone, "you ought to know, that I am not to be trifled with. But however insincere you may choose to be, you shall not find *me* so. My character has ever been celebrated for its sincerity and frankness, and in a cause of such moment as this, I shall certainly not depart from it." (Austen 439)

Here, Seth Grahame-Smith's version reads:

> "Miss Bennet," replied her ladyship, in an angry tone, "you ought to know, that I am not to be trifled with. But however insincere you may choose to be, you shall not find *me* so. My character has ever been celebrated for its sincerity and frankness, just as my killing powers have been celebrated as having no equal." (285)

Instead of merely offering Elizabeth Bennet a chilly reception, in Grahame-Smith's intervention, Lady Catherine issues her a duel. His additions mention not only zombies but also ninjas, pointing to the economic reality of Regency England that had been effaced in Austen's original text: namely, the fact that the English were supported by an empire stretching from the Caribbean to the Orient.

Voigts-Virchow muses, "What are the elements that make Austen texts so susceptible to being mashed-up, to become material in 'cultural jazz' and to be turned into this carnivalesque market place of affinity culture? In response, one may venture the classic, out-of-copyright status, the history of Austenite 'literature as furniture' reception, the modest scale and limited scope of her secluded universe, her domestic, anti-sublime aesthetics marked by a lack of emotional intensity (of which Charlotte Brontë complained), the clearly gendered texts and audience contexts, the ethnic 'purity' and national canonicity, the inherently conservative middlebrow iconicity" (44).

I can speak only to those (now several) versions of zombified mash-ups that infuse the undead into Austen's classic works, but I think the answer is to be found somewhere between the domesticity and the limited national and racial perspective of the original novels.

Edward Said cites Jane Austen's *Mansfield Park* as the perfect example of the kind of willful blind spot in the treatment of empire characteristic of European literature of the period. Said remarks how the eponymous property of *Mansfield Park* is tied to Thomas Bertram's slave plantation, but Austen "sublimates the agonies of Caribbean existence to a mere half-dozen passing references to Antigua" (291). Empire is kept decidedly offstage in the work of such authors, of which Austen is but one example in Said's estimation: "Yet most cultural historians, and certainly all literary scholars, have failed to remark the geographical notation, the theoretical mapping and charting of territory that underlies Western fiction, historical writing, and philosophical discourse of the time" (290). Reinfusing the Caribbean zombie, or even the Egyptian mummy, in canonical works points to this omission in the originals, still present though perhaps less obvious in the adoption of the other figures found in the recent Austen revisions, commonly but often inadequately referred to as "mash-ups" for their combination of genres: the sea monster, lycanthrope, and vampire.[7]

Instead of providing a more detailed bibliographic tour of this strain in contemporary literature, which generally unintentionally highlights the cultural appropriation of the zombie only by impotently repeating the gesture, I want to illustrate the way that some in the visual arts have taken the lead toward a use of the zombie that is more fertile. In examining various "textual zombifications," I want to consider whether the better among them amount to avant-garde apologism for the cinematic and cultural appropriation of the zombie or, even, recognition of the artistic conquests that figure as part of colonial empire's cultural apparatus.

My resistance to discussing Rhys's novel in this book was also personal. The spark—I imagine it now as if it occurred in Frankenstein's laboratory—that ignited in me the desire to first look critically at the zombie came out of a graduate course in which we were reading *Jane Eyre* as a transatlantic text. In brief, Bertha Mason was my first zombie. She led me to Lewton's 1943 film, *I Walked with a Zombie*, and to Jean Rhys's 1966 novel.[8] And now, all grown up, I want to get as far away from her as possible.

For the present discussion, I find that the most useful aspect of *Wide Sargasso Sea* is found in a line that has nothing to do with zombies. The poignantly unnamed character, who is clearly recognizable as Brontë's Rochester, refuses at some point any longer to call his wife "Antoinette," since her mother's name was Annette, and he begins to fear that she will inherit mental illness in her bloodline. Instead he calls her "Bertha," the name by which the reader knows Brontë's mad Creole. Antoinette says to her husband, "Bertha is not my name. You are trying to make me into someone else, calling me by another name. I know, that's obeah too"

(147). To me this line reveals the larger project of the novel: it is a bit of Obeah; it works some Vaudou on *Jane Eyre*, but in self-defense. The novel's appropriation of a European classic is not the same as the zombie's rebranding as an "American" cinematic monster, nor is it like the erasure of the identity of the renamed African slave that is referenced in the husband's change of Antoinette's name (like Olaudah Equiano become Gustavus Vassa; like Alex Hayley's Kunta Kinte become Toby). The latter examples rename for the sake of complete conquest, the former for cultural recovery: Rhys's novel allegorizes the subject of colonial empire striking back against such renamings, reclaiming what was once its own. A bit of Obeah itself, the textual zombifications that most interest me are those, like *Wide Sargasso Sea*, that have resistive potential to work against colonial empire and the postcolonial infrastructure that remains in its place.

In the spirit of this chapter's devotion to the visual arts, let's take, for example, a piece by Jean Hérard Céleur, Haitian sculptor and member of the Atis Rezistans collective, whose work I discuss briefly later: it is a roughly hewn wooden sculpture like a fetish but also an image of a saint, decorated with cast-off mass-produced junk—pieces of car tires, computer parts, the pan of an oscillating fan made into a halo, a crown of nails that pays homage to the Congolese nkisi.[9] Like many textual zombifications, this artist's work reappropriates or rescues something that has been damaging to or denigrated in his own culture. Céleur's sculpture consciously riffs on both Vaudou and Catholic iconography and plays in the key of cultural *métissage*. It acculturates and creolizes structures that have been forced on his people; with its inclusion of cheap, disposal circuit boards, his work sounds a lament for the country's dependency on the cell phone manufacturer and provider Digicel, Haiti's largest employer (Strom). In his atelier, sculptures made of salvaged materials extend to the ceiling. Outside, in downtown Port-au-Prince, a horizontal column of trash, mostly Styrofoam, blankets a water channel and looks to me at first like snow: so much poverty amid such a gross of commodities is, like the zombie, a paradox that isn't at all incidental.

As both Colin Dayan and Don Consentino note in separate discussions on the art of contemporary Haiti, such craftsmanship made from *objets trouvés* has a long-standing history in Haiti.[10] In her preface to the book produced out of the Fowler exhibition, Edwige Danticat writes that the Atis Rezistans of the Grand Rue emblematize the Haitian effort, especially pertinent in the wake of the 2010 earthquake, "to gather what is lost, as we ourselves have been lost[,] . . . to pick up our shattered pieces and build a world anew, be it in words or tears, ink on paper, sequins or glitter or paint on cloth or canvas, spray paint on rubble, discarded wood or metal, or even human remains" (Danticat 19). In doing so, this practice also intervenes to make something new not *with* the master's tools but *of* the master's tools. Renaming is easy; it's resurrection that is hard.

We have seen the way that American cinema zombified the folkloric Haitian zombie, turning a figure about colonial empire and enslavement to work in their own fields, and we have regarded the reconstitution of the zombie, post-Duvalier, as a symbol of empowerment for the Haitian people. In this chapter, I consider the way that figurations of the zombie in art metaphorize precisely this drama: the enslavement, the deployment of the myth, and the myth's rescue—or if that is too hopeful a term—its use by others more faithful to the zombie's original significations. In the visual arts, the zombie myth itself becomes an object to be salvaged.[11]

Art History

In the visual arts, the tradition of pseudo-allusion or not-quite-homage has a long history. In his essay "The Glorious Company," the eminent art historian Leo Steinberg presents a catalog of what have been variously called "appropriations," "cannibalizations," "borrowings," or pictorial "quotations," as he traces, for example, the distinct posture of a bowing horse from an antique ornament to a sixteenth-century Titian to a seventeenth-century Van Dyck to John Trumbell's 1790 *Portrait of George Washington*. "The possibilities," Steinberg explains of the artists' motives, "run from want of invention and labor saving . . . to an elaborate symbolism of supercession," or a means of "suing for membership in that glorious company of horsethieves which is the performing cast of the history of art" (9). Whatever the reasons for the piracy, the act itself is often discussed in the language of resurrection: Rembrandt "revives" the old, forgotten Haarlem master Heemskerck (28); "By altering their environment, a latter-day artist can lend moribund images a new lease on life" (25). But this phenomenon of *Wanderungen eines Motivs*, which permeates the history of art and for which Steinberg can find no *mot juste*, noting the insufficiency of that term migrating motifs—"as if the motif itself had the wanderlust and itch to shift from one work to another"—also seems to reveal something about the zombie myth's actual operation (9).

In the preface to their book *Art about Art* (1978), in which Steinberg's essay serves as an introduction, Jean Lipman and Richard Marshall describe the phenomenon of artistic reference thus: "The content or style, or both, of earlier works of art has been integrated into new works that comment, critically or satirically, on the art that provided the point of departure. It is the contemporary American artist's obvious practice, however, to make the borrowed art a recognizable, even blatant, element of the composition" (6). Steinberg himself clarifies the difference between the wandering motif and the intentional reference by comparing an anonymous etching circa 1640 that borrows various figures from different masters to a 1960 cover of the *New Yorker* drawn by Saul Steinberg, which includes easily identifiable artistic predecessors in the form of typographical designs and ornaments: "the seventeenth century draftsman disguised his ready-mades by integration, whereas Steinberg divulges all, *like a conjurer airing his paraphernalia*" (19–20; emphasis mine). The language here is telling; we might compare this to Foster's description in the epigraph of the spectral shadowing of artistic influence; the latter imparts a sense of being haunted, the former a willful act of sorcery.

If Steinberg, Lipman, and Marshall differentiate between modes of imitation that resemble incorporation (the inclusion of a foreign element, either apparent or oblique) and those that redirect an homage—something perhaps like reincarnation, as when Marcel Duchamp reinvents the Mona Lisa, or Andy Warhol or Robert Rauschenberg or Jasper Johns do—what interests me here is a type of artistic revivification that works more like zombification: when the style or content of a text or work is replicated precisely in order to do work that is specifically contra the context or associations we have with the original. Take, for example, the appropriations of the American artist Robert Colescott (1925–2009), which earn a handful of mentions in Lipman and Marshall's book but no in-depth discussion.

In the collection *African American Visual Aesthetics*, Lowery Stokes Sims calls Colescott "a forerunner of postmodernism" (101), noting his "method of deconstructing European traditions" (102). In *Laughing Fit to Kill: Black Humor in the Fictions of Slavery*, Glenda Carpio includes the work of Colescott in her discussion of a comedy of the grotesque for the way his paintings restage "well-known images from the high-art tradition" in order to critique racial stereotypes, such as Emanuel Leutze's *George Washington Crossing the Delaware*, Willem de Kooning's *Woman I*, Picasso's *Les Desmoiselles d'Avignon*, and others. In place of the familiar figures, Colescott inserts brash and jarring gendered and racialized tropes that draw on archaic or exoticized notions of blackness as well as images from popular culture.

In his appropriation of de Kooning's *Woman I*, for example, Colescott's *I Gets a Thrill Too When I See De Koo* (1978), the name of which, as Carpio notes, recalls the word coon but is also so mellifluous as to evoke the title of a blues song, features a horrific caricature of a mammy figure, in do-rag and with large, sagging breasts. A more detailed discussion of Colescott's work is not needed here. Carpio's important argument draws our attention to the way Colescott's appropriations are well-placed interventions that not only trouble contemporary attitudes to race and gender but speak back to elements of the artistic predecessors he possesses as well. In his imitation of abstract impressionism's scattered brush strokes, the fact that her breasts and grimacing face are the most defined area of her figure, claims Carpio, Colescott's mammy highlights the issue of embodiment: Which bodies get to be? Which body parts are privileged? Carpio writes, "*I Gets a Thrill* signifies on both the antebellum culture of which Mammy is a symbol *and* on the context of de Kooning's painting" (151).

Colescott's (re)appropriation of modernist works acts as a critique of the period's "primitivist" tendencies, including the use of Africanized faces, as seen in Colescott's redo of Picasso's *Les demoiselles d'Avignon* (1907) as *Les desmoiselles d'Alabama* (1985).[12] Art historians and critics like Ann Gibson and Lowery Sims have discussed the way that African American artists like Colescott retaliated against the troubling, exoticizing appropriation of African forms by modernists. *Selon* Georges Bataille, in the words of Sims, "the appropriation of symbols from the arts of nonwhite cultures had become problematic; as their 'transpositioning' negated their primary meaning" (104). Of particular interest here, Sims quotes Gibson on this technique: "[It] 'involves the mimicry of a style or statement,' but also a redirection of its accepted message: 'a repetition with a difference'" (108). This is a key element of the category I call textual zombification: in its most potent distillation, it specifically appropriates a form in order to redirect our attention to the period or conventions of the original, its limitations or failures. This territory already delineated in art history overlaps, as in a Venn diagram, with the larger field of textual zombies I delineate herein.

To give a concrete illustration of the borders of this province, we might say that *Les desmoiselles d'Alabama* draws closer to a textual zombification than, say, Colescott's revision of Vincent van Gogh's *The Potato Eaters* (1885), *Eat Dem Taters* (1975), which replaces European peasants with grimacing, cartoonish caricatures of African Americans. Because it is difficult to tell what if any critique this levels at van Gogh, or the postimpressionist period he represents, there doesn't seem to be a clear "redirection" of the original painting, even if this "restatement"—as John Russell called the work in a review of a retrospective at the New Museum of Contemporary Art—visibly lambasts Colescott's own contemporary society and its "myth of the happy darky."

Like Steinberg, Colescott has been called a conjurer: Carpio includes Colescott in league with fellow conjurers Kara Walker and Ishmael Reed because he "operates like a houngan and a boco, bringing to life the stereotypes that flourished under slavery" (148). Carpio notes the difference between the "conjuring" of Colescott and Walker and the "light humor of spoofing" of other appropriations, like Duchamp's mustachioed Mona Lisa (142). For Carpio, the conjuring occurs in the dislocation of stereotypes, the power that comes from laughing at them.

If Ishmael Reed's "Neo-HooDoo aesthetic," as seen in works like *Mumbo Jumbo* (1972), involves parody and bricolage, as Neil Schmitz writes, we can think of this type of "conjure," as Reed titled a collection of poems in 1972, as a composite composition: an improvised jazz variation, or a syncretic fusion, like Vaudou, of different source material.[13] Lisa Saltzman has called Kara Walker's work "a form of pictorial séance" that "brings back the bodies, the historical subjects, of the antebellum South, and renders concrete the ways those bodies, and that history, continue to haunt a nation" (57–58). Walker's images transform the types of idyllic silhouettes found in Edwardian nurseries into a nightmare plantation where bodies are violated, experience or inflict violence, sometimes becoming unrecognizable human-nonhuman hybrids in the process. The prevalence of metaphors comparing this type of work to sorcery is telling. In her discussion of Wifredo Lam's syncretic process, "combining the formal aspects of cubism and the spontaneous experimentation of surrealism," Sims writes that the artist discovered "a visual framework that correlated with the concepts of African Cuban belief systems: metamorphosis, hybridization, infusion," and the same seems to be implied of Walker, Reed, and Colescott. These artists' counter-appropriation is similar to what occurs in the zombie's recent artistic redirections that I profile in this chapter.

The key to this type of magic is in its transformation and combination of recognizable imagery: the same type of practice that we find in the creolization of the French language in Haiti or the melding of the Catholic saints with African belief systems in Vaudou. It is not a conjuring of something out of nothing but of salvaging something known, ordinary, innocuous, and even sometimes banal, into a symbol of resistance: like turning a jar of Vick's Vaporub into a powerful fetish object said to contain a dead man's soul, or recasting a racial stereotype so that it mocks the original mocker. Or, more extremely, when the tool of his oppression, like the machete used to cut cane, is turned against the master. Audre Lorde said, "The master's tools will never dismantle the master's house," but with a little Vaudou—by definition *not* the master's tools but something new made of them—might not the house itself be called upon to crush him flat?

I am not claiming that every reanimation of a previous work, such as Colescott's restatements, are textual zombies. Such willful resemblances of predecessor texts remind me of zombies, it is true, because they have a similar form but a new and often opposite use. But, then, I see zombies everywhere. An ecologist might think of them in the language of recycling, like the newest eco-friendly trend in Mardi Gras beads, Zom-Beads, made from recycled materials; a biologist, in terms of Batesian mimicry. I am not trying to brand all remakes that infuse an element of satire or critique as textual zombies; rather, I am exploring the ways that zombies are used in reanimations of texts, genres, or forms as a means of noting the larger cultural work of critique that they do. Although the category of textual zombification might be expanded to include works that do not literalize this technique by including zombies in them, for the present I am sounding only those waters where "there be zombies." That is, I limit this study of textual zombifications to pieces that replay or reanimate former texts while specifically drawing on the imagery of the zombie, as in the work of the San Francisco–based contemporary artist George Pfau.

As an introduction to Pfau's work, which I return to later in the chapter, I submit for examination his large-scale oil painting, *Zombies Ascending an Escalator* (2012). An overt restaging of Marcel Duchamp's *Nude Descending a Staircase* (1912), Pfau intertwines in the original work's cubist lines, which suggest the movement of limbs and the form of a woman walking, a scene from Romero's film *Dawn of the Dead* (1978) of zombies climbing the wrong way up an escalator. Though the scale of the zombies differs from the woman that the viewer still, out of habit, sees in the painting's angles, their articulation is in keeping with the abstract style of the original (which itself recalled Eadward Muybridge's 1887 serialized photographs of a nude woman walking down stairs), one that has been often revised or rerendered, as in a digitized reimagination called *Cheap Imitation* by David Rokeby (2002). As such, Pfau, like Rokeby, joins the "glorious company" of postmodern imitators and draws attention to what this mode does, its layering of significations upon those of its predecessors, which doubtlessly includes a commentary on photography, film, and what Benjamin called "art in the age of mechanical reproduction." Setting off the movement of bodies in his version with a reddish hue that is absent from Duchamp's original, Pfau makes immediately visible his intervention in the iconic image. The red color and horizontal lines in Pfau's painting suggest the toothed steps of the escalator and also faintly suggest the canvas-high female form in the original, as if they might be the bones of a spinal column or rib cage, the scarlet ribbon of the escalator recalling arteries and blood.

The enfolding of an image from an iconic zombie film into one of the classic images of modern art reveals that such imitation is inherently a kind of zombification of the predecessor work. In Pfau's piece the commentary of the textual zombification draws from the social critique of Romero's *Dawn of the Dead* regarding waste capitalism and the frenetic and yet constant pace of production and consumption, concretized (in the film as it is here) in the zombie's relentless cannibalism as in the escalator's unceasing movement even at the end of human civilization. In appropriating Duchamp's staircase, and superimposing on it an image from popular culture and a zombie film that had recently been remade at that—in 2004, by Zack Snyder—Pfau links Romero's critique of capitalism to the postmodern propensity to repeat, restage, remake: a merging of what Fredric Jameson notes in *Postmodernism, or the Cultural Logic of Late Capitalism*, is "the problem of postmodernism . . . at one and the same time an aesthetic and a political one" (55).

But if Jameson's interest in the examples of postmodern art he probes, like the difference between Andy Warhol's *Diamond Dust Shoes* and van Gogh's rendering *A Pair of Boots*, is on the "new depthlessness" and its "consequent weakening of historicity" (6), there is nonetheless a kind of textual zombification that emphasizes history to pose an explicitly postcolonial critique. Leaving aside textual zombies in the literary mode, like *Wide Sargasso Sea* or, perhaps (I say, begrudgingly), *Huck Finn and Zombie Jim*, what I propose to do here is curate an imaginary exhibition of real works with the intention of highlighting textual zombies as they exist in diverse media in the visual arts. This showcases those works that preserve the zombie's original critique of imperialism, using it to remind the viewer of the dehumanization of empire's subjects, or that comment on the zombie myth's own commodification. Often one finds that the postmodern, postcolonial mode of repetition with a difference illustrates the enduring effects of that oppressive past. Or else the depthless circuitry works to great political commentary, prompting us to question what has changed from the colonial period that first gave rise to the zombie myth to today's era of advanced globalized capitalism.

Antechamber and Chamber: You and Others

If this volume has given short shrift to zombie narratives that exist in video games and in texts of other varieties—in comic books and graphic novels, on radio shows and in other media—it is not because the author thinks these are unworthy of attention but rather because others are more suited to and have already done this work. For example, in a forthcoming collection called *Undead Souths*, Taylor Hagood discusses plantation zombies in Alan Moore's graphic novel *Swamp Thing* and a comic called *The Goon*.[14] The opening sequence of *Resident Evil 5*, which depicts a viral zombie outbreak in Africa, and which sets up the first player shoot-'em-up action in a way that allows for massive violence perpetrated against black bodies, begs to be read in the light of the zombie's complicated colonial history, and this work has been tackled by scholars like Tanner Higgin, whose dissertation was titled "Gamic Race: Logics of Difference in Videogame Culture."[15]

Zombie games now exist in a variety of forms, from Facebook applications to trading card and board games to live zombie tag played widely on college campuses. Though most video games that involve zombies belong to the larger category "first person shoot 'em ups," in which zombies are, it is now widely held, a convenient enemy—"all of the fun of killing someone with none of the guilt," as an undergraduate student explained to me—there are others, such as *Plants vs. Zombies*—a game in which slow-moving zombies try to make it past pea-shooting plants—that are not your garden variety blood fest. Some nonzombie video games, like *Call of Duty* and *Black Ops 2*, have a "Zombie Mode," and the zombie game *Left 4 Dead* has a mode where the gamer can *be* the zombie.

Beyond video games, in recent years a variety of avenues for people to play dead have been opened. In events like "Humans vs. Zombies" tag, or Zombie Walks, Zombie Mobs, Zombie Pub Crawls, Zombie Proms, or Zombie Runs, and coordinated *Thriller* dances patterned after Michael Jackson's 1983 video, which are discussed in the book's epilogue, the living dead have an extratextual un-life, one bound only by the contours of the freshman quad, for instance, or the city limits. These types of communally made zombie stories often involve the participation of makeup artists or the participants' own displays of ghoulish artistry and costume design; they challenge us to rethink whether the zombie, in this sense a collective and collaborative property, ever really left the domain of folklore. There are also many websites devoted to "zombie preparedness" that allow fans to facilitate meet-ups in real life, in online forums, and in chat rooms to co-create fantasies in which zombies have attacked and to build collaborative narratives about their survival strategies.[16]

Like the undead zombie, Robert Kirkman's graphic novel *The Walking Dead* is a story without a foreseeable end, and the multimodality of the series, existing in the form of a book, a television show, and, most recently, a video game, has been of interest to scholars for its reflection on the aptness of the transformability of the zombie—a creature that has and continues to mutate within and across genres. Whole volumes have been devoted just to this narrative in its various iterations.[17] Set as it is in the environs of Atlanta, *The Walking Dead* television show has drawn some attention to issues of race and the legacy of slavery. No doubt, a discussion of any of these forms of Kirkman's narrative and many others like it would fit within the pages of this book, but although I find fascinating those narratives or texts in which the form parallels the content—as with the seriality and multimodality of *The Walking Dead*, or where the narrative seems to be in conversation with the media in which it is ensconced, as when live zombie performance defies traditional boundaries of page and screen—my interest here is in elucidating this category of texts that themselves mimic zombification.

The emergent trend of the DIY zombie, for example, can be seen in a host of online applications, such as makemezombie.com, Zombieme.com, and deadyourself.com, where people can zombify themselves using only the technology of their computer's camera and a simple program to alter their image. Participants select from skin pallor shades and options like bruises and bloody gashes to remake themselves as zombies. Many such programs are offered free as publicity machines for movie releases, like the film *Zombieland* (2009) or the start of a season of AMC's *The Walking Dead*. In the same camp, there are a few viewer-interactive independently made short zombie films that are available online that I regret not being able to treat here, such as "Deliver Me to Hell," an advertising campaign for a company called Hell Pizza, in which the viewer chooses the actions of the protagonist to propel the narrative forward. The fact that such applications are deeply commodified, tied to television and film promotion, or are considered goods and services in their own right should not be overlooked. This was a startling and disturbing feature of what many characterized as the zombie boom or "zombie renaissance" (in Kyle Bishop's terms) of the first decade of the twenty-first century:

As the practice of zombifying oneself in an expression of powerlessness within the greater ideological network of capitalism—a trend that is most visible in the zombie walk phenomenon—came itself to be packaged and sold as entertainment, the bite was taken out of the zombie metaphor.

There is also at least one online outlet that invites people to insert themselves into a zombie movie: JibJab, an online e-card service, offers a Halloween e-card that features the customer and a friend inserted in footage from Romero's film *Night of the Living Dead*. This is achieved in a rather low-tech manner: passport-sized photos are uploaded into a program that pastes the new faces over those of the actors in the film. A simple animation program allows for the mouths to move to redubbed dialogue from a pastiche of scenes that are patched together to create a forty-five-second clip. The effects of this application, aptly called "Night of the Living Dead*ish*," may be rudimentary and the result comic, but nonetheless this intervention is indicative of a much larger and significant trend within the zombie mythos: the Mobius-like appropriation and counter-appropriation of the zombie commodity.

It has long been celebrated that, due to a copyright snafu, Romero's original zombie film has remained squarely in the public domain. This seems karmically satisfying if one remembers that, as stated in chapter 2, the origins of the zombie's entrance into cinema was due to its lack of copyright protection as a creature of folklore, but it is also fitting of the anticapitalist turn that the "American zombie" would take, in large part because of Romero's recasting of the figure—particularly in *Dawn of the Dead*—as a critique of consumerism. Because *Night of the Living Dead* is in the public domain, people have been able to make unofficial sequels of the film (the most recent of which is called *Night of the Living Dead: Resurrection* [2012], directed by James Plumb) and to stage live theater versions of the plot (*Night of the Living Dead Live!*) without having to pay Romero. Without fear of litigation, Romero's classic film can be screened anywhere and the film's images or vocal tracks can be hijacked; artists have remixed and recut the film in a variety of ways. For example, *Night of the Living Dead: Reanimated* (2009) is an illustrated version of the film that uses the original sound track and actor's voices set to a composite of artwork produced by about 120 artists and artist collectives from around the world.[18] Rather than list a director, the credits announce that the film is "*curated* by Mike Schneider." There are as many different styles as there are artists, and the diversity acts in defiance of the homogeneity we associate with zombification. In a kind of prologue to the film, a man in Dracula drag on a campy stage set complete with coffin winkingly admits the appropriation inherent in such a project: "One thing you can say about *Night of the Living Dead: Reanimated* is that it is the story of one group that rises up to consume the other."

My own imaginary curated exhibition of zombies in the visual arts and media would officially begin in an alcove with a row of computer terminals on which guests can use various functions to zombify themselves or use basic programs like that of the JibJab greeting card company to insert themselves in existing zombie movies. These would not be new programs but those that currently exist, with commercial purposes clearly labeled. The zombie, beginning with Romero's *Dawn of the Dead* and elevated by the anticonsumerist zombie walks of the first decade of the twenty-first century, had been visible as a sign of dissatisfaction with one's own embeddedness in the consumerist matrix, though it was itself an appropriation of a folkloric figure previously symbolizing colonial oppression. This first stage in the exhibition would highlight the neat trick wherein the act of self-zombification was offered or sponsored by various corporations or companies in a further appropriation of this symbol, wresting from it the subversive, antimaterialist/anticolonial message of the living dead and making it into one more saleable commodity or entertainment experience.

Whereas one can easily zombify herself online using an online application like those described above, artists like Bill Killen and Rob Saccheto offer their services to produce painted portraits for those who commission them, rendering their subjects as zombies from photographs for a fee exchanged via PayPal. There are many commercial artists whose work graces the pages of pulp fiction novels and comic books, or is used in video games or to create special effects in films, but the intersection of horror and the arts is beginning to garner serious critical interest.[19]

Following the antechamber with its invitation to self-zombify, the first room of my exhibition would aim to re-create the discordance of a zombie horde by melding the work of commercial artists—including, perhaps, a Schell Studios' zombie sculpture, like the type that might be used in a film or on the set of *The Walking Dead*; or the oil paintings of David Palumbo, an artist whose darker works have been used as book covers and as *Magic the Gathering* cards; or the horrifying special effects creations of the film artist Giancarlo Brajdic (afterlifemediasfxstudio.com)—with those whose work is laureled as fine art and which critics, curators, or the artists themselves have associated with the figure of the zombie. Take as examples of the latter the zombielike imagery of Matthew Barney's acclaimed *Cremaster Cycle* (1994–2002), or the many works by Adam Helms titled *Zombie* (2011–12), blown-up photographs silkscreened onto felt or cow skin, or Stephen Hendee's 2005 neon graveyard, titled *Some Zombies Stayed Home Last Night and Did Nothing* (stephenhendee.com). I would add to this uncanny and discordant collective the work of contemporary Haitian artists whose art is inspired by the Vaudou and folklore of their own culture. I include, for example, the work of the Atis Rezistans collective in Port-au-Prince, like the previously mentioned sculpture of Jean Hérard Céleur, whose tall figures made of wood, repurposed car tires, metal parts from discarded electronics, and defunct household appliances often recall the zombie or make reference to African ancestry and Vaudou rituals with their inclusion of items like bent nails and human bones. Danticat says that the striking juxtapositions in such works (as between a giant wooden erection and a human skull) are examples of a practice of artistic "maronaj." Adjoin to these sculptures the work of other Haitian artists that obliquely suggest the zombie: the surrealist, spiritual images of the painter Edouard Duval-Carrié; Mario Benjamin's *Untitled* series of 2000—zombielike visages made of spray paint and oil on canvas mounted on light boxes; Jean Phillippe Jeannot's altar bottle of Mazaka, a mixed media sculpture of a human body emerging from a coffin constructed of doll parts and wood; and perhaps even the ghoulish grimaces in the works of the Haitian American artist Jean-Michel Basquiat.

In riotous contradiction, my own attempt at métissage (rather than marronage), such pieces would be interspersed with the work of artists who are explicitly and concretely using the form of the zombie as it appears in Haitian Vaudou, as well as that which comes through its whitewashing in American popular culture. In the former group, I would include pieces like Dubreus Lhérisson's *Jan Zombi* (2003), in the style of the Vaudou *drapo*, sequined flags; various paintings by Wilson Bigaud and Hector Hyppolite that depict zombies, such as Bigaud's *Zonbi* (1953) and Hyppolite's *Zombis* (1946) or *Baron Samedi* (1975); or Frantz Zépherin's *The Resurrection of the Dead* (2007). In the latter category, we find the *Zombie Golf* installation by the art collective BANK (1994),[20] Richard Hawkins's ink-jet pictures of decapitated heads with titles like *zombie ben purple, 1997,* and *disembodied zombie ben green, 1997*; or Chad Robertson's series called "Rise" (2006) of ghostly and discombobulating images inspired by the films of Romero; or the improvisational video piece *Afterlifers: Walking and Talking* (2004) by the media artists HalfLifers.[21]

As a model for the kind of hodgepodge I hope to create, one could hardly do better than a show curated by the artist Travis Louie at the

Last Rites Gallery in Manhattan in spring 2012 called Zombie: 50 Artists Interpret the Word "Zombie."[22] This exhibition offered many fine inclusions that I would introduce in my own zombie cotillion, such as an example of the horror photography of Joshua Hoffline. And yet what is most telling about the larger phenomenon of zombies in the arts is the sheer number of textual zombies included in Louie's exhibition. Among the fifty selections, one finds many appropriations-as-zombifications, including Robert Kato Destefan's *The Walken Dead*, a silicone bust of the actor Christopher Walken as zombie, "with hand punched hair"; Stefano Alcantara's *The First One*, a zombified Christ; John Cebollero's simply and aptly titled *Repetition*, which is reminiscent though not an overt reprisal of Edvard Munch's *The Scream* (1893–1910); Mark Texeira's *Smile*, Mona Lisa zombified; Chris Seaman's *Lamb to the Slaughter*, a redo of Hans Holbein's portrait of Henry VIII (1698); Mark Garro's *Zom Sawyer*, a more surrealistic interpretation of Tom Sawyer, with perhaps a dash of Ralph Waldo Emerson in the mix, in an oil painting of giant transparent eyeballs and a figure fishing beneath a tree; Rick "Dienzo" Blanco's two pieces, *Blue Boy Rising*, after Thomas Gainsborough's *The Blue Boy* (1770), and *Boardwalking Dead*, a portrait of the actor Steve Buscemi of the show *Boardwalk Empire* as a zombifed version of his character, Nucky Thompson; and Dave DeVries's *Undying Hatred*, separate portraits zombifying DC Comics' characters Batman and the Joker. The last, nearly a zombification of a zombification, pays homage to Marvel's limited series *Marvel Zombies* (2005–6), by Robert Kirkman, author of *The Walking Dead* graphic novel.

Along with the pieces already mentioned, my cabinet of zombie curiosities would include photographs of the Canadian artist and model Rick Genest, who goes by "Zombie Boy" and whose body is his canvas, having transformed himself into an image of walking death with skeletal tattoos covering the majority of his person; Tony Dowler's large-scale, highly detailed watercolor map of Seattle as imagined after the zombie apocalypse; Jeriah Hildwine's series of paintings titled *Living Dead Girls* (2012) and his female *Zombie Hunter Portraits* (2012); as well as images of *The Safe House*, designed by KWK Promes and lauded on the Internet as the world's first "Zombie Proof House," and other architectural marvels that have been celebrated for their presumed ability to withstand hordes of the undead.

The exhibition thus far, with rooms cluttered with pieces of mixed media of diverse genres and by various artists, is orchestrated to create a feeling of crowding, oversaturation, and perhaps even, in confronting so

FIGURE 1 Jillian Mcdonald, *Zombie Loop*, 2006. Video installation, dimensions variable. (Photo by Aron Namewirth, courtesy of ArtMovingProjects.)

many copies—works that themselves zombify a well-known original—to produce an uncanny sensation. The next three rooms of our imaginary gallery, however, would each be devoted to the oeuvre of a single artist whose figurations of living death do much to showcase the concept of the textual zombie proper, illuminating both our culture's fascination with the zombie myth and the potential of the figure to comment on the zombie's appropriation itself.

Jillian Mcdonald: Double Vision

In Jillian Mcdonald's video installation piece *Zombie Loop*, the viewer is positioned between two simultaneously running screens: on one is projected the image of a lumbering, lunging zombie, and on the other we see the hapless victim, ceaselessly running, casting nervous glances over her shoulder. The two figures are clearly treading the same rural roadside, and they are plainly played by the same person. Both are Mcdonald herself, wearing the same cotton frock in each video. Aside from the transformative makeup and stiff gait of the zombie, the figures are identical. Much could be said about this doubling of the character of zombie and victim for what it illustrates is the crux of the zombie's ability to terrify: its emphasis on the uncanny process of "depersonalization," whereby someone previously known to the spectator becomes something strange, foreign (Dendle 4).

Mcdonald's oeuvre is thick with the undead, including lenticular images that, depending on the viewer's position vis-à-vis the photograph, show the transformation of a human figure into a grotesque zombie (*Zombie Portraits*, 2007); video installations that juxtapose zombies and vampires (*Alone Together in the Dark*, 2009); high-resolution videos of hauntingly beautiful zombies (*Field of the Dead and Undead*, 2011, and *A Prairie Horror*, 2011); as well as video-staging events, in which participants are invited to play dead, for example, an all-night performance piece staged at the Scotiabank Nuit Blanche art festival in Toronto in 2009 that dramatized a zombie film shoot and drew inspiration from Toronto's annual zombie walk, the first of its kind.[23]

Mcdonald's work deserves serious attention. Known mostly for her digital trespassing, in which she inserts her own image into films alongside celebrities, Mcdonald might say that her work questions what kind of catharsis the cinemagoer seeks. Often she creates a fantasy in which the female fan can objectify the male body, and her accessibility invites the ordinary woman to occupy her space just as she has occupied the place of the star or starlet. Most famous is *Screen Kiss* (2005), in which the artist positions herself as a jilted fan desperate to get the attention of the actor Billy Bob Thornton, a video of various kissing scenes from fairly easily identifiable Hollywood movies. Mcdonald has inserted herself into the shot in place of the lover and shares a digital kiss with Johnny Depp (twice, once in *Sleepy Hollow*, 1999, and once, in drag, in *Before Night Falls*, 2000), Vincent Gallo, Billy Crudup, Ben Stiller, Angelina Jolie, Daniel Day Lewis, Gary Oldman, and Ewan McGregor.[24] Leaving this aspect of her work aside, I could still devote a whole room of my exhibition just to that subset of her works—which is but a subset of her zombie portfolio—that could be considered textual zombies.

In pieces like *Field of the Dead and Undead*, for example, Mcdonald investigates the zombie's uncanny embodiment by illustrating the moment of its transformation, but in *Zombie Loop* we find something different: that moment is both present and absent.

Mcdonald explains that the viewer's location positioned between two walls on which the images are projected puts him or her simultaneously in the place of both zombie and victim. One is not able to see the two screens at the same time but must turn to look either at the fleeing damsel, and thus find him or herself in the zombie's place as pursuer, or at the zombie, and thus step into the role of prey. Of course, there is a third location offered, as one perceives oneself as the spectator witnessing an ongoing drama. In its structure, then, *Zombie Loop* explores the role of the viewer; however, the spectator is pushed away as much as embraced. The climax of the piece, the anticipated attack and subsequent transformation of the victim into a zombie, is continually deferred. Because the projected images are run on a continuous loop, "no one ever gets attacked, and no one ever gets eaten" (Mcdonald, pers. comm.). As such,

FIGURE 2 Jillian Mcdonald, *Zombie Portrait: Changah*, 2007. Lenticular object, 40 × 30 in. (Photo by Sean Colon, courtesy of the artist.)

the viewer may experience the work as a suspension of action. However, because the zombie is plainly the same woman as the victim, there is also the sense that the spectator has been deprived of the pivotal moment of metamorphosis. And thus the piece is a "loop" not just in technical terms but also as a description of the effect it has on the viewer, who may feel an alternation between relief and frustration, as well as a push and pull between the ambivalent positioning in the (non)event. *Zombie Loop* thus provides a different understanding of the textual zombie than those (like even her nonzombic digital invasions of film) that dramatize appropriation.

Alternatively, we might say that textual zombies are texts that approximate the zombie in their form as well as in their content. *Zombie Loop*'s precise balance between parallel perspectives of the same woman as damsel and zombie emulates the zombie myth's dialecticality. The inescapable video loop draws attention to the embodiment of the zombie and the relentless hunger that is never satisfied: this is also like the chain of significations, ever building one on the next, in the cycle of appropriation and counter-appropriation seen in the zombie myth's history.

In a room across from Jillian Mcdonald's *Zombie Loop*, I would display a video of her live performance piece *Horror Makeup*, decorating the walls in between with several of her lenticular *Zombie Portraits*, for their literalization of the parallax image that the zombie projects.

In the 2005 performance event, *Horror Makeup*, Mcdonald got on a subway with her makeup kit. Over the course of her ride she transformed herself not into a professional woman ready for work—an everyday occurrence often witnessed during a morning commute—but into a hideous, decaying zombie. A film of the live performance was displayed in Brooklyn, New York, from September 8 to October 15, 2006, and the exhibition notes explain some of the issues that are piqued by this hair-raising display: "This work takes cues from the legion of women who

FIGURE 3 Jillian Mcdonald, *Horror Makeup*, 2006. Performance and video, 6:30 min. (Video stills courtesy of the artist.)

perform beauty rituals on the subway in a curious private zone where they are unaware of anything outside their activity, and the rising cult of zombies in popular culture, where zombie gatherings and zombie lore flourish. Locating the audience physically in the subway performance space positions them as both voyeurs and potential victims" (Mcdonald, *Horror Makeup* exhibition notes).

The piece self-consciously draws on one of the most fascinating features of the zombie myth, the interruption and confusion of private and public space. As the artist suggests, this conflation is very much a feature of the recent phenomenon of zombie gatherings, but it also speaks to that definitive element of the zombie, which some, like Viktor Shklovsky, have claimed is the basis for all art—the boundary transgression between strange and familiar.[25] Mcdonald's was a zombie performance aside from the fact that it performed a woman's transformation into a zombie because it presented the live viewer, the first-generation audience of unwitting subway spectators, with an unfamiliar element in a familiar setting.

The performance was chronicled by a hidden camera and by a journalist for the *New York Times* who wrote, "Only when she slipped in a pair of green teeth and began daubing her face with fake blood did people start to stare, exchange meaningful glances and roll their eyes. When the train reached Morgan Avenue in Bushwick, the woman stood, grimaced delicately and staggered to the doorway. As the man with the messenger bag hurried out behind her, one of the noisy women hissed, 'I think it's performance art'" (Kino).

The woman, of course, was right. And as a performance art piece, we can think of this text as not being bound to a medium. The film of *Horror Makeup* is not the piece. The piece is the "happening" that occurred on that subway train in 2006. The original event is irrecoverable, and what we have of it, the record, is merely its digital trace. This performance is sort of an antizombie: an ephemeral ghost, as opposed to the enduring corpse it leaves behind. As such, we might consider this work as an example of an extratextual zombie: Mcdonald's *Horror Makeup* event allows the zombie to step out from the pages of the book, the cinematic screen, the ones and zeros of a computer game's code, and live (or not live, as the case may be) in our world, as a metaphor bound to no medium. And yet this extratextual zombie is still a textual zombie after all: in its form it seems like a reanimation of the kind of performance event staged by the artist Adrien Piper, who "carried out a series of 'self-transformations' in which she intentionally disfigured herself in order to provoke responses from people in the streets, the subway, the Metropolitan Museum of Art, and the library" (Brentano 51).[26] *Horror Makeup* is itself a kind of reanimation of the history of performance art.

I enjoy pondering these moments when the zombie seems to be more than just a metaphor but something rather like tone painting in music, an effect that provides commentary on itself and its own technē, as if underscoring the *meta* (as in "with" self; in metamorphosis, self-transformation) in *meta*phor (from meta-pherein, "to carry over," in which meta connotes "after" or "beyond"). If a metaphor is a word that bears the meaning for another, then perhaps all metaphors are zombies. But one of the questions this book seeks to answer ultimately is what kind of catharsis is sought by the wielder of the zombie metaphor, and Mcdonald's work allows us to watch the itch being scratched as she pries the zombie free from its Hollywood frame.

Her work makes use of images from movies (cinematic appropriations or zombifications) in various ways: a high-definition video, *Apocalypse Zombie* (2009), repurposes a scene from the film *The Quiet Earth* (1985). *The Screaming* (2007), an eleven-minute video, is a composite of various scenes from horror films, including Lucio Fulci's *Zombi 2* (1979).[27] Either of these pieces might be found in my exhibition. As a transition to the next room, however, I would display a series of drawings dating from 2010.

In ink, watercolor, and gold and silver pencil on paper, Mcdonald's *Body Count Drawings, Zombie Series*, is simple and low-tech compared to her digital, video, and web-based works but just as visually striking. The artist renders a visual "body count" of the films *Night of the Living Dead* and *Day of the Dead* on separate sheets of paper, creating a field crowded with "All the Undead" of each film. On another sheet, she provides us with a sparer collection of the easily recognizable dead, numbered in the

FIGURE 4 Jillian Mcdonald, *Body Count All the Undead in "Day of the Dead,"* 2010. Ink and watercolor and gold pencil on paper, 30 × 22 in. (Courtesy of the artist.)

order in which they die in the film and with a corresponding key. Visually, this work reminds me of George Pfau's interactive web painting, *Zombieindex.us* (2013), which is the next stop on our tour.

George Pfau: Blurred Lines

A large watercolor, colored pencil, and ink drawing of a pan-zombie horde, *Zombieindex.us* (pronounced "us") is online and interactive. On the page called "Zombies," viewers can zoom in on the various figures for a closer look at each one. Some are rendered in sharp detail in black and white, others in vibrant color; still others are a series of dots or a smear of color only abstractly suggesting a human form or a mass of connective tissue. On the page titled simply "Names"—which in its pictorial construction might remind one of the Vietnam Memorial in Washington, DC—the viewer is invited to click on the red letters in a collection of Pfau's influences. Hyperlinks provide channels to a barrage of articles, book reviews, Youtube clips, websites, and other points of interest for the zombie enthusiast. The zombie jubilee presented in the drawing and the live names provide a plethora of information fitting for the typical cinematic zombie mob and of the best films' critiques of capitalist surplus. Standing (or sitting) before it, one is mobbed by this piece: the scope and spectrum of the bodies included in the image and the sheer amount of information provided in the hyperlinks are overwhelming. This, too, then, is a moment in which we find the form of the artwork approximate the content.

A zombie expert in her own right, Annalee Newitz, author of *Pretend We're Dead*, writes of the piece on io9.com, "The zombie's plurality is what artist George Pfau has tried to capture in his latest piece of interactive art, *Zombie Index*. When you go to the site, you'll see an intricate painting of thousands of figures, each standing in for a different kind of zombie. There are orgy zombies and flesh-eating zombies, alongside plague zombies and crap I can't even identify."

Of the piece, Pfau has written, "The visual ideas I've been thinking about involve the amount of information necessary for a figure, or human, or zombie to be recognized. So, I've included a lot of variety in this regard: from stick figures, to blobs, to outlines, to full color renderings. Lots of the images are invented, but many actually recognizable, and nameable, as in depictions of Michael Jackson, or Tarman from *Return of the Living Dead*, etc." (artist's statement).

In its appropriation of recognizable figures, *Zombieindex.us* is a textual zombie. My favorite inclusions are in deference to the Haitian zombie: Clairvius Narcisse, Baron Samedi, and the skeletal zombies of a 1950 painting by Wilson Bigaud. It even includes textual zombies within textual zombies, as some of Pfau's own compositions are miniaturized and included in the *Zombieindex*, like *Zombie Maison*, a recasting of Louise Bourgeois's *Femme Maison* (1947), in which in Pfau's intervention the house from *Night of the Living Dead* is perched atop the female body. But the piece also challenges us to think about what a zombie *is* and why Pfau includes each of the figures that he does. It acts something like a reverse "Where's Waldo," where each figure encountered must be considered, not passed over—shifting the emphasis from the individual celebrated under capitalism to something like a truly equivalent, if terrifying, collective.

If I would begin the room devoted to George Pfau's textual zombies with a large touch screen version of *Zombieindex.us*, I might flank this installation with projections of some of Pfau's video art. A two-minute piece called *zombie (swallows the world, swallowed by the world)* reminds me somewhat of Bill Viola's *The Crossing* (1996) in its creation of a state of suspended uncertainty. In Pfau's video a suffused golden light is blocked by a vaguely human shape that seems to be slowly advancing toward the camera; though it is only two minutes long, the viewer's deprivation of focus, confounding the eye's efforts to make sense of the form that appears to emerge, creates a sense of potentially stressful anticipation, even as the aureate glow is warm and inviting.

Another video, *Between I and Us* (2012), is a collaboration with the blues singer Augusta Lee Collins that weaves together lyrics from Otis Redding and Etta James and "snippets of dialogue from zombie films like *Night of the Living Dead* and *28 Days Later*" (Pfau, artist's statement). Central to this piece, and to all of Pfau's explorations of the zombie form (including sculptures made out of human skin and other materials), is the "blurry line that divides and connects one body to another, or a body to its surroundings" (Pfau, artist's statement); here the melding happens at the level of language.

Yet some of his most stunning textual zombifications are pin sharp in their distinction between the body and the surrounding environment. A few illustrations zombify Umberto Boccioni's futurist sculpture *Unique Forms of Continuity in Space* (1913), combining the hard angular form of the original with the content of a waterlogged zombie from Lucio Fulci's *Zombi 2*. A series of letterpress prints depicts zombies that are recognizable from iconic films rendered in the style of medical illustrations, combining traditional Renaissance postures—like the man holding his own skin open to reveal his innards—with the familiar form of the large, bald zombie ripped from *Dawn of the Dead*;[28] or a skeletal study of Tarman from *Return of the Living Dead* (1985), or a map of the circulatory system of the cheerleader from *Land of the Dead*. For the sake of the extreme disjunction between these black-and-white, thin-line drawings of the medical series and Pfau's Zombiescapes (2012–13), wherein moments from zombie films are re-created as colorful impressionistic oil paintings, I would hang them on opposite walls.

Pfau borrows a style we associate with the impressionist painters, in muted pastel color palette, dappled light and mottled shadow, and short brush strokes ranging from precise to pointillist. He explains that the influence for this stylistic adoption was the need to create human forms "on the verge of recognition" (Pfau, artist's statement). In this series, of which there are at least twenty-nine paintings, ranging in size from small (9 by 16 in.) to medium (14 by 22 in. and 40 by 30 in.), Pfau is most interested in the blurriness of the zombie, the body's breakdown in life as well as death, and the way that an impressionist style can approximate the diffusion of the body into its environment. Pfau writes, "The landscapes are rendered in oil on linen allowing for a situation in which figures visibly blend into their environment, and vice versa" (Pfau, artist's statement). Indeed, in contemplating such works, the viewer must squint. Does this dot of paint symbolize a patch of dirt or a human head? Is it the head of a zombie or a human?[29]

Pfau's Zombiescapes render scenes from popular horror cinema, what Robin Wood called "our collective nightmares" (78), into breathtaking landscapes. Most simply, these paintings are legible as textual zombies for their appropriation of both the material of the movies and an array of artistic styles associated with impressionism, pointillism, and neo-impressionism. Even an image of an indoor mall from (you guessed it) *Dawn of the Dead* or a street scene of the Winchester pub from *Shaun of the Dead* (2004) becomes a thing of beauty. And yet there's much more to these paintings than just this transmission to a new stylistic medium. The composition is not Pfau's own design, for he excises a precise shot from these films, but the choice of which moment to render on canvas is significant. The true genius here is perhaps, like that of a film editor, knowing where to cut.

Some of the chosen moments are still and quiet, what we might expect of a landscape painting: a snowy field, a Ferris wheel at night, a bridge with no one on it, the light suggestive of early morning. Others seem curious subject matter for the frame: a helicopter in a field, with blues, greens, and yellows that seem right out of van Gogh's paint box; a car abandoned on a roadside, human figures distant, off-center, apart. Still others are brimming with human forms: a mass in a parking lot done in all the hues of Claude Monet's series on the cathedral at Rouen, or a mob of dabs, the same drab color as the trees, watched over by the visage of Ché Guevara, painted on a building's facade, an extraction from the film *Juan of the Dead*. Appropriate both to the zombie's paradoxical nature and to the cinematic medium itself run at twenty-four frames per second, Pfau's Zombiescapes seem to move and yet do not move, as the eye strains to focus the pixilated images into recognizable forms.

Seen together, the hum of tension—perhaps the staccato brush strokes contribute to the feeling—is palpable, as the viewer peruses the collection of freeze frames. Because of the buzzing, pointillist brush strokes, there seems to be movement within the stillness and noise within the silence. Looking at some of the arrangements—a prison yard with figures on either side of high fences, a car crash with figures milling about the streets—the suspension of action becomes doubly uncanny since the scenes are already familiar from the moving pictures that are their antecedents.

FIGURE 5 George Pfau, *Landscape (Zombi 2)*, 2012. Oil on linen, 14 × 22 in. (Courtesy of the artist.)

Pfau will tell you his choice to adopt the impressionist style came out of not only his interest in the zombie's penetrability, its blurry borders; he was also influenced by Camille Pissarro above other artists of the period for his anarchist politics (pers. comm.).[30] Even at the surface level, Pissarro is a wise choice for the nineteenth-century artist's attention to the rural laborer, the cityscape as well as the landscape, and the antibourgeois element in French society, themes endemic in his work that communicate with the long history of the zombie myth and its development in cinema. An art historian might make much of the fact that Pfau reincarnates Pissarro rather than another impressionist. Especially common in Pissarro's oeuvre is a preference for certain viewpoints, looking down upon an urban scene from a greater height—what seems to be a common angle in zombie movies, perhaps suggestive of the possibility of a survivor stranded above the throng—and the prevalence of certain motifs, particularly the road, both for its thematic of the journey or the trial and the structural feature of dividing the canvas or the frame.[31]

But a deeper look at Pissarro's biography reveals a commonality with the zombie's origins: Pissarro was born in 1830 on St. Thomas, an island in the West Indies, "to a French Jewish father from Bordeaux, and a mother with Creole origins from Santo Domingo" (Pissarro, *Pioneering*

FIGURE 6 George Pfau. *Landscape (Dawn of the Dead, Parking Lot)*, 2011. Oil on linen, 14 × 22 in. (Courtesy of the artist.)

Modern Painting 17). That he was the *only* impressionist artist with direct ties to the Caribbean makes him the ideal candidate for zombification.[32]

Indeed, Pissarro was not merely born in St. Thomas, but grew up there. Because of a scandal that rendered the family social pariahs in the community, he attended school alongside the children of slaves. Though his early works featured St. Thomas landscapes, such as *A Creek in St. Thomas* (1856) or *Antillian Landscape, St. Thomas* (1856), and even depicted black figures, such as *Woman Carrying a Pitcher on Her Head* (1855) or *Two Women Chatting by the Sea* (1856), these works are realist and not exemplary of the impressionist style that Pissarro is commonly credited with fathering. Though many scholars attribute Pissarro's unique perspective on French society to his outsider status—as a Jew, a Danish citizen born in St. Thomas, and his time in Venezuela and the American colonies—"he left for Paris in 1855, never to return to the New World" (Pissarro, *Pioneering Modern Painting* 17), and it is thought that Pissarro did not paint St. Thomas or its subjects after 1857 (Stern). Nonetheless, one art historian notes the lasting influences of his early experiences.

> Camille Pissarro must have carried these images of nature as seen in St. Thomas and Venezuela with him to France in 1855 and it is worth pondering whether he ever recounted his memories to Paul

FIGURE 7 Camille Pissarro, *Rue de l'Épicerie, Rouen*, 1898. Oil on canvas, 32 × 25 5/8 in. (81.3 × 65.1 cm). Metropolitan Museum of Art. (Courtesy of Artstor.)

Gauguin when they met towards the end of the 1870s. Certainly Pissarro reached Paris with his interest in landscape and peasant life already aroused—the two subjects which he was later to develop at length.... Add to this the advantage of seeing landscape under the intense light of the tropical zone and one can appreciate how Pissarro arrived in Paris as a nascent Impressionist painter. (Lloyd 19)

Whether or not one is convinced that the quality of sunlight in the Caribbean may have influenced Pissarro's impressionist style is irrelevant to the point at hand. The correlation I mean to draw out here is that of Pissarro to Paul Gauguin and influence to appropriation.

Textual zombies are reanimations of the texts or images of others to represent zombies figuratively or narratively, textually as well as literally, and the works of Mcdonald and Pfau showcased here are prime examples. Is Pfau's textual zombification of Pissarro a means of paying homage to the only impressionist painter who had a direct relationship with the slaves of the Caribbean? Or is it more sinister, a punishment for his having turned away from them to represent European laborers and their plight?

I favor the former interpretation because Pfau's treatment of these isolated frames from zombie movies strikes me as profoundly loving, a compliment to both Pissarro and various film directors that stages a conversation between them about the differences between influence and appropriation. But if the tension between the two possible readings is ambivalent, that, too, is in keeping with the zombie's paradoxicality.

What is no more than subtext in the work of Pfau—a labor demanding biographical research and meditation on the larger meaning of impressionism and the place and time period out of which it comes, the acme of European bourgeois society, built on the backs of the poor at home and slaves abroad—is explicit in another textual zombie, which definitively involves a tropological insistence on repetition in order to revisit and rewrite/right a history of political, colonial, and postcolonial oppression. In the next work I want to examine, a textual zombification plays with repetition and revision to critique (post)colonial appropriation in a manner in which the figure of the zombie signifies an act of redemptive or resistive counter-appropriation. In a tidy reversal, Pissarro's real-life protégé, Paul Gauguin (who instead of moving from the colonies to the French capital like his mentor, sojourned from Paris to the Polynesian islands to the benefit of his artistic career), is zombified by the artist Debra Drexler in an installation devoted entirely to his transformation.

The Zombification of Paul Gauguin

In March 2005 New York's Annex "White Box" gallery exhibited a multimedia installation by Debra Drexler called *Gauguin's Zombie*.[33] The exhibition displayed an eclectic assemblage of objects: a fax machine framing an outgoing message, various printouts of e-mails, and homemade picket signs with cryptic slogans like "Something is stirring at the National Ethnographic Museum!" A shaggy hut constructed of palm fronds stood in one area of the gallery, offering museum patrons a three-dimensional re-creation of a Tahitian lean-to. By means of these objects, as well as woodcarvings and woodcuts, vibrant watercolors alongside fictive journal entries, and oil paintings ranging in size, a bizarre tale is spun.

The *Gauguin's Zombie* installation weaves the following macabre yarn. In what is presumably the present day, an ethnographic museum decides to display the embalmed cadavers of famous artists. Calling the exhibition "The Fathers of Modern Art," they plan to display the corpses of the artists rather than their works. During the "restoration process," however, something unspecified causes Gauguin to reanimate. At the same time, protesters objecting to the display demand that the bodies be repatriated. Gauguin, now an animate corpse, is put on a plane to Paris.

In France, Gauguin's zombie feels lost and alone even though he is always followed by the Tahitian *tupapa'u*, specter of death. He tries to take pleasure in the things he loved in life, like prostitutes, but he is now a putrid corpse, shunned by all. Eventually he meets Vinnie Begone, a postmodern artist whom he mistakes for Vincent van Gogh. Begone's oeuvre consists of the solicitation of copies of great works by master forgers. When he finds this ersatz (or erstwhile) Gauguin and discovers that this awkward, noisome man can perfectly replicate the works of the postimpressionist, he organizes a new show to consist of what he incorrectly assumes are counterfeit Gauguins. For a while, Gauguin's zombie finds joy in re-creating his own artworks, but ultimately he feels unfulfilled, and the exhibition concludes with Zombie Gauguin longing to return to the region where he died.

The viewer's experience of the exhibition as a work of textual zombification can be conveyed by a cursory glance at the large-scale oil paintings: the zombie theme is conveyed as much through the form as the content of the works. Nearly each painting in the exhibition incorporates some element from one of Gauguin's classic pieces, reworks one or more of his painting's poses, or is very nearly an exact replica, with

FIGURE 8 Debra Drexler, *Gauguin's Zombie*, 2002. Installation at Honolulu Museum of Art, featuring *Old Habits*, oil on canvas, 72 × 72 in. (Courtesy of Honolulu Museum of Art and the artist.)

a few minor alterations. In one of the images above Drexler reworks an original, *Hina Te Fatou* (also called "The Moon and the Earth") (1893), putting Gauguin's zombie in the supplicating pose of the young female figure and transforming the head of the male god into a travel poster. *Zombie Employment* is a composite of Gauguin's original masterpiece *Where Do We Come From? What Are We? Where Are We Going?* (1897) and Gauguin's *Van Gogh Painting Sunflowers* (1888), but here it sets Vinnie Begone in the role of van Gogh, as if the two are painting side by side in his studio. One of Gauguin's most recognizable pieces, *Two Tahitian Women* (1899), in which one of two half-clad women is holding a bowl of what appears to be fruit or flowers, becomes in Drexler's reimagination the scene of Gauguin's reanimation: the women are (re)attired in medical scrubs, and the bowl contains some mysterious element of the embalming process; the newly reanimated Gauguin rises from a crouch, naked, in a posture suggesting birth.

Drexler's reworkings of Gauguin's paintings are a zombie project as well as a project representing the zombie: these are essentially the dead works of Gauguin made strange and given new life, but they

FIGURE 9 Paul Gauguin, *Two Tahitian Women*, 1899. Oil on canvas, 37 × 28 1/2 in. (94 × 72.4 cm). Metropolitan Museum of Art. (Courtesy of Artstor.)

FIGURE 10 Debra Drexler, *Gauguin's Zombie*, 2002. Installation at Honolulu Museum of Art, featuring entry woodcarving and *The Awakening*, oil on canvas, 72 × 74 in. (Courtesy of Honolulu Museum of Art and the artist.)

are definitively refashioned as a critique of Gauguin's work, and its, I would say, starkly uncritical chronicle of empire. Drexler's operation on Gauguin functions as a biting (but, I think, accurate) assessment that Gauguin's representation of the people of Tahiti is like a zombie: substanceless surface, form without content. Drexler's installation also points to a troubling absence in Gauguin's oeuvre: the acknowledgment of his act of cultural appropriation. In this way—and in the subplot of the false forgeries that Gauguin's zombie produces for Vinnie Begone, who bears an eerie resemblance to Gauguin's long dead friend van Gogh—Drexler highlights the zombie's sense of uncanny return, but most concretely the textual zombification of Gauguin's originals dramatize the zombie as a figure of appropriation and counter-appropriation.

Drexler's exhibition offers us a concise framework in which to examine many of the central elements of the zombie narrative. The emphasis on narrative déjà vu and the play with repetition and revision neatly parallel the use of the zombie in Caribbean literature, raising the specter of the cyclical nature of history discussed in the previous chapter.[34] Most important, however, *Gauguin's Zombie* offers us an opportunity to examine the central elements of the most successful "textual zombies" and to articulate the difference between insensitive and resistive acts of cultural appropriation.

Perhaps it is best to start by asking a simple question: Why does Drexler choose the French artist Paul Gauguin to zombify? Though Gauguin's politics may have been anticolonial when it suited him, there is no doubt that he came to Tahiti because of a deeply entrenched exoticism and that his work portrays a rather one-sided view of colonialism. Stephen Eisenman has argued that postcolonial criticism has been too quick to dismiss Gauguin. In *Gauguin's Skirt*, Eisenman claims that Polynesian sexuality is depicted as a powerful force in the artist's work. This may be true, but Gauguin nonetheless benefited from his power as a white male colonialist in Polynesian Tahiti, in more ways than one. It therefore seems appropriate that it should be Gauguin, rather than, for example, van Gogh—who never left Europe—who becomes a zombie in Drexler's installation.

There are myriad differences between Polynesian Tahiti, which was annexed by France in 1880, and the Caribbean slave colony that broke free of France in 1804 to become Haiti, the land we most commonly associate with the zombie. But the peoples of both territories—the Polynesian natives and the descendants of African slaves—have both been denigrated as bloodthirsty cannibals, naive and childlike, mystical and superstitious by external powers seeking to justify their intervention in the country or their control of the people. Both places are legible as postcolonial communities, and the wider scholarly interest in looking at the ways that such cultures employed modes of resistance against empire is helpful to our understanding of the Haitian zombie, specifically.

Eisenman writes:

> Far from being merely passive victims . . . colonized peoples have historically employed some of the very Orientalist rhetorics described by Said as a means of forging collective identities and fashioning resistance movements. At the heart of colonialist discourses themselves, argue Spivak and Bhabha, lie potentially significant ambivalences and aporias. Colonial novels, artworks, letters, and official documents may in fact, Bhabha argues be 'hybrid' texts that 'reverse the effects of colonial disavowal [of native worth], so that 'denied knowledges enter upon the dominant discourse and estrange the basis of its authority.' Rather than buttressing repressive regimes, colonial arts and literatures may actually undermine their ideological legitimacy, or at least offer potential paths for future cultural and political resistance. (19)

Eisenman's synthesis of Gayatri Spivak, Homi Bhabha, and Edward Said is useful here, for it appositely describes the way in which the zombie myth is such a hybrid text, a site of deep ambivalence that comes out of an explicitly "denied knowledge," Vaudou, one that can be configured as a source of power affecting (or infecting) would-be colonizers or oppressors.

Let's linger for a moment on Gauguin's original work, *Ta Matete* (The Marketplace), and Drexler's reimagination of it as *Lost in Paris*. The women in Gauguin's original painting are explicitly prostitutes—a few of them hold the sanitation cards that women in the profession were made to carry (Eisenman 155). In Drexler's zombified version of the painting, everything is nearly the same: the colors are brighter and the skirts are shorter; one girl seems to have morphed into a man, and the sanitation cards have become cigarettes. In the background, Gauguin's zombie lumbers through the park, following the specter of death. The painting is titled simply *Lost in Paris*, but the following description from the zombie's journal sheds some light on the scene: "I saw in the central district some young women and young girls, tranquil of eye, pure Tahitians, some of whom would perhaps [have] gladly shared my life. However, I did not approach them. They actually made me timid with their sure look, their dignity of being, and their pride of gait."

In fact, these lines come directly from Gauguin's real-life memoir, *Noa Noa*. The original text is married in the zombie's journal with various other passages from Gauguin's real writings as well as Drexler's own inventions. Here the natives are transplanted, and they become immigrants powerfully occupying the space of the Parisian park; this is an inverse image to Gauguin's own transplantation and his cultural colonization of Tahiti. And it raises, I think, an interesting point about immigration as the fair turnabout for colonization and of the deep hypocrisy displayed when citizens complain about the drain on the nation's economy that illegal immigrants pose when many targets of their ire come from the same colonial outposts that were politically and economically undermined by that nation's unjust mining of their resources.

Gauguin's own words and images are often repurposed in this exhibition, perhaps none more successfully than the use of his masterpiece's title, *Where Do We Come From? What Are We? Where Are We Going?*, as some of the first words the zombie speaks after his reanimation. The revivification of Gauguin as a zombie resembles precisely the flip that occurs in Haitian folklore and literature (detailed in chapter 3). Either the enslaved zombie becomes powerful, rebelling against his curse, or,

FIGURE 11 Debra Drexler, *Gauguin's Zombie*, 2002. *Lost in Paris*, oil on canvas, 72 × 95 in. (Courtesy of the artist.)

as we see here, the former colonizer becomes the oppressed, colonized, and disempowered zombie in a rewriting of the zombie myth. Paul Gauguin—an expatriate who benefited materially and professionally from his position in a colonial outpost, whose most well known art is an act of cultural appropriation of the subject matter of Tahiti and even the people's artistic style—is zombified in Drexler's work in a direct act of creative resistance. In Drexler's installation, Gauguin's Zombie is sent back to France where he is haunted by the Tahitian specter of death. Gauguin's work, an artistic appropriation itself, is counter-appropriated by Drexler's textual zombification.

In contrast to this type of direct artistic conjury, and more in line with the shadowing of artistic influence described by Foster in the chapter's epigraph, Derek Walcott writes in a poem about Camille Pissarro, "the great works we admire / civilise and colonise us, they chain our hands / invisibly."[35] In spite of the comparisons to slavery and colonialism in this description of what Harold Bloom called the "anxiety of influence" Walcott's own work—in its dialogue with the great European epics of Dante and Homer—and the textual zombifications described herein, demonstrate that it doesn't have to be this way: one can reincarnate, possess, and even zombify the masters.

Coda

It was not intentional that my Kreyol section titles in the introduction to this book, "Ki sa sa ye?, Ki Zombi? Pou ki moun Zombi sa ye?, Ki kote nou prale?" ("What is that? What zombie? Whose zombie?; Where are we going?"), should faintly echo the title of Gauguin's masterpiece, reappropriated by Drexler: *Where Do We Come From? What Are We? Where Are We Going?* But this happy coincidence affords me an opportunity to draw out a bit further the issue of intentionality as it relates to the zombie and its appropriations. At times, as we have seen, the zombie is willfully redirected to bear one's own burden—and in so doing, the myth itself resembles the metaphor that is one half of its heart, the slave laboring for another. It feels in keeping with the zombie's historicity (as a figuration of, and one produced out of, the transatlantic slave trade) to see this evidenced most starkly when it is white film directors that take up the Caribbean figure of the living dead to represent the travails of their own cultural moment, but one must be careful in articulating the history of appropriation and counter-appropriation of the zombie. For the various "reclamations" of the zombie I have pointed to here, be it a blaxploitation film like *Sugar Hill* or the reconstitution of the zombie in Haitian literature after its deeply entrenched associations with Papa Doc Duvalier and his Tonton Macoutes, or a work like Drexler's multimedia art exhibit *Gauguin's Zombie*, are, in point of fact, merely further appropriations, new uses of the myth, even if these uses critique those who had previously confiscated it. What such instances of counter-appropriation emphasize, however, is the zombie myth's potential to effect figurative resistance as much as figurative exploitation; that the myth can be turned against those who have been the abusers is analogous to the other half of its heart: the metaphor of the rebel slave in arms. And for this use of the myth, I reserve the word conjure.

It is an imperfect word, to be sure: conjure too often has a sense of something made out of thin air, whereas the types of conjure I have addressed in this chapter in relation to art, like Reed's Neo-Hoodoo aesthetic, draw on salvage, syncretism, métissage—not making something of nothing, but repurposing the things around us or changing them. In the opening of this chapter, I quoted Antoinette accusing Rochester of working his own brand of "obeah" in trying to change her name; in the type of conjure I'm describing, the zombie, once a slave metaphor, is changed into a figure of resistance. The word conjure also has in its etymology a whiff of the rebel slaves' conspiracy, of those who would swear (jurare) to join together (con), to fight a common enemy. The Bois Caïman ceremony was, thus, doubly an act of conjure: an oath and a Vaudou ceremony. And there is a way that, it seems to me, the use of conjure performed on the figure of the zombie is not an individual but a collective task, belonging not to an isolated author or auteur filmmaker but to the myth's collectivity itself, in the aggregated substance of the long history of a metaphor's significances and its transmissions.

The zombie's history can be sketched as a series of appropriations and counter-appropriations, a metanarrative of a figural tool wielded by those who would make it signify what they would. But it might also be thought of in terms of the migrating motif, as Steinberg describes it, one animated by the accrued historical significance of the myth. In such a reading, the spirit of its history—accumulated over the centuries in its various uses—is infused into the zombie myth and visible in the figure itself: a dialectical metaphor symbolizing both slavery and rebellion, capture and resistance, confiscation and the work of conjure that combats it.

Epilogue: The Occupation of Metaphor

On a chilly October day, I was standing in Toronto, Canada, the city that famously (or infamously) incubated, in 2003, a phenomenon that has since been described as propagating and spreading like a virus. Thea Munster, engineer of the Zombie Walk movement, is a small woman wearing full zombie makeup, handing out flyers for the upcoming event. It reads: "The 6th Annual Toronto Zombie Walk 2008. Sunday October 19, Shuffling Starts at 3 pm. Starting Point: Trinity Bellwoods Park, Destination: Bloor Cinema."

* * *

A headline in the *San Francisco Chronicle* reads simply, "Zombies Invade Apple Store." In the accompanying picture, a woman in fake blood and traces of face paint in her stringy blond hair bites the corner of a sleek Apple desktop monitor (McCullagh).

* * *

On a warm autumn afternoon, three students thunder past me on the campus of the University of South Florida. A backpack is vaulted through the air; a student wearing a bandanna on his arm dives across the threshold of the student center, leaps to his feet, and holds up his arms, declaring with his gestures his successful entry into the safe zone. The two "zombies" in hot pursuit (students wearing bandannas on their heads), come to a halt, grumble disappointedly, and slink off.

On October 30, 2009, Londoners turned up for an event called "Parliament of the Living Dead," which was listed on crawlofthedead.com. Perhaps many of those in attendance had also been at the "Zombie Walk and Protest" held at Parliament two months earlier, in August. In reality, however, this is a publicity stunt organized by the video game manufacturer Capcom Entertainment to publicize its latest game, *Dead Rising 2* (Hussain). Staged during the time of the student protests, the event's organizers may have hoped to co-opt a bit of the excitement and momentum of the student protest movement and redirect it to the purchase of quality zombie shoot-'em-ups.

* * *

In front of the presidential palace in Santiago, Chile, hundreds of students dressed as the living dead perform a choreographed dance to Michael Jackson's "Thriller" to protest an educational system they claim is "rotten" and "dead" (*Huffington Post,* June 25, 2011). A similar student protest making use of Michael Jackson's "Thriller" was staged at UC Davis in 2010, spoofing the chancellor's budget cuts and the tuition hikes that preserve the inflated salaries of top-tier administrators at the expense of students and adjunct instructors. And while I can't say for certain that the Chile protest was inspired by the one in Davis, California, the "Thriller" protest held at UC Berkeley in July 2012 at the UC Regents' meeting drew direct inspiration from the YouTube video that students had seen of the Chilean "Thriller" protest.[1] In keeping with the viral nature of the contemporary cinematic zombie, such events reveal the communicability of culture on a global Internet: "And round and round it goes" (Charlie Eaton, pers. comm., October 11, 2013).

* * *

A young woman sits in a London jail cell dressed as a zombie; she has been arrested for "potential breach of the peace" (Parsons). Outside, the world watches as Prince William and Kate Middleton are wed in an ostentatious display of archaic tradition and wealth, much of which was accumulated by an empire on which the sun never set.

* * *

It's a beautiful May day in Miami, and a naked man on a roadside is mauling a homeless person; he bites off pieces of the man's flesh with his teeth. Witnesses will later say that the attacker is feral, that it was like something out of a horror movie, as he chewed off nearly 50 percent of the indigent's face and destroyed one of his eyes. The police have to shoot the assailant dead to get him to stop. Before the victim has fully convalesced, the site of what is quickly dubbed the "Miami Zombie Attack" will become a pivotal point of interest for tourists on the "True Crime Tour," eager for a glimpse of the spot where the atrocity took place (David Ovalle, pers. comm., April 29, 2013).

* * *

On the Internet a company called Zombie Industries offers life-sized, three-dimensional tactical mannequins that "bleed" when you shoot them. They offer a Nazi, a terrorist, a scantily clad woman (Alexa, a.k.a. "The Ex"), and, before it was removed, a model that looked suspiciously like President Obama, called "Rocky" or "Barocky."[2]

* * *

In Atlanta in June 2013, Georgian runners sprint past throngs of zombies, trying to outrun the hordes that seek not to bite them but to pop the latex balloons strapped to their waists. When they're hit, a red powder sprays the runners in an imitation of blood. As it does, will the memory of images of the Boston Marathon bombing hang in the air?

* * *

A hacked digital roadside in Austin, Texas, borrows the apparatus that normally warns of traffic disruptions to the smooth workings of that capitalist fiction, perpetuated by the engine Lauren Berlant calls *Cruel Optimism*, the fantasy of the everyday "good life." Instead, it proclaims, parodically but not perhaps dishonestly: "Caution, Zombies Ahead!" (Brown). The sign provides a bit of wry levity for the early morning commuter, or even a moment of consideration: who or what are the "zombies" we face in our own real lives?

Zombies in Protest and Play

I have elected to begin here—or more properly, to begin the ending here—in a manner that provides a synchronic snapshot of zombies in the early twenty-first century, rounding out the largely diachronic scope of what came before. Observed individually, each image in this composite portrait of the contemporary zombie mythos does the same thing as the road sign: it commandeers the zombie metaphor, seizing the signifier's switchboard and reprogramming it to transmit an alternate message. Taken together, they provide a picture of the zombie in the bizarre cultural moment when at the beginning of the new millennium zombies were everywhere—not just on the silver screen and in the bookstore, but on the sidewalk and on the Internet. Perhaps, in the face of facts predicting looming ecological crisis and on the heels of a political strategy that embraced a rhetoric of permanent warfare and an economic downturn brought about by the failure of neoliberalist policies, it came out of an inability to imagine the future—as if everyone living at that time felt a little bit dead already.

In Wade Davis's *The Serpent and the Rainbow*, a source describes to Davis the amount of shame that is associated with zombification in Haiti in order to clarify that it is unlikely that Clairvius Narcisse, a man who came forward and claimed to be a real-life zombie, had done so in order to get attention. He says, "In Haiti a zombi is a complete outcast. Would a leper stand upon Hyde Park Corner and boast of his disease?" (29). The point of comparison that equates the social stigma associated with zombieism in Haiti to that of leprosy in the United Kingdom seems valid and worth remembering, though today one is much more likely to find zombies in public than lepers.

Consider, for example, this advertised call for a "Zombie picnic" in (of all places) Hyde Park: "Hyde Park, Greater London Saturday, April 30, 2011, 12:30 pm–8:00 pm. The idea is that we get as many people as humanly possible to come to Hyde Park dressed as zombies and have a picnic. It's just meant to be a fun event where you get to come to London, scare commuters, meet new people and generally just be your weird selves . . ." (plancast.com). As the original poster makes clear, the point of such events is explicitly *not* to make money but "just to get a load of people together to have fun." In doing so, such events returned to the zombie an element of the folkloric, communally made, extratextual narrative that we associate with the original Haitian zombie. An integral part of the exercise of such zombie performances is the experience of freeing oneself from the capitalist matrix, doing labor without expecting any recompense besides enjoyment, and the striking display of an organized congregation of individuals taking over public space.

In the decade since Thea Munster organized the first Zombie Walk, we saw a cultural trend that appeared viral-like in its operations and in its transmission—an aspect that is fitting for the zombie's most recent instantiation in cinema as virally contagious. Simone do Vale described such events in a short piece called "Trash Mob: Zombie Walks and the

Positivity of Monsters in Western Pop Culture" as "a movement that in less than three years has managed to spread like a real plague along several Canadian and North American cities, and infected countries like Brazil, England, Poland, and Australia, [which] has spread through the internet" (191).

The first and what will perhaps be the last, the Toronto Zombie Walk, cost nothing and didn't accept donations for many years. It was affiliated with no charity, corporation, or organization and thereby insisted on its own purposelessness. People got together, dressed up like zombies, and walked through town. But, as Thea Munster once told me, as most zombie events began to take on some charitable aspect—like suggestions that participants bring a canned food item or booths to raise awareness about various issues—the line became hard to hold. Eventually, even Toronto's annual event merged into a "zombie walk and Halloween parade," sponsored by *Fangoria Magazine* and the Ontario tourism board and in support of the Heart and Stroke Foundation. Its 2014 website, torontozombiewalk.ca, allowed vendors to bid for space at the upcoming event: capitalism had officially devoured the dream that the zombie walk could disrupt the machine (even temporarily!) and turned the movement into one more marketable commodity, a pop-up venue to generate revenue. The effect of these philanthropic and corporate adoptions was, indeed, an anesthetization of the zombie walk that made it more palatable to mainstream society and divorced it from its revolutionary resonance. Nowhere is this conquest of the zombie walk more concretely demonstrated than in the example of the faux-walk described among my collection of zombie portraits, in which a video game manufacturer staged an event that resembled this kind of profitless performance in order to hand out swag to a targeted demographic.

The popularity of these events has at last begun to wane, as can be plainly seen by looking at the date stamps on registered zombie walk forums. Increasingly, one finds zombie runs sprouting up like mushrooms in their place—including one in the little town where I live, Clemson, South Carolina, which doesn't even have its own movie theater. But such events are explicitly purposeful—for fitness—and they raise money. And though runners can choose to play either a human (and pay a $25 registration fee) or a zombie ($20, or if you do your own makeup, $10), they also pivot the zombie narrative from the directionless wandering of pitiful hordes to the human's outrunning of a swift, strong enemy (clemsonzrun.com). As such, they emphasize a narrative of survival rather than invite identification with the undead.

Simone do Vale had presciently noted the vulnerability of the zombie walk to increased commodification (198–99). Aware of the kinship between carnival and revolt as it is discussed by Mikhail Bakhtin in *Rabelais and His World*, I described such zombie events as "voided signifiers," writing in an essay titled "Playing Dead: Zombies Invade Performance Art . . . and Your Neighborhood": "Munster's events have the shape and form of insurrection, but, like a zombie, are just contour, devoid of sense" (220). In an essay published in *Generation Zombie* (2011) at nearly the same time, "Mass Psychology and the Analysis of the Zombie: From Suggestion to Contagion," Phillip Mahoney comes to a similar conclusion: "Like a typical flash mob . . . the zombie walk may be said to manifest the empty form of the social itself, essentially demonstrating nothing other than the very ability of people to organize en masse" (125). Mahoney also writes that "on message boards and websites devoted to zombie walks, the term 'zombie' operates as what Ernesto Laclau, in his book on populism, calls an 'empty signifier,' a term which 'can be attached to the most diverse social contents,' precisely because it has no particular content of its own" (125). I preferred the language of voided to empty signifiers, because it is a mistake to claim that the zombie, as Mahoney writes, "has no particular content of its own" (125). Indeed, I see now that even the term voided is insufficient: the zombie has a deep historical content stretching back to its roots in the Haitian Revolution—and before that, to its connection to the transatlantic slave trade—that I don't think can ever be erased. The zombie refuses to be a palimpsest: its history bleeds through our attempts to write over it, and the trace is visible, like ghost graffiti coming through the whitewash.[3] The zombie signifier is not always already empty, and if there is an attempt to evacuate it and make it stand for something new, this is more like an *occupation* of the zombie metaphor, one that, I would say, never successfully evicts the myth's history.

The zombie mob phenomenon may have been inaugurated in Canada in 2003, but its popularity really began to rise in the United States in 2005, during a period of relative calm but pervasive social dissatisfaction. Writing about the uses of images of the living dead in social protests and their blank deployment in zombie walks in an article called "'Sois mort et tais toi': Zombie Mobs and Student Protests," I drew a link between the largely unpopular Iraq war and zombie performances. I concluded that although students might not feel it was worth their time to overtly demonstrate their disaffection with the system, these zombie events were nonetheless productive of a kind of inchoate catharsis for the participants that was directly related to the urge to retaliate against the status quo. Demonstrations against the US invasion of Iraq had had no impact on an administration determined to go to war in 2003; my sense—gleaned from evidence about political uninterest on college campuses and research on zombie mobs in general—was that the type of citizen participating in the earliest wave of zombie mobs (before they were cosponsored by your local Halloween Headquarters and Mountain Dew) may have found in such events a means of conveying this muteness. The general population was somatically cut off from immediate connection to the war by the Bush administration's restriction of media images, which prohibited even the publication of images of the coffins of US casualties in 2006. Perhaps, I theorized, on the level of the collective unconscious, the contemporary zombie mobs becoming ever more popular at the time were making visible the corpses that could not be shown. Or maybe they were symbolizing, too, the bodies of the "enemy" civilians, who, as Judith Butler writes in *Precarious Life*, could not be mourned.[4] Were zombie mobs at first a way a particular demographic made visible the undeadness of an intangible enemy or performed mourning when it could not mourn publicly without incurring the wrath of right-wingers, for whom any public expression of grief connoted a lack of support for the troops? Or maybe these events were an expression of participants' own sense of themselves as insensible—in both senses of the word: incapable of perception and incapable of being perceived—blinded by the administration's control of the press, and unable to make themselves heard. Once, I wondered what would happen to the zombie mob in a time of widespread social upheaval when there were *real* mobs. And what I found in the last years of the first decade of the new millennium was that the zombie was often taken up into protests, as a symbol of demonstrators' dissatisfaction or their sense of frustration with the system.

The tastefulness of using the undead in protest has already been questioned, and it is clear that the imagery needs to be handled carefully. As stated in the introduction, the living dead zombie cannot signify revolutionary resurrection but only a perpetual state of undeadness. As such, the zombie can make visible the populace's sense of its own inability to protest; it can serve as an icon, lamenting the fact that their voices are not being heard. But because of the dual nature of the zombie, its historical representation of *both* slavery and slave rebellion, it seems to work only as a figure of ambivalence or disempowerment.

Take, for instance, an image from the Egyptian protest artist Ganzeer that depicts dwindling optimism after the Arab Spring (fig. 12). In the

FIGURE 12 Ganzeer, Egyptian protest poster, 2013. Digital production for online distribution, 800 x 1241 pixels, dimensions variable in print. (Reprinted by permission of the artist.)

style of a movie poster advertising coming attractions, it depicts the people's choice between Mohamed Morsi and Hosni Mubarak as a choice between a zombie and a vampire. The tagline here reads: "One will eat your brains. The other will suck your blood." The title implies that the nation is caught "Between a Zombie and a Blood-Sucker," and the fine print below the image identifies principal players in the drama: Morsi, Mubarak, the Motherland, the media, and the armed forces.[5] Therefore, the zombie is invoked here as an expression of frustration, the only way, I think, that the image *can work* as a protest icon. This explains one of the problems with the Occupy Wall Street zombies that I articulated at the outset of this book.

Here, at the end, having taken full stock of the history of the figure, we can ask again of the OWS zombies: What did it mean for those who donned zombie dress-up to wield or inhabit the zombie metaphor, and what are the implications when we make use of the zombie to signify dissatisfaction in the wealthiest and most powerful nations of the world? Isn't it deeply insensitive (to the point of being intellectually negligent) to make a symbol of slavery stand for our own cultural ennui?

As we've seen, the zombie represents the uncanny return of history, but this trope operates in a diverse manner: the figure is equally capable of representing the disconcerting presence of a tyrannical past or—particularly in Haitian literature—the triumphal *reawakening* of the resistance for the future. It is fitting that the myth itself undergoes various "revolutions" and that it continually dramatizes the startling recurrence of the past (and this is done structurally as well, in the form of the textual zombies described in chapter 4), as of the reemergence of one who was thought to be dead. And yet, like the zombie itself, which is not a resurrected body but a reappearance of the form without the substance—the body returned without its soul—the image of the zombie will always make visible that which is absent and irrevocably lost for the present: as a symbol of rebellion, it is tempered by its simultaneous representation of permanent enslavement and thus incapable of effecting change. As is reflected in the duality of its undecidable dialecticality (living/dead, self/other, human/animal), the zombie exists only as a material mirage, its direct power limited to discursive operation, one that is permanently mired in the tension between the dichotomy of the imaginary and the real.

If I ultimately refuse to concede the revolutionary potential of the zombie mob, I nonetheless underscore that I agree wholeheartedly with those like David McNally, Annalee Newitz, Robert Latham, and scores of others who read the zombie as an apt reflection of capitalism's living deadness.[6] In my previous work on zombie performances and protests, I concentrated on the occupation of space and overlooked the zombie's relationship to time. In particular, I am intrigued by those who relate the zombie's nonlinearity to an experience of time under neoliberalism, or "late late capitalism," as Rebecca Schneider says (155), connecting zombie performance, and the living deadness of theater more broadly, to a "future, that is, in ruins. The future: the late late past" (158).

In a special issue of the *Drama Review*, Schneider writes that "to *seem as if* dead is not to be dead, and the *seeming* impossibility of OWS's demands become their living potentiality. To act as living dead ricochets relations among zombies on the move *between* the states of living and dead labor—that is, they purposefully stand precisely in and as the interval of crisis that Marx identified, in order to make that very precarity *count*" (160; original emphasis). If Schneider notes the OWS zombie's usefulness as "reflection machines . . . aimed to catch the visages of those who worship corporate wealth" (153) or as bringing to light "what Lauren Berlant has termed 'slow death'—those within capitalism who are 'marked for wearing out'" (152), this nonetheless occurs within the flexible space of movable theater: *seems*, not *is*. Likewise, there is no real dezombification here but only the rehearsal of it, which may, in the end, only further undergird the cultural apparatuses of ideology, providing the populace with a kind of release valve to prohibit true action.

In his useful essay "Zombies of Immaterial Labor: The Modern Monster and the Death of Death," Lars Bang Larsen concludes, "Sooner or later, the opacity of our fascination with the zombie exhausts sociological attempts at reading of it. There is ultimately no way to rationalize the skepticism the zombie drags in" (11).[7] So, then, what's the use? I appreciate Schneider's term reflection machines. For years I've been misquoting Judith Halberstam's Skin Shows, which proclaims that "Monsters are meaning machines" (21). Somehow I transcreated this in my memory to "Monsters are mirror machines." This slip reveals a major difference between my discussion of the zombie's uses and Halberstam's description of the "technology of monsters," in which the hegemonic society employs the monster to demonize "Parasites and Perverts" and other social undesirables: the Jew in Dracula, the transsexual in Silence of the Lambs. "Gothic," Halberstam writes, "is the production of difference through a repetition of sameness" (179). Inarguably, the zombie has and still does operate in this register in American cinema: it represents the African in early film and, more recently, the homeless, the drug addicted, and the mentally disabled as monsters. Yet my own sense of the zombie's technology is the double way it operates as a "mirror," reflecting, first, a people's monstrous (in the sense of "outrageously unjust") historical and lived condition and allowing, second, the Haitian to project/deflect/redirect his own mistreatment onto the very forces that oppress him. In the zombie, we see the production of sameness, written over the surface of hierarchical difference. As Haitians know, dezombification begins with the realization of one's deadness. If we were to become more cognizant of what it means to use the zombie metaphor, perhaps we, too, could awaken from our living dead state. But we have to start with understanding the full historical complexity of the myth and its appropriations.

Remember that, as far as intellectual property law is concerned, there was no zombie Ur-text; the zombie made for a convenient cinematic monster in the early decades of the twentieth century precisely *because* it came from folklore, and thus no author was owed copyright fees (Jaime Russell 19). This is a lot like the comedian Eddie Izzard's bit about empire in his special *Dress to Kill* (1999), in which he spoofs imperialism's warped rationalization with the biting mantra, "No flag, no country." No documents, no narratives. Yet we have seen in this book the way that in Haitian literature and folklore, in the visual arts, and even in some notable examples in cinema, the zombie is reclaimed and given new direction in the last half of the twentieth century: some acknowledge the problematic appropriation of the figure, while others, turning the mirror outward, suggest that the fascination with this monster of Haitian origin signals the Blancs' successful cultural colonization by the Caribbean imaginary. Simultaneously, and to my mind, most important, the zombie is historically a figuration of both slavery and slave rebellion. It is bound to this pairing in a way I do not think can or should be undone. The myth's history is the second major obstacle (other than its innate bifurcation) to considering the zombie an icon of revolution, but the figure nonetheless begs us to think more carefully about cultural transmission and appropriation.

Just as the phrase and strategy of "occupation" is never empty but crowded with colonial ghosts and memories of human suffering, the zombie myth's diverse "occupations" by those who would make use of its imagery (particularly its ability to symbolize, simultaneously, both disempowerment and resistance) is not really so different from the colonists who, like Moreau de St. Méry, compared their plight, unrepresented in the National Assembly, to the pitiable condition of the African slaves. There is no comparison. And to invoke the zombie, descendant of an

African soul-capture mythology and citizen of Haiti, is to drag also the specter of the African slave into our economy of self-reference. Whether the intention is to make reference to the African slave or to efface this history in zombie narratives, either amounts to an appropriation.

The zombie, some will argue, has transcended its transatlantic form. They'll cry that the meanings of myths, like words, change over time, and thus this is all a moot point; they'll say that the zombie is no longer always immediately visible as a standard-bearer for themes of slavery and rebellion. And this is true: zombies lug behind them fears of global pandemic or ecological catastrophe, terrorism, and endless wars waged against invisible enemies, or global economies and the sovereignty of the nation-state.

There is an even more convincing argument to be made that zombies no longer "belong" to the Americas, if they ever did. Zombie movies have been made around the world, and people now call a variety of living dead "zombies," even when they come from France and are more clearly related to the European revenant, as in the film *Les Revenants* (2004); from Spain, where they are still tinged with Catholic fear of demon possession, as in *Rec* (2007); and Sweden, when the movie itself, *Dead Snow* (2009), spoofs the youth culture's obsession with Hollywood monsters, and the treasure-guarding living dead is more clearly related to the Scandinavian *draguar* (Bishop, "Non-Zombies of Dead Snow"). Zombie films have recently risen in Israel and in Pakistan shouldering the burdens of their society's most pressing concerns.[8] A special segment on zombies produced by the American outlet Al Jazeera in October 2013 reported that the countries with the highest number of Google searches for the word zombie were Indonesia, the Philippines, and Vietnam—all, it bears emphasizing, former colonial outposts. Despite the ever increasing cultural heterogeneity of the "zombie," and its global transmission through media—this *sharing* (at best) or willful appropriation of a slave culture's narrative (at worst)—will always be evocative of the age of global empire that made such a widespread universal mythology possible and the infrastructure of ideological, economic, and political control that remains in place after its supposed end. For, as everyone knows, the real zombie we are concerned with here is Empire, in the sense meant by Michael Hardt and Antonio Negri: "the idea of Empire reappears, not as a territory, not in the determinate dimensions of its time and space, and not from the standpoint of a people and its history, but rather simply as the fabric of an ontological human dimension that tends to become universal" (385).

I think I can leave off here, with a final note regarding what the zombie's atemporality, at least, is trying to tell us. Slavery and Empire may have changed forms under advanced capitalism, but they are not over. The zombie's model is especially relevant for understanding how exploitation and "antagonisms to exploitation" work together in the service of Empire: "articulated across the global networks of production and determine crises," for "crisis is coextensive with the postmodern totality of capitalist production: it is proper to imperial control" (Hardt and Negri 385). Resistance itself becomes subsumed as a part of the mechanism. And yet the figure of the zombie lives on as long as Empire functions, and the myth remains important to our conception of how it works. This, too, is an act of resistance. And once more the zombie's dialectic resists resolution.

Nonetheless, the zombie metaphor seems always to have a life of its own: there is something forceful, even malevolent about the way the zombie undermines the potential success of protest at the same time that it embodies revolutionary drive—no matter how much the Zuccotti Occupiers wanted it to signify otherwise. Or perhaps we should, as the bokors that Degoul cites as his informants advise us, take our obsession with the walking dead as evidence of our own cultural possession, our being worked upon by the spiritual powers of the Vaudoun lwa: who is colonizing whom? Either way, people are going to get pissed off.

I was made keenly aware of this when I received hate mail after being quoted in a widely disseminated Associated Press news article on the popularity of the zombie. In the interview, I sought to express the fact that the zombie is not wholly alive, or wholly dead, and thus not a symbol of complete and successful rebellion but of profound ambivalence, disempowerment as well as resistive struggle. The article quoted me as saying, "If you were to ask the [zombie walk] participants, I don't think that all of them are very cognizant of what they're saying when they put on the zombie makeup and participate" (Kinnard). The amount of ire that my supposition drew—including threats that a liberal "juice-boxer" like me (a term that apparently means preppie, elitist, or trustfunder) should leave the South—leads me to think that I was onto something.

I did not mean to suggest that a more wide-scale study of the various types of people who participate in zombie walks, mobs, or zombie cosplay would be useless. It would be valuable to know what the participants' stated motivations (if any) are for playing a part in such events—my own research is limited to correspondence with organizers of the earliest and most overtly political zombie events—especially as the few published ethnographies that exist in this area do not help. But my interest is the way the metaphor speaks above and beyond the individual motivations of those comprising the crowd. It is not my project to psychoanalyze participants to see what latent tensions the zombie walkers might be expressing—be they their own fears of death or insecurity about the body's openness and orifices, or even, should it possibly bubble to the surface, imperial guilt—nor is it to determine what they *mean to say* in invoking the zombie metaphor. Rather, my goal is to truly turn away from the human subject altogether (its conscious or unconscious motivations) and ask, in a posthuman approach, what *the zombie myth says*. As in linguistics, the zombie signifier does not merely convey whatever the survivalist shooting zombie target practice wants it to signify (zombies are immigrants, parasites on our national resources) nor even the Occupy protester chomping dollar bills in face paint (Wall Street bankers are zombies, greedily gaming the system at the expense of the people). But the slave and the rebel slave are always there, too. Whether or not fans are aware of the zombie's past, putting on makeup and dressing as a living corpse is more than just "fun," and it is more than just a reflection of their own disempowerment under advanced capitalism: it is also a concrete dramatization of the occupation of a myth that was about conquest, colonialism, and slavery. I submit that this message overwrites the human-playing-zombie, no matter what his or her intention is in performing living-deadness, and telegraphs another implication—one about the colonial framework of appropriation and occupation on which our current society is based.

As I learned from the gentleman who called me a "juice-boxer" and many others like him, people tend to react badly when you say to them, "You think that when you dress like a zombie it says X, but really it says Y." One supposes it makes them feel as if they have no control, even over their own thoughts or actions—rather like the zombies, funnily enough, they were imitating in the first place.

In Haiti in fall 2013, I asked the Grand Ati of Vaudou, Max Beauvoir, why he thought Americans were so obsessed with the zombie. His answer was slowly delivered and forcefully determined: "It is an act of aggression." I cannot disagree even though I'm not sure, now, that I know exactly what he meant. I was hoping he would second the opinion of Degoul's informants—that the United States had been culturally invaded by zombies in fair turnabout for their military occupation of Haiti and continued economic and political interventions in the country. I prefer to think that the ambiguity of the pronoun in Beauvoir's statement is in keeping with the zombie's profound ambivalence. Is it an act of aggression that the United States confiscates the Haitian zombie or a

Haitian act of retaliation that the United States is possessed by it? I prefer to leave it there, without deciding.

The zombie myth has outgrown its old skin. It is no longer just "about" slavery or rebellion, but these elements of the zombie myth are not merely scars written on the surface of the body, which can be sloughed. Rather, they are like genetic material in its DNA: the zombie today remains colored by its original makeup and its history—a myth about conquest and colonialism that was itself commandeered and colonized—to the point that this myth about the appropriation of human labor has become a myth "about" cultural appropriation itself.

The zombie today acts as an illustration of the power of myths in a transnational context and in an increasingly technologized global community: revealing how myths traveled once on slave ships and how they do now, in a matter of seconds, whirring through cyberspace; how they are used as a common language to bridge cultural divides but still remind us that they have their own histories. They will talk over us about where they come from, and what they once meant. Zombies may not often speak, but I believe that the transatlantic zombie, now global, more mythos than myth, *does*: it implores us to listen to what it signifies about the operations of the culture industry and cautions us to think about what we do when we put zombies to work in the fields of our own cultural concerns, whether or not we give them a new name.

Notes

Introduction

1. A stylized mask of Guy Fawkes, leader of the Gunpowder plot that attempted to blow up the House of Lords in 1605, became a symbol adopted by various antigovernment protesters after being popularized by the graphic novel and subsequent film, *V for Vendetta*. On the incidence of clown-gang disruptions in France and elsewhere, see Zach Goldhammer, "Scary Clowns are Terrorizing France," *The Atlantic*, October 31, 2014.

2. Foster writes, "I . . . don't deny that—that we live in the wake not only of modernist painting and sculpture but of postmodernist deconstruction of these forms as well, in the wake not only of the prewar avant-gardes but of the postwar neo-avant-gardes as well" (125).

3. The association between zombies and capitalist critique has been deeply entrenched since *Dawn of the Dead* (1978). In his book *Hollywood from Vietnam to Reagan* (1986) Robin Wood wrote that Romero's "zombies represent, on the metaphorical level, the whole dead weight of patriarchal consumer capitalism, from whose habits of behavior and desire not even Hare Krishnas and nuns, mindlessly joining the conditioned gravitation to the shopping mall, are exempt" (118). Instead of looking for the seeds of this critique in the larger zombie mythos, most see the element germinate in Romero's intervention in the mythology and leave it there. In fact, the zombie provided a grotesque caricature of the power relations that undergird capitalism long before Romero.

4. Romero famously cited Richard Matheson's vampires from the novel *I Am Legend* as an influence for his film *Night of the Living Dead* (1968), but he was also influenced by the living dead of EC Comics, which were, in turn, influenced by the voodoo zombies of the pulps. Regardless of the filmmaker's influences, however, fans were quick to dub Romero's "ghouls" "zombies," as also happened with the nondead "infected" of Danny Boyle's 2002 *28 Days Later*, thus extending the mythology to

include divergent types of creatures. This pivot of the mythology is discussed in more detail in chapter 2.

5. Whereas the sociologist Ulrich Beck uses the term zombie categories to describe social structures and categories that no longer exist in the prior sense but remain in use in society, I am interested in the vitality of the zombie as a useful concept for describing everything from moribund social structures and outmoded institutions to processes of conceptual or cultural appropriation. In a strange way, even a term like zombie category or zombie bank is itself a categorical zombie.

6. Franco Moretti discusses the relationship that exists between the Monster and Frankenstein as a kind of master/slave dialectic in *Signs Taken for Wonders*: "On the one hand, the scientist cannot but create the Monster. . . . On the other hand, he is immediately afraid of it and wants to kill it, because he realizes he has given life to a creature stronger than himself and of which he cannot henceforth be free" (85).

7. Canetti even recounts the story of a preacher's congregation of twenty thousand feigning simultaneous death and subsequent resurrection in August 1801 as a part of their spiritual rebirth; comparisons of the scene to a battlefield were in abundance (60–61).

8. On this point about cross-cultural transmission, see Ashis Nandy's *The Intimate Enemy* and Partha Mitter's *Much Maligned Monsters*.

9. An accompanying footnote makes clear that in these lines Warner is thinking in particular of *The Tempest* and its portrayal of magic as it is inflected by the history of imperialism; her study of the zombie concentrates mainly on early texts, with Jean Rhys's *Wide Sargasso Sea* as a lone exception (see my chapter 4).

10. The Jewish Golem is not only a protector of the Jews and "resistance fighter," defending the community from oppression and aggression, but also *their slave*: "he performed the hardest tasks: sweeping, straightening, chopping wood, hauling water, and so forth" (Neugroschel 83); until he rebels when the Rabbi forgets to deanimate him on the Sabbath. Mary Shelley's *Frankenstein* is similarly ambivalent. The monster does not just suggest oppression and rebellion, though it has famously been read as an allegory about political revolt and the Shelleys' antislavery politics are well known. (See, for example, Marilyn Butler, *Romantics, Rebels, and Reactionaries*; and Tim Morton, *The Poetics of Spice*, for discussion of Shelley's boycott of "blood sugar.") But rather, like the zombie myth itself, some critics have noted the split registers (both conservative and radical) upon which the novel's imagery works. See note 12, below.

11. On this point, see Cathy Gelbin's *The Golem Returns* (36); and Ruth Bienstock Anolik's essay, "Reviving the Golem, Revisiting Frankenstein" (155n11).

12. In fact, Baldick notes the way that the novel was used subsequently to cast aspersions on the movement: "George Canning spoke in the House of Commons in a debate on West Indian slave emancipation, remarking of the slave that 'To turn him loose in the manhood of his physical strength, in the maturity of his physical passion, but in the infancy of his uninstructed reason, would be to raise up a creature resembling the splendid fiction of a recent romance'" (60). Lloyd-Smith, too, notes the way that, like Frankenstein, the Haitian Revolution was invoked by both abolitionists and pro-slavery advocates. He quotes Eric Sundquist's *To Wake the Nations: Race in the Making of American Literature*: "Like a prism, the trope of San Domingo reflected all conflicting sides of the tangled question of bondage" (qtd. in Lloyd-Smith 218).

13. I think it is telling that zombification receives but a short note in Leslie Desmangles's important work on the cosmology of Vodou, *The Faces of the Gods* (195n7), wherein he describes it only through its association with the bizango secret society, as studied by Wade Davis and others.

14. This confluence is made visible in a Portuguese trader's commissioned carving of an ivory saltcellar in the Sierra Leone region in the fifteenth century, in the image of a mermaid, which Henry John Drewal reads as a point of collision of the mythologies. See "The Beauteous Beast."

1 / Slavery and Slave Rebellion

1. For a discussion of this "glaring discrepancy between thought and practice" as it relates to this region, see Susan Buck-Morss's "Hegel and Haiti" (821).

2. My comparison of the zombie to Hegel's dialectic is different from that of Kyle Bishop in *American Zombie Gothic* (70–73), for I am thinking about the way the zombie itself incarnates in one body the slave/master duality of reciprocal power and servitude. Hegel writes in *Phenomenology of Spirit*, "The object in which the lord has achieved his lordship has in reality turned out to be something quite different from an independent consciousness. What now really confronts him is not an independent consciousness, but a dependent one. He is, therefore, not certain of being-in-itself as the truth of himself. On the contrary, his truth is in reality the unessential consciousness and its unessential action.... The truth of the independent consciousness is accordingly the servile consciousness of the bondsman" (116–17). But Frantz Fanon wisely cautions that as we examine the reality of the white slaveholder in a postcolonial context, "the master differs basically from the master described by Hegel. For Hegel there is reciprocity; here the master laughs at the consciousness of the slave. What he wants from the slave is not recognition but work" (*Black Skin, White Masks* 220).

3. See also Eli Friedlander, "The Measure of the Contingent."

4. Wade Davis, a Harvard scientist, wrote about his journey to discover the contents of the zombie powder, the drug that was used to induce a deathlike state in zombification victims. Davis's central finding was that the presence of tetrodotoxin in the powder, a poison from the puffer or porcupine fish that causes all-over paralysis, may have accounted for the phenomenon. His critics claimed that his research was fraudulent and that there was not enough tetrodotoxin in the samples produced by Davis to cause such a phenomenon (see studies by Yasumoto and Kao). Supporters assert that the Haitian bokor probably knows more about tetrodotoxin than Blanc scientists, for example, what times of year the fish's poison would be most potent. See also the A&E documentary *Zombies*, from the series The Unexplained.

5. Although the surrounding island nations share similar cultural heritages and there were slave revolts of various degrees in Jamaica, Guadeloupe, and elsewhere, only Haiti achieved independence as a result of slave rebellion. Tacky's Rebellion of 1760 in Jamaica is considered the most significant slave rebellion other than the Haitian Revolution. For slavery and revolt in Jamaica, see Trevor Burnard's *Mastery, Tyranny, and Desire*; and Vincent Brown, *The Reaper's Garden*.

6. The various theories of the origins of these concepts and their development from African mythologies are chronicled most thoroughly in Ackermann and Gauthier, "The Ways and Nature of the Zombi." They write, "Many scholars have long been

aware of the dualism of the zombie concept; however, this has gone largely unnoticed by the general public outside of Haiti. Most investigators have focused on the flesh-and-blood zombi, a body without a soul.... The other variety of the zombi, a soul without a body, remains little known if at all, both to scholars and to the general public" (467). They conclude, "The primary belief from which all others derive seems to be that the soul can be influenced by magic. Capture or enslavement of the soul, from either a dead or living victim, and the misuse of the soul appear as further developments.... From zombification of the soul, it is only a small mental step to zombification of the body" (490).

7. Though we principally think of the "zombie" as a soulless embodied creature, the other type of zombi is still very much a part of Haitian culture: disembodied zombies, sometimes called the zombi astral or "zonbi," have been written about by Elizabeth McAlister in *Rara!* and "A Sorcerer's Bottle."

8. In the passage in which the word appears, Moreau de St. Méry is describing the passion of the people for their amorous rendezvous, for which they will travel long distances in the middle of the night to see their beloveds. Here the author is remarking that the promise of a liaison with the lover is the only thing that can get the people to surmount their fear of zombis and walk about by night. He writes, "A young beauty, the color of ebony, who is normally made to tremble in every limb by a zombie story, keeps watch for her lover, and opens the door without letting it make a sound, and she has but one fear, to have her expectations interrupted" (1:52). The note at the bottom of the page reads, "Mot creol qui signifie esprit, revenant." This is from the original publication of 1797.

9. For a more detailed description of the European revenant, which was often a corpse of someone familiar possessed by an evil spirit and made to roam, see Nancy Caciola, "Wraiths, Revenants, and Ritual in Medieval Culture."

10. I have tried to preserve the orthography of these older texts as much as possible, including or omitting punctuation and accents where the original text does, though I have changed the long s to our modern s throughout.

11. Joseph Murphy writes that "eighteenth-century slave traders distinguished at least seventy different African ethnicities present in Haiti, of which the Arada were but one" (15). The Arada were said to come from the area called Guinea, in West Africa.

12. As others such as Jaime Russell and Marina Warner note (though I went to see it in the British Library for myself), Coleridge wrote in the margin on page 24 of the second volume, "R. Pitta syllogized. Zombi is the name of the Angolan God. But the Angolan God is the Devil. Ergo, Zombi is the name of the Devil. The logic limps in the article 'the,' instead of 'a.'"

13. "Zemi" is described as connoting "both the spirit of the dead and the familiar soulless 'walking dead'" (Daniel Cohen 39). I am not able to corroborate this definition; the *Encyclopaedia Britannica* lists the word as signifying only gods or the stone idols made to represent a household deity. For a definition of duppy, see *Folklore: A Quarterly Review* 15 (1909): 90.

14. This same passage is pointed to by Elizabeth McAlister in her essay "Slaves, Cannibals, and Infected Hyper-Whites" as a probable ancestor of the zombie-bouteille she describes at length elsewhere. For other depictions of nkisi, minkisi, and Congo beliefs, see Simon Bockie, *Death and the Invisible Powers*; and Jason Young, *Rituals of Resistance*.

15. However, in *Fantastic Metamorphoses, Other Worlds*, Marina Warner notes that elsewhere in Hearn's oeuvre he quotes a girl saying that zombies look "like people." For Warner, this signifies that the term later "widened out to enfold ghosts and spectres of all kinds" (128).

16. Legends and the names for various entities vary throughout the Caribbean. An early "zombie story" (1920) by Henry S. Whitehead and included in Peter Haining's anthology *Zombie! Stories of the Walking Dead*, describes the Jumbee of the Virgin Islands. The word Jumbee is often cited in the etymological histories of zombie, though the exact nature of their intertwined history is unclear. In Whitehead's story, "Jumbee" is used as a catchall phrase to refer to several different kinds of entities: there is a shape-shifting dog that grows larger with each step (80); the "Hanging Jumbee," a trio of apparitions that float in the air with a cloud of mist obscuring their feet (78); and a figure more like a revenant or ghost.

17. Though it is clear that Dutertre suggests the name, it may have been Père Labat who first used the phrase "Le Pays des Revenants" (Warner 155). I have been unable to find the phrase in Labat's *Voyage aux isles*.

18. In the introduction to the 1993 edition of *Voyage aux isles*, Michel LeBris writes, "The most shocking thing is to see how P. Labat became, for the negres of Martinique, a sort of bogeyman, a zombi, a revenant, that must be feared and venerated. To misbehaving children, the mothers cry, 'I will make P. Labat come get you!'" (xiii). Hearn, too, makes much of the fact that the people of Martinique believe that the ghost of Pere Labat haunts the island. Though he may not have drawn attention to Martinique's brand of zombi, he has, according to popular legend, become one of their most famous. He is said to roam the night carrying a lantern (Hearn 152).

19. This scene is addressed in Garraway, cited previously, and Montague Summers, *The Vampire* (318).

20. This aspect of the mythology is probably described in the most detail by Davis, regarding the case of Clairvius Narcisse particularly. See *Ethnobiology of the Haitian Zombie* and *The Serpent and the Rainbow*.

21. Edward Long describes the duppy as a relatively benign ghost of a friend or loved one (2:416).

22. Descourtliz also mentions, among references to charms that make one insensible to pain, spells that induce sickness in an enemy, invisible force fields that can be installed to protect property, and the use of poisons by certain sorcerers to punish those that cross the Vaudoux (116–18).

23. It seems especially pertinent that the soul is taken to a faraway desert land, as Africans were kidnapped and taken from their homeland to labor as slaves, first via the trans-Saharan trade (seventh to fourteenth centuries) and later via the transatlantic slave trade in the colonies.

24. Though doubts have been cast on Dapper's use of sources, critics saying that his tome amounts to little more than a compendium of previously published sources—Dapper himself never visited the dark continent—his discussion of the Loanga region is singled out by Adam Jones in his article "Decompiling Dapper: A Preliminary Search for Evidence" as one of the places where Dapper relied most on unpublished accounts, specifically, the testimonials of sea captains and the writings of employees of the Dutch East India Trading Company.

25. In *Slavery and Social Death*, Orlando Patterson emphasizes that in records kept between 1701 and 1810 under 20 percent of slaves were logged as genuine prisoners of war; after European demand for slaves had been made known, "wars" between African tribes were largely economically motivated, thinly veiled kidnapping expeditions (119).

26. It is not always clear in the zombie myth what effect salt will have: merely to awaken the zombie to its unnatural state or to arouse violence. Métraux writes, "Zombies have to be fed, but care must be taken never to allow them a taste of salt. One grain is enough to dispel their lethargy and renew their will to power" (*Haiti* 96). It might be a slight stretch to note that salt was one of the first traded commodities, thus linking the mythology to the development of global exchange. Salt was also used as a currency by ancient societies; Marco Polo returned from the Orient with pressed salt cakes on which the Tibetans had impressed the faces of their leaders (Wright 259). Thus salt was one of the very first examples of the commodity fetish. Most simply, though, salt was also used in burial and baptism ceremonies among the Congolese to keep away witches (J. R. Young 167). It was also a preservative used to embalm the dead, so it is no surprise that it should be this ingredient that allows the zombie to remember that it is no longer living.

27. Though knowledge of herbs is part of the African shaman's arsenal, it was believed in traditional African mythology that all disease was the result of sorcery, and sorcery, good or evil, was produced by the spirits who favored the shaman. See Patricia Ann Lynch and Jeremy Robert's *African Mythology A–Z* (97–103).

28. See *The Journals of Mary Shelley: 1814–1844*, ed. Paula R. Feldman and Diana Scott-Kilvert. The readings listed in the Journals have been made searchable by a database published at the University of Pennsylvania: www.english.upenn.edu/Projects/knarf/MShelley/reading.html.

29. See also on this point, *Inquiring Spirit: A New Presentation of Coleridge from His Published and Unpublished Prose Writings*, ed. Kathleen Coburn (52).

30. See Tim May, "Coleridge's Slave Trade Lecture."

31. Long recounts how in one instance a man was called out to demonstrate this invulnerability under the power of the potion and was killed for all to see; this, Long says, brought the practice of Obeah into disrepute for some time (418).

32. The famous "Three-finger'd Jack," a.k.a. Jack Mansong, was a runaway Jamaican slave, Obeah man, leader, and, to some, folk hero. He is discussed in Benjamin Moseley's "A Treatise on Sugar" (1799); William Burdett's 1801 "The Life and Exploits of Three Fingered Jack, the Terror of Jamaica, With a Particular Account of the Obi," which was later dramatized for the stage; and in sentimentalized accounts like *Obi, or The History of Three-Fingered Jack in a Series of Letters*, an epistolary novel by William Earle (1804). Moseley's account of the criminal Three-Fingered Jack is preceded by a description of the Obeah man's powers, which include "the application of poisons (193). See also in this vein, *Hamel, the Obeah Man (1827)*, by Cynric R. Williams.

33. The point of inducing suspended animation seems to be the desire for the organs to be fresh when harvested from the victim; see St. John 236–41. On cannibalism and St. John, see especially Mimi Sheller, *Consuming the Caribbean*.

34. This story is attributed to the Haitian paper *L'Oeil*; other sources from which St. John draws include another Haitian newspaper, *Le Peuple*, a clerical journal called *La Vérité*, the French newspaper *Le Moniteur Officiel*, *British Daily News*, and *The New*

York Evening Post and *The World*. This illustrates that interest in stories of Haitian cannibalism and Vaudou was far-reaching in the 1880s.

35. Besides W. B. Seabrook's *Magic Island*, we might include among this second wave of zombie dissemination *The White King of La Gonave* by Wirkus, both of Craige's books, and Stamper's *Beyond the Seas*. Add to these the artist Richard A Loederer's *Voodoo Fire in Haiti* (1932), translated from the German in 1935, and two very different anthropological works by women: Zora Neale Hurston's *Tell My Horse* (1938) and Edna Taft's *A Puritan in Voodoo Land (1938)*. The first wave, then, would include scant references to figures called "zombies" that resemble our modern-day acceptance of the term only in part, from Blessebois's *Zombi du Gran Perou* (1697) to Lafcadio Hearn's *Country of Comers-Back (1889)*.

36. See Buck-Morss for a discussion of the European invocation of slavery (836).

37. Cf. Vincent Brown, "Social Death and Political Life in the Study of Slavery"; and Walter Johnson, "On Agency."

38. For other discussions of the slave as a kind of living dead or the way sovereignty is established through the exercise and pronouncement of death, see Georgio Agamben, *Homo Sacer*; Achille Mbembe, "Necropolitics"; Russ Castronovo, *Necrocitizenship*; and Fanon, *The Wretched of the Earth*. For a discussion of death and its implications for resistance, see Ian Baucom's *Specters of the Atlantic*; Vincent Brown's *The Reaper's Garden*; and Trevor Burnard's article "Jamaica as America, America as Jamaica," in which he writes of Brown's argument, "There is an intrinsic problem with seeing Jamaica as a land haunted by death; death overwhelms life" (207).

39. Though Brown discusses many aspects of the "mortuary politics" exhibited in the sugarcane colony in his "political history of death" in Jamaica" (10), including strategies used by the masters to keep slaves in line (e.g., the exhibition of corpses), here I am referring to the part of his argument that describes slave strategies like infanticide and suicide but also burial ceremonies and conceptions of the afterlife. Brown writes, "In Jamaican slave society and its transatlantic hinterlands, at least, death tended and nurtured the activities of the living, cultivating their understanding of the world and their struggle to shape it. In this reaper's garden, death helped to constitute life, and the dead were an undeniable presence" (The Reaper's Garden 255).

40. Though a revered general during the revolution, Christophe would oust Jean-Jacques Dessalines from power, declare himself king of Haiti, and become a corrupt and unpopular monarch. He shot himself with a silver bullet in 1820 rather than face removal from power by a political coup.

41. Elsewhere in the book, Herskovitz describes this "unnatural" death of sorcery as precisely that which leads to the production of the zombie: "On occasion, an apparent death is felt not to be a real death, but rather the simulacra of death brought about by the machination of a sorcerer." The enslaved corpse is only allowed to return "to the grave when the time decreed by God for his natural death is reached, or if he is accidentally fed salt" (245–46).

42. Code Noir, 1685. Article II: all slaves will be baptized and instructed in Catholicism. Article III: all other religions prohibited from practice (reprinted in Dubois and Garrigus 14).

43. The leader Boukman, of the above quotation, was (by most accounts) a Vaudou priest who led the Bois Caïman ceremony prior to the first slave revolt in August 1793. On the doubtfulness of certain aspects of the ceremony's representation, Geggus

cautions that "one should note that the historicity of the Bois Caïman ceremony hangs by quite a slender thread. There is a contemporary document, a deposition by one of the conspirators, which provides basic details of the meeting of the organizers, but it mentions nothing about a religious ceremony. . . . That Boukman himself was actually a houngan is not obvious from these [early] accounts" (Geggus 18).

44. The source for this information is an online article by W. F. Burton Sellers, "Heroes of Haiti." See L'ouvertureproject.org for a wiki of resources on the Haitian Revolution.

45. Makandal worked through *pacotilleurs*, slaves selling petty trifles to other slaves; "he had adepts and followers within slave society and within the parameters of the plantation system who, as pacotilleurs, as domestic slaves on errand, or as 'occasional' maroons, actively procured and distributed various poisons, potions, and other 'remedies'" (Fick 61).

46. See Dubois, *Avengers* 51, in contrast to Fick 63.

47. Jean Zombi is also discussed in Milo Rigaud's 1953 work, "La tradition voudoo et le voudoo haïtien, son temple, ses mystères, sa magie."

48. The man known as Jean Zombi may have been so called because he was considered to be more than a man, a cross between a human and a supernatural figure, as reflects earlier etymologies of the word, where it meant merely "spirit." As Dayan notes, he is a member of the pantheon of Petro lwa, worshipped as a god (Haiti, History, and the Gods 36).

49. Dalmas writes, "Flames had consumed one hundred sugar works; and twenty-thousand slaves, once peaceful and submissive, were now so many cannibals, threatening Cap Français with the same fate" (excerpt translated by and published in Dubois and Garrigus 93).

50. Léger mentions a third, though I cannot find other references to this man: "Hallaou pretended to be immune from death by virtue of a white cock which never left him" (356).

51. Fick quotes De Vassière: "The frequent punishments and torture which their compatriots suffer before their eyes creates no fear in them whatsoever, and it must be said that the victims endure the most cruel torments with an unequalled steadfastness, appearing on the scaffold and at the stake with ferocious courage and tranquility" (qtd. in Fick 70; De Vassière, *La Société* 249).

52. The translator's note here reads: "This word is unclear in the letter; it could either be transe (trance) or trame (conspiracy), but the context of the document makes it probable that it is the latter" (Dubois and Garrigus 94). For an investigation of the role Vaudou played in the revolution, however, the word trance would be just as suitable, given that the letter's oblique suggestion is that there is some kind of unseen "motor" powering the slaves.

53. On both these points, see Fick 42 and note 292, respectively.

54. The allusion is to C.L.R. James's *The Black Jacobins: Toussaint L'Ouverture and the San Domingo Revolution* (1938).

55. See again on death as rebellion, Brown's *The Reaper's Garden*.

2 / "American" Zombies

1. Most likely, this zombie is put to work in the service of the bokor who performed the ceremony, as they are typically depicted as having many zombies in their employ.

2. Gary Rhodes, for example, notes a reference to "concombre zombi," which is elsewhere implicated in zombie making, in Henry C. Castellanos, *New Orleans as It Was: Episodes of Louisiana Life* (1905); in Castellanos's discussion of "philters, drugs," and "gris-gris," it is mentioned as the Jamestown weed (elsewhere jimsum weed), sometimes put in coffee—presumably for the recreational effects produced when the sedative is used in small doses (Rhodes 75). Thus the same ingredients used in zombie-making in Haiti may serve different purposes in the American South.

3. Davis's *Passage of Darkness* famously pronounced that the principal ingredient involved in the process of zombification is tetrododoxin, a paralyzing poison from the puffer fish, and that the workings of these witch doctors, who seemingly raise the soulless dead to labor for them, was scientifically possible, the result of a paralytic agent that induces a state resembling death, and a combination of mind-numbing drugs that keep the victim in a subservient state.

4. A darker and more dubious modern myth claims that Laveau provided Madame Delphine Lalaurie, the most famous sadist and slave torturer of New Orleans, with the zombie powder for use in her husband's experiments (Love and Shannon 98).

5. On this subject, there are several good essays in Martin Munro and Celia Britton, eds., *American Creoles*.

6. This prescription for undoing a hex, to "draw the enemy's 'wine,'" is corroborated by Hurston's account of Hoodoo beliefs (*Of Mules and Men* 289).

7. The powders that Morton found in all of his hats and that a secretary in the office ingested in a cup of water, swelling her lips grotesquely, sound something like the zombification powders described by Davis in his pharmacological study of the Haitian zombie, *Passage of Darkness*, and his recounting of his adventures, *The Serpent and the Rainbow*.

8. The description then continues: "In his vest pocket was a large packet of tinder and phosphate and lime. On his chest he had a little sack full of hair, herbs, and bits of bone, which they call a fetish." Dubois writes of this arsenal, "The law of liberty, ingredients for firing a gun, and a powerful amulet to call on the help of the gods: clearly, a potent combination" (Dubois, *Avengers* 102–3).

9. This lack of zombies in the South is further corroborated by Gary Rhodes in his *White Zombie*. He nonetheless notes this article of March 30, 1919, from the *New Orleans Item*: "Mammy Zoe Appeases Gran' Zombi and Saves Brides Wedding Gown" (75). This, too, clearly refers to the deity Zombi rather than the walking dead, as does Natalie Vivian Scott's play *Zombi* (Rhodes 77–78). Rhodes also discusses another early text, *Drums of Damballa* (1932), by H. Bedford-Jones, which does describe the zombi as "a resurrected corpse that obeyed the orders of the voodoo priest" (Rhodes 82) but may be borrowing from Seabrook.

10. Further, this use of a "zombie salve" would suggest that Louisiana Voodooists possessed such a command of medicinal ingredients that they could produce varying levels of results, from complete zombification to a slight immunity to pain that would still allow the performer to play his part. It should be noted that the ingredient Davis identifies as the agent of the zombie powder, tetrododoxin, is valued for its pain-killing properties. Minuscule doses can produce in late-stage cancer patients a weeklong reprieve from their constant suffering. See *Wired Magazine*, "Puffer Fish Pain-Killer." Though we cannot know whether the salve here contains this same compound.

11. For example, Faustin Wirkus and Taney Dudley's *The White King of La Gonave* (1931), John Houston Craige's *Black Baghdad* (1933) and *Cannibal Cousins* (1934), and W. J. Stamper's *Beyond the Seas* (1935).

12. Before the American occupation began in July 1915, there were three political coups within a year, resulting in changes of power from President Oreste to President Zamor to President Théodore. This political instability led to American concerns about investments in the country and figured as a major motivation for the military occupation. See Mary Renda, *Taking Haiti*.

13. Hutter was the pen name of Garnett Weston, screenwriter of *White Zombie* for the director, Victor Halperin (Haining 14). Markman Ellis discusses this story and some of the others of this early period in his *History of Gothic Fiction*.

14. It is relatively rare to find lucid zombies in Haitian folklore; at best, when they do speak, it tends to be in simple, monosyllabic phrases, and the Haitian zombie speaks either through its nose or in a very nasal voice. Ackerman and Gautier note that this detail about the zombie's nasal voice may come from a Ghanaian legend about the dead breaking their noses on the banks of the river Nsatshi (479).

15. The narrator deduces from this that Marie must be 150 years old; this detail of a zombie's longevity, too, seems to depart from the Haitian mythology.

16. In his *History of Gothic Fiction*, Markman Ellis reads this story as an overt critique of the Haitian Revolution; Ellis writes that Hutter "cannily rewrites the zombie trope as a counter-revolutionary argument, reversing Seabrook's gothic identification of the zombie with the slaves of modern capitalism" (229).

17. This narrative is evidenced, for example, in a firsthand account told by the former Marine William J. Stamper in his collection *Beyond the Seas*. In a piece called "Ti Michel," Stamper describes a Haitian man who confesses that he once came home to find his daughter being raped and strangled by a police officer. He killed the officer, but it was too late to save his daughter. In recounting his personal tragedy to the Marine, the Haitian emphasizes how corrupt Haiti was before the American presence: "There was no law in those days before the Americans came to our shores, no justice. The gendarme [police officer] swaggered up to your counter, bought your rum, and spat in your face for payment. He mistreated your family, and if you reported it to the Commandant, you were kicked and clubbed for your trouble. Don't you think Ti Michel would have had a chance for a fair trial if you had been here then, Monsieur?" (Stamper 147–48).

18. From time to time the theme of slave rebellion overtly resurfaces in zombie fiction. For example, a 2004 story by Derek Gunn, "A Diabolical Plan" (published in *The Undead Zombie Anthology*, edited by D. L. Snell and Elijah Hall), revisits the colonial period—specifically, 1791, the year of the slave revolt on Saint Domingue—and depicts a battle between British and French ships trolling their imperial interests. The French have discovered contagious viral zombies on an island in their control and have taken them aboard in the hope of releasing the walking dead on British soil.

19. A rare exception to this trend is found in the film *The Devil's Daughter* (1934), in which a black woman of Haitian ancestry pretends to work "Obeah" on her half sister from New York in order to maintain control of the ancestral plantation. However, there is no actual magic in this narrative, as the threat of a zombielike spell turns out to just be a ruse. See Chera Kee's "Women of Color as Zombie Masters," in which she describes this film and several of the others that I discuss here.

20. See, e.g., Edna Aizenberg, "'I Walked with a Zombie': The Pleasures and Perils of Postcolonial Hybridity"; Ellen Draper, "Zombie Women When the Gaze Is Male"; Lizabeth Paravisini-Gebert, "Women Possessed"; Rhodes, *White Zombie*; and Shannon Rose Riley, "Cannibals, Zombies, and the Cultural Performance of 'Going Native.'"

21. See Armond White's unpopular review of *12 Years a Slave*, "Can't Trust It," in which he writes, "Northrup's travail merely makes it possible for some viewers to feel good about feeling bad.... *12 Years a Slave* lets them congratulate themselves for 'being aghast at slavery.'" For a counterpoint, see Wesley Morris's review of the film, "Song of Solomon."

22. Though there is a Cambodian man capable of raising the dead in *Revolt of the Zombies*, he is quickly killed off and a white man takes over the role of zombifier.

23. The same year, a television episode of the series *The Saint*, called "Sibao," depicts Simon Templar's adventures in Haiti. Though much Vaudou is depicted, the ultimate conflict is that a white villain is seeking to marry into a powerful Vaudouist's family to gain the secrets of the cult. The zombie also doesn't seem to be the puppet of anyone so much as a natural phenomenon. The protagonist is told, "This is Haiti, Mr. Templar. Those who die violently avenge themselves. This is the land of the undead. The living dead, if you like. The zombie."

24. Another 1974 film, *Night of the Sorcerers*, originally *La noche de los brujos*, depicts an African cult that makes white women into vampire-zombie "leopard women." Apart from the opening scene of their sacrifice, however, all of the violence perpetrated in the film is by the white "zombies."

25. Barbara Bruce, "Guess Who's Going to Be Dinner: Sidney Poitier, Black Militancy, and the Ambivalence of Race in Romero's *Night of the Living Dead*." See also Robert Lightening's essay "Interracial Tensions in *Night of the Living Dead*"; and not only for a discussion of race in the film but also a general overview of its most salient themes and foundational scholarship (like that of Robin Wood and R. H. W. Dillard), see Stephen Harper's essay "*Night of the Living Dead*: Reappraising an Undead Classic."

26. Many film critics find this explanation of the outbreak unconvincing, either because it is only mentioned in passing and is never clarified in the film or because they feel there is reason to doubt the veracity of the television reports. Jennifer Cooke shares this skepticism and feels that the ill-defined origin of the phenomenon in *Night of the Living Dead* underscores that zombies "confront us as the inexplicable, the irrational, in a world we would like to think of as rational and explainable; they are what confounds science in a world where science is perceived to be at the forefront of progress" (170). Many draw a similar conclusion about the zombie's illustration of the limits of human progress, but I feel that this aspect of the myth is specifically linked to the horrors of slavery out of which the zombie originally arose.

27. Despite the tantalizing tagline of *Dawn of the Dead* (1978), "When there is no room in hell, the dead will walk the earth," critics agree that Romero's zombie is decidedly "nonsupernatural" (Kay and Gordon 95). Rebecca May suggests, in her preface to *Zombology, Library of the Living Dead*, that zombies sometimes allegorize overpopulation. What we might see in this line is a clever antithesis that codes the predominant fear the zombie begins to represent from the late 1970s on: "When there is no more room on Earth, we'll end up beneath it."

28. This collision of mythologies was in large part the subject of my doctoral dissertation, "The Modern Zombie: Living Death in the Technological Age."

29. I think, too, of Lincoln's description in his second inaugural address of plantation owners "wringing their bread from the sweat of other men's faces" and of Michel de Montaigne's essay "Of Cannibalism," but the concept has also been applied to postcolonial exoticism and even tourism. See bell hooks, "Eating the Other"; and C. Richard King, "The (Mis)uses of Cannibalism in Contemporary Cultural Critique."

30. The last text that Jennifer Cooke examines in *Legacies of Plague* is Bruce LaBruce's film that combines the zombie with the art-house film and gay pornography, *Otto: Or, Up with Dead People*. Cooke discusses, among other things, the commentary that the film makes about the AIDS epidemic. See also on the themes of contagion and zombielike creatures, Priscilla Wald, *Contagious*.

31. For example, the blogger at concatenation.org divides the genre into zombies "BR," Before Romero, and "AR," After Romero.

32. In his *Zombie Movie Encyclopedia*, Peter Dendle notes that this tactic is also mentioned in *Creature with the Atom Brain* and "put to the test" in *Dr. Orloff's Monster* (1964) (6). Dendle likewise notes that the decayed, rotting zombie precedes Romero but is also considered a mainstay of the "new-style zombie" (5).

33. Romero has spoken about this connection in various interviews; see, e.g., Mariana McConnell, "Interview: George A. Romero on *Diary of the Dead*." See also Deborah Christie's discussion of the connection between the novel and the film in "A Dead New World: Richard Matheson and the Modern Zombie," in Christie and Lauro, *Better Off Dead* (2011).

34. A critique of capitalism has been directly associated with the modern zombie myth since Romero's films drew a comparison between the capitalist consumer and the unabating hunger of the zombie horde; in fact, as we've seen, the thematic concern with the human as commodity stretches farther back in time, to the zombie's origins under colonial, precapitalist rule. For a discussion of the theme of consumerism in *Dawn of the Dead*, see Stephen Harper, "Zombies, Malls, and the Consumerism Debate"; Matthew Walker, "When There's No More Room in Hell, the Dead Will Shop the Earth"; and Kevin Wetmore's discussion of the film and its 2004 remake in *Back from the Dead*. Though it is usually this film that is cited as providing a link between zombies and capitalist critique, for a broader discussion of zombies and capitalism, see Annalee Newitz, *Pretend We're Dead*; and David McNally, *Monsters of the Market*.

35. After seeing the film in this context, Andy Warhol's *inter/view* magazine critic, George Abagnalo, wrote, "It should open at an art house and run for at least a month, because it is a work of art"; quoted in *Birth of the Living Dead*. See also Abagnalo and Ork's 1969 interview with Romero, in Tony Williams, ed., *George A. Romero: Interviews*.

36. For a sketch of the survivalist subculture that dialogues with the zombie narrative, see Christopher Zealand, "The National Strategy for Zombie Containment."

37. The British film *Shaun of the Dead* (2004) has a somewhat similar ending: after the outbreak has been contained some zombies are integrated into commercial entertainment and used on game shows. On *Fido*, See Michele Braun's essay "It's So Hard to Get Good Help These Days."

38. See, e.g., James Lowder, *Triumph of the Walking Dead*; and Dawn Keetley, "We're All Infected."

39 There is a similar theme underlined in *Voodoo Man* (1944), also starring Bela Lugosi, at the picture's end, when the scriptwriter protagonist turns his adventures into a screenplay for his boss, saying, "There's your horror story. . . . Why don't you get that actor Bela Lugosi [for the part of the Voodoo Man]? It's right up his alley."

40. These eye coverings are seen in the aforementioned *Zombies on Broadway* and are mentioned in Andre Cajun's description of performative zombies in *Louisiana Voodoo*.

3 / Haitian Zombis

1. For a discussion of zombie bottles, see again Elizabeth McAlister, "A Sorcerer's Bottle."

2. I tend to use the terms *houngan* or *oungan* and *bocor* or *bokor* interchangeably, though Hurston writes, "Some maintain that a real and true priest of Voodoo, the houngan, has nothing to do with [zombification]. That it is the bocor and priests of the devil—worshipping cults—who do these things. But it is not always easy to tell just who is a houngan and who is a bocor" (*Tell My Horse* 189).

3. For the sake of reconstruction after the revolution, forced labor was instituted under the regulations put in place by Toussaint L'Ouverture. See, for one description among many, Ludwell Lee Montague's *Haiti and the United States, 1714–1938*: "This plan of reconstruction, conceived by an ex-slave, was effective in restoring order and a certain degree of prosperity, but, for the time at least, it relegated the freedmen to something akin to their former status" (8). See also Thomas Ott, *The Haitian Revolution, 1789–1804*; and Madison Smartt Bell, *Toussaint Louverture: A Biography*.

4. See Davis, *The Serpent and the Rainbow*, where zombification is defined as "a social sanction imposed by recognized corporate groups whose responsibility included the policing of that society" (213).

5. I have not found that early twentieth-century accounts of the zombie, like those by William Seabrook, Zora Neale Hurston, Edna Taft, and others, bear this description of the use of the zombie as moral punishment, though the tendency of the secret societies to punish their enemies is affirmed. Neither is this feature of zombification described in Maya Deren's *Divine Horsemen*, written in 1953, or Alfred Métraux's writings on the subject.

6. Wade Davis, the most vocal proponent of this theory, develops Michel Laguerre's assertion that the secret societies "represented a legitimate political and juridical force in the vodun society" (Davis, Serpent and the Rainbow, 215). In an interesting application of this aspect of the mythology, Paravisini-Gebert's claims in "Women Possessed" that "many of Hollywood's zombie films employ this punishment function of zombification as a plot element, particularly in the presentation of women zombified as punishment for adultery or lustful behavior" (56n6).

7. "Papa Doc" Duvalier ruled from 1957 to 1971, "Baby Doc" from 1971 to 1986. As is well known, François Duvalier published a monograph on Vaudou (with Lorimer Denis) titled *L'Evolution graduelle du vaudou* (The Gradual Evolution of Voodoo); adopted the symbolic top hat associated with Baron Samedi, lord of the cemetery; and encouraged at every turn the sense that he was more than human. He once said, it is oft repeated, "My enemies cannot get me, I *am* already an *immaterial* being!" (*Time*, "Death and the Legacy of Papa Doc Duvalier").

8. See, e.g., Jean Price-Mars, *Ainsi parla l'oncle*, and the discussion of it in Michel Laguerre, *Voodoo and Politics in Haiti*; and Maximilien Laroche, "Imaginaire populaire et littérature."

9. Economic interests are greatly implicated in the American occupation. See especially the discussion of Hasco, a sugar company, in Mary Renda, *Taking Haiti*.

10. Amy Wilentz singles out several modern-day zombies in her *New York Times* op-ed. She writes, "There are many reasons the zombie, sprung from the colonial slave economy, is returning now to haunt us. Of course, the zombie is scary in a primordial way, but in a modern way, too. He's the living dead, but he's also the inanimate animated, the robot of industrial dystopias.... He's labor without grievance. He works free and never goes on strike. You don't have to feed him much. He's a Foxconn worker in China; a maquiladora seamstress in Guatemala." She also makes this point in her book *Farewell, Fred Voodoo* (96).

11. Although contrapasso literally means "suffer the opposite," many of the sinners in Dante's *Comedia* actually continue to suffer their sins into the afterlife or must experience what they inflicted on others. The zombie's "contrapasso," then, is that the occupying nation is figured as being invaded by the Caribbean island's mythology.

12. See, e.g., Michel-Rolph Trouillot's *Silencing the Past*, which begins with a description of the inherent fluidity between "the sociohistoric process" and "our knowledge of that process" (3) and "the reluctance with which theories of history have dealt with this ambiguity" (4), before accounting for the forces and interests inherent in the production of Haitian "history" and the role that silencing plays in determining that history.

13. See also Farmer's many other works on the subject, such as *The Uses of Haiti* and his discussion of Haiti in *Pathologies of Power*. For a sense of the complication of charity and neocolonial intervention in Haiti, see Patrick Bellegarde-Smith, "A Man-Made Disaster."

14. Exactly what happened in the US-backed ousting of President Aristide in 1990 and then again in 2004 is beyond the purview of this history of a Haitian myth, but it should not be doubted that this was a move made in the interest of American business and not for the sake of "restoring democracy," as Noam Chomsky emphasizes in *Getting Haiti Right This Time*. Aristide's removal from power reveals the neocolonial reality in which Haiti is mired (1), to which the zombie myth also reacts. See also Peter Hallward's excellent book *Damming the Flood*.

15. Carpentier takes poetic license here. In point of fact, Sans-Souci was actually modeled after the palace of Frederick the Great (Loederer 238).

16. The body of the king, who commited suicide rather than be apprehended by the mob, was, in fact, as the novel states, actually hidden in a pool of mortar at the Citadel La Ferrière, presumably to keep his corpse from being torn apart by the crowd. In Carpentier's book, however, the king's death echoes his cruel execution of a bishop, whom he ordered immured and left to die.

17. Paravisini-Gebert reads this novel as revealing "Carpentier's hopelessness concerning the Haitian land and its people" (123). See "The Haitian Revolution in Interstices and Shadows." I take a more optimistic approach, in line with those who focus on the ritualistic repetition of the novel, interpreting it as being equally revealing of the usefulness of literary retellings.

18. According to Degoul's informants, the knowledge of how to make zombies is often depicted as coming from the Christian god, but there is no implication that it

is Christ himself who raises these dead for Haitians. Christ is not appealed to as the source of Haitian power; rather he is reclaimed in their vernacular: *Christ was a witch doctor!* In an alternate version of this origin story, Elizabeth McAlister relates a story in which Jesus is figured as the first zombi; in this narrative, the soldiers guarding Jesus' tomb were Haitian and stole the secret of his revivification. As McAlister states, this strand acknowledges the sorcerer's opposition to Christianity. McAlister, "The Jew in the Haitian Imagination" (92); and "Slaves, Cannibals, and Hyper-Whites" (467).

19. Though Makandal is never explicitly named in this passage, true to Chantal's description, his poisons were often put in the water supply of "les Blancs." Another description makes the claim that the ancestors are also responsible for the yellow fever epidemic that was a factor in the revolution (Degoul, "Dos a la vie, dos a la mort" 248).

20. In a national decree of April 4, 2003, Aristide proclaimed, "Vodou is henceforth to be fully recognized as a religion, empowered to fulfill its mission throughout the country consistent with the constitution and the laws of the Republic, pending the adoption of a law relating to its legal status" (qtd. in Pettinger 423).

21. In his 1973 history of the Haitian Revolution, Thomas Ott called Haiti's relationship with the Dominican Republic its "most troubled foreign relationship," which seems shocking given all the pressure and intervention imposed by France and the United States. Ott cites Trujillo's slaughter of 12,000 Haitian migrant workers in 1937 and escalating tensions in the 1960s (192–93).

22. Almost in the same breath, Colbert justifies a recent example of American intervention: "At the same time, when the Americans penetrated Haitian soil, in 1994, it was us who had invited them. . . . [I]f it hadn't been for that, they wouldn't have been able to do it. Because . . . we have Vaudou. . . . we have devils." Colbert is referring here to the American military intervention under President Bill Clinton after Aristide was removed from power for the first time. (31)

23. Fanon is describing the role of storytellers in Algeria in the 1950s (*The Wretched of the Earth* 241).

24. On this point, Dash quotes Fanon (*Black Skin, White Masks*, 177): "It is a vigorous style, alive with rhythms, struck through and through with bursting life. . . . The new movement gives rise to a new rhythm of life and to forgotten muscular tensions, and develops the imagination" (Dash 333). The ellipsis is present in Dash's quotation.

There are other places where Fanon's imagery is more concretely reminiscent of awakening or resurrection. Fanon also writes: "The storytellers who used to relate inert episodes now *bring them alive* and introduce into them modifications which are increasingly fundamental" (Fanon, "National Culture" 155; emphasis mine). Or, in his description of the way revolutionary consciousness affects the people's craftsmanship of the human figure: "The inexpressive or overwrought mask *comes to life* and the arms tend to be raised from the body as if to sketch an action" (*Wretched of the Earth* 242; emphasis mine).

25. As Wilentz notes in "A Zombie Is a Slave Forever," "A Taste of Salt" was the name of a literacy campaign initiated by liberation theologians in Haiti after the fall of the Duvalier regime. With all the use that Papa Doc Duvalier made of the iconography of the zombie, and particularly of Baron Samedi, this appropriation of the terminology by the opposition is all the more salient. See, on this point, the chapter "Voudou Is His Arm" in Diederich and Burt's *Papa Doc* (1969) and James Ferguson's *Papa Doc, Baby Doc*. See also Wilentz, *Farewell, Fred Voodoo*.

26. Trouillot writes that "Ignace Nau inaugurated in Haiti the literary genre of historical fiction" (17). Combining the historical novel with the fantastical elements of local folklore, Nau was one of the first to implement what would become a central feature of "la literature antillaise."

27. The first novel written entirely in Kreyol is Frankétienne's 1975 *Dézafi*, which is discussed later in the chapter.

28. There are zombies mentioned to varying degrees in many texts I do not describe here—like Jean-Claude Fignolé's *Les possédés de la pleine lune* (1987) or *Aube tranquille* (1990), or Stanley Péan's *Zombi Blues* (1996), or Lyonel Trouillot's *Thérèse en mille morceaux* (2000), or Magloire Saint-Aude's *Veillée*, published posthumously in 2003.

29. See also Léon-François Hoffmann's "The Haitian Novel during the Last Ten Years" for its discussion of the difficulty of publishing literature critical of the dictatorship during the Duvalier regime.

30. Although its focus is not on figures of the living dead, Jana Evans Braziel's tellingly titled *Duvalier's Ghosts* also bears some relevance, particularly in its attention to the work of Edwige Danticat.

31. In 2002, when Frankétienne revisited and rewrote the Creole *Dézafi* yet again, the text was updated to emphasize the present-day Haitian society. Douglas claims that through the addition of extra words and hyperbolic statements, Frankétienne indicates stylistically, if not thematically, that the people's struggle continues.

32. See also Glover's discussion of the rebellion of Frankétienne's zombies in "Exploiting the Undead," and her discussion of the novel in *Haiti Unbound*. See also Lucy Swanson, "Zombie Nation?," for a detailed discussion of the significance of bois nouveau and the zombi's ability to wake to consciousness.

33. See, e.g., Antoine Dalmas, *Histoire de la revolution de Saint Domingue*, which described slaves removing their masters' eyes with a red hot *tire-bouchon* (corkscrew), disemboweling a pregnant colonist, and stoning the fetus to death (209).

34. For an example of contemporary folkloric rebel zombies that turn against their master and "eat" him, see McAlister, "Slaves, Cannibals, and Hyper-Whites" (468).

35. I especially like the discussion of this trend in McAlister's "Slaves, Cannibals, and Infected Hyber-Whites": "The living take charge of their history when they mimetically perform master-slave relationships with the dead. The production of spiritual (and bodily) zonbis shows us how groups remember history and enact its consequences in ritual arts. The slave trade and colonial slavery—whose *modus operandus* was to cast living humans as commodities—are quite literally encoded and reenacted in this living object. Just as slavery depended on capturing, containing, and forcing the labor of thousands of people, so does this form of mystical work reenact the same process in local terms. It is, as [Michael] Taussig famously put it, history as sorcery" (McAlister 464–65; original emphasis). She is referring to Michael Taussig, *Shamanism, Colonialism, and the Wild Man: A Study in Terror and Healing*.

36. I include in this category texts that revise the work of others or that play with repetition and recurrence in a manner recalling the zombie motif. Textual zombies are discussed at length in the next chapter.

37. Both Paravisini-Gebert's chapter "Women Possessed" and Glover's "Exploiting the Undead" discuss these interrelated texts.

38. The narrator repeatedly describes her inability to tell the difference between night and day, and as such, she is a good model for a third possibility of what the

former zombie might look like, neither "bois nouveau" nor deanimated. Indeed, Glover reads her as such—a not wholly returned being but one who suffers docilely in an in-between state.

39. See, for biographical information on these authors, Raymond Leslie Williams, *The Columbia Guide to the Latin American Novel since 1945*.

40. See Dayan, "France Reads Haiti," for a discussion of Hadriana's whiteness and other complicated aspects of the novel.

41. Lucas writes, "In *Hadriana de tous mes rêves* (1988), René Depestre *exploits* the suggestive potential of vaudou zombification in order to draw out a compensatory oneiric surreality, and to impart a poetic force to a reflection upon death" (61; emphasis mine). See again Glover, "Exploiting the Undead."

4 / Textual Zombies in the Visual Arts

1. Though they may not have used the term textual zombie, many have already done the work of looking at Rhys's invocation of zombies in regard to her intervention in Charlotte Brontë's *Jane Eyre* narrative in order to infuse into the classic text a subliminal critique of colonialism. See especially Sandra Drake, "All That Foolishness / That All Foolishness"; and Thomas Loe, "Patterns of the Zombi in Jean Rhys's *Wide Sargasso Sea*." Also: Romita Choudhury, "'Is there a Ghost, a Zombie There?'"; Judith L. Raiskin, *Snow on the Canefields*; and Carine M. Mardorossian, "Opacity as Obeah in Jean Rhys's Work," for her critique of Raiskin's interpretation of the appropriation of the zombie for white Creole empowerment.

2. In the novel the zombi is defined as "a dead person who seems to be alive or a living person who is dead. A zombi can also be the spirit of a place, usually malignant but sometimes propitiated with sacrifices or offerings of flowers and fruit" (107). "Obeah" is equated with Vaudou and given "another name in South America" (107).

3. See Sutherland, "Rigor/Mortis." As a body that is animate though it be dead, the zombie inherently suggests not only the regimentation of the body under systems of power and ideology, as Sutherland rightly notes of American zombie films; more broadly, the figure also suggests a recasting of the past and a rewriting of a previous mythology.

4. This list is by no means comprehensive. For example, to truly treat the subject one would have to include those texts that also mirror the original, such as the Romeo and Juliet theme of Isaac Marion's novel (2011) and movie *Warm Bodies* (2013), in which a zombie and a human fall in love.

5. While one might suppose that there could be potential in a narrative that returns to the zombie its previous associations with slavery, I have little hope for this alternate version, in which the slaves have been freed because of an influx of zombie labor resulting from a plague. Desperate to get away from his revivified, abusive Pap, Huck joins the docile zombie Jim; the central dilemma of our great protagonist Huck is not whether to free an enslaved friend but whether to put down a "Bagger" who might become dangerous.

6. For another take on this Austenian revision, see Andrea Ruthven's "*Pride and Prejudice* and Post-Feminist Zombies."

7. In addition to two other installations of *Pride and Prejudice and Zombies*, subtitled *Dawn of the Dreadfuls* and *Dreadfully Ever After* (both by Steve Hockensmith, 2010 and 2011), there is also *Sense and Sensibility and Sea Monsters* (Ben H. Winters, 2009), *Mansfield Park and Mummies* (Vera Nazarian, 2009), *Emma and the Werewolves*

(Adam Rann, 2009) ,and several vampire books. Brontë's *Jane Eyre*, it should be mentioned, has also been inducted into the mash-up genre, as a vampire huntress called *Jane Slayre* (Sherri Browning Erin, 2010).

8. Some question whether Rhys had seen the 1949 Val Lewton film, *I Walked with a Zombie* (a version of *Jane Eyre* set on a fictional Caribbean isle called Saint Sebastien), when writing her 1966 novel (see David Thomson, *"Have you seen . . . ?": An Introduction to 1,000 Films*). It was Lewton who brought in the themes from *Jane Eyre* that are visible in the film; these elements are absent in the articles by Inez Wallace of the same name (Haining 16). In fact, Rhys began the book much earlier. A letter she wrote in October 1945 described a novel, which the editors say was an early version of *Wide Sargasso Sea*, as "half finished" (*Letters of Jean Rhys*, ed. Francis Wyndham and Diana Melly, 39–40)—and, as Emily Taylor Meyers points out in her dissertation, "Transnational Romance: The Politics of Desire in Caribbean Novels by Women" (2009), Rhys claimed to have had the idea for the novel in her childhood, though the final version was begun in 1957 (Meyers 35, 53). Although it isn't one of the handful of films noted in these collected letters, Rhys was an avid moviegoer. If she had seen it, we might wonder whether Rhys's choice of the surname "Cosway" for Antoinette might have been subconsciously influenced by the film's leading man, played by Tom Conway.

9. I am not describing any one particular piece here, and therefore I give no title or date; rather, I am characterizing Céleur's sculpture as I saw it in his atelier on the Grand Rue in Port-au-Prince when I visited in 2013.

10. In *Kafou: Haiti, Art, and Vodou*, Colin Dayan connects the "bricolages and assemblages" of the Atis Rezistans artists to the blacksmith and sculptor Georges Liautaud: "Taking the materials condemned as junk . . . [they] reconstruct a world of transformation and belief in our twenty-first century terrors" (33).

11. See, for an in-depth discussion of salvage's aesthetics and its political importance in relation to Caribbean history and politics, Angela Naimou, *Salvage Work*.

12. For a similar work, see Fred Wilson, *Picasso: Whose Rules (with Video)* (1991), also based on Picasso's *Demoiselles*, in which the artist supplants some of the women's faces with a Kifwebe mask. This work is discussed in Ann Gibson's "The African American Aesthetic and Postmodernism."

13. Reed writes in his "Neo-HooDoo Manifesto" that Neo-HooDoo, in contrast, "takes its 'organization' from Haitian VooDoo. . . . Neo-HooDoo believes that every man is an artist and every artist is a priest" (27). See also Neil Schmitz, "NeoHoodoo: The Experimental Fiction of Ismael Reed."

14. Zombies in other comics (such as the superhero Voodoo reanimate Simon Garth, resurrected from the July 1953 issue of the Stan Lee comic *Menace* (5) "Zombie!" in the Tales of the Zombie series, 1973–75) have been largely ignored. See Peter Paik, "Zombies and Other Strangers."

15. For other scholarship on zombies and video games, see Tanya Krzywinska, "Zombies in Gamespace," and Ron Scott, "'Now I'm Feeling Zombified,'" both in Shawn McIntosh and Marc Leverette, eds., *Zombie Culture*.

16. See Christopher Zealand, "The National Strategy for Zombie Containment."

17. See, e.g., the collection edited by Dawn Keetley, *We're All Infected*.

18. There is also a thirty-second version of the film, something like a fifteen-minute *Hamlet* one supposes, albeit animated, and "with bunnies" (http://www.angryalien.com/0206/NOLDbuns.asp).

19. On the small scale, one finds events like "Art Is Undead," held at the Capricorn studios in Ybor City, Florida, which featured work by local artists (http://www.examiner.com/article/art-is-undead-zombie-art-event-tampa-july-9th); while a show called "The Modern Monster" at Queens's Nails in San Francisco, California, curated by Jeanne Gerrity, drew work from high-profile artists across North America (http://www.sfaqonline.com/2013/03/the-modern-monster-at-queens-nails-san-francisco/). Even more broadly, the London-based curator Caryn Coleman has organized various exhibitions on horror in the arts, like Empty Distances at the Mark Moore Gallery in Los Angeles and The Art of Fear exhibition of artist films in Brooklyn, New York.

20. Former BANK member John Russell has various other pieces that are informed by or make reference to zombies, for example, his "Dear Living Person" letter in *Mute 3.1* (2001) and the performance piece *Return of the Living Dead III: Clement Greenberg Is a Conceptual Artist; Flatness and Shapism* (2008).

21. Anthony Discenza and Torsten Burns, better known as "HalfLifers," embrace "a rigorously low-fi aesthetic" in their videos of their improvisational performances, as noted on the boxed set of their work, *Halflifers* (http://www.vdb.org/titles/halflifers-complete-history-1992–2010). In AfterLifers, they play at being both zombies and experts on zombies.

22. In Travis Louie's curated exhibition, there were also a few pieces that drew on Haitian folkloric influences in their creation of works inspired by the word zombie. See especially Jasmine Worth's *Zombi*, a figure of a Madonna, zombified, with a what appears to be a Haitian veve drawn on her forehead; Travis Louie's own *There Are Three Types of Zombie Root*, a graphite and acrylic wash of a floating head accompanied by three botanical illustrations referring to the science of zombification; Katelan V. Foisy's *Le Gran Zombie*, a three-dimensional decorated and painted wooden cabinet, with various Voodoo symbols and paraphernalia; and Kelley Hensing's *Idol of the Bokor*, a rich painting of a Haitian bokor, acrylic on board, in a decorative frame with nails protruding from it.

23. See my "Playing Dead: Zombies Invade Performance Art, and Your Neighborhood" for a more detailed discussion of the relationship between these two events.

24. This aspect of Mcdonald's oeuvre consists of pieces like the website MeandBillyBob.com, including videos, unauthorized duets, and chronicles of other performance-based projects, such as a piece in which she replicates Billy Bob's tattoos on her own body (http://meandbillybob.com/), and visual love letters to other stars of the screen, like "To Vincent with Love," a website where viewers can choose in which order they watch four short videos of the artist inserted into Gallo's film *Buffalo 66* again, overlaid with an unauthorized duet. It can be viewed at http://artport.whitney.org/gatepages/artists/mcdonald/.

25. I am thinking here of the Russian formalist concept "ostranenie." Ironically, this is the idea that art defamiliarizes life in order to prevent "over-automatization," a condition in which the individual will "function as though by formula." See Viktor Shklovsky, "Art as Device." In these zombie gatherings, then, we may see people play the automaton in order to prevent it from becoming a reality.

26. For a detailed description of the history of performance art that may provide more context for the work of Jillian Mcdonald and suggest many other fruitful comparisons that I do not have the space to explicate here, see RosaLee Goldberg, *Performance Art: From Futurism to the Present*.

27. In *The Screaming*, Mcdonald encounters famous movie monsters and screams in place of the hapless heroine—she grafts herself into classics like Lucio Fulci's *Zombi 2*, Stanley Kubrick's *The Shining*, and Ridley Scott's *Alien*—but here we find a different

outcome than in the original texts: her screams have power, and she defeats her foes with ear-piercing shrieks. A performance piece, unrecorded, called *Dead of the Night* (2010), replayed the plot of George Romero's *Night of the Living Dead*, with actors depicting central characters from *other* zombie movies, intercepting and interrupting the action. See jillianmcdonald.net.

28. See, for one example among many, Giulio Casser's (1556–1616) illustration of the abdominal cavity.

29. To emphasize the point, Pfau displays in his studio and exhibits of the work blown-up photographs of the figures in these paintings alongside the paintings themselves, to show how little the individual's form differs from its immediate surroundings.

30. See, e.g., chapter 2, "We Field Women," of T. J. Clark's *Farewell to an Idea*, in which he reads Pissarro's 1891 painting *Two Young Peasant Women* in relation to the artist's anarchist politics.

31. On this point, of the importance of the trope of the road and the "path" in Pissarro, see Leonard Lopate's interview with Karen Levitov, curator of an exhibition at the Jewish Museum.

32. Nonetheless, in *Cézanne/Pissarro, Johns/Rauschenberg*, Joachim Pissarro notes that both Camille Pissarro and Paul Cézanne had mothers of Creole origins: "The term 'Creole' in French can refer to persons of two different origins: one of European descent born in the French West Indies or in Latin America, or a descendent of French or Spanish settlers; or one of mixed Creole and black descent. It was presumably in the former sense that both Pissarro's and Cézanne's mothers were described of Creole origins, although very little is known about the genealogy of either woman" (215n30).

33. *Gauguin's Zombie* was previously shown in Hawaii in 2002 and 2003. One can see an interactive virtual gallery online that re-creates the exhibition at http://www2.hawaii.edu/~drexler/. As one puts the cursor over the various items on the opening screen, they move in small ways and point to links. If you put the cursor over the body, it sits up; if you click on the canvas, you are relayed to a page where you can see the art up close.

34. Drexler's installation keeps intact the most salient features of the mythology, even if it does bend it in places. For example, Drexler's ambiguous description of the cause of the corpse's reanimation, which it is suggested is the result of some combination of the chemicals used in the process of making the corpses ready for public viewing, is directly in line with the cinematic zombie's emphasis on scientific rather than supernatural means: Gauguin's is a secular rather than divine reawakening. In contrast, much of Gauguin's story is relayed through the zombie's vivid journal entries of his firsthand experiences, even though most zombies, by definition, have no consciousness, and only a few outliers can speak.

35. See Walcott's long poem *Tiepolo's Hound* and Diane Mehta's review of it in *Agni*.

Epilogue

1. It had been posted on YouTube a year before the event in Chile. See http://www.youtube.com/watch?v=q-GZ-hrciBk. Charles Eaton, an organizer of the event at Berkeley, told me of their inspiration (pers. comm.).

2. See, e.g., the MSN news write-up of May 17, 2013, "Did NRA Ban Zombie Targets That Resemble Obama?," http://news.msn.com/us/did-nra-ban-zombie-targets-that-resemble-obama.

3. This attempt to rewrite the zombie's significance is visible in other places as well. In the same piece, Mahoney emphasizes the zombie narrative's connection to themes of crowds and revolts; this is indebted to a herd mentality and the zombie's inherent brain-deadness, and while Mahoney connects themes of contagion in zombie films to voodoo mind control, Romero's intervention in the genre is still given too much credit. To my mind, all these aspects of the mythos clearly predate the zombie's cinematic development and derive from its roots as a folkloric being tied to the Haitian Revolution, in which rebel slaves had been problematically figured as animals and senseless automatons; the rebellion was even characterized as a communicable fervor that slaveholders feared would expand beyond the island. Therefore, zombies do not evoke rebellion because they are contagious; they are contagious because they have long symbolized rebellion.

4. Butler's *Precarious Life* (2004) considers, "Who counts as human? Whose lives count as lives? And finally, What *makes for a grievable life?*" (20; original emphasis). Examining the way violence against "enemy combatants" is figured (or more often, not figured), Butler describes the way such people are seen as "unreal" and, dare I offer, zombielike.

5. A translation and discussion of this poster can be found at Global Voices online, Aug. 21, 2013, http://globalvoicesonline.org/2013/08/21/egypt-caught-between-a-zombie-and-a-bloodsucker/.

6. See McNally, *Monsters of the Market*; Newitz, *Pretend We're Dead*; Latham, *Consuming Youth*. Chris Harman and John Quiggan have written, respectively, on *Zombie Capitalism* (2009, subtitled *Global Crisis and the Relevance of Marx*) and *Zombie Economics* (2010, *How Dead Ideas Still Walk among Us*); see also Henry A. Giroux's *Zombie Politics and Culture in the Age of Casino Capitalism* (2011).

7. Larsen reminds us that the zombie "also straddles the divide between industrial and immaterial labor, from mass to multitude, from the brawn of industrialism to the dispersed brains of cognitive capitalism" (8). Most terrifying of all, zombie walks might be conceived of as working within cognitive capitalism: "Immaterial capitalism's tropes of self-cannibalization render it more ambiguous than ever whether the abject is a crisis in the order of subject and society, or a perverse confirmation of them" (10). Schneider, too, has been struck by the same terrible thought: "Is theatre's circulation of living ruin a reanimation of dead capital in some way that promotes the machinery of the entire operation?" (159). Is this labor that people do when they perform zombiedom, not in some frightening way, also protecting the capitalist system? Put another way, do we play dead to master our enslavement to the system in order to *subvert* it—what we've said is impossible, because of the inseparable dialecticality of the living dead—or to *make it more tolerable*, thus ensuring its survival?

8. See, for Pakistani zombie films, *Hell's Ground* (2007); for Israeli films, see *Poisoned* (2011), *Cannon Fodder* (2013), and *Another World* (2014). See especially Matthew Rovner's piece in the *Jewish Daily Forward*, "What's Behind Israel's Zombie Outbreak?"

Filmography

Feature Films

Army of Darkness. Dir. Sam Raimi. 1992.
Astro-Zombies. Dir. Ted V. Mikels. 1968.
Beverly Hills Bodysnatchers. Dir. Jonathan Mostow. 1989.
Bio-Zombie (Japan). Dir. Wilson Yip. 1998.
Birth of the Living Dead. Dir. Rob Kuhns. 2013
The Blind Side. Dir. John Lee Hancock. 2009.
The Brain That Wouldn't Die. Dir. Joseph Green. 1962.
The Crazies. Dir. George Romero. 1973.
Creature with the Atom Brain. Dir. Edward L. Cahn. 1955.
Dawn of the Dead. Dir. George Romero. 1978.
Dawn of the Dead. Dir. Zack Snyder. 2004.
Day of the Dead. Dir. George Romero. 1985.
Dead Alive (a.k.a. *Braindead*). Dir. Peter Jackson. 1992.
Dead Meat. Dir. Conor McMahon. 2004.
Diary of the Dead. Dir. George Romero. 2007.
Django Unchained. Dir. Quentin Tarantino. 2012.
Dr. Blood's Coffin. Dir. Sidney J. Furie. 1961.
The Earth Dies Screaming. Dir. Terence Fisher. 1964.
Fido. Dir. Andrew Currie. 2006.
Frankenstein. Dir. James Whale. 1931.
The Ghost Breakers. Dir. George Marshall. 1940.
The Help. Dir. Tate Taylor. 2011.
The Horror of Party Beach. Dir. Del Tenney. 1963.
I Am Legend. Dir. Francis Lawrence. 2007.

I Eat Your Skin. Dir. Del Tenney. 1964.
The Incredibly Strange Creatures Who Stopped Living and Became Mixed-Up Zombies?! Dir. Ray Dennis Steckler. 1964.
Invasion of the Body Snatchers. Dir. Don Siegel. 1956.
Invasion of the Body Snatchers. Dir. Phillip Kaufman. 1978.
Invisible Invaders. Dir. Edward L. Cahn. 1959.
I Walked with a Zombie. Dir. Jacques Tourneur. 1943.
I Was a Zombie for the FBI. Dir. Marius Penczner. 1982.
Juan de los Muertos (Spain/Cuba). Dir. Alejandro Brugués. 2011
King of the Zombies. Dir. Jean Yarbrough. 1941.
Land of the Dead. Dir. George Romero. 2005.
Last Man on Earth. Dir. Ubaldo Ragona. 1964.
The Living Dead at Manchester Morgue (a.k.a. *Let Sleeping Corpses Lie*). Dir. Jorge Grau. 1975.
Night of the Living Dead. Dir. George Romero. 1968.
Night of the Living Dead. Dir. Tom Savini. 1990.
Night of the Living Dead: Reanimated. Dir. Mike Schneider. 2009.
La noche de los brujos (Spain). Dir. Amando de Ossario. 1974.
Omega Man. Dir. Boris Sagal. 1971.
Otto, or Up with Dead People. Dir. Bruce LaBruce. 2008.
Ouanga. Dir. George Terwilliger. 1935.
Plague of the Zombies. Dir. John Gilling. 1966.
Plan Nine from Outer Space. Dir. Ed Wood. 1958.
Quartermaas 2. Dir. Val Guest. 1957.
Raisins de la mort (France). Dir. Jean Rollin. 1978.
Re-Animator. Dir. Stuart Gordon. 1985.
Resident Evil. Dir. Paul W. S. Anderson. 2002.
The Return of the Living Dead. Dir. Dan O'Bannon. 1985.
La Revanche des mortes-vivants (France). Dir. Pierre B. Reinhard. 1987.
Revenge of the Zombies. Dir. Steve Sekely. 1943.
Revolt of the Zombies. Dir. Victor Halperin. 1936.
SARSWars: Bangkok Zombie Crisis (Thailand). Dir. Taweewat Wantha. 2004.
Serpent and the Rainbow. Dir. Wes Craven. 1988.
Severed. Dir. Carl Bessai. 2005.
Shaun of the Dead. Dir. Edgar Wright. 2004.
Shrunken Heads. Dir. Richard Elfman. 1994.
Slaves. Dir. Herbert J. Biberman. 1969.
Sugar Hill. Dir. Paul Maslansky. 1974.
Teenage Zombies. Dir. Jerry Warren. 1959.
Toxic Zombies. Dir. Charles McCrann.1980.
12 Years a Slave. Dir Steve McQueen. 2013.
28 Days Later. Dir. Danny Boyle. 2002.
28 Weeks Later. Dir. Juan Carlos Fresnadillo. 2007.

Voodoo Island. Dir. Reginald LeBorg. 1957.
Voodoo Man. Dir. William Beaudine. 1944.
White Zombie. Dir. Victor Halperin. 1932.
Zombex. Dir. Jesse Dayton. 2013.
Zombi 2. Dir. Lucio Fulci. 1979.
Zombi 3. Dir. Lucio Fulci. 1988.
The Zombie Diaries. Dir. Michael Bartlett and Kevin Gates. 2006.
Zombieland. Dir. Ruben Fleischer. 2009.
Zombie Prom. Dir. Vince Marcello. 2006.
The Zombies of Mora Tau. Dir. Edward L. Cahn. 1957.
Zombies on Broadway. Dir. Gordon Douglas. 1945.

Shorts

Night of the Living Dead in 30 Seconds, Reenacted by Bunnies. Short video. Prod. Jennifer Shiman. http://www.angryalien.com/0206/NOLDbuns.asp. Web. 24 July 2014.

Series

Al Jazeera+ online content, pilot episode, "Why Do We Love Zombies?" filmed 10.30.2013 circulated internally, unreleased.
American Horror Story: Coven. Creator Ryan Murphy. FX, 2013–14.
American Horror Story: Inside the Coven (Featurettes). Creator Ryan Murphy. FX, 2013–14.
The Man from U.N.C.L.E. "The Very Important Zombie Affair." 1965. Creator Sam Rolfe. NBC, 1965–68.
Miami Vice. "Tale of the Goat." 1985. Creator Anthony Yerkovich. NBC, 1984–90.
The Saint. "Sibao," 1965. Creator Robert S. Baker/Roger Moore. ITC, 1962–69.
The Unexplained. "Zombies." A&E Documentary Series, 2008.
Walking Dead. Creator Frank Darabont. AMC, 2010–present.

Works Cited

Ackermann, Hans-W., and Jeanine Gauthier. "The Ways and Nature of the Zombi." *Journal of American Folklore* 104.414 (Autumn 1991): 466–94. Print.
Agamben, Georgio. *Homo Sacer: Sovereign Power and Bare Life*. Stanford, CA: Stanford UP, 1998. Print.
Aizenberg, Edna. "'I Walked with a Zombie': The Pleasures and Perils of Postcolonial Hybridity." *World Literature Today* 73.3 (Summer 1999): 461–69. Print.
Alaux, Gustav d'. *L'Empereur Soulouque et son empire*. Paris: J. W. Randolph, 1861. Print.
Alexis, Jacques Stephen. *Les arbres musiciens*. Paris: Gallimard, 1957. Print.
———. "Of the Marvellous Realism of the Haitians." *Post-Colonial Studies Reader*. Ed. Bill Ashcroft, Gareth Griffiths, and Helen Tiffin. 2nd ed. London: Routledge, 2006. Print.
———. *Romancero aux etoiles*. Paris: Gallimard, 1988. Print.
All That Is Interesting. "The First Zombie-Proof House." 26 Apr. 2011. http://www.all-that-is-interesting.com. Web. 24 July 2014.
All Things Zombie. http://www.allthingszombie.com. Web. 24 July 2014.
AMC. "Disaster Films." http://www.filmsite.org/disasterfilms.html. Web. 24 July 2014.
Anolik, Ruth Bienstock. "Reviving the Golem, Revisiting Frankenstein." *Connections and Collisions: Identities in Contemporary Jewish-American Women's Writing*. Ed. Lois Rubin. Newark: U of Delaware P, 2005. Print.
Apple, Lauri. 3 Oct. 2011. http://gawker.com/5846013/hey-occupy-wall-street-dressing-up-like-zombies-is-dumb. Web. 24 July 2014.
Arendt, Hannah. *The Human Condition*. 1958. Chicago: U of Chicago P, 1998. Print.

Arthur, Charles, and Michael Dash, eds. *Libète: A Haiti Anthology*. London: Latin American Bureau Publishing, 1999. Print.
Austen, Jane. *Pride and Prejudice*. 1813. Cirencester, UK: CRW Publishing, 2003.
Austen, Jane, and Seth Grahame-Smith. *Pride and Prejudice and Zombies*. Philadelphia: Quirk Books, 2009. Print.
Badley, Linda. *Film, Horror, and the Body Fantastic*. Westport, CT: Greenwood Press, 1995. Print.
———. "Zombie Splatter Comedy from Dawn to Shaun: Cannibal Carnivalesque." *Zombie Culture: Autopsies of the Living Dead*. Ed. McIntosh and Leverette. Lanham, MD: Scarecrow Press, 2008. Print.
Bakhtin, Mikhail. *Rabelais and His World*. Trans. Hélène Iswolsky. Bloomington: Indiana UP, 1984. Print.
Baldick, Chris. *In Frankenstein's Shadow: Myth, Monstrosity, and Nineteenth Century Writing*. Oxford: Oxford UP, 1990. Print.
Ballowe, Hewitt Leonard. *Creole Folk Tales: Stories of the Louisiana Marsh Country*. Baton Rouge: Louisiana State UP, 1948. Print.
———. *The Lawd Sayin' the Same: Negro Folk Tales of the Creole Country*. Baton Rouge: Louisiana State UP, 1947. Print.
Baucom, Ian. *Specters of the Atlantic: Finance Capital, Slavery, and the Philosophy of History*. Durham, NC: Duke UP, 2005. Print.
Beck, Ulrich, and Elisabeth Gernsheim. *Individualization: Institutionalized Individualism and Its Social and Political Consequences*. London: Sage, 2002. Print.
Bell, Madison Smartt. *Toussaint Louverture: A Biography*. New York: Pantheon Books, 2007. Print.
Bellegarde-Smith, Patrick. "A Man-Made Disaster: The Earthquake of January 12, 2010—a Haitian Perspective." *Journal of Black Studies* 42.2 (Mar. 2011): 264–75. Print.
Benedek, C., and L. Rivier. "Evidence for the Presence of Tetrodotoxin in a Powder Used in Haiti for Zombification." *Toxicon* (1989): 473–80. Print.
Benjamin, Walter, and Hannah Arendt. *Illuminations*. [1st ed.] New York: Harcourt, Brace & World, 1968. Print.
Berkeley Journal of Sociology. "Understanding Occupy." 7 Dec. 2011. Web forum. http://occupyduniya.wordpress.com/2011/12/07/berkeley-journal/. 27 July 2014.
Bewell, Alan. *Romanticism and Colonial Disease*. Baltimore: Johns Hopkins UP, 1999. Print.
Bhabha, Homi K. *The Location of Culture*. London: Routledge, 1994. Print.
Bishop, Kyle. *American Zombie Gothic: The Rise and Fall (and Rise) of the Walking Dead in Popular Culture*. Jefferson, NC: McFarland, 2010. Print.
———. "The Non-Zombies of *Dead Snow*, or, How US Pop Culture Killed Eight

Norwegian Med Students." Paper presented at the annual conference of the International Association for the Fantastic in the Arts, 2013.

Blessebois, Pierre-Corneille de. *Le Zombi du Gran Perou*. Rouen, 1697. Accessed via Google Books.

Bloom, Harold. *The Anxiety of Influence: A Theory of Poetry*. New York: Oxford UP, 1973. Print.

Bockie, Simon. *Death and the Invisible Powers: The World of Kongo Belief*. Bloomington: Indiana UP, 1993. Print.

Bodin, Ron. *Voodoo: Past and Present*. Louisiana Life Series, No. 5. Lafayette: Center for Louisiana Studies, 1990. Print.

Boluk, Stephanie, and Wiley Lenz, eds. *Generation Zombie: Essays on the Living Dead in Popular Culture*. Jefferson, NC: McFarland. 2011. Print.

Boon, Kevin. "The Zombie as Other: Mortality and the Monstrous in the Post-Nuclear Age." *Better Off Dead: The Evolution of the Zombie as Posthuman*. Ed. Christie and Lauro. New York: Fordham UP, 2011. Print.

Booth, William. "Voodoo Science." *Science*, no. 240 (15 Apr. 1988): 274–77. Print.

Braham, Persephone. "The Monstrous Caribbean." *The Ashgate Research Companion to Monsters and the Monstrous*. Ed. Asa Simon Mittman and Peter Dendle. Farnham, Surrey: Ashgate, 2012. Print.

Braun, Michele. "It's So Hard to Get Good Help These Days: Zombies as a Culturally Stabilizing Force in Fido." *Race, Oppression, and the Zombie: Essays on the Cross-Cultural Appropriations of the Caribbean Tradition*. Ed. Moreman and Rushton. Jefferson, NC: McFarland, 2011. Print.

Braziel, Jana Evans. *Duvalier's Ghosts: Race, Diaspora, and US Imperialism in Haitian Literatures*. Gainesville: U of Florida P, 2010. Print.

Brentano, Robyn. *Outside the Frame: Performance and the Object: A Survey History of Performance Art in the USA since 1950*. Cleveland: Center for Contemporary Art, 1994. Print.

Brickhouse, Anna. *TransAmerican Literary Relations and the Nineteenth-Century Public Sphere*. Cambridge: Cambridge UP, 2004. Print.

Brodie, B. C. *Further Experiments and Observations on the Action of Poisons on the Animal System*. Philosophical Transactions of the Royal Society of London, vol. 102 (1812): 205–27. Print.

Bromley, Gordon Leigh. "American Zombie." Reprinted in Haining, ed., *Zombie! Stories of the Walking Dead*. London: W. H. Allen & Co., 1985. Print.

Brooks, Max. *World War Z: An Oral History of the Zombie War*. New York: Three Rivers Press, 2006. Print.

———. *The Zombie Survival Guide: Complete Protection from the Living Dead*. New York: Three Rivers Press, 2003. Print.

Brown, Chris N. "Keep Austin Zombie Free." 26 Jan. 2009. http://nofearofthefuture.blogspot.com. Web. 27 July 2014.

Brown, Eric S. *Unabridged, Unabashed, and Undead.* n.p.: CreateSpace Independent Publishing Platform, 2009. Print.
Brown, Karen McCarthy. *Tracing the Spirit: Ethnographic Essays on Haitian Art.* Davenport, IA: Davenport Museum of Art, 1995. Print.
Brown, Vincent. *The Reaper's Garden: Death and Power in the World of Atlantic Slavery.* Cambridge, MA: Harvard UP, 2008. Print.
———. "Social Death and Political Life in the Study of Slavery." *American Historical Review* (Dec. 2009): 1231–49. Print.
Bruce, Barbara. "Guess Who's Going to Be Dinner: Sidney Poitier, Black Militancy, and the Ambivalence of Race in Romero's *Night of the Living Dead*." *Race, Oppression, and the Zombie: Essays on Cross-Cultural Appropriations of the Caribbean Tradition.* Ed. Moreman and Rushton. Jefferson, NC: McFarland, 2011. Print.
Buck-Morss, Susan. "Hegel and Haiti." *Critical Inquiry* 26.4 (Summer 2000): 821–65. Print.
Burdett, William. *The History and Adventures of Jack Mansong, the Famous Negro Robber, and Terror of Jamaica.* London: A. Neil, 1801. Accessed via Google Books. 24 July 2014.
Burnard, Trevor. "Jamaica as America, America as Jamaica: Hauntings from the Past in Vincent Brown's *The Reaper's Garden*." *Small Axe* 14.1, 31 (March 2010): 200–211. Print.
———. *Mastery, Tyranny, and Desire: Thomas Thistlewood and His Slaves in the Anglo-Jamaican World.* Chapel Hill: U of North Carolina P, 2004. Print.
Burton Sellers, W. F. "Heroes of Haiti." 11 Jan. 1999. World History Archives, Hartford Web Publishing. http://www.hartford-hwp.com/archives/43a/168.html. 24 July 2014.
Butler, Judith. *Precarious Life: The Powers of Mourning and Violence.* London: Verso, 2004. Print.
Butler, Marilyn. *Romantics, Rebels, and Reactionaries: English Literature and Its Background, 1796–1830.* Oxford: Oxford UP, 1981. Print.
Caciola, Nancy. "Wraiths, Revenants, and Ritual in Medieval Culture." *Past & Present,* no. 152 (Aug. 1996): 3–45. Print.
Cajun, Andre, *Louisiana Voodoo.* 2nd ed. New Orleans: Harmanson, 1946. Print.
Calmet, Dom Augustine. *Treatise on the Vampires of Hungary and Surrounding Regions.* Paris, 1746.
Canavan, Gerry. "We Are the Walking Dead: Race, Time, and Survival in Zombie Narrative." *Extrapolation* 51.3 (2010): 431–53. Print.
Canetti, Elias. *Crowds and Power.* Hamburg: Classen Verlag, 1960. Print.
Carpentier, Alejo. *The Kingdom of This World.* Trans. Harriet de Onís. New York: Farrar, Straus & Giroux, 2006. Print.
Carpio, Glenda. *Laughing Fit to Kill: Black Humor in the Fictions of Slavery.* Oxford: Oxford UP, 2008. Print.

Carroll, Noel. *The Philosophy of Horror, or, Paradoxes of the Heart*. New York: Routledge, 1990. Print.
Castronovo, Russ. *Necrocitizenship: Death, Eroticism, and the Public Sphere in the Nineteenth-Century United States*. Durham, NC: Duke UP, 2001. Print.
Certeau, Michel de. *The Practice of Everyday Life*. 1984. Berkeley: U of California P, 1988. Print.
Césaire, Aimé. *Discourse on Colonialism*. Trans. Joan Pinkham. New York: Monthly Review Press, 1972. Print.
———. *Notebook of a Return to the Native Land*. Trans. Clayton Eshleman and Annette Smith. Middletown, CT: Wesleyan UP, 2001. Print.
Chamoiseau, Patrick. *Creole Folktales*. Trans. Linda Coverdale. New York: New Press, 1994. Print.
———. *Texaco*. Trans. Rose-Myriam Réjouis and Val Vinokurov. New York: Pantheon Books, 1997. Print.
Chester, Toni. "Zombies before Romero." Concatenation. http://www.concatenation.org/articles/zombies_before_romero.html. Web. 24 July 2014.
Chivallon, Christine, and Dorothy S. Blair. "Images of Creole Diversity and Spatiality: a Reading of Patrick Chamoiseau's *Texaco*." *Cultural Geographies* 4 (July 1997): 318–36. Print.
Chomsky, Noam, Paul Farmer, and Amy Goodman. *Getting Haiti Right This Time: The U.S. and the Coup*. Monroe, ME: Common Courage Press, 2004. Print.
Choudhury, Romita. "'Is There a Ghost, a Zombie There?': Postcolonial Intertextuality and Jean Rhys's *Wide Sargasso Sea*." *Textual Practice* 10.2 (1996): 315–27. Print.
Christie, Deborah "A Dead New World: Richard Matheson and the Modern Zombie." *Better Off Dead*. Ed. Christie and Lauro. New York: Fordham UP, 2011. Print.
Christie, Deborah, and Sarah Juliet Lauro, eds. *Better Off Dead: The Evolution of the Zombie as Posthuman*. New York: Fordham UP, 2011. Print.
Clark, T. J. *Farewell to an Idea: Episodes from a History of Modernism*. New Haven, CT: Yale UP, 1999. Print.
Clover, Carol J. *Men, Women, and Chainsaws: Gender in the Modern Horror Film*. London: BFI, 1992. Print.
Clover, Joshua. "Swans and Zombies: Neoliberalism's Permanent Contradiction." *The Nation*, 25 Apr. 2011. Web.
Coates, Carrol F. "A Note on Franketienne's *Les Affres d'un défi*." *Callaloo* 19.3 (Summer 1996): 756–61. Print.
Coburn, Kathleen, ed. *Inquiring Spirit: A New Presentation of Coleridge from His Published and Unpublished Prose Writings*. Toronto: U of Toronto P, 1979. Print.
Cohen, Daniel. *Raising the Dead*. New York: Cobblehill Books, 1997. Print.
Cohen, Jeffrey Jerome, ed. *Monster Theory: Reading Culture*. Minneapolis: U of Minnesota P, 1996. Print.

Cole, Phillip. *The Myth of Evil: Demonizing the Enemy*. Westport, CT: Praeger, 2006. Print.

———. "Rousseau and the Vampires: Towards a Political Philosophy of the Undead." *The Undead and Philosophy: Chicken Soup for the Soulless*. Ed. Greene and Mohammed. Chicago: Open Court, 2006. Print.

Coleridge, Samuel Taylor. "Rime of the Ancient Mariner." *The Oxford Book of English Verse, 1250–1900*. Ed. Sir Arthur Thomas Quiller-Couch. Oxford: Clarendon, 1919. Print.

Colon, Yves. "A Victory for Voodoo? Gaffes in US Taken as a Sign." *Miami Herald*, 17 Sept. 1994. Print.

Comaroff, Jean, and John Comaroff. "Alien-Nation: Zombies, Immigrants, and Millennial Capitalism." *Codesria Bulletin* 3–4 (1999). *South Atlantic Quarterly* 101.4 (Fall 2002): 779–805. Print.

Common Routes: Saint Domingue and Louisiana. Exhibition notes. New Orleans Historic Williams Center. March 2009.

Computer and Videogames. "Capcom Plans Parliament Zombie Stunt." 16 Aug. 2010. http://www.computerandvideogames.com/259994/capcom-plans-parliament-zombie-stunt/. Web. 24 July 2014.

Comstock, Andrew. *Spectral America: Phantoms and the National Imagination*. Madison: U of Wisconsin P, 2004. Print.

Consentino, Donald. *In Extremis: Death and Life in 21st-Century Art*. Exhibition catalog. Fowler Museum. Los Angeles: UC Regents, 2012. Print.

Cooke, Jennifer. *Legacies of Plague in Literature, Theory, and Film*. New York: Palgrave Macmillan, 2009. Print.

Cosby, Andrew, et al. *Zombie Tales*. Vol. 1. n.p.: Boom Studios, June 2007. Print.

Craige, John. *Black Baghdad*. New York: Minton, Balch, & Co., 1933. Print.

———. *Cannibal Cousins*. New York: Minton, Balch, & Co., 1934. Print.

Daily Mail. "Wall Street Demonstrators Dressed as 'Corporate Zombies' Lurch Past Stock Exchange as Protests Spread beyond America." 4 Oct. 2011. www.dailymail.co.uk/news/article-2044983/Occupy-Wall-Street-protesters-dressed-corporate-zombies-lurch-past-stock-exchange-protests-spread-America.html. Web. 27 June 2014.

Dalmas, Antoine. *Histoire de la Revolution de Saint-Domingue*. Paris: Mame Frères, 1814. Print.

Danticat, Edwige. *After the Dance: A Walk through Carnival in Jacmel, Haiti*. New York: Crown Publishers, 2002. Print.

———. Preface to *In Extremis: Death and Life in 21st-Century Art*. Ed. Consentino. Exhibition catalog. Fowler Museum. Los Angeles: UC Regents, 2012. Print.

Dapper, Olfert. *Description de l'Afrique: Naukeurige beschrijvinge der Afrikaensche gewesten, and Naukeurige beschrijvinge der Afrikaensche Eylanden (1668)*. Amsterdam, 1686. Landmarks in Anthropology. New York: Johnson Reprint Corporation, 1970. Print.

Dash, Michael. "In Search of the Lost Body: Redefining the Subject in Caribbean Literature." *Post-Colonial Studies Reader.* Ed. Bill Ashcroft, Gareth Griffiths, and Helen Tiffin. 2nd ed. London: Routledge, 2006. Print.

———. "Postcolonial Thought and the Francophone Caribbean." *Francophone Postcolonial Studies: A Critical Introduction.* Ed. Charles Forsdick and David Murphy. London: Arnold, 2003. Print.

Daston, Lorraine, and Katharine Park. *Wonders and the Order of Nature.* New York: Zone Books, 1998. Print.

Davis, Rod. *American Vaudou: Journey into a Hidden World.* Denton: U of North Texas P, 1998. Print.

Davis, Wade. "The Ethnobiology of the Haitian Zombi." *Journal of Ethnopharmacology* 9 (1983): 85–104. Print.

———. *Passage of Darkness: Ethnobiology of the Haitian Zombie.* Chapel Hill: U of North Carolina P, 1989. Print.

———. *The Serpent and the Rainbow.* New York: Warner Books, 1985. Print.

Dayan, Joan (also known as Colin Dayan). "The Call of the Gods, The Making of History." *Kafou: Haiti, Art, and Vodou.* Ed. Leah Gordon. Nottingham: Notthingham Contemporary, 2012. Print.

———. "France Reads Haiti: René Depestre's *Hadriana dans tous mes rêves.*" *Yale French Studies* 83 (1993). Special issue, Post/Colonial Conditions: Exiles, Migrations, and Nomadisms 2:154–75. Print.

———. *Haiti, History, and the Gods.* Berkeley: U of California P, 1998. Print.

Degoul, Franck. "Dos à la vie, dos à la mort: Une exploration ethnographique des figures de la servitude dans l'imaginaire haïtien de la zombification." Diss. 2006. Bibliothèque et Archives Canada, 2007. Print.

———. "'We Are the Mirror of Your Fears': Haitian Identity and Zombification." Trans. Elisabeth Lore. *Better Off Dead: The Evolution of the Zombie as Posthuman.* Ed. Christie and Lauro. New York: Fordham UP, 2011. Print.

Deleuze, Gilles. *Difference and Repetition.* Trans. Paul Patton. New York: Columbia UP, 1994. Print.

Deleuze, Gilles, and Felix Guattari. *Anti-Oedipus: Capitalism and Schizophrenia.* Minneapolis: U of Minnesota P, 2003. Print.

Dendle, Peter. *The Zombie Movie Encyclopedia.* Jefferson, NC: McFarland, 2001. Print.

Depestre, René. *The Festival of the Greasy Pole.* Trans. Carrol F. Coates. Caraf Books. Charlottesville: U of Virginia P, 1990. Print.

———. *Hadriana dans tous mes rêves.* Paris: Editions Gallimard, 1998. Print.

Deren, Maya. *Divine Horsemen: The Living Gods of Haiti.* 1953. New Paltz, NY: McPherson, 1983. Print.

Derrida, Jacques. *Specters of Marx: The State of the Debt, the Work of Mourning, and the New International.* New York: Routledge, 1994. Print.

Descourtilz, M. E. *Voyage d'un naturaliste, et ses observations . . .* Paris: Dufart Père, 1809. Paris: Plon, 1935. Print.

Desmangles, Leslie. *The Faces of the Gods: Vodou and Roman Catholicism in Haiti*. Chapel Hill: U of North Carolina P, 1992. Print.

De Vassière, Pierre. *Saint Domingue: La societé et la vie creoles sous l'ancien régime (1629–1789)*. Paris: Perrin, 1909. Print.

de Vere, Maximilian Schele. *Americanisms: The English of the New World*. New York: Charles Scribner & Co., 1872. Print.

Dewisme, C. H. *Les zombis, ou le secret des morts-vivants*. Paris: Grasset, 1957. Print.

Diederich, Bernard, and Al Burt. *Papa Doc: Haiti and Its Dictator*. 1969. Victoria, Australia: Penguin Books, 1972. Print.

Dillard, Tom. "Deep into That Darkness Peering: An Essay on Gothic Nature." *ISLE* 16.4 (2009): 685–95. Print.

Dillard, R. H. W. "*Night of the Living Dead*: It's Not Just a Wind That's Passing Through." *American Horrors: Essays on the Modern American Horror Film*. Ed. Waller. Urbana: U of Illinois P, 1987. Print.

Douglas, Rachel. *Frankétienne and Rewriting: A Work in Progress*. Lanham, MD: Lexington Books, Rowman & Littlefield, 2009. Print.

Drake, Sandra. "All That Foolishness/That All Foolishness: Race and Caribbean Culture as Thematics of Liberation in Jean Rhys's *Wide Sargasso Sea*." *Critica* 2.2 (Fall 1990): 97–112. Print.

Draper, Ellen. "Zombie Women When the Gaze Is Male." *Wide Angle* 10.3 (1988): 52–62. Print.

Drewal, Henry John. "The Beauteous Beast: The Water Deity Mami Wata in Africa." The *Ashgate Research Companion to Monsters and the Monstrous*. Ed. Asa Simon Mittman and Peter Dendle. Aldershot: Ashgate, 2012. Print.

Drexler, Debra. *Gauguin's Zombie: An Installation*. http://www2.hawaii.edu/~drexler/. Web. 24 July 2014.

Dreyfus, Hubert, and Paul Rabinow, eds. *Michel Foucault: Beyond Structuralism and Hermeneutics*. 2nd ed. Chicago: U of Chicago P, 1983. Print.

Drezner, Daniel. *Theories of International Politics and Zombies*. Princeton, NJ: Princeton UP, 2011. Print.

Dubois, Laurent. *Avengers of the New World: The Story of the Haitian Revolution*. Cambridge, MA: Harvard UP, 2004. Print.

———. *A Colony of Citizens: Revolution and Slave Emancipation in the French Caribbean, 1787–1804*. Chapel Hill: U of North Carolina P, 2004. Print.

Dubois, Laurent, and John D. Garrigus, eds. *Slave Rebellion in the Caribbean, 1789–1804: A Brief History with Documents*. Bedford Series in History and Culture. New York: Palgrave Macmillan, 2006. Print.

Dumesle, Hérard. *Voyage dans le nord d'Hayti, ou révélations des lieux et des monuments historiques*. Les Cayes: Impr. du gouvernement, 1824. Accessed via Google Books. 24 July 2014.

"Duppy." *Folklore: A Quarterly Review* 15. London, 1909. Print.

Duvalier, François, and Lorimer Dennis. *L'Evolution stadiale du vodou* (The

Gradual Evolution of Voodoo). Port-au-Prince: Imprimerie de l'Etat, 1944. Accessed via Google Books. 24 July 2014.

Earle, William. *Obi or, The History of Three-Fingered Jack. In a Series of Letters from a Resident in Jamaica to His Friend in England.* London: Printed for Earle and Hemet, No. 47, Albemarle-Street, Piccadilly, 1800. Accessed via Google Books. 24 July 2014.

Edwards, Bryan. *Civil and Commercial History of the British West Indies in Two Volumes* (1793). London: Printed for J. Parsons, Paternoster-Row; and J. Bell, Oxford-Street, 1794. Accessed via Google Books. 24 July 2014.

———. "Civil and Commercial History of the British West Indies in Two Volumes." Excerpt. *African American Religious History: A Documentary Witness.* Ed. Milton C. Sernett. Durham, NC: Duke UP, 1999. Print.

Eisenman, Stephen. *Gauguin's Skirt.* London: Thames and Hudson, 1997. Print.

Ellis, Markman. *The History of Gothic Fiction.* Edinburgh: Edinburgh UP, 2005. Print.

Emery, Mary Lou. *Jean Rhys at "World's End": Novels of Colonial and Sexual Exile.* Austin: U of Texas P, 1990. Print.

The Encyclopaedia Brittanica (Great Britain). Vol. 4 pt. 1, 1797. Print.

Encyclopèdie ou Dictionnaire raisonné des sciences, des arts et des métiers (France). Vol. 11. Paris: Briasson, 1765.

Estok, Simon. "Theorizing in a Space of Ambivalent Openness: Ecocriticism and Ecophobia." *ISLE* 16.2 (2009): 203–25. Print.

Etienne, Gérard. *Le nègre crucifié: Récit.* Montreal: Editions Francophones & Nouvelle Optique. 1974. Print.

Examiner. "Art Is Undead: Zombie Art Event in Tampa." 4 July 2011. Examiner.com. Web. 24 July 2014.

Fandrich, Ina Johanna. *The Mysterious Voodoo Queen, Marie Laveaux: A Study of Powerful Female Leadership in Nineteenth-Century New Orleans.* New York: Routledge, 2004. Print.

Fanon, Frantz. *Black Skin, White Masks.* New York: Grove Press, 1967. Print.

———. "National Culture." *Post-Colonial Studies Reader.* Ed. Bill Ashcroft, Gareth Griffiths, and Helen Tiffin. 2nd ed. London: Routledge, 2006. Print.

———. *The Wretched of the Earth.* New York: Grove Press, 1963. Print.

Farmer, Paul. *Pathologies of Power: Health, Human Rights, and the New War on the Poor.* Berkeley: U of California P, 2005. Print.

———. *The Uses of Haiti.* Monroe, ME: Common Courage Press, 2004. Print.

———. "What Happened in Haiti: Where the Past Is Present." *Getting Haiti Right This Time: The U.S. and the Coup,* by Noam Chomsky, Paul Farmer, and Amy Goodman. Monroe, ME: Common Courage Press, 2004. Print.

Faulkner, William. *Requiem for a Nun.* New York: Random House, 1951. Print.

Feldman, Paula R., and Diana Scott-Kilvert, eds. *The Journals of Mary Shelley: 1814–1844.* Oxford: Clarendon Press, 1987. Print.

Ferguson, James. *Papa Doc, Baby Doc: Haiti and the Duvaliers*. Oxford: Basil Blackwell, 1987. Print.
Fick, Carolyn. *The Making of Haiti: The Saint Domingue Revolution from Below*. Knoxville: U of Tennessee P, 1990. Print.
Fignolé, Jean-Claude. *Aube tranquille*. Paris: Editions du Seuil, 1990. Print.
———. *Les possédés de la pleine lune*. Paris: Editions du Seuil, 1987. Print.
Finkplamingoes. "Mark Yudof's Thriller." Online video clip. YouTube. 2 June 2010. http://www.youtube.com/watch?v=q-GZ-hrciBk. Web. 27 July 2014.
Folk-Lore: A Quarterly Review of Myth, Tradition, Institution, & Custom [incorporating the *Archæological Review* and the *Folk-Lore Journal*]. Journal of the Folk-Lore Society (Great Britain) 15. London, 1909. Print.
Foster, Hal. *Design and Crime and Other Diatribes*. New York: Verso, 2002. Print.
Foster, Hal, Rosalind Krauss, Yves-Alain Bois, and Benjamin Buchloh. *Art since 1900: Modernism, Antimodernism, Postmodernism*. Vol. 2: *1945 to the Present*. London: Thames and Hudson, 2005. Print.
Foucault, Michel. "The Subject and Power." *Michel Foucault: Beyond Structuralism and Hermeneutics*. 2nd ed. Ed. Dreyfus and Rabinow. Chicago: U of Chicago P, 1983. Print.
Frankétienne. *Dézafi* (1975); ou *Les Affres d'un défi* (1979). Paris: J. M. Place, 2000. Print.
Frazer, Sir James George. *The Golden Bough*. New York: Macmillan, 1950. Print.
Freeland, Cynthia A. *The Naked and the Undead: Evil and the Appeal of Horror*. Boulder, CO: Westview Press, 2000. Print.
French, Howard, "Is Voodoo the Weapon to Repel the Invaders?" *New York Times*, 24 June 1994, A4. Print.
Friedlander, Eli. "The Measure of the Contingent: Walter Benjamin's Dialectical Image." *boundary2* 35.3 (Fall 2008): 1–26. Print.
Froude, James Anthony. *The English in the West Indies, or, The Bow of Ulysses*. New York: Charles Scribner's Sons, 1888. Print.
Fuchs, A. P., ed. *Dead Science*. Winnipeg: Coscom Entertainment, 2009. Print.
Gagne, Paul R. *The Zombies That Ate Pittsburgh: The Films of George A. Romero*. New York: Dodd, Mead, 1987. Print.
Garraway, Doris. *The Libertine Colony: Creolization in the Early French Caribbean*. Durham, NC: Duke UP, 2005. Print.
Gates, Brian, ed. *Afro-Caribbean Religions*. London: Ward Lock Educational, 1980. Print.
Gauguin, Paul. *Two Tahitian Women* (1899). Metropolitan Museum of Art, New York. ARTstor. http://library.artstor.org/library/secure/ViewImages?id=%2FDFMaiMuOztdLSowdD5%2BQXou> Accessed 8 July 2014.
Geggus, David. *Slave Resistance Studies and the San Domingue Slave Revolt*. Occasional Papers Series, vol. 4. Latin American and Caribbean Center, Florida International University, 1983. Print.

Gelbin, Cathy. *The Golem Returns: From German Romantic Literature to Global Jewish Culture, 1808–2008*. Ann Arbor: U of Michigan P, 2011. Print.

Giangregorio, Anthony, ed. *Book of the Dead: A Zombie Anthology*. n.p.: Living Dead Press, USA, 2009. Print.

———. *Dead Worlds: Undead Stories*. n.p.: Living Dead Press, USA, 2009. Print.

Gibson, Ann. "The African American Aesthetic and Postmodernism." *African American Visual Aesthetics: A Postmodern View*. Ed. David C. Driskell. Washington, DC: Smithsonian Institution Press, 1995. Print.

Gilroy, Paul. *The Black Atlantic: Modernity and Double-Consciousness*. Cambridge, MA: Harvard UP, 1995. Print.

Giroux, Henry A. *Zombie Politics and Culture in the Age of Casino Capitalism*. New York: Peter Lang, 2011. Print.

Glissant, Edouard. *Le discours antillais*. Paris: Seuil, 1981. Print.

Global Voices. "Egypt: Caught between a Zombie and a Bloodsucker!" 21 Aug. 2013. Globalvoicesonline.com. Accessed 27 June 2014. Web.

Glover, Kaiama. "Exploiting the Undead: The Usefulness of the Zombie in Haitian Literature." *Journal of Haitian Studies* 11.2 (Fall 2005): 105–21. Print.

———. *Haiti Unbound: A Spiralist Challenge to the Postcolonial Canon*. Liverpool: Liverpool UP, 2010. Print.

———. "New Narratives of Haiti; or, How to Empathize with a Zombie." *Small Axe* 16.3 39 (2012): 199–207. Print.

Goldberg, Jeff. "These Zombies Are Not a Metaphor." *The Apocalypse Reader*. Ed. Justin Taylor. New York: Thunder's Mouth Press, 2007. Print.

Goldberg, RosaLee. *Performance Art: From Futurism to the Present (2001), or A Theatre without Theatre*. Barcelona: Museu d'Art Contemporani de Barcelona, 2007. Print.

Golden, Christopher, ed. *The New Dead: A Zombie Anthology*. New York: St. Martin's Griffin, 2010. Print.

Goldhammer, Zach. "Scary Clowns are Terrorizing France." The Atlantic. 31 Oct. 2014. http://www.theatlantic.com/international/archive/2014/10/clown-killer-quest-ce-que-est/382092/. Web.

Golman, Harry, and Kenneth Strickfaden. *Dr. Frankenstein's Electrician*. Jefferson, NC: McFarland, 2005. Print.

Gordon, Avery. *Ghostly Matters: Haunting and the Sociological Imagination*. Minneapolis: U of Minnesota P, 2008. Print.

Gouveia, Keith, ed. *Bits of the Dead*. Winnipeg: Coscom Entertainment, 2008. Print.

Grant, Barry Keith. *The Dread of Difference: Gender and the Horror Film*. Austin: U of Texas P, 1996. Print.

Grant, Drew. "'Zombies' Occupy Wall Street [Slide show]." *The Observer*. http://observer.com/2011/10/do-zombies-capitalism-or-communism-in-occupy-wall-street-protests-slideshow/. 4 Oct. 2011.

Greene, Richard, and K. Silem Mohammed, eds. *The Undead and Philosophy: Chicken Soup for the Soulless.* Chicago: Open Court, 2006. Print.

Guinness Book of World Records. "Largest Gathering of Zombies." http://www.guinnessworldrecords.com. Web. 24 July 2014.

Hagood, Taylor, Eric Gary Anderson, and Daniel Cross Turner, eds. *Undead Souths: The Gothic and Beyond.* Baton Rouge: Louisiana State University Press, forthcoming.

Hahn, Patrick. "Dead Man Walking: Wade Davis and the Secret of the Zombie Poison." 4 Sept. 2007. Biology-Online.org. Web. 24 July 2014.

Haining, Peter, ed. *Zombie! Stories of the Walking Dead.* London: W. H. Allen & Co., 1985. Print.

Haitian Internet Newsletter. "Dead Haitian Woman Found Alive in Haiti Three Months Later." Sept. 3, 2008. http://www.haitianinternet.com/articles/dead-haitian-woman-found-alive-in-haiti-3-months-later.html. Web. 24 July 2014.

Halberstam, Judith. *Skin Shows: Gothic Horror and the Technology of Monsters.* Durham, NC: Duke UP, 1995. Print.

Hallward, Peter. *Damming the Flood: Haiti, Aristide, and the Politics of Containment.* London: Verso, 2007. Print.

Hantke, Steffen. *American Horror Film: The Genre at the Turn of the Millennium.* Jackson: UP of Mississippi, 2010. Print.

Hardt, Michael, and Antonio Negri. *Empire.* Cambridge, MA: Harvard UP, 2000. Print.

Harman, Chris. *Zombie Capitalism: Global Crisis and the Relevance of Marx.* Chicago: Haymarket Books, 2009. Print.

Harper, Stephen. "Night of the Living Dead: Reappraising an Undead Classic." *Bright Lights Film Journal.* http://brightlightsfilm.com/50/night.php#.UrD-W12RDtc8. Web. 24 July 2014.

———. Zombies, Malls, and the Consumerism Debate: George Romero's *Dawn of the Dead*." *Americana: The Journal of American Popular Culture* 1.2 (Fall 2002). Web. 24 July 2014.

Hauser, Larry. "Revenge of the Zombies." http://www.philpapers.org. Web. 24 July 2014.

Hayles, Katherine N. *How We Became Posthuman: Virtual Bodies in Cybernetics, Literature, and Informatics.* Chicago: U of Chicago P, 1999. Print.

Hearn, Lafcadio. *Two Years in the French West Indies.* 1889. New York and London: Harpers & Brothers, 1890. Print.

Hegel, G. W. F. *The Phenomenology of the Spirit.* 1807. Trans. A. V. Miller. Oxford: Oxford UP, 1977. Print.

Heidegger, Martin. *Poetry, Language, Thought.* 1st ed. New York: Harper & Row, 1971. Print.

Herskovitz, Melville Jean. *Dahomey, an Ancient West African Kingdom.* Vol. 2. Chicago: Northwestern UP, 1967. Print.

———. *Life in a Haitian Valley*. 1937. New York: Octagon Books, 1964. Print.
Hoffman, Léon-François. "The Haitian Novel during the Last Ten Years." *Callaloo* 15.3 (Summer 1992): 761–69. Print.
hooks, bell. "Eating the Other." *Black Looks: Race and Representations*. Boston: South End Press, 1992. Print.
Hochschild, Adam. *King Leopold's Ghost: A Story of Greed, Terror, and Heroism in Colonial Africa*. New York: Houghton Mifflin, 1999. Print.
Horkheimer, Max, and Theodor Adorno. *Dialectic of Enlightenment: Philosophical Fragments*. Stanford, CA: Stanford UP, 2002. Print.
Horror Movies. "World Zombie Day Bites 2009." Posted by Meh, Mar. 25, 2009. http://www.horror-movies.ca/horror_14719.html. Web. 24 July 2014.
Huffington Post. "Chile 'Thriller' Protest: Students Stage Michael Jackson Dance for Education Rally." 25 June 2011. Web. 27 July 2014.
Huggan, Graham. "A Tale of Two Parrots: Walcott, Rhys, and the Uses of Colonial Mimicry." *Contemporary Literature* 35.4 (Winter 1994): 643–60. Print.
Humans vs. Zombies. http://humansvszombies.org. Web. 24 July 2014.
Hurbon, Laënnac. *Les mystères du vaudou*. Paris: Gallimard, 1993. Print.
Hurston, Zora Neale. *Mules and Men*. London: J. B. Lippincott Co., 1935. Print.
———. *Tell My Horse*. Philadelphia: J. B. Lippincott Co., 1938. Print.
Hussain, Tamoor. "Capcom Plans Parliament Zombie Stunt." 16 Aug. 2010. ComputerandVideogames.com. Web. 24 July 2014.
Hutter, G. W. "Salt Is Not for Slaves." Reprint. *Zombie! Stories of the Walking Dead*. Ed. Haining. London: W. H. Allen & Co., 1985. Print.
Jacobus X. "Untrodden Fields of Anthropology: Observations on the Esoteric Manners and Customs of a Semi-civilized People . . . " Vol. 2. New York: American Anthropological Society, 1898. Web. Accessed via archive.org.
James, C. L. R. *The Black Jacobins: Toussaint L'Ouverture and the San Domingo Revolution*. 1938. 2nd ed. New York: Vintage Books, 1989. Print.
James, Edward. *Science Fiction in the 20th Century*. Oxford: Oxford UP, 1994. Print.
Jameson, Fredric. *Postmodernism, or the Cultural Logic of Late Capitalism*. Durham, NC: Duke UP, 1990. Print.
JibJab. "Night of the Living Deadish." Jibjab.com. Web. 24 July 2014.
Johnson, Barbara. "The Last Man." *The Other Mary Shelley: Beyond "Frankenstein."* Ed. Audrey Fisch, Anne K. Mellor, and Esther H. Schor. New York: Oxford UP, 1993. Print.
Johnson, Walter. "On Agency." *Journal of Social History* 37 (2003): 113–24. Print.
Jonassaint, Jean. *Des romans de tradition haïtienne sur un récit tragique*. Montreal: CIDIHCA/L'Harmattan, 2002. Print.
Jones, Adam. "Decompiling Dapper: A Preliminary Search for Evidence." *History in Africa* 17 (1990): 171–209. Print.
Jones, Beth. "Zombie Protest Spurring Debate: Students Protest Budget at Special Olympics Event." *Associated Press*, 9 June 2011. Web.

Jones, Nicole. "Zombies Lurch Down Telegraph to Support Public Libraries." *Oakland North*, 23 May 2011. Web. http://oaklandnorth.net/2011/05/23/zombies-lurch-down-telegraph-to-support-libraries-brains/.

Jones, Stephen, ed. *The Mammoth Book of Zombies*. New York: Carroll and Graf, 1993. Print.

Joseph, Raymond A. "US Invaders of Haiti vs. Battalions of Zombies: The Americas." *Wall Street Journal*, 17 June 1994, A15. Print.

Kahn, Janine. "Zombie Prom, Wicked, and the Seven Deadly Sins: Your Monday Morning Hangover." *SFWeekly* blogs, 9 Feb. 2009. Web. blogs.sfweekly.com/shookdown/2009/02/zombie_prom_wicked_and_the_sev.php.

Kay, Glenn, and Stuart Gordon. *Zombie Movies: The Ultimate Guide*. Chicago: Chicago Review Press, 2008. Print.

Kee, Chera. "They Are Not Men . . . They Are Dead Bodies: From Cannibal to Zombie and Back Again." *Better Off Dead: The Evolution of the Zombie as Posthuman*. Ed. Christie and Lauro. New York: Fordham UP, 2011. Print.

———. "Women of Color as Zombie Masters." Wayne State University Brown Bag Lunch Presentation. 2012. Web. Academia.edu. https://www.academia.edu/4102508/Wayne_State_Humanities_Center_Brown_Bag_Luncheon_Women_of_Color_as_Zombie_Masters. Accessed 6 Sept. 2014.

Keetley, Dawn, ed. *"We're All Infected": AMC's "The Walking Dead" and the Fate of the Human*. Jefferson, NC: McFarland, 2014. Print.

Kendall, David, ed. *The Mammoth Book of Zombie Comics*. Philadelphia: Running Press, 2008. Print.

Kenemore, Scott. *The Zen of Zombie: Better Living through the Undead*. New York: Skyhorse Publishing, 2007. Print.

King, C. Richard. "The (Mis)uses of Cannibalism in Contemporary Cultural Critique." *Diacritics* 30.1 (Spring 2000): 106–23. Print.

Kinnard, Meg. "Researcher: Zombie Fads Peak When Society Unhappy." *Associated Press*, 3 Mar. 2013. Web.

Kino, Carol. "Watch the Closing Doors, and Mind the Zombies." *New York Times*, 30 July 2006. Web.

Kirk, Robert. *Zombies and Consciousness*. Oxford: Oxford UP: 2007. Print.

———. "Zombies vs. Materialists." *Proceedings of the Aristotelian Society* 48 (1974): 135–52. Print.

Kirkman, Robert, et al. *The Walking Dead*. Image Comics, 2003–present. Print.

Knellwolf, Christa, and Jane Goodall, eds. *Frankenstein's Science: Experimentation and Discovery in Romantic Culture, 1780–1830*. Burlington, VT: Ashgate, 2008. Print.

Knepper, Wendy. *Patrick Chamoiseau: A Critical Introduction*. Jackson: UP of Mississippi, 2012. Print.

Koch, Christof. "On the Zombie Within." *Nature* 411 (21 June 2001): 893. Print.

———. *The Quest for Consciousness: A Neurobiological Approach*. Englewood, CO: Roberts & Co., 2004. Print.

Kordas, Ann. "New South, New Immigrants, New Women, New Zombies: The Historical Development of the Zombie in American Popular Culture." *Race, Oppression, and the Zombie: Essays on Cross-Cultural Appropriations of the Caribbean Tradition*. Ed. Moreman and Rushton. Jefferson, NC: McFarland, 2011. Print.

Koven, Mikel J. *Blaxploitation Films*. Sparkford, UK: Kamera Books, 2010. Print.

Kristeva, Julia. *Powers of Horror: An Essay on Abjection*. New York: Columbia UP, 1982. Print.

Kwon, Miwon. *One Place after Another: Site-Specific Art and Locational Identity*. Cambridge, MA: MIT Press, 2002. Print.

Labat, Jean Baptiste. *Nouveau Voyage aux Isles de l'Amerique*. 1724. Ed. Michel LeBris. Paris: Phébus Libretto, 1993. Print.

Lacey, Marc. "New Head of Voodoo Brings on the Charm." *New York Times*, 4 Apr. 2008. Web.

Laferrière, Dany. *Pays sans chapeau*. Dijon-Quetigny: Motifs, l'Imprimerie Darantiere, 2010. Print.

Laguerre, Michel S. *Voodoo and Politics in Haiti*. New York: St. Martin's Press, 1989. Print.

Laroche, Maximilien. "Imaginaire populaire et littérature: Le houngan, le zombi et le mécréant." *Notre Librairie*, no. 133 (Jan.–Apr. 1998): 82–89. Print.

———. "The Myth of the Zombi." *Exile and Tradition: Studies in African and Caribbean Literature*. Ed. Roland Smith. New York: Africana Publishing Co., 1976. Print.

Larsen, Lars Bang. "Zombies of Immaterial Labor: The Modern Monster and the Death of Death." *e-flux journal* 15 (Apr. 2010). Web.

Latham, Rob. *Consuming Youth: Vampires, Cyborgs, and the Culture of Consumption*. Chicago: U of Chicago P, 2002. Print.

Lauro, Sarah J. "The Eco-Zombie." *Generation Zombie: Essays on the Living Dead in Popular Culture*. Ed. Boluk and Lenz. Jefferson, NC: McFarland, 2011. Print.

———. The Modern Zombie: Living Death in the Technological Age." Ph.D. diss., University of California, Davis, 2011. Print.

———. Playing Dead: Zombies Invade Performance Art... and Your Neighborhood." *Better Off Dead: The Evolution of the Zombie as Posthuman*. Ed. Christie and Lauro. New York: Fordham UP, 2011. Print.

———. "Sois mort et tais toi." *Zombies in the Academy: Living Death in Higher Education*. Ed. Whelan, Walker, Moore. Bristol, UK: Intellect Press, 2013. Print.

Lauro, Sarah J., and Karen Embry. "A Zombie Manifesto: The Non-Human Condition." *boundary 2* 35.1 (Spring 2008): 85–108. Print.

Leconte, Frantz-Antoine, ed. *Haïti: Le Vodou au troisième millénaire*. Montreal: Editions du CIDIHCA, 2002. Print.

Lederer, Susan. *Exhibition Frankenstein: Penetrating the Mysteries of Nature*. New Brunswick, NJ: Rutgers UP, 2002. Print.

Lee, Stan. "Zombie!" *Menace* #5, July 1953. Atlas Era Menace. Vol. 1. New York: Marvel Publishing, 2009. Print.

Lefebvre, Henri. *Critique of Everyday Life*. 1947. London: Verso, 2008. Print.

Léger, Jacques Nicolas. *Haiti, Her History and Detractors*. New York: Neale Publishing Co., 1907. Print.

Lightening, Robert. "Interracial Tensions in Night of the Living Dead." *CineAction* 53 (2000): 22–29. Print.

Lincoln, Abraham. "Second Inaugural Address." *Norton Anthology of American Literature*. Ed. Nina Baym and Robert Levine. New York: W. W. Norton, 2012. Print.

Lipman, Jean, and Richard Marshall. *Art about Art*. New York: Dutton, 1978. Print.

Littlewood, Roland, and Chavannes Douyon, "Clinical Findings in Three Cases of Zombification." *Lancet*, no. 350 (1997): 1094–96. Print.

Lloyd, Christopher. *Camille Pissarro*. New York: Rizzoli, 1981. Print.

Lloyd-Smith, Alan. "A Thing of Darkness: Racial Discourse in Mary Shelley's Frankenstein." *Gothic Studies* 6.2 (Oct. 2004): 208–22. Print.

Loe, Thomas. "Patterns of the Zombi in Jean Rhys's Wide Sargasso Sea." *World Literature Written in English* 31.1 (1991): 34–42. Print.

Loederer, Richard. *Voodoo Fire in Haiti*. New York: Literary Guild, 1935. Print.

Lomax, Alan. *Mister Jelly Roll: The Fortunes of Jelly Roll Morton, New Orleans Creole and "Inventor of Jazz."* 1950. Berkeley: U of California P, 2001. Print.

Long, Carolyn Morrow. *A New Orleans Voudou Priestess: The Legend and Reality of Marie Laveau*. Gainesville: U of Florida P, 2006. Print.

Long, Edward. *History of Jamaica or General Survey of the Ancient and Modern State of That Island*. London: Lowndes, 1774. Print.

Lopate, Leonard. "Camille Pissarro: Jewish Impressionist Painter." WNYC, 25 Oct. 2007. Web. Wnyc.org. 27 July 2014.

Lorde, Audre. "The Master's Tools Will Never Dismantle the Master's House." *Sister Outsider: Essays and Speeches*. Trumansburg, NY: Crossing, 1984. Print.

Lott, Eric. *Love and Theft: Blackface Minstrelsy and the American Working Class*. New York: Oxford UP. Print.

L'ouvertureproject.org. http://thelouvertureproject.org/index.php?title=Main_Page. Web. 24 July 2014.

Love, Victoria Cosner, and Lorelei Shannon. *Mad Madame Lalaurie: New Orleans' Most Famous Murderess Revealed*. Charleston, SC: History Press, 2011. Print.

Lovecraft, H. P. "Herbert West, ReAnimator." Home Brew. 1922. http://www.hplovecraft.com/writings/texts/fiction/hwr.aspx. Web.

Lowder, James, ed. *The Best of All Flesh: Zombie Anthology*. Lake Orion, MI: Elder Signs Press, 2009. Print.
———. *Triumph of the Walking Dead: Robert Kirkman's Epic on Page and Screen*. Dallas: Benbella Books, 2011. Print.
Lowenstein, Adam. *Shocking Representation: Historical Trauma, National Cinema, and the Modern Horror Film*. New York: Columbia UP, 2005. Print.
Lucas, Rafaël. "The Aesthetics of Degradation in Haitian Literature." *Research in African Literatures* 35.2 (2004): 54–74. Print.
Luckhurst, Roger. *Science Fiction*. Cambridge: Polity Press, 2005. Print.
Lutz, Leora. "The Modern Monster at Queen's Nails." SFAQ online. http://www.sfaqonline.com/2013/03/the-modern-monster-at-queens-nails-san-francisco/. Web. 24 July 2014.
Lynch, Patricia Ann, and Jeremy Robert. *African Mythology A–Z*. 2nd ed. New York: Chelsea House, 2010. Print.
MacCormack, Patricia. *Cinesexuality*. Aldershot: Ashgate, 2008. Print.
MacGaffrey, Wyatt. *Religion and Society in Central Africa: The BaKongo of Lower Zaire*. Chicago: U of Chicago P, 1986. Print.
Mahoney, Phillip. "Mass Psychology and the Analysis of the Zombie: From Suggestion to Contagion." *Generation Zombie: Essays on the Living Dead in Modern Culture*. Ed. Boluk and Lenz. Jefferson, NC: McFarland, 2011. Print.
Maltzman, Josina Manu. "The Problem with Occupation in the Occupy Movement." 21 Nov. 2011. http://mondoweiss.net/2011/11/the-problem-with-occupation-in-the-occupy-movement.html. Web. 27 July 2014.
Mardorossian, Carine M. "Opacity as Obeah in Jean Rhys's Work." *Journal of Caribbean Literatures* 3.3 (2003): 133–42. Print.
Marsh, Richard. *A Spoiler of Men*. 1905. Richmond, VA: Valancourt Books, 2009. Print.
"Mary Shelley's Reading." http://knarf.english.upenn.edu/MShelley/reading.html. Web. 24 July 2014.
May, Rebecca, ed. *Zombology: A Zombie Anthology*. n.p.: Library of the Living Dead Press, 2009. Print.
May, Tim. "Coleridge's Slave Trade Lecture: Southey's Contribution and the Debt to Thomas Cooper." *Notes and Queries* 55.4 (2008): 425–29. Print.
Mbembe, Achille. "Necropolitics." *Public Culture* 15.1 (Winter 2003): 11–40. Print.
———. "On the Postcolony." *Post-Colonial Studies Reader*. Ed. Bill Ashcroft, Gareth Griffiths, and Helen Tiffin. 2nd ed. London: Routledge, 2006. Print.
M'biti, John. *African Religions and Philosophy*. London: Heinemann, 1970. Print.
McAlister, Elizabeth. "The Jew in the Haitian Imagination." *Invisible Powers: Vodou in Haitian Life and Culture*. Ed. Claudine Michel and Patrick Bellegarde-Smith. New York: Palgrave Macmillan, 2006. Print.

———. *Rara! Vodou, Power, and Performance in Haiti and Its Diaspora*. Berkeley: U of California P, 2002. Print.
———. "Slaves, Cannibals, and Infected Hyper-Whites: The Race and Religion of Zombies." *Anthropological Quarterly* 85.2 (2012). Print.
———. "Sorcerer's Bottle: The Art of Magic in Haiti." *Sacred Arts of Haitian Vodou*. Ed. Donald Consentino. Los Angeles: UCLA Fowler Museum of Cultural History, 1995. Print.
McClusky, Thorp. "While Zombies Walked" Reprint. *Zombie! Stories of the Walking Dead*. Ed. Haining. London: W. H. Allen & Co., 1985. Print.
McConnell, Mariana. "Interview: George A. Romero on *Diary of the Dead*." *Cinema Blend*, Jan. 14, 2008 Web. 17 August 2014.
McCullagh, Declan. "Brain-Eating Zombies Invade SF Apple Store." Cnet news, May 26 2007. Web. http://news.cnet.com/8301–17938_105-9723086-1.html.
Mcdonald, Jillian. "Horror Make-up." Lecture, Exhibition notes. Brooklyn, NY. 2006.
———. "Me and Billy Bob." http://meandbillybob.com. Web. 24 July 2014.
———. "Movie Stars and Monsters." Lecture. Marin Headlands, Marin, CA. 4 Sept. 2008.
———. "To Vincent with Love." http://artport.whitney.org/gatepages/artists/mcdonald/. Web. 24 July 2014.
———. 2007. "Zombie Portraits." http://jillianmcdonald.net/projects/zombie_lenticular.html. Web.
McGarry, Molly. *Ghosts of Futures Past: Spiritualism and the Cultural Politics of Nineteenth-Century America*. Berkeley: U of California P, 2008. Print.
McIntosh, Shawn, and Marc Leverette, eds. *Zombie Culture: Autopsies of the Living Dead*. Lanham, MD: Scarecrow Press, 2008. Print.
McNally, David. *Monsters of the Market: Zombies, Vampires, and Global Capitalism*. Chicago: Haymarket Books, 2011. Print.
Mecum, Ryan, *Zombie Haiku*. Cincinnati, OH: How Books, 2008. Print.
Mehta, Diane. "*Walcott*, Pissarro, and the Search for Tiepolo's Hound." *Agni* 52 (2000): 299–307. Print.
Meik, Vivian. "White Zombie." Reprint. *Zombie! Stories of the Walking Dead*. Ed. Haining. London: W. H. Allen & Co., 1985. Print.
Mercer, Kobena, "Monster Metaphors: Notes on Michael Jackson's 'Thriller.'" *Screen* 27.1 (1986): 26–43. Print.
Merchant, Carolyn. *The Death of Nature*. San Francisco: Harper & Row, 1980. Print.
Métraux, Alfred. *Haiti: Black Peasants and Their Religion*. Trans. Peter Lengyl. London: George G. Harrap & Co., 1960. Print.
———. *Le Vaudou Haïtien*. Paris: Gallimard, 1958. Print.
———. *Voodoo in Haiti*. Trans. Hugo Charteris. New York: Oxford UP, 1959. Print.
Meyers, Emily Taylor. "Transnational Romance: The Politics of Desire in Caribbean Novels by Women." Ph.D. diss., University of Oregon, 2009.

Michel, Claudine, and Patrick Bellegarde-Smith, eds. *Invisible Powers: Vodou in Haitian Life and Culture*. New York: Palgrave Macmillan, 2006. Print.

Mitter, Partha. *Much Maligned Monsters: History of European Reactions to Indian Art*. Oxford: Clarendon Press, 1977. Print.

Moers, Ellen. *Literary Women*. Garden City, NY: Doubleday, 1976. Print.

Moglen, Helene. *The Trauma of Gender: A Feminist Theory of the English Novel*. Berkeley: U of California P, 2001. Print.

Montague, Ludwell Lee. *Haiti and the United States, 1714–1938*. Durham, NC: Duke UP, 1940. Print.

Montaigne, Michel de. *Essays*. Trans. J. M. Cohen 1958. London: Penguin Books, 1993. Print.

Moreau de St Méry, M. L. E. *Description de la partie francaise de l'Isle de Saint Domingue*. Vol. 1. Philadelphia, 1797. Print.

——. Speech of July 23, 1789, before the National Assembly. *European Magazine* (July 1789): 208. London. Print.

Morehead, John. "Zombie Walks, Zombie Jesus, and the Eschatology of Postmodern Flesh." *The Undead and Theology*. Ed. Kim Paffenroth and John Morehead. Eugene, OR: Pickwick Publications, 2012. Print.

Moreman, Christopher, and Cory Rushton, eds. *Race, Oppression, and the Zombie: Essays on the Cross-Cultural Appropriations of the Caribbean Tradition*. Jefferson, NC: McFarland, 2011. Print.

Moretti, Franco. *Signs Taken for Wonders: On the Sociology of Literary Forms*. London: Verso, 1983. Print.

Morris, Wesley. "Song of Solomon: A Review of *12 Years a Slave*." *Grantlands*, 24 Oct. 2013. Web.

Morton, Timothy. *Ecology without Nature*. Cambridge, MA: Harvard UP, 2007. Print.

——. *The Poetics of Spice: Romantic Consumerism and the Exotic*. Cambridge: Cambridge UP, 2000. Print.

——, ed. *A Routledge Sourcebook on Mary Shelley's Frankenstein*. London: Routledge, 2002. Print.

Moseley, Benjamin. *A Treatise on Sugar*. London: G. G. and J. Robinson, 1799. Accessed via Google Books.

MSN News. "Did NRA Ban Zombie Targets That Resemble Obama?" 17 July 2013. http://news.msn.com/us/did-nra-ban-zombie-targets-that-resemble-obama. Web. 27 July 2014.

Mulrain, George MacDonald. *Theology in Folk Culture: The Theological Significance of Haitian Folk Culture*. Frankfurt am Main: Verlag Peter Lang, 1984. Print.

Mulvey, Laura. "Visual Pleasure and Narrative Cinema." *Screen* 16.3 (1975): 6–18. Print.

Munro, Martin. "Petrifying Myths: Lack and Excess in Caribbean and Haitian Histories." *Interpreting the Haitian Revolution and Its Cultural Aftershocks*.

Ed. Martin Munro and Elizabeth Walcott-Hackshaw. Kingston, Jamaica: U of the West Indies P, 2006. Print.

———. *Shaping and Reshaping the Caribbean in the Work of Aimé Césaire and René Depestre*. London: Maney Publishing, 2000. Print.

Munro, Martin, and Celia Britton. *American Creoles: The Francophone Caribbean and the American South*. Liverpool: Liverpool UP, 2012. Print.

Murphy, Joseph M. *Working the Spirit: Ceremonies of the African Diaspora*. Boston: Beacon Press, 1994. Print.

Nakashima-Brown, Chris. "Keep Austin Zombie-Free." Web. 26 Jan. 2009. nofearofthefuture.blogspot.com.

Naimou, Angela. *Salvage Work: U.S. and Caribbean Literature amid the Debris of Legal Personhood*. New York: Fordham UP, 2015.

Najman, Charles. *Dieu seul me voit*. Paris: Editions Balland, 1981. Print.

Nandy, Ashis. *The Intimate Enemy: Loss and Recovery of Self under Colonialism*. 2nd ed. New Delhi: Oxford UP, 2013. Print.

Nau, Ignace. *Isalina, ou, Une scène créole: Récit*. Ed. Hénock Trouillot. Port-au-Prince: Editions Choucoune, 2000. Print.

Neugroschel, Joachim. *The Golem*. New York: W. W. Norton, 2006. Print.

Newitz, Annalee. *Pretend We're Dead: Capitalist Monsters in American Pop Culture*. Durham, NC: Duke UP, 2006. Print.

———. "This interactive painting can explain why we are still obsessed with zombies." io9.com 05 Mar 2013. Web.

New Orleans Bulletin. 29 May 1875. Print.

Nuckols, Ben. "Humans vs. Zombies: New Sport Sweeping College Campuses." *The Herald Online* (Sierra Vista, AZ), 9 Dec. 2008. http://www.svherald.com/articles/2008/12/10/sports/features/doc493f5267c6f98956874247.txt. Web.

Ott, Thomas O. *The Haitian Revolution: 1789–1804*. Knoxville: U of Tennessee P, 1973. Print.

Paffenroth, Kim. *Gospel of the Living Dead: George Romero's Visions of Hell on Earth*. Waco, TX: Baylor UP, 2006. Print.

Paik, Peter. "The Gnostic Zombie and the State of Nature: On Robert Kirkman's *The Walking Dead*." Unpublished.

———. "Zombies and Other Strangers." 26 Jan. 2011. U of Minnesota P blog. http://www.uminnpressblog.com/2011/01/zombies-and-other-strangers-thoughts-on.html. Web.

Palumbo, David. "The Fantasy Art of David Palumbo." This Is Cool. http://www.this-is-cool.co.uk/the-fantasy-art-of-david-palumbo/. Web. 24 July 2014.

Paravisini-Gebert, Lizabeth. "The Haitian Revolution in Interstices and Shadows: A Re-Reading of Alejo Carpentier's The Kingdom of This World." *Research in African Literatures* 35.2 (Summer 2004): 114–27. Print.

———. "Women Possessed: Eroticism and Exoticism in the Representation of Woman as Zombie." *Sacred Possessions: Vodou, Santeria, Obeah, and the*

Caribbean. Ed. Olmos and Paravisini-Gebert. New Brunswick, NJ: Rutgers UP, 2000. Print.
Parrinder, Geoffrey. *Mythologies africaines*. Paris: Odege, 1969. Print.
Parsons, Rob. "Zombies Held in Police Swoop." *Evening Standard* (London), 20 May 2011. Web. Accessed via WorldCat.
Pastras, Phil. *Dead Man's Blues: Jelly Roll Morton Way Out West*. Berkeley: U of California P, 2001. Print.
Patterson, Orlando. *Slavery and Social Death: A Comparative Study*. Cambridge, MA: Harvard UP, 1982. Print.
Peake, Bryce. "He Is Dead, and He Is Continuing to Die: A Feminist Psycho-Semiotic Reflection on Men's Embodiment of Metaphor in a Toronto Zombie Walk." *Journal of Contemporary Anthropology* 1.1 (2010): 50–71. Print.
Péan, Stanley. *Zombi Blues*. Montreal: La Courte Echelle, 1996. Print.
Pensky, Max. "Method and Time: Benjamin's Dialectical Images." *The Cambridge Companion to Walter Benjamin*. Ed. David Ferris. Cambridge: Cambridge UP, 2004. Print.
Penzler, Otto, ed. *Zombies! Zombies! Zombies! The Most Complete Collection of Zombie Stories Ever Published*. New York: Vintage Books, 2011. Print.
Perkowski, Jan Louis. *The Darkling: A Treatise on Slavic Vampirism*. Columbus, OH: Slavica, 1989. Print.
Perron, Bernard. *Horror Video Games Essays on the Fusion of Fear and Play*. Jefferson, NC: McFarland, 2009. Print.
Pettinger, Alasdair, "From Vaudoux to Voodoo." *Modern Language Studies* 40.4 (2004): 415–25. Print.
Pfau, George. Artist statements and works. http://www.georgepfau.com/. Web. 27 July 2014.
Phillips, Kendall R. *Projected Fears: Horror Films and American Culture*. Westport, CT: Praeger, 2005. Print.
Pierre, Romulus. *Les Zombis en furie*. Port-au-Prince: Ateliers Fardin, 1978. Print.
Pissarro, Camille. *Rue de l'Épicerie, Rouen*. 1898. New York: Metropolitan Museum of Art, ARTstor. Web. Accessed 8 July 2014.
Pissarro, Joachim. *Cézanne/Pissarro, Johns/Rauschenberg: Comparative Studies on Intersubjectivity in Modern Art*. Cambridge: Cambridge UP, 2006. Print.
———. *Pioneering Modern Painting: Cézanne and Pissarro, 1865–1885*. New York: Museum of Modern Art, 2005. Print.
Plancast. http://www.plancast.com. Web. 24 July 2014.
Plancy, Collin de. *Dictionnaire infernal, ou Biblioteque universelles, sur les etres, les personnages, les livres, les faits, et les choses . . .* 2nd ed. Paris, 1826. Print.
Pratt, Mary Louise. "Arts of the Contact Zone." 1991. *Ways of Reading*. 5th ed. Ed. David Bartholomae and Anthony Petroksky. New York: Bedford/St. Martin's, 1999. Print.

Price-Mars, Jean. *Ainsi parla l'oncle*. Trans. Magdaline W. Shannon. Washington, DC: Three Continents Press, 1983. Print.
Prichard, H. Hesketh. *Where Black Rules White: A Journey across and about Hayti*. 1900. London: Thomas Nelson & Sons, 1910.
Poupeye, Veerle. *Caribbean Art*. London: Thames & Hudson, 1998. Print.
Powell, Anna. *Deleuze and Horror Film*. Edinburgh: Edinburgh UP, 2005. Print.
Puckett, Newbell Niles. *Folk Beliefs of the Southern Negro*. Chapel Hill: U of North Carolina P, 1926. Print.
Quiggan, John. *Zombie Economics: How Dead Ideas Still Walk among Us*. Princeton, NJ: Princeton UP, 2010. Print.
Raiskin, Judith L. *Snow on the Canefields: Women's Writing and Creole Subjectivity*. Minneapolis: U of Minnesota P, 1996. Print.
Reed, Ishmael. *Mumbo Jumbo*. Garden City, NY: Doubleday & Co., 1972. Print.
———. *New and Collected Poems, 1964–2006*. New York: Carroll & Graf, 2006. Print.
Reinhardt, Catherine A. *Claims to Memory: Beyond Slavery and Emancipation in the French Caribbean*. New York: Berghahn Books, 2006. Print.
Renda, Mary A. *Taking Haiti: Military Occupation and the Culture of U.S. Imperialism, 1915–1940*. Chapel Hill: U of North Carolina P, 2001. Print.
Revert, Eugène. *Les Antilles*. Paris: A. Collin, 1954. Print.
Rhodes, Gary D. *White Zombie: Anatomy of a Horror Film*. Jefferson, NC: McFarland, 2006. Print.
Rhys, Jean. *Wide Sargasso Sea*. New York: W. W. Norton, 1966. Print.
Rigaud, Milo. *Jésus ou Legba? ou, Les dieux se battent*. Ecole du symbolisme Afro-Haitien. L'Imprimerie Yvers. Niort: P. Nicolas, 1933. Print.
———. *Secrets of Voodoo*. 1953. Trans. Robert B. Cross. San Francisco: City Lights Books, 1985. Print.
———. *La tradition voudoo et le voudoo haïtien, son temple, ses mystères, sa magie*. Port-au-Prince: Editions Fardin, 1953. Print.
Riley, Shannon Rose. "Imagi-Nations in Black and White: Cuba, Haiti, and the Cultural Performance of Difference in U.S. National Projects, 1898–1940." Ph.D. diss., University of California, Davis, 2006.
Robinson, Michelle, ed. *Edouard Duval-Carrié: The Migration of the Spirit*. Davenport, IA: Figge Art Museum, 2005. Print.
Romero, George A., and Tony Williams. *George A. Romero: Interviews*. Jackson: UP of Mississippi, 2011. Print.
Rovner, Matthew, "What's behind Israel's Zombie Outbreak?" *Jewish Daily Forward*, 17 Oct. 2013. http://blogs.forward.com/the-arty-semite/185456/whats-behind-israels-zombie-outbreak/#ixzz2kjNirpWu. Web. 27 June 2014.
Russell, Jaime. *Book of the Dead: A Complete Guide to Zombie Cinema*. Surrey, UK: FAB Press, 2006. Print.
Russell, John. "Turbulent Restatements from Robert Colescott." *New York Times*, 3 Mar. 1989. Web. http://www.nytimes.com/1989/03/03/

arts/review-art-turbulent-restatements-from-robert-colescott. html?pagewanted=all&src=pm. 27 June 2014.

Ruthven, Andrea. "Pride and Prejudice and Post-Feminist Zombies." *Weaving New Perspectives Together: Some Reflections on Literary Studies.* Ed. María Alonso Alonso, Jeannette Bello Mota, Alba de Béjar Muíños, and Laura Torrado Mariñas. Newcastle upon Tyne: Cambridge Scholars Publishing, 2012. Print.

Safire, William. "Zombie." *New York Times Magazine*, 17 May 2009. Web.

Said, Edward. "Overlapping Territories, Intertwined Histories." *Twentieth Century Literary Theory: A Reader.* 2nd ed. Ed. K. Newton. London: Palgrave, 1997. Print.

Saint-Lot, Marie José Alcide. *Vodou, a Sacred Theatre: The African Heritage in Haiti.* Coconut Creek, FL: Educa Vision, 2003. Print.

Sale, George, et al. *An Universal History from the Earliest Accounts to the Present Time.* Vol. 16, pt. 2. London: C. Bathhurst, 1760. Accessed via Google eBook.

Saltzman, Lisa. *Making Memory Matter: Strategies of Remembrance in Contemporary Art.* Chicago: U of Chicago P, 2006. Print.

Savory, Elaine. *The Cambridge Introduction to Jean Rhys.* Cambridge: Cambridge UP, 2009. Print.

Saxon, Lyle, Edward Dreyer, and Robert Tallant, eds. *Gumbo Ya-Ya: A Collection of Louisiana Folk Tales.* 1945. Gretna, LA: Pelican Publishing Co., 1991. Print.

Schell Sculpture Studio. schellstudio.com/gallery/thumbnails.php?album=12. Web. 24 July 2014.

Schmitz, Neil. "NeoHoodoo: The Experimental Fiction of Ismael Reed." *20th Century Literature* 20.2 (Apr. 1974): 126–40. Print.

Schneider, Bret, and Omair Hussain, "An Interview with Hal Foster." *Platypus Review* 22 (Apr. 2010). Web. http://platypus1917.org/2010/04/08/an-interview-with-hal-foster/.

Schneider, Rebecca. "It Seems as If . . . I Am Dead: Zombie Capitalism and Theatrical Labor." *Drama Review* 56.4 (Winter 2012): 150–62. Print.

Schneider, Steven Jay. *Fear without Frontiers: Horror Cinema across the Globe.* Godalming, UK: FAB, 2003. Print.

Schwartz-Bart, Simone. *Between Two Worlds.* 1979. Trans. Barbara Bray. New York: Harper & Row, 1981. Print.

———. *Bridge of Beyond (Pluie et vent sur telumée miracle).* Trans. Barbara Bray. New York: Atheneum, 1974. Print.

Seabrook, William. *The Magic Island.* New York: Harcourt, Brace & Co., 1929. Print.

Sharpe, Jenny. *Ghosts of Slavery: A Literary Archaeology of Black Women's Lives.* Minneapolis: U of Minnesota P, 2003. Print.

Shaviro, Steven. *The Cinematic Body: Theory Out of Bounds.* Vol. 2. Minneapolis: U of Minnesota P, 1993. Print.

Sheller, Mimi. *Consuming the Caribbean: From Arawaks to Zombies*. London: Routledge, 2003. Print.
Shelley, Mary. *Frankenstein, or the Modern Prometheus*. 1818. New York: Dover Publications, 1994. Print.
———. *The Last Man*. Ed. Anne McWhir. Peterborough, ONT: Broadview Press, 1996. Print.
Shklovsky, Viktor, "Art as Device." *Theory of Prose* (1917). Reprint. Normal, IL: Dalkey Archive Press, Illinois State University, 1990. Print.
Skal, David J. *The Monster Show: A Cultural History of Horror*. New York: W. W. Norton, 1993. Print.
Sims, Lowery Stokes. "African American Artists and Postmodernism: Reconsidering the Careers of Wifredo Lam, Romere Bearden, Norman Lewis, and Robert Colescott." *African American Visual Aesthetics: A Postmodern View*. Ed. David C. Driskell. Washington, DC: Smithsonian Institution Press, 1995. Print.
Slater, Jay. *Eaten Alive! Italian Cannibal and Zombie Movies*. London: Plexus, 2002. Print.
Smith, Caleb. *The Prison and the American Imagination*. New Haven, CT: Yale UP, 2009. Print.
Smith, Rowland, ed. *Exile and Tradition*. New York: Dalhousie UP, 1976. Print.
Snell, D. L., and Travis Adkins, eds. *The Undead*. Vol. 2, *Skin and Bones*. Franklin, TN: Permuted Press, 2007. Print.
———. *The Undead*. Vol. 3, *Flesh Feast*. Franklin, TN: Permuted Press, 2007. Print.
Snell, D. L., and Elijah Hall, eds. *The Undead: Zombie Anthology*. Franklin, TN: Permuted Press, 2005. Print.
Sontag, Susan. *AIDS and Its Metaphors*. New York: Farrar, Straus & Giroux, 1989. Print.
Southey, Robert. *History of Brazil*. London: Longman, Hurst, Rees, and Orme, 1810. Print.
Spivey, Virginia. "Jillian Mcdonald." *Art Papers* (May–June 2008): 72–72. Web.
Stamper, W. J. *Beyond the Seas: A Collection of Short Stories Filled with Mystery, Adventure, and Lure of Foreign Countries as Experienced and Narrated by a Marine Officer on Duty beyond the Seas*. [Norfolk, Va.]: n.p., 1935. Print.
Stern, David. Comment on "Camille Pissarro at the Jewish Museum." 12 Oct. 2007. http://louisproyect.org/2007/10/12/camille-pissarro-at-the-jewish-museum/. Web. 27 July 2014.
Sternberg, Esther M. "Walter B. Cannon and 'Voodoo' Death: A Perspective from 60 Years On." *American Journal of Public Health* 92.10 (Oct. 2002): 169–81. Print.
Stiles, Kristine, and Peter Selz, eds. *Theories and Documents of Contemporary Art: A Sourcebook of Artists' Writings*. Berkeley: U of California P, 1996. Print.

Stinson, Elizabeth. "Zombified Capital in the Postcolonial Capital: Circulation (of Blood) in Sony Labou Tansi's Parentheses of Blood." *Race, Oppression, and the Zombie: Essays on Cross-Cultural Appropriations of the Caribbean Tradition*. Ed. Moreman and Rushton. Jefferson, NC: McFarland, 2011. Print.
St. John, Spenser. *Hayti, or the Black Republic*. 1884. Accessed via Google Books. Web.
Strom, Stephanie. "A Billionaire Lends a Hand in Haiti." *New York Times*, 6 Jan. 2012. Web.
Summers, Montague. *The Vampire: His Kith and Kin*. 1928. Park, NY: University Books, 1960. Print.
Sundquist, Eric J. *To Wake the Nations: Race in the Making of American Literature*. Cambridge, MA: Belknap Press, 1993. Print.
Sutherland, Megan. "Rigor/Mortis: The Industrial Life of Style in American Zombie Cinema." *Framework: Journal of Cinema and Media* 48.1 (Spring 2007): 64–78. Print.
Swanson, Lucy. "Zombie Nation? The Horde, Social Uprisings, and National Narratives." *Cincinnati Romance Review* 34 (Fall 2012): 13–33. Print.
Taft, Edna. *A Puritan in Voodoo Land*. 1938. Detroit: Tower Books, 1971. Print.
Tallant, Robert. *Voodoo in New Orleans*. New York: Macmillan, 1946. Print.
Taylor, Fabienne Boncy, and Joel C. Timyan. "Notes on Zombia antillarum." *Economic Botany* 58.2 (2004): 173–83. Print.
Thomson, David. *"Have You Seen . . . ?": An Introduction to 1,000 Films*. New York: Knopf, 2008. Print.
Tiffin, Helen. "Postcolonial Literatures and Counter-Discourse." *Post-Colonial Studies Reader*. Ed. Bill Ashcroft, Gareth Griffiths, and Helen Tiffin. 2nd ed. London: Routledge, 2006. Print.
Time. "Death and the Legacy of Papa Doc Duvalier." 17 Jan. 2011. http://content.time.com/time/magazine/article/0,9171,876967,00.html. Web. 27 June 2014.
Trésor de la langue française: Dictionnaire de la langue du XIXe et du XXe siècle (1789–1960). Vol. 16. Institut National de la Langue Française. Nancy: Gallimard, 1994. Print.
Tripp, Andrew. "Zombie Marches and the Limits of Apocalyptic Space." *Nomos Journal*, 7 Aug. 2012. Nomosjournal.org. Web.
Trouillot, Lyonel. *Thérèse en mille morceaux*. Arles, France: Actes Sud, 2000. Print.
Trouillot, Michel-Rolph. *Silencing the Past: Power and the Production of History*. Boston: Beacon Press, 1995. Print.
Vale, Simone do. "Trash Mob." *The Domination of Fear*. Ed. Mikko Canini. At the Interface/Probing the Boundaries. Amsterdam: Rodopi, 2010. Print.
Victor, Gary. *Je sais quand Dieu vient se promener dans mon jardin*. Paris: Vents d'ailleurs, 2007. Print.
———. *Treize nouvelles vaudou*. Montreal: Mémoire d'encrier, 2007. Print.

Video Data Bank. "Halflifers: The Complete History, 1992–2010." http://www.vdb.org/titles/halflifers-complete-history-1992-2010. Web. 24 July 2014.

Vint, Sheryl. "Abject Posthumanism: Neoliberalism, Biopolitics, and Zombies." *Monster Culture in the 21st Century*. Ed. Marina Levina and Diem-my T. Bui. New York: Bloomsbury Press, 2013. Print.

Voigts-Virchow, Eckart. "Pride and Promiscuity and Zombies, Or: Miss Austen Mashed Up in the Affinity Spaces of Participatory Culture." *Adaptation and Cultural Appropriation: Literature, Film, and the Arts*. Ed. Pascal Niklas and Oliver Lindner. Berlin: De Gruyter, 2010. Print.

Walcott, Derek. "A Muse of History." *Post-Colonial Studies Reader*. Ed. Bill Ashcroft, Gareth Griffiths, and Helen Tiffin. 2nd ed. London: Routledge, 2006. Print.

———. *Tiepolo's Hound*. New York: Farrar, Straus & Giroux, 2000. Print.

Wald, Priscilla. *Contagious: Cultures, Carriers, and the Outbreak Narrative*. Durham, NC: Duke UP, 2008. Print.

Walker, Matthew. "When There's No More Room in Hell, the Dead Will Shop the Earth: Romero and Aristotle on Zombies, Happiness, and Consumption." *The Undead and Philosophy: Chicken Soup for the Soulless*. Ed. Greene and Mohammed. Chicago: Open Court, 2006. Print.

Wallace, Inez. "I Walked With a Zombie." Reprint. *Zombie! Stories of the Walking Dead*. Ed. Haining. London: W. H. Allen & Co., 1985. Print.

Waller, Gregory, ed. *American Horrors: Essays on the Modern American Horror Film*. Chicago: U of Illinois P, 1987. Print.

Warner, Marina. *Fantastic Metamorphoses, Other Worlds*. Oxford: Oxford UP, 2004. Print.

Webb, Jen, and Sam Byrnand. "Some Kind of Virus: The Zombie as Body and as Trope." *Body and Society* 14 (2008): 83–98. Print.

Wetmore, Kevin. *Back from the Dead: Remakes of George Romero Films as Markers of Their Times*. Jefferson, NC: McFarland, 2011. Print.

Whelan, Andrew, Ruth Walker, and Christopher Moore, eds. *Zombies in the Academy: Living Death in Higher Education*. Bristol, UK: Intellect Press, 2013. Print.

White, Armond. "Can't Trust It." *City Arts: New York's Review of Culture*, 16 Oct. 2013. Web. http://cityarts.info/2013/10/16/cant-trust-it/.

Wilentz, Amy. *Farewell, Fred Voodoo: A Letter from Haiti*. New York: Simon & Schuster, 2013. Print.

———. A "Zombie Is a Slave Forever." *New York Times*, 30 Oct. 2012. Web.

Williams, Cynric R., and Candace Ward. *Hamel, the Obeah Man*. 1827. Peterborough, ONT: Broadview Press, 2010. Print.

Williams, Raymond Leslie. *The Columbia Guide to the Latin American Novel since 1945*. New York: Columbia UP, 2007. Print.

Williams, Tony. *The Cinema of George A. Romero: Knight of the Living Dead*. London: Wallflower, 2003. Print.

Wired Magazine. "Puffer Fish Pain-Killer." 30 Nov. 2003. Web.

Wirkus, Faustin, and Taney Dudley. *The White King of La Gonave: The True Story of the Sergeant of Marines Who Was Crowned King on a Voodoo Island.* New York: Doubleday, Doran & Co., 1931. Print.

Wood, Robin. *Hollywood from Vietnam to Reagan.* New York: Columbia UP, 1986. Print.

Worland, Rick. *The Horror Film: An Introduction.* Malden, MA: Blackwell, 2007. Print.

Wright, Thomas, ed. *The Travels of Marco Polo, the Venetian.* London: Henry G. Bohn, 1854. Print.

Wyndham, Francis, and Diana Melly, eds. *The Letters of Jean Rhys.* New York: Viking, 1984. Print.

Yasumoto, Takeshi, and C. Y. Kao. "Tetrodotoxin and the Haitian Zombie." *Toxicon,* no. 24 (1986): 747-49. Print.

———. Tetrodotoxin in 'Zombie Powder.'" *Toxicon,* no. 28 (1990): 129-32. Print.

Young, Elizabeth. *Black Frankenstein: The Making of an American Metaphor.* New York: New York UP, 2008. Print.

Young, Jason R. *Rituals of Resistance: African Atlantic Religion in Kongo and the Lowcountry South in the Era of Slavery.* Baton Rouge: Louisiana State UP, 2007. Print.

Zealand, Christopher, "The National Strategy for Zombie Containment: Myth Meets Activism in Post 9/11 America." *Generation Zombie: Essays on the Living Dead in American Culture.* Ed. Boluk and Lenz. Jefferson, NC: McFarland, 2011. Print.

"Zemi" search. *Encyclopaedia Britannica.* Web. http://www.britannica.com/EBchecked/topic/656371/zemi. 24 July 2014.

Zizek, Slavoj. *Enjoy Your Symptom!* Hoboken, NJ: Taylor and Francis, 2013. Print.

———. *Looking Awry: An Introduction to Jacques Lacan through Popular Culture.* Cambridge, MA: MIT Press, 1991. Print.

Zombie Crawl New York. http://nyczombiecrawl.com. Web. 24 July 2014.

Zombie Hub. http://zombiehub.com. Web. 24 July 2014.

Zombie Industries. http://zombieindustries.com/. Web. 24 July 2014.

Zombie Me. http://Zombieme.com. Web. 24 July 2014.

Zombie Research Society. http://www.zombieresearch.org. Web. 24 July 2014.

Zombie Walk. http://www.zombiewalk.com. Web. 24 July 2014.

Index

28 Days Later (Boyle), 95, 97, 172, 203n4

Ackermann and Gauthier, 38, 73, 205n6
Adorno, Theodor, 5
Africa: regions and people, characterizations of, general, 16, 86–87, 96, 101, 155, 159, 196, 203n24; Angola, 16, 37–38, 73, 206n12; Arada, 37, 41, 206n11; Camma, 45; Congo, 37–38, 51, 73, 86, 152, 206n14, 208n26; Dahomey, 44, 73, 130; Gobbi, 45; Guinea, 14, 36, 206n11; Loango, 38, 46
African slave, 17, 20, 27, 37, 50, 59, 79, 84, 121–22, 141, 152, 182, 197, 207n23, 208n25; folklore, mythology and religions, 6, 8, 10, 12, 15, 17, 20, 32–34, 38, 41–47, 50–53; 60, 66, 69, 70, 72, 74, 109, 111, 121–22, 156, 163, 198, 205n6; herbal knowledge, 58–59, 66, 208n27
Alaux, Gustave d', 51–53, 58
American Zombie (Bromley), 86–87
Appropriation: appropriation of the zombie myth, 4–5, 10–11, 15, 25, 33, 67, 69, 78, 89, 98, 101, 103–4, 105, 107, 109, 161–62, 164–165, 167, 171, 173, 197–200, 204n5; artistic and cultural appropriations, 148–56, 169, 177, 181–186; counterappropriation (or reappropriation), 25, 100, 103, 106, 120, 126, 177, 184–86
Agamben, Georgio, 209n38

AIDS, 95, 126, 214n30
Alexis, Jacques Stephen, 108–9, 115, 127, 138–42
American Horror Story (AMC), 105–7
Aristide, Jean-Bertrand, 113, 116, 122–23, 133, 135, 216n14, 217n19, 217n22
Article 249 of the Penal Code, 42–43
Atis Rezistans, 152–53, 163, 220n10
Austen, Jane, 149–51, 219n6

Bakhtin, Mikhail, 192
Baron Samedi, 104–5, 126, 128, 163, 171, 215n7, 217n25
Baseball, 108
Basquiat, Jean-Michel, 163
Beauvoir, Max, the Grand Ati of Vaudou, 76, 200
Beck, Ulrich, 204n5
Benjamin, Walter, 5, 31, 158
Berlant, Lauren, 189, 196
Bhabha, Homi, 10–11, 120, 182–83
Bigaud, Wilson, 163
Black Jacobins, 61, 63, 210n54
Black magic, 19, 35, 61, 86, 94, 103
Black Republic, 7, 29, 48–50, 71, 110
Blackface, 10–11, 13, 69, 104
Blancs, 43, 63, 69, 197, 217n19
Blaxploitation, 104, 185
Blessebois, Pierre-Corneille de, 34–36, 41, 209n35

Blood Enriched Classics, 149
Bloom, Harold, 184
Blues, 67, 155, 172–73
Body Count (Mcdonald), 169–70
Bois Caïman, 28–29, 56, 71, 118, 186, 209–10n43
bois nouveau, 132–34, 137, 218–19n32, 219n38
Bokor: vaudou practioner, 81, 87, 91,199, 205n4, 221n22; zombie's master, 50, 55, 73, 102, 126, 210n1, 215n2. *See also* Houngan
Boukman, 55–56, 117–18, 209–10n43
Boyle, Danny, 95, 97, 203n4
Bricolage, 156, 220n10
Bromley, Gordon, 86–87
Brontë, Charlotte, 146–51, 219n1, 220n7
Brown, Vincent, 20, 38, 53, 205n5, 209n37, 209n38
Buck-Morss, Susan, 29, 205n1, 209n36
Bush, George W., 193
Butler, Judith, 193, 223n4

Canavan, Gerry, 102
Cannibals, 3, 14–15, 32, 49, 60, 62, 93, 94, 96, 98–99, 101, 102, 134, 158, 206n14, 208n33, 209n34, 212n11, 213n20, 214n29; cannibalism, used to denigrate people, 14, 49, 60, 182, 210n49; figurative cannibalism, 99, 153, 223n7; zombies as, 3, 15, 32, 90, 93, 96–99, 102
Capitalism, 6, 9, 12–13, 18, 20, 25, 79, 85, 127, 158–59, 161, 171, 191, 199, 200, 203n3, 212n16, 214n34, 223n6–7; zombie as critique of, 31, 44, 77–79, 97–98, 114, 121, 158, 196. *See also* Neoliberalism
Capois, François (aka Capois-la-Mort), 55–56, 60
Carnival, 125–26, 128, 133, 138, 140, 142–43, 145, 192
Carpentier, Alejo, 57, 114–20, 125, 216n15–17
Castro, Fidel, 91, 130
Catholicism, 72, 144–45, 152, 156, 198, 209n42
Césaire, Aimé, 147, 149
Chamoiseau, Patrick, 137, 143–44
Chomsky, Noam, 216n14
Christian, 85, 121, 144, 216n18; Christianity, 6, 36, 217n18; Jesus Christ, 121, 217n18

Christophe, Henri, 54, 82, 91, 102, 110, 117–20, 209n40; and his Citadel La Ferrière, 118–19, 216n16
Clinton, Bill, 114, 217n22
Code Noir, 55, 209n42
Cohen, Jeffrey Jerome, 9–10, 18
Cold War, 93
Coleridge, Samuel Taylor, 37, 47–48, 206n12, 208n29, 208n30
Colonialism, 6, 11–13, 17–19, 44–47, 77, 84, 95, 97, 105, 107, 121, 143, 182, 184, 200–201, 219n1. *See also* Empire; Imperialism
Comaroff, Jean and John, 44–5
Comedians, The (Greene), 128–30
Comic books, 123, 159, 162, 164, 203n4, 220n14
Communists, Communism, 89, 130; anti-Communist, 130
Contact zones, 17, 89, 114. *See also* Pratt
Contagion, contagious, 15 18–19, 22, 32, 70, 77, 92–97, 102, 190–92, 212n18, 214n30, 223n3. *See also* Zombie, viral
Corps cadavre, ko kadav, 40, 43, 73, 142
Craige, John H., 209n35, 212n11
Cuba, 57, 71–72, 101–2, 133, 156

Danse macabre, 6
Dante, 6, 114, 184, 216n11
Danticat, Edwidge, 126, 138, 152–53, 163, 218n30
Dapper, Olfert, 45–46, 52, 207n24
Davis, Wade, 33, 39, 55, 91, 110–11, 113, 190, 205n13, 207n20, 211n7, 215n4, 215n6; study of the puffer fish poison, 66, 205n4, 211n3, 211n10
Dawn of the Dead (Romero), 9, 31, 97, 157–58, 160–62, 172–73, 175, 203n3, 213n27, 214n34
Dawn of the Dead (Snyder), 158
Day of the Dead (Romero), 95–96, 169–70
Dayan, Colin (Joan), 19, 59–61, 63, 121, 152, 210n48, 219n40, 220n10
Degoul, Franck, 113–14, 121–23, 199–200, 216n18, 217n19
Dendle, Peter, 19, 96, 165, 214n32
Depestre, René, 34, 115, 127; *Hadriana dans tous mes reves*, 137–43, 219n41
Deren, Maya, 19, 110, 121, 215n5
Derleth, August, 21, 82–84, 87
Derrida, Jacques, 2, 19

Descourtilz, M.E., 41–42, 60
Desmangles, Leslie, 19, 205n13
Dessalines, Jean-Jacques, 51, 55, 117, 209n40
Dézafi (Frankétienne), 131–34, 142, 218n27, 218n31–32
Dialectical image, 5, 31
Diederich, Bernard & Al Burt, 123, 130–31, 217n25
Digicel, 108, 152
Dominican Republic, 123, 217n21
Dracula, 161, 196
Drexler, Debra, 177–85, 222n33, 222n34
Drogue, 54–55
Duchamp, Marcel, 154, 156–58
Dutertre, Père, 40, 207n17
Duval-Carrié, Edouard, 163
Duvalier, François "Papa Doc," 16, 22, 62, 103, 113–34, 122–23, 126–32, 136, 140, 185, 215n7, 217n25, 218n29–30
Duvalier, Jean-Claude, "Baby Doc," 22, 103, 111, 113–14, 122, 130, 133, 153, 215n7, 218n29–30

Eco-criticism, 133
Eco-Zombie, 95
Edwards, Bryan, 46–49
Egypt: ancient, 6, 139; Arab Spring, 193–94, 223n5; mummy, 151; Osiris and Isis myth, 6, 121
Empire, 8, 12, 15, 17, 20, 29, 34, 46, 79, 89, 99, 101, 121, 142, 144, 150–53, 181–82, 197–99; British Empire, specifically, 150, 188; Hardt and Negri's *Empire*, 198–99

fan-fic, 149
Fanon, Frantz, 5, 7, 124, 205n2, 209n38, 217n23–24; on a "literature of combat," 124–25
Farmer, Paul, 116, 216n13
Faulkner, William, 114
Faust, 64
Fetish: commodity, 68, 208n26; object, 38, 48, 152, 156, 211n8
Fido (Currie), 101, 214n37
Flesh-eating, 22, 92, 171. *See also* Cannibalism
Folklore: general, 6, 8, 22, 69, 160–61, 197; African, 8, 43; Caribbean, 5, 17, 20, 22, 29, 80–82, 109, 112–15, 120–25, 134, 163, 183, 197, 212n14, 218n26; US South, 73–74
Foster, Hal, 2, 146, 154, 184, 203n2
Foucault, Michel, 19, 30, 32
Frankenstein's monster, 5, 103, 151
Frankenstein (Shelley), 13–15, 93–94, 204n6, 204n10–12
Frankenstein (Whale), 93–94
Frankétienne, *Dézafi*, 131–34, 142, 218n27, 218n31–32
Freud, Sigmund, 138; Freudian psychoanalysis, 19
Fulci, Lucio, 95, 169, 172, 221n27

Gandolfo, Jerry, 64, 67, 76, 110
Ganzeer, 193–95
Gauguin, Paul, 177–85
Gauguin's Zombie (Drexler), 178–85, 222n33–34
Gilroy, Paul, 10–11
Give man zombie (Ba Moun), 64–65, 67–68
Glissant, Edouard, 144, 147
Glover, Kaiama, 131–32, 218n32, 218n37, 219n38, 219n41
Golem, 14–15, 204n10–11
Gore, Al, 135
Gothic, 47, 196
Grahame-Smith, Seth, 149–50
Great Depression, The, 80
Greene, Graham, 128–30
Griot (storyteller), 124, 143
Guadeloupe, 34, 137, 205n5

Hadriana dans tous mes reves (Depestre), 137–43, 219n41
Haiti: American Occupation of, 4, 11, 12–13, 20–21, 23, 32, 50, 54, 63, 69–70, 80–82, 84, 113, 143, 147, 200, 212n12, 216n9; Haitian Revolution, 7–8, 10, 15, 20, 27–29, 32–34, 42, 47–48, 51–63, 76, 81, 109, 116–18, 122, 192, 204n12, 205n5, 210n44, 212n16, 215n3, 217n21, 223n3. *See also* Port-au-Prince
Halberstam, Judith, 18, 196
Halloween, 161, 191, 193
Halperin, Victor, 86, 94, 212n13
Hardt, Michael and Antonio Negri, 198–99
Harper, Stephen, 213n25, 214n34
Hasco (also HASCO, Haitian-American Sugar Company), 78–79, 84, 100, 127, 216n9

Hauntology, 2, 19
Hearn, Lafcadio, 39–40, 207n15, 207n18, 209n35
Hegel, G. W. F., 4–5, 29–32, 53, 205n1–2; Master/Slave (or Bondsman) dialectic, 5, 13, 29, 30, 32–33, 204n6, 205n2; Spirit of history, 4
Heidegger, Martin, 4
Hérard Céleur, Jean, 152, 163
Herbal acumen: medicine, 58, 66, 75; weapon, 33, 48–50, 59; vaudou, 49–50, 58; zombie-making, 33, 48–50, 58–61, 66, 75–76
Herskovitz, Melville J., 16, 44–45, 54–55, 209n41
Hollywood cinema, 5, 21, 87, 89–94, 98, 106, 123, 134, 144, 166, 169, 198,
Hoodoo, 65–69, 156, 185
Horror fiction, 80–87. *See also* Pulp fiction
Horror film, 18, 21–22, 25, 37, 73, 89–107
Horror of Party Beach, The (Tenney), 92–93
Horror Makeup (Mcdonald), 167–69
Hotel Oloffson, 133
Houngan (or oungan), a Vaudou priest, 5, 46, 53, 58, 87, 93, 109, 115, 117, 121–22, 130–32, 142, 144, 156, 210n43, 215n2
House in the Magnolias, The (Derleth), 21, 82–84, 87
House on Skull Mountain (Honthaner), 91, 102, 104
Hurbon, Laënnec, 20–22, 42, 49, 110
Hurston, Zora Neale: in Haiti, 64–65, 69, 113, 138, 209n35, 215n2, 215n5; in US South, 65–66, 74, 211n6
Hutter, G.W., 21, 81–83, 212n13, 212n16
Hyacinthe, 52–54, 60
Hyppolite, Hector, 126, 163

I am Legend (Matheson), 97, 203n4, 214n33
Isalina (Nau), 115, 125–28, 218n26
I Walked With a Zombie (Lewton), 82, 86, 103, 151
I Walked With a Zombie (Wallace), 82, 86, 89
Imperialism, 158, 197, 204n9. *See also* Colonialism; Empire
Israel, 198, 223n8

Jackson, Michael, 159, 188
Jamaica, 15, 20, 46–48, 53, 71, 115, 137, 205n5, 208n32, 209n38–39

James, C. L. R., 210n54
Jameson, Frederic, 158
Jane Eyre (Brontë), 146–48, 151–52, 219n1, 220n7–8
Jazz, 64, 67, 150, 156
Jones, Darby, 103–4
Jones, Duane, 91, 99
Juan de los Muertos (Brugués), 101–2, 173

Kingdom of this World, The (Carpentier), 57, 114–20, 125, 216n15–17
King of the Zombies (Yarbrough), 86, 88–89, 94
Kirkman, Robert, 160, 164
Kooning, Willem de, 154–55

L'Ouverture, Toussaint, 53, 55, 82, 110, 116, 141, 210n44, 215n3
Labat, Père, 40–41, 207n17–18
LaBruce, Bruce, 95, 214n30
Laferrière, Dany, 38–39, 115, 135–37, 142–44
Lalaurie, Delphine, 105–7, 211n4
Land of the Dead (Romero), 31, 97, 172
Laroche, Maximilien, 53, 77, 216n8
Larsen, Lars Bang, 196, 223n7
Laveau, Marie, 66–67, 105–6, 211n4
Lazarus, 7, 121
Lee, Stan, 87, 220n14
Léger, Jacques Nicolas, 28, 54–56, 210n50
Leonard, Sheldon, 89, 103
Lewton, Val, 82, 103, 151, 220n8
Lincoln, Abraham, 214n29
literary zombification (textual zombification), 148, 151–52, 155, 157–58, 172, 177–78, 181, 184
literature of combat, 124–26, 137
living dead, other figurations: Chinese hopping ghost, 12; dlukula, 44; draguar, 198; duppy, 38, 42, 74, 206n13, 207n21; Egyptian mummy, 151; ghosts, 2, 15, 19, 22, 36, 38, 40, 45, 75, 109, 112, 115, 126, 135, 207n15–16, 207n18, 207n21; grims, 6; Raw-Head-And-Bloody-Bones, 74; revenants, 84, 98, 108, 139, 198, 206n8–9, 207n16, 207n17–18; shipoko, 44; vampire, 6, 41, 148, 151, 165, 195, 203n4, 207n19, 213n24, 220n7; vekongi, 44
Loa or lwa, 38, 55, 60, 73, 104, 123, 199, 210n48; Damballah Ouedou, 142; Li

INDEX / 261

Gran Zombi, Le Grand-Zombi, 73, 106. *See also* Baron Samedi
Lomax, Alan, 68–69
Long, Edward, 46–48, 207n21
Lorde, Audre, 157
Lott, Eric, 10–11, 69
Louie, Travis, 163–64, 221n22
Louisiana, 70–75, 211n2, 211n10, 215n40
Lovecraft, H.P., 96
Lucas, Rafaël, 142–43, 219n41
Lugosi, Bela, 87, 100, 103, 215n39

Machete, 53–54, 81, 96, 105, 137, 157
Machine: body as, 98; rebel slaves as machines run amok, 28, 61
Mad Cow Disease, 95
Mad scientist, 93–94, 96, 100
Magical realism, 115
Makandal, François, 56, 210n45, 217n19
Martinique, 27, 39–40, 70, 72, 207n18
Marx, Karl, 5, 68, 196; Marxism, 19, 140
Mash-ups, 149–51
Master/Slave dialectic, 5, 13, 29, 30, 32–33, 204n6, 205n2. *See also* Hegel, G.W.F.
Matheson, Richard, 97, 203n4, 214n33
Mbembe, Achille, 209n38
McClusky, Thorp, 21, 87
Mcdonald, Jillian, 165–70, 177, 221n23, 24, 26, 27
McNally, David, 5, 195, 214n34, 223n6
Meik, Vivien, 21, 86–87
Meta-myth, 22, 111, 122–23
Métissage, 67, 152, 163, 185
Métraux, Alfred, 208n26, 215n5
Mixed-race, mulatto/a, 59, 88–90, 103, 119
Montero, Mayra, 133–35
Moreau de St. Méry, Médéric-Louis-Elie, 27–29, 36, 41, 50–51, 63, 197, 206n8
Moretti, Franco, 204n6
Morton, Jelly Roll, 64–65, 67–70, 100, 105, 211n7
Munster, Thea aka Thea Faulds, 187, 190–92
Myal. *See* Obeah

Narcisse, Clairvius, 171, 190, 207n20
Nau, Ignace, 115, 125–28, 218n26
Neoliberalism, 190, 196
New Orleans, Louisiana, 38, 64–67, 71–76, 83, 100, 105, 107, 211n2, 211n4, 211n9
Newitz, Annalee, 19, 171, 195, 214n34, 223n6

Night of the Living Dead (Romero), 32, 91–92, 96–99, 161–62, 169, 171–72, 203n4, 213n25–26, 222n27
Nkisi (zumbi), 38, 152, 206n14
Nzambi, 37–38, 73

Obama, Barack, 106, 189, 222n2
Obeah (Myal), 15, 46–48, 146, 148, 151–52, 185, 208n31–2, 212n19, 219n1–2
Occupy Wall Street (OWS), 2–4, 11–12, 23, 195, 200
Ouanga (Terwilliger), 86–87, 89–90, 103
Ouanga (charm), also spelled "wanga," 55, 81

Palm of Darkness, In the (Montero), 133–35
Patterson, Orlando, 20, 52–53, 208n25
Pays Sans Chapeau (Laferrière) 38–39, 115, 135–37, 142–44
Pétion, Alexandre, 91, 102
Pfau, George, 157–58, 170–77, 222n29
Pissarro, Camille, 174–77, 184, 222n30–32
Plague, 47, 93, 96–97, 117, 171, 191, 214n30, 219n5. *See also* Contagion; Zombie, viral
Plantation, 3, 8, 17, 28, 55–58, 61, 64, 66, 70, 78–79, 81–83, 87, 89, 93, 99, 110–11, 113, 117, 119–20, 132, 151, 156, 159, 212n19, 214n29; plantation system, 58, 78, 210n45
Poison, 16, 37, 40–42, 44, 46, 49, 54–61, 66–67, 74, 91, 116–17, 122–23, 133–34, 139–40, 146, 205n4, 207n22, 208n32, 210n45, 211n3, 217n19; to fake death, 16, 37, 42, 44, 49, 55; slaves poisoning masters, 46, 56–61, 116–23; in zombie-making, 46, 49, 55, 67, 91, 139–40
Port-au-Prince, Haiti, 38, 79, 108, 128, 130, 135, 152, 163, 220n9
Postcolonialism, 4, 9, 11, 17, 19, 25, 30–31, 55, 61, 84–85, 99, 108, 115, 120, 124–25, 127, 133, 143–44, 146–48, 152, 158, 177, 182, 205n2, 214n29
Postmodernism, 148, 154, 157–58, 178, 199
Power relations, 11, 29–31, 203n3
Pratt, Mary Louise, 114
Pride and Prejudice (Austen), 149–51, 219n6
Pride and Prejudice and Zombies (Grahame-Smith), 149–50
Protest, 1–6, 12, 20, 23–24, 129, 178, 188–89, 192–96, 199–200, 203n1. *See also* Occupy Wall Street and Zombie walks

Pulp fiction, 3, 10, 85–87, 162

Rebel slave, slave in revolt, 8, 10, 14, 20, 28, 30–31, 33, 54–55, 58–62, 76, 97, 122, 185–6, 200, 223n3
Reconstruction: Haiti, 215 n. 3; U.S., 67
Reed, Ishmael, 156, 185
Resident Evil, (various) 95, 159
Resurrection, 6–7, 27–29, 62, 74, 93, 121, 153, 193, 204n7, 217n24; in contradistinction to zombie, 7, 29, 62, 193
Return of the Living Dead (O'Bannon), 171–72
Revenge of the Zombies (Sekeley), 88, 96, 100, 105
Revolt of the Zombies (Halperin), 86, 100, 213n22
Revolution: American, 27; as contagious, 70; French, 51, 70–1; Haitian, 7–8, 10, 15, 20, 27–29, 32–34, 42, 47–48, 51–63, 76, 81, 109, 116–18, 122, 192, 204n12, 205n5, 210n44, 212n16, 215n3, 217n21, 223n3
Rhys, Jean, 146–48, 151–52, 204n9, 219n1, 220n8
Rime of the Ancient Mariner (Coleridge), 47–48
Romero, George: *Dawn of the Dead*, 9, 31, 97, 157–58, 160–62, 172–73, 175, 203n3, 213n27, 214n34; *Day of the Dead*, 95–96, 169–70; as father of the modern zombie, 92–99, 214 n.31–33; *Land of the Dead*, 31, 97, 172; *Night of the Living Dead*, 32, 91–92, 96–99, 161–62, 169, 171–72, 203n4, 213n25–26, 222n27
Root doctors, 66, 72. *See also* Houngan; Herbal medicine
Russell, Jaime, 21, 197, 206n12

Sacrifice: of humans, 49, 90; ritual, as of an animal, 28, 90, 118–19, 219n2; self-sacrifice, 62; zombies as sacrifice, 64–65, 68, 213n24
Said, Edward, 120, 150–51, 183
Saint Domingue, 8, 14, 16, 24, 27–29, 32–34, 36–37, 41, 44, 48, 50–51, 55–56, 70–71, 77–78, 212n18, 218n33

Salt, as zombie cure, 21, 45–46, 65–66, 80–83, 92, 115–17, 124, 131–34, 137, 142–44, 208n26, 209n41, 217n25
Salt is not for Slaves (Hutter), 21, 81–83, 212n13, 16
Satan, or the Devil, devils: selling one's soul to the Devil, 64, 74; Vaudou's association with, 49, 68, 206n12, 215n2, 217n22
Seabrook, William, 32, 43–44, 78–82, 84, 110, 127, 142, 209n35, 211n9, 212n16, 215n5
Secularism, 15–16, 37, 46, 96–98, 222n34
Sheller, Mimi, 208n33
Shelley, Mary, 14–15, 47, 93–94, 204n10, 208n28
Slavery, as social death, 20, 52; zombie as metaphor for, 3, 7, 9–24, 63. *See also* African slave; Master/Slave dialectic; Patterson, Orlando; Plantation, Rebel Slave
Song of the Slaves (Wade), 84–85
Sorcery, 15–16, 20, 35, 37, 41, 44, 48, 52–53, 58, 98, 109, 115, 125, 149, 154, 156, 208n27, 209n41
Soulouque, Faustin, 48, 51
Southey, Robert, 37
Spivak, Gayatri, 182–83
St. John, Spenser, 49, 58, 208n33
Sugar, 20, 44, 59, 78–79, 84, 108, 113, 128–29; bloodsugar, 204n10; sugar cane, 8, 56, 79, 127–28, 209n39, 216n9
Sugar Hill (Maslansky), 104–5, 107, 185

Tahiti, 178–84
Talisman, 38, 53–54, 56, 61, 106; gris-gris, 211n2. *See also* Ouanga (charm)
Tenney, Del: *Horror of Party Beach*, 92–93, 96; *I Eat Your Skin*, 90
Tetrododoxin, 67, 91, 205n4, 211n3, 211n10
Textual zombies, 23, 138, 146–86, 195, 218n36. *See also* Literary zombification
Three-Finger'd Jack, (aka Jack Mansong), 208n32
Thriller (Jackson), 159, 188
Ti Joseph, 79–81, 142
Tontons Macoutes, 16, 22, 103, 126, 128, 133, 185

Transatlantic Slave Trade, triangle trade, 9, 17–20, 38, 50, 85, 98, 107, 185, 192, 207n23
Trouillot, Michel-Rolph, 19, 120, 216n12

US Armed Forces: Marines, 20, 32, 54, 63, 141, 212n17; Coast Guard, 126; GIs, 141
US Occupation of Haiti. *See* Haiti, US Occupation of

Van Gogh, Vincent, 155, 158, 173, 178–79, 181–82
Vaudou, 5, 15–16, 19–22, 38, 40, 46–50, 61–69, 72–77, 81, 88–94, 96–98, 103–4, 106, 108–45, 152, 156–57, 163, 183, 186, 199–200, 207n22, 209n34, 209n43, 210n52, 213n23, 215n7, 217n22, 219n41, 219n2; cosmology of, 14, 16, 20, 72, 205n13; depiction in cinema, 89–91, 93–107; role in rebellion of slaves, 54–58, 61, 72, 81. *See also* Lwa
Veve, 62, 106, 221n22
Video-based art, 163, 165–69, 171–72, 221n21, 221n24
Videogames, 1, 95, 102, 124, 159–60, 162, 191, 220n15; Capcom Entertainment, 188
Virus. *See* Zombie, viral
Voodoo doll, 35, 92
Vumbi, 38–9

Walcott, Derek, 147, 184–85, 222n35
Walker, Kara, 156
Walking Dead, The (AMC) 2, 102, 160, 162; scholarship on, 214n38
Walking Dead, The (Kirkman), 160, 164
Wallace, Inez, 82, 86, 220n8
Warhol, Andy, 154, 158, 214n35
Warner, Marina, 13, 47, 146, 204n9, 206n12, 207n15
Wellman, Manly Wade, 84–85
While Zombies Walked (McClusky), 21, 87
White Zombie (Halperin), 86, 87, 94, 100, 103, 212n13
White Zombie (Meik), 21, 86–87
Wide Sargasso Sea (Rhys), 146–48, 151, 158, 204n9, 219n1, 220n8

Wilentz, Amy, 110–12, 114, 216n10, 217n25
Witch doctor, 16, 22, 33, 46, 67, 89, 94, 102, 148, 211n3, 217n18. *See also* Houngan
Witches, 35, 43–44, 105–6, 208n26
Wood, Ed, 93, 100
World Series, 108, 113
World War Z (Forster), 32

Yellow fever, 61, 117, 217n19

Zombi 2 (Fulci), 169, 172, 174, 221n27
Zombi 3 (Fulci), 95
Zombi, Angolan deity, 37–38, 73, 206n12
Zombi astral, 36, 206n7
Zombi bouteille, 36, 38, 44, 206n14
Zombi, Jean, 59–61, 210n47
Zombi Salve, 75–76, 211n10
Zombie dialectics, 4–6, 10, 13–14, 19, 23, 25, 30–31, 33–34, 104, 167, 186, 195, 199, 223n7
Zombieindex.us (Pfau), 170–71
Zombie Loop (Mcdonald), 165–67
Zombie master, 81, 83, 87, 132, 139, 141
Zombie, Miami, 189
Zombie mob, 77, 159, 171, 192–93, 195
Zombie picnic, 190
Zombie powder, 39, 66–69, 130, 135
Zombie preparedness, 160
Zombie runs, 2, 159, 191
Zombies as puppets, 106–7, 213n23
Zombiescapes (Pfau), 172–75
Zombies of Mora Tau, The (Cahn), 89, 96
Zombies on Broadway (Douglas), 94, 103–4, 107, 215n40
Zombie's techne, 55, 58–59, 114, 124, 169
Zombie tag, "Humans vs. Zombies" tag, 159
Zombie, viral, 8–9, 92, 95–96, 107, 159, 187, 188, 190, 212n18
Zombie walks, 1–3, 23, 159, 161–62, 166, 187–88, 190–92, 199–200, 223n7
Zombification as punishment, 76, 110, 215n5–6
Zombis de ronde, 35
Zonbi, 14, 163, 206n7
Zong massacre, 84
Zuccotti Park, 2, 199
Zumbi, nkisi, 38

About the Author

Sarah Juliet Lauro is coauthor of "A Zombie Manifesto: The Nonhuman Condition in the Era of Advanced Capitalism," *boundary 2* (Spring 2008), and coeditor of *Better Off Dead: The Evolution of the Zombie as Posthuman* (2011). She has published many other essays and articles on zombies and other phenomena in literature, film, and popular culture. This, her first book, was selected as one of the First Book Institute's projects in its inaugural session at Penn State in 2013.

She has recently coedited two special issues, one for the journal *South Carolina Review* that is devoted to the topic "The Spectral South"; another for the *Journal of the Fantastic in the Arts* titled "After/Lives: What's Next for Humanity?" Lauro is an assistant professor in the English department of the University of Tampa, where she teaches courses on Hemispheric literature.